From Messianism to Collapse

Soviet Foreign Policy, 1917–1991

Books by David MacKenzie

The Serbs and Russian Pan-Slavism, 1875–1878

The Lion of Tashkent:
The Career of General M. G. Cherniaev

A History of Russia and the Soviet Union

A History of the Soviet Union

Ilija Garašanin: Balkan Bismarck

Apis: The Congenial Conspirator

Imperial Dreams/Harsh Realities:
Tsarist Russian Foreign Policy, 1815–1917

Dedication

To the valiant Russian people for their courage in the struggle to overcome the disastrous legacy of Soviet Communist rule.

Acknowledgments

My warm thanks go to my colleagues from UNC-Greensboro, Dr. Karl Schleunes and Dr. Ronald Cassell, for reading portions of the manuscript and providing suggestions. Dr. Teddy Uldricks of UNC-Asheville read the entire volume and provided valuable suggestions for the text and for the suggested readings. My graduate assistant, Mr. John Coman, did some of the work on the index. I would like to thank my students at UNC-Greensboro for their patience and encouragement.

David MacKenzie

From Messianism to Collapse

Soviet Foreign Policy, 1917–1991

David MacKenzie
University of North Carolina
at Greensboro

Harcourt Brace College Publishers

Fort Worth   Philadelphia   San Diego   New York   Orlando   Austin
San Antonio   Toronto   Montreal   London   Sydney   Tokyo

Publisher   Ted Buchholz
Acquisitions editor   Drake Bush
Assistant editor   Kristie Kelly
Project editor   steve Norder
Production manager   Wendy Temple
Senior art director   Serena Manning
Photo editor   Lili Weiner
Cover designer   Sok James Hwang
Maps   Academy Artworks

Illustration credits: p. 6, The Bettmann Archive; p. 21, UPI/Bettmann; p. 27, Novosti from Sovfoto; p. 28, AP/Wide World Photos; p. 65, UPI/Bettmann; p. 92, UPI/Bettmann; p. 93, UPI/Bettmann; p. 102, UPI/Bettmann; p. 124, UPI/Bettmann; p. 131, The Bettmann Archive; p. 159, UPI/Bettmann; p. 219, UPI/Bettmann; p. 223, AP/Wide World Photos; p. 239, Reuters/Bettmann; p. 253, Reuters/Bettmann; p. 262, AP/Wide World Photos

Library of Congress Catalog Card Number: 93-80890

Address for Editorial Correspondence: Harcourt Brace College Publishers, 301 Commerce Street, Suite 3700, Fort Worth, TX 76102.

Address for Orders: Harcourt Brace & Company, 6277 Sea Harbor Drive, Orlando, FL 32887. 1-800-782-4479, or 1-800-433-0001 (in Florida).

ISBN: 0-15-501303-3

Printed in the United States of America

4 5 6 7 8 9 0 1 2 3   016   9 8 7 6 5 4 3 2 1

PREFACE

This volume is the sequel to the author's *Imperial Dreams/Harsh Realities: Tsarist Russian Foreign Policy, 1815–1917* (Harcourt Brace, 1993), which treats Russian foreign relations until the Bolshevik Revolution of November 1917. *From Messianism to Collapse* surveys Soviet foreign policy and its ideological bases from the Bolshevik seizure of power until the USSR's dissolution in December 1991, with a postscript on the immediate aftermath of that collapse. The Soviet regime inaugurated its tyrannical rule with messianic dreams of world revolution and the establishment of a world socialist order. Even after overly optimistic initial expectations of proletarian revolutions in Europe and anti-colonial revolts in the Third World had passed, the Soviet regime under Stalin and his successors continued efforts to expand their dominion by force, subversion, and propaganda throughout the globe. Beginning in the 1970s appeared signs of decline and disintegration that culminated in December 1991 in the utter collapse of Soviet power and the creation of a weak, ineffective successor: the Commonwealth of Independent States. The world-shaking events of 1989–1991, placing Soviet foreign policy and its legacy in a wholly new light, stimulated me to attempt a new synthesis.

Derived in large measure from materials collected during fifteen years of teaching a course on Russia and the Soviet Union in world politics since 1815, this volume is designed primarily for college undergraduates and general readers. Therefore the emphasis is on clarity and conciseness, rather than on exhaustive scholarship. Suggested readings have been appended to each chapter to assist students and readers to deepen their knowledge of events.

David MacKenzie

Greensboro, N.C. 1994

CONTENTS

ILLUSTRATIONS

MAPS

IDEOLOGY, AIMS, AND INSTRUMENTS

THE IDEOLOGICAL BASES

Initially intransigently hostile towards the capitalist West, the Bolshevik regime of V. I. Lenin and L. D. Trotskii embarked on a foreign policy fundamentally different from that of tsarist Russia and featuring radically new aims and means. Bolshevik leaders dramatized their allegedly complete break with what they called the "reactionary policies of tsarism" and with an ineffective Provisional Government that they considered a tool of world capitalism. However, subsequently, as the influence of Marxist-Leninist ideology waned within the USSR and upon Soviet foreign policy, there was an increasing reaffirmation of many objectives and interests from the tsarist Russian past.

Foreign scholars and political leaders have debated the significance of ideology in Soviet foreign policy. Did Marxist-Leninist principles actually determine it and prescribe Soviet actions abroad? Did Soviet leaders truly view the world through rose-tinted glasses? Especially, ex-Communists in the West viewed the doctrines of Marxism-Leninism, despite some obvious contradictions over matters of detail, as a blueprint for world revolution and socialist dominion. Ever since 1917, they emphasized, Soviet leaders had explained that their indispensable and over-riding aim was to create a world Communist system by every possible means, including war and the violent overthrow of established governments everywhere. Soviet leaders, they argued, had never repudiated Lenin's famous statement issued in March 1919 to the Eighth Congress of the Russian Communist Party:

> We live not only in one country but in a system of countries, and for the Soviet Republic to exist for long side by side with imperialist nations is impossible. One of the two systems will ultimately triumph over the other. But before that happens, there is bound to be a series of terrible conflicts between them.[1]

---

[1]Quoted in B. Lazitch and M. Drachkovitch, *Lenin and the Comintern*, vol. I, (Stanford, CA, 1972), p. 127.

Lenin's declaration suggested to some an inevitable and protracted conflict between the new Soviet Russia and the opposing capitalist states until one side or the other triumphed, and that Soviet leaders believed so fervently in Marxism-Leninism they would never cooperate with capitalist countries. However, this view overlooked periods of such cooperation. Every Soviet move in foreign policy, argued advocates of that school of thought, must be examined to discover how it promoted the overall goal of world revolution directed from Moscow. Because Soviet leaders could never be trusted, it would be pointless, even harmful, to conclude agreements with the USSR.

Another group of scholars viewed Soviet foreign policy increasingly in its national context as a continuation, with different rhetoric, of the main features of tsarist Russian policies. They contended that geographical position, climate, culture, and historical experience provide a country with a set of basic interests and outlooks toward the external world regardless of the nature and ideology of the regime in power. These scholars sought motives for Soviet actions abroad in Russia's traditional urge to secure firm access to the seas and to warm water ports; the desire for security, especially on its vulnerable western frontiers; the protection or domination of fellow Orthodox and Slavic peoples in eastern Europe and the Balkans; and an expansionist manifest destiny in Asia. Such observers regarded Soviet foreign policy under Joseph V. Stalin and his successors as increasingly pragmatic, realistic, and power-oriented. Therefore, they contended, the capitalist West might well achieve accommodation with Soviet Russia based on power politics and mutual interests.

As the "Cold War" between the Soviet Union and the West cooled, a middle path won increasing scholarly acceptance in the West. Soviet foreign policy came to be viewed as a complex combination of ideological and traditional national elements. Initially, under Lenin and Trotskii—from 1917 through 1920—ideological beliefs and aims had clearly been uppermost. Soviet foreign policy then had diverged radically and dramatically from traditional, largely conservative tsarist policies. Later, with world revolution clearly no longer imminent, pragmatism and nationalism had prevailed increasingly among Soviet policymakers. As Marxist-Leninist ideology gradually eroded, they had turned to more traditional objectives based on geographical and power-political considerations. However, neither ideology nor geopolitics could be disregarded. In most Soviet foreign policy decisions both elements were present. To assess their interaction, one must comprehend the essentials of Marxist-Leninist theory and the domestic conditions that prompted Soviet decisions.

MARXISM-LENINISM AND ITS IMPLICATIONS FOR SOVIET FOREIGN POLICY

In the 1840s, Karl Marx and Friedrich Engels, two German "city boys," originated the theory that Lenin (V. I. Ulianov) adapted and utilized to bring the Bolshevik Party to power in Russia in November 1917. However,

Lenin greatly altered—some would say distorted—Marxism in order to apply it to Russian conditions. The Marxist philosophy of dialectical materialism rested on the belief that the conflict of opposites continues to produce change until a state of perfection is achieved, that everything is constantly becoming something else. Marx applied the dialectical method of the German idealist philosopher G. W. F. Hegel to the historical process in the form of the class struggle. Historical development, he argued, was based on the conflict between a class owning the means of production—land, factories, mines—and a subjected or exploited class. Such exploitation would persist as long as the productive means remained privately owned. Marx and Engels were optimists who believed that each society, itself reflecting its economic foundations, embodied greater productivity and more freedom than its predecessor. Believing firmly in the western idea of progress, they predicted that perfection would eventually be attained in a socialist society without private property, and thus without exploitation or war. History would pass inevitably on the basis of inexorable laws through a series of stages beginning with primitive communism, slavery, feudalism, and capitalism. During the capitalist phase, ushered in by the French Revolution of 1789, which Marx himself lived under, the means of production, he affirmed, were owned by a shrinking minority of entrepreneurs and factory owners exploiting the labor of the proletariat, the increasingly large class of factory workers. When capitalism achieved full development, the overwhelming majority of the population would be exploited and increasingly class-conscious proletarians would absorb within their ranks most peasants and much of the middle class. Then the proletariat, led by the Communists—its most class-conscious element—would revolt and take control of the state and society.

Initially, Marx and Engels believed that the shift from private capitalism to socialism would require a violent revolution because the private capitalists would not relinquish voluntarily their control over the economy and state. However, by the 1870s, witnessing the growth of the workers' movement and their voting power in western Europe, Marx concluded that a peaceful transition from capitalism to socialism might be possible in advanced parliamentary countries such as England, Holland, and the United States. In any case, capitalism would be overthrown only where it had developed fully. A vast mass of miserable and exploited factory workers would face a handful of greedy monopolists no longer able to sell their goods. The revolution would be "democratic" because it would be carried through by the vast majority against a tiny oppressing minority.

Replacing the capitalist state—the "dictatorship of the bourgeoisie"—would be a proletarian state—"the dictatorship of the proletariat." Marx borrowed these phrases from the French revolutionary Auguste Blanqui, and used them repeatedly in his correspondence. However, he never described fully how the dictatorship of the proletariat would be organized or how it would rule. In his *Critique of the Gotha Program* (1875) Marx described the dictatorship of the proletariat as a transitional stage when the state would continue to act as an organ of coercion run by the proletarian majority against a minority of former bourgeois exploiters and thus constituting a "democratic dictatorship." Its tasks would be to eliminate bourgeois ways and habits, reeducate former exploiters, and prepare the way for a perfect, classless socialist society.

A convinced internationalist, Marx greatly underestimated the power and appeal of modern nationalism. Believing that a worker's primary loyalty would be to his class, rather than to his country, he argued that workers would form spontaneously an international alliance to overthrow capitalism everywhere, but that capitalism would be superseded by socialism only where socioeconomic conditions were ripe. Thus a socialist revolution, Marx believed, could not be imposed on backward peoples who were not yet ready for it. Nonetheless, predicted Marx, capitalism eventually would fall everywhere as the victim of its own internal contradictions, a worldwide socialist system would take its place, and international wars would end. Thus his phrase: "Workingmen of all lands unite!"[2]

Finally, Marx predicted that once it had achieved its goals, the dictatorship of the proletariat would "wither away" because the compulsive aspects of the state would no longer be needed. The result would be communism when society would "inscribe on its banners: 'from each according to his ability, to each according to his needs.' "[3] The Marxist system, based on the belief in absolute, inevitable laws of history operating without the need for individual leadership, was designed for the advanced industrial societies of western Europe and the United States. Indeed, Marx and Engels remained very unsure whether their predictions would apply to Russia and even more backward countries, and if so, how they would be implemented.

Late in life, Marx learned Russian and corresponded with Russian socialists, who in the 1870s were overwhelmingly Populists who believed in a peasant socialism based around the Russian village commune *(mir)*. A leading Populist, Georgii Plekhanov, argued that socialism in Russia could triumph without capitalist development because it could be formed around that traditional institution. However, after fleeing into exile in Switzerland, Plekhanov soon became a convert to Marxism and the first important Russian Marxist ideologist. In Switzerland in the mid-1880s, Plekhanov established the Liberation of Labor group as the nucleus for an eventual Russian Marxist party. In *Our Differences* (1885) Plekhanov, repudiating his former Populist faith, affirmed that capitalism was already becoming the dominant economic form in Russia and was inevitable, progressive, and revolutionary. Only the proletariat, argued Plekhanov, could organize a true revolution and lead the Russian peasantry to socialism. The task of the

---

[2]Karl Marx and Friedrich Engels, *The Communist Manifesto* (New York, 1948), p. 44.

[3]Karl Marx, *Critique of the Gotha Program* (1875), quoted in R. N. Carew Hunt, *The Theory and Practice of Communism: An Introduction* (London, 1950), p. 73.

intelligenstsia would be to aid the proletariat to acquire knowledge and organize in order to become a conscious revolutionary force. One could not just sit back and await the triumph of the revolution. Retaining a good balance between the determinist and voluntarist aspects of Marxism, Plekhanov remained confident that the laws of history were moving Russia and the world inexorably onward towards socialism. He affirmed that both western Europe and Russia had to pass through all stages of historical development on the way to socialism.

About Plekhanov his most famous pupil, Vladimir I. Lenin, declared: "He reared a whole generation of Russian Marxists."[4] Beginning his own revolutionary activity in St. Petersburg in 1893, Lenin explained Marxism to workers' groups. Lenin was soon arrested by the tsarist authorities and sent into comfortable exile in Siberia, where he wrote a lengthy volume, *The Development of Capitalism in Russia* (1899), which reaffirmed Plekhanov's arguments against the Populists. Returning to European Russia, Lenin insisted that violent revolution was the only way to achieve socialism and rejected assertions by European socialists, notably Eduard Bernstein, that it could be attained by gradual, peaceful, democratic methods. Whereas Marx had predicted confidently that socialism would triumph inevitably through the operation of inexorable historical laws, Lenin impatiently wished to "give history a push." Emphasizing the voluntaristic aspects of Marxism, Lenin argued the necessity for organization, leadership, and conscious action by the proletariat. To combat tsarist autocracy, argued Lenin in a key pamphlet, *What Is To Be Done?* (1902), an autocratic party of professional revolutionaries led by intellectuals had to be built in Russia based on rigid discipline and the subordination of the rank and file to the top leadership. He borrowed that concept not from Marx but from the Russian revolutionary tradition epitomized by the Populist and terrorist "People's Will" organization, which had assassinated Alexander II in 1881. Lenin wrote in *State and Revolution* (1917) shortly before the Bolshevik power seizure: "The substitution of a proletarian for the capitalist state is impossible without a violent revolution. . . ."[5] Recalling that Marx late in life had stated that in England and the United States socialism might triumph without destroying the existing state machinery, Lenin wrote that "Today this distinction of Marx's becomes unreal" because the British and Americans had sunk during World War I to the low level of other imperialist governments.

As to the means of achieving a socialist revolution, Lenin, as an active revolutionary and the creator of the militant Bolshevik faction within Russian socialism, revised Marxism arbitrarily to make it fit the very different

---

[4]Quoted in Hunt, p. 130.

[5]V. I. Lenin, *The State and Revolution* (1917), in Robert C. Tucker, ed., *The Lenin Anthology* (New York, 1975), p. 325.

VLADIMIR ILICH LENIN *(1870–1924)*, FOUNDER OF THE BOLSHEVIK
PARTY; CHIEF LEADER OF THE NOVEMBER REVOLUTION OF *1917;* CHIEF
SOVIET LEADER, *1917–1924*

conditions prevalent in peasant Russia while claiming to be a loyal Marxist.
By April 1917 he had rejected the basic Marxian tenet that capitalism would
be overthrown only after achieving full development and only when the
industrial proletariat comprised the vast majority of the population. In
Russia, then at an early stage in the growth of a proletariat, that traditional
Marxian concept would require a long wait. Whereas Marx had dismissed
the peasantry as an incurably petty bourgeois element destined to be
absorbed into the proletariat before a socialist revolution, Lenin after 1905

accepted the peasantry as the proletariat's indispensable ally in achieving socialism.

Although denounced by many fellow socialists as using Blanquism or anarchism, Lenin justified his willingness to resort to a minority seizure of power with several arguments. As early as 1905 Lenin had suggested that capitalism, like a chain, might break at its weakest link—Russia. In Russia, he argued, operated a well-organized Bolshevik Party ready to lead the proletariat forward to victory. Large-scale capitalist industry had taken root in the principal Russian cities creating a highly class-conscious but poorly paid and disgruntled industrial proletariat. The emergence of worker soviets (councils) in 1905 and 1917 represented the prototype of the dictatorship of the proletariat that with proper leadership could triumph in Russia. Western Europe, claimed Lenin in 1917, was ripe for a socialist revolution that would assist a socialist victory in Russia and help keep socialism in power. After Trotskii's return to Russia in May 1917, Lenin welcomed him and his followers into the Bolshevik Party. He appropriated Trotskii's idea of "permanent revolution." Rather than await full development of capitalism, Russia could move directly to socialism by revolution.

A key pamphlet of Lenin, derived from the writings of European socialists, Rudolph Hilferding and J. A. Hobson, was *Imperialism, the Highest Stage of Capitalism* (1916). There Lenin argued that finance or monopoly capitalism, then prevalent in the world, had sprung directly from earlier competitive capitalism:

> Imperialism is capitalism in that stage of development in which the domination of monopoly and finance capital has taken shape; in which the export of capital has acquired pronounced importance; in which the division of the world by international trusts has begun, and in which the partition of all the territory of the earth by the greatest capitalist countries has been completed.[6]

The division of the world among leading capitalist powers as they sought markets, raw materials, and bases had caused constant quarrels over the spoils and ultimately World War I, a conflict that Lenin predicted would provoke the demise of capitalism. Imperialism, he claimed, would collapse from the internal contradictions that had produced war and presumably would provoke wars among leading capitalist powers. That in turn would spark revolts in their colonies, which would fight wars of national liberation. Breaking at its weak Russian link, capitalism would yield to worldwide socialist revolution. Becoming a major foundation for Soviet foreign policy, Lenin's pamphlet would long remain the established and authoritative doctrine in Soviet Russia.

---

[6]V. I. Lenin, *Imperialism, the Highest Stage of Capitalism* (New York, 1917), p. 89.

While in exile in neutral Switzerland, Lenin expressed unremitting hostility towards World War I, a feeling he brought with him to Russia in April 1917. Thus in *Socialism and War* (1915), written in preparation for an antiwar socialist conference at Zimmerwald, he wrote:

> ...This war is an imperialist war.... Capitalism in its imperialist stage has turned into the greatest oppressor of nations. ... This is a war, firstly, to increase the enslavement of the colonies ... by means of a more concerted exploitation of them. ... Tsarism is waging a war to seize Galicia and finally crush the liberties of the Ukrainians, and to obtain possession of Armenia, Constantinople, etc.[7]

Returning to a Russia in April 1917 ruled by the democratic Provisional Government with these same views, Lenin presented to Bolshevik Party meetings his famous "April Theses" that soon afterwards were published in that party's newspaper, *Pravda:*

> In our attitude towards the war, which under the new government of Lvov and Company [Provisional Government], unquestionably remains on Russia's part a predatory imperialist war owing to the capitalist nature of that government, not the slightest concession to "revolutionary defensism" is permissible. The class-conscious proletariat can give its consent to a revolutionary war ... only on condition: a) that the power pass to the proletariat and the poorest sections of the peasants aligned with the proletariat; b) that all annexations be renounced in deed and not in word; c) that a complete break be effected in actual fact with all capitalist interests ...

Lenin, therefore, concluded there could be "no support for the provisional government ..."[8] Soon adopted by the Bolshevik Party, these "April Theses" became the key element in its program which helped sweep it into power that November.

THE BOLSHEVIKS SEIZE POWER, NOVEMBER 1917

The successful Bolshevik coup of November 6–7, 1917,* in Petrograd permitted the inauguration of Soviet foreign policy based on Lenin's program. The Provisional Government, led initially by Foreign Minister Paul Miliukov, chief leader of the Constitutional Democrats, sought to continue fighting in World War I with the western Allies for their agreed imperialist war aims. Miliukov's resignation in May 1917 in the face of vehement opposition from the Petrograd Soviet scuttled that policy. Moderate socialists headed by Alexander Kerenskii attempted to keep Russia fighting without seeking imperialist gains. A convinced democrat committed ideologically to the Allied cause, Kerenskii

---

[7]Tucker, pp. 183ff.
[8]Tucker, pp. 296–97.
*New Style dates of the calendar used in Western Europe are given here unless otherwise indicated.

realized that Russia could not repudiate its wartime alliances and remain a credible great power. Thus on May 18 Foreign Minister M. I. Tereshchenko, seeking to assuage pressures from the Petrograd Soviet, pledged to seek a peace "without annexations and indemnities" while rejecting any idea of a separate peace by Russia. War Minister Kerenskii staked everything on a Russian military offensive against the Austrians, launched July 1, to restore army discipline and dramatize Russia's continued role in the war. However, after the offensive ground to a halt, a German counteroffensive provoked a disastrous retreat by the rapidly disintegrating Russian armies.

This military defeat triggered the disorders of the "July Days" in Petrograd, which nearly brought down the Provisional Government. After order was restored, a struggle developed between Kerenskii's moderate left and conservatives backing the new army commander-in-chief, General Lavr Kornilov, who also was supported by the Allies. A poorly planned abortive military coup by Kornilov in early September discredited the conservatives and undermined morale in the army. The Bolsheviks, having spearheaded the defense of Petrograd against Kornilov, now won strong support from radical workers and soldiers there and in Moscow. After the soviets of the two capitals gave the Bolsheviks their first majorities, the Bolsheviks took control of them. In the face of galloping inflation, declining real wages, and dwindling urban food supplies, industrial workers became increasingly discontented and revolutionary. With the army in full disintegration, peasants seizing the land, and nationalities pressing for full independence, Lenin realized in October 1917 that the time had come for his party to strike decisively for political power. To wait for the Constituent Assembly, which would not support them, would be pointless, he told his party comrades. Returning to Petrograd in disguise in late October, Lenin finally convinced his reluctant comrades on the Central Committee that it was time to act decisively. Because the Provisional Government had almost no loyal troops, the actual power seizure was virtually bloodless. Acting under cover of the Second All-Russian Congress of Soviets that convened on November 7 as the Winter Palace fell and the ministers of the Provisional Government were arrested, an all-Bolshevik government was formed led by Lenin, Trotskii, and Joseph Stalin, the chief leaders of the only Russian party committed to take Russia speedily out of World War I.

The Bolsheviks had won the power competition of 1917 for a variety of reasons. As the chief opposition to a weak and ineffective Provisional Government, they profited from the army's disintegration, the economic collapse, and general discontent. With Lenin and Trotskii, the Bolsheviks enjoyed a great advantage in leadership and organization. Their program based on Lenin's "April Theses" promised "Bread, land, and peace," slogans popular with Russia's war-weary masses. The Bolsheviks were aided greatly by the indecisiveness, failures, and divisions of their opponents, who proved unable to mobilize their followers (especially the Socialist Revolutionaries, who split irrevocably and whose peasant followers were scattered in villages throughout Russia). The other major political parties were all compromised by their participation in a Provisional Government that had failed to govern or to redeem its promises. But now Lenin and Trotskii realized that the Bolsheviks must move swiftly to carry out their own promises and program or they would face a similar overthrow.

AIMS AND INSTRUMENTS OF SOVIET FOREIGN POLICY

Assuming power in November 1917, Bolshevik leaders believed fervently that revolution was imminent in Germany and western Europe and that only its speedy triumph would allow a weak Soviet Russia to survive. Convinced that all capitalist countries necessarily would be extremely hostile to the new Soviet state, Bolshevik leaders concluded that they would seek to combine against it and destroy it, just as the Paris Commune of 1870–1871 had been destroyed by conservative France. Thus, out of an instinct of self-preservation, Soviet foreign policy was launched on an internationalist basis of promoting a world revolution which was believed to be imminent. However, as early as March 1918 when Soviet Russia signed a separate peace with Germany and its allies, the pragmatic aim of preserving the Soviet power base in Russia tended to take precedence even over promoting world revolution, although Soviet leaders continued to believe that this was inevitable.

Several corollary aims stemmed from this basic defensive objective of early Soviet foreign policy. One objective was to prevent the formation of a capitalist coalition of powers against Soviet Russia by dividing world capitalism in accordance with Lenin's theory of imperialism. Another aim was to strike at world capitalism where it was weakest in the colonial world by seeking the support of peoples of Africa and Asia exploited, the Bolsheviks believed, by European imperialism. Finally, Soviet leaders fostered the creation of Communist parties in other countries and sought to exert control or influence over them.

Which instruments did Soviet foreign policy utilize in order to attain its objectives? Despite its initial military weakness, Soviet Russia possessed a variety of means to forward its aims and often employed them in flexible combinations. Beginning in 1919 Communist parties emerged in many countries from splits in socialist parties that Soviet leaders welcomed. Although small and weak at first, they looked for inspiration and example primarily to Moscow, and especially to the Comintern, as the center of the world's first and only socialist state. Coordinated after 1919 by the Comintern (Third International) and subjected to increasing control and discipline from the Soviet Communist Party after 1921, they became important instruments of Soviet foreign policy. Within some capitalist countries Communist parties comprised a fifth column, alienating moderate democratic socialists, who often became militantly anti-Soviet and anti-Communist. In democratic and parliamentary countries the legal Communist apparatus predominated propagating pro-Soviet positions in parliaments, leading labor unions, and opposing anti-Soviet governments and policies. Illegal, underground apparatuses that conducted subversion and sabotage, assumed control when Communist parties were banned, as happened increasingly in eastern Europe.

A normal instrument of foreign policy, employed at first in a highly untraditional manner, was diplomacy. Trotskii, as the first Soviet foreign commissar, at first believed that diplomacy would prove unnecessary because of the supposed imminence of world revolution. When the new Soviet state had to deal diplomatically with triumphant imperial Germany, it at first repudiated completely the norms, dress, and behavior of traditional European secret diplomacy. Instead Trotskii appealed over the heads of the Central Powers' delegation at Brest-Litovsk directly to the workers and soldiers of Europe. Unlike the old diplomacy, infant Soviet diplomacy, instead of seeking to resolve problems or achieve permanent accommodation with capitalist powers, continued the war against "imperialism" by other means. Under Trotskii its methods were most unorthodox, becoming flexible and ingenious under his successor, Foreign Commissar Georgii Chicherin.

Propaganda was an instrument employed effectively by the Soviet state throughout its existence. At first the Soviet view was spread among German troops and workers behind the front by distribution of thousands of leaflets. Later, free or inexpensive magazines, newspapers, and books propagated and circulated Soviet arguments. Radio propaganda was employed most effectively in colonies and underdeveloped countries.

For great powers when diplomacy failed the final resort had always been the threat or use of force. For Soviet Russia prior to World War II this usually was not a viable option because of its military weakness. The first attempt to employ force in order to expand the Soviet revolution and foster uprisings in Germany during the Soviet offensive in the Soviet-Polish War stimulated Polish national resistance and ended in failure. Not until 1939–1940 would the Soviet government again utilize this dangerous instrument. During the 1920s it appeared at times as if these varied tools, notably the Comintern and Soviet diplomacy, were working at cross purposes, but actually all of them were coordinated carefully in Moscow by the Communist Party directed by Lenin or Stalin.

Suggested Readings

A FEW GENERAL WORKS:

Fleron, Frederic J., Jr., et al., eds., *Soviet Foreign Policy: Classic and Contemporary Issues.* New York, 1991.

Strausz-Hupe, Robert, et al. *Protracted Conflict.* New York, 1959.

Ulam, Adam. *Ideologies and Illusions: Revolutionary Thought from Herzen to Solzhenitsyn.* Cambridge, MA, 1976.

Uldricks, Teddy. *Diplomacy and Ideology: The Origins of Soviet Foreign Relations, 1917–1930.* London, 1980.

ON MARXISM-LENINISM:

Baron, Samuel H. *Plekhanov: The Father of Russian Marxism.* Stanford, CA, 1963.

Carew-Hunt, R. N. *The Theory and Practice of Communism: An Introduction.* London, 1950

_____. *Marxism: Past and Present.* New York, 1954.

Daniels, Robert. *A Documentary History of Communism.* 2 vols. Hanover, NH, 1984.

Lenin, V. I. *Imperialism: The Highest Stage of Capitalism.* New York, 1939.

_____. *Selected Works.* 12 vols. New York, 1943.

_____. *Collected Works.* 45 vols. Moscow, 1960–1970.

_____. *What Is To Be Done?* Trans. Joe Fineberg and G. Hanna. London, 1988.

Lukacs, Gyorgy. *Lenin: A Study on the Unity of His Thought.* Trans. N. Jacobs. Cambridge, MA, 1971.

Marx, Karl. *Critique of the Gotha Program.* New York, 1938.

Marx, Karl and Friedrich Engels. *Selected Works.* 2 vols. Moscow, 1951.

_____. *The Communist Manifesto.* Hammondsworth, England, 1985.

Meyer, Alfred G. *Communism.* New York, 1960.

_____. *Leninism.* Cambridge, MA, 1957.

Tucker, Robert C., ed. *The Lenin Anthology.* New York, 1975.

_____. *The Marx-Engels Reader.* 2nd ed. New York, 1978.

Wilson, Edmund. *To the Finland Station: A Study in the Writing and Acting of History.* New York, 1972.

THE BOLSHEVIK REVOLUTION:

Daniels, Robert. *Red October: The Bolshevik Revolution of 1917.* New York, 1967.

Koenker, D. and W. G. Rosenberg. *Strikes and Revolution in Russia, 1917.* Princeton, NJ, 1990.

Pipes, Richard. *The Russian Revolution.* New York, 1990.

Rabinowitch, A. *The Bolsheviks Come to Power.* New York, 1976.

Reed, John. *Ten Days That Shook the World.* New York, 1919.

THE FIRST REVOLUTIONARY ERA, 1917–1920

Soviet Russia underwent frequent changes in its basic orientation in foreign affairs from the Bolshevik Revolution until it was invaded in World War II. Five well-defined periods from 1917 to 1941 reflected different Soviet approaches toward world capitalism, its avowed mortal foe. Domestic Soviet problems and policies influenced greatly the course that Soviet leaders adopted abroad. For each period, therefore, major internal Soviet developments parallel external policies. Extreme policies at home were duplicated or reflected in Soviet foreign policy.

THE ERA OF "WAR COMMUNISM," 1917–1921

The Bolshevik triumph in Petrograd on November 7, 1917, brought the party to power there with relative ease. However, Bolshevik leaders soon faced complex and interrelated problems that at times appeared insoluble. Overnight a small opposition party had become the established authority, and the Bolsheviks had to establish a regime in a hostile world under conditions of near military and economic collapse. Could they redeem their promises where the Provisional Government had failed? Could they retain state power against formidable foreign and domestic foes, then establish socialism in a largely peasant country?

Their first task was to complete the seizure of power throughout Russia. After defeating General N. N. Krasnov's forces near Petrograd, the Bolsheviks subdued Moscow after a week's fighting against military cadets loyal to the Provisional Government. Within two months local Bolshevik detachments of soldiers and workers leading local soviets took control of major European Russian cities. Initially, the Bolsheviks exercised little effective control in rural areas or in non-Russian borderlands. During 1917, the Bolsheviks, like other major parties, had pledged to convene the Constituent Assembly that was to decide on a permanent regime; now they were too weak to prevent it from meeting. Prepared by the Provisional Government, the elections to that body were the freest held in Russia until near the end of Soviet power. The Bolsheviks garnered roughly one-quarter of the votes while the peasant Socialist Revolutionaries (SRs) obtained 58 percent and dominated the

Constituent Assembly. Convened January 18, 1918, it passed anti-Bolshevik resolutions then was dissolved at Lenin's order; Red troops prevented it from reconvening.

The Bolsheviks soon achieved a one-party state. Defeating a right-wing Bolshevik faction that urged including other socialist parties, Lenin then brought a few Left SRs temporarily into his government and claimed it represented the proletariat (Bolsheviks) and poor peasants (Left SRs). That completed the split of the SRs which, during 1917, had possessed the greatest mass following in Russia. When Russia left World War I in March 1918, the Left SRs resigned, sought to overturn Lenin's regime, and were banned. Already in December 1917 the Constitutional Democrats (Kadets) were proscribed as a "bourgeois" party; moderate socialists were forced to dissolve during 1918. By 1921 only the Bolshevik Party remained legal and completely dominated the soviets. Decrees abolished all tsarist organs of local self-government. A Soviet secret police was created—the Cheka (Extraordinary Commission)—and began a systematic Red terror. Finally, in July 1918, at Lenin's order, the Romanov family (the former Tsar Nicholas II, his wife Alexandra, and their six children) was killed in Sverdlovsk in the Urals to remove any threat of a monarchist restoration.

The Bolshevik regime moved swiftly to undermine traditional social institutions such as the family and church in order to clear the way for a new socialist society. Only civil marriage was recognized, divorce became simple, and adultery and bigamy were decriminalized. The church was separated from the state and lost the right to own property. The Orthodox hierarchy was destroyed, many clergy were arrested, and all Orthodox Church property was nationalized. Twenty years of persecution of all religions as "the opium of the people" began; thousands of churches were destroyed or converted to other uses.

Initially, an inexperienced Bolshevik regime, retaining only a few large estates as state farms, allowed peasants to seize the rest and divide them into small plots. Lenin's Decree on Land (November 1917) abolished private ownership of estates and apparently fulfilled a major Bolshevik pledge. Worker committees seized control of factories, completing the ruin of private capitalism. All railroads, banks, and foreign trade were nationalized.

Bolshevik economic policies from June 1918 to early 1921 are usually called "War Communism." This began in June 1918 with nationalization of large-scale Russian industries before the outbreak of the major civil war. Soviet interpretations of this as an essential wartime measure are inaccurate. Lenin himself admitted that the government's abrupt decisions had been ideologically motivated and had been mistaken:

> Carried away by a wave of enthusiasm . . . , we thought that by direct orders of the proletarian state, we could organize state production and distribution

of products communistically in a land of petty peasants. Life showed us our mistake.[1]

The elaborate hierarchy of boards created to administer industry proved most inefficient. Nevertheless, in December 1920 most remaining industries were also nationalized. By then Russia's industrial production had fallen to a fraction of the 1913 level.

In agriculture "War Communism" proved equally disastrous. In May 1918 the Bolsheviks decided on drastic measures to feed the starving cities. Red Army detachments aided "committees of the poor" in seizing from better-off and middle peasants all grain above a bare minimum for subsistence. Deprived of incentives, the peasantry reduced farm output to about half the prewar level. That sparked a terrible famine in 1920–1921 in the Volga region and a wave of peasant revolts. The proletarian–poor peasant alliance used by the Bolsheviks to take power was undermined. Once the Russian Civil War ended, economic "War Communism" became intolerable and threatened to bring down the Soviet regime. Such doctrinaire extremism revealed the impracticality of seeking to achieve socialism immediately in a backward country.

Fragmented by the Bolshevik takeover, opposition forces revived early in 1918 as an anti-Communist White movement united only by hatred of the Bolsheviks (Reds). In the Caucasus former tsarist generals organized a Volunteer Army under Generals Lavr Kornilov and Anton Denikin. Made up of many tsarist officers and landholding Cossacks, it became the finest White fighting force. Facing a disparate White movement, including monarchists, moderates, and socialists was a new Red Army, created in January 1918 from a nucleus of Red Guards. By late 1918 under War Commissar Lev Trotskii it became a regular army based on conscription, severe discipline, and commanded by former imperial officers whose families were often held hostage. Fought at first with small Russian forces of uncertain morale and loyalty, the Civil War grew in extent and ferocity. Entire regions changed hands repeatedly in a fratricidal struggle that saw numerous atrocities committed by both sides and large areas left devastated. Attacks on the Bolshevik citadel in central Russia came from Estonia against Petrograd, from Siberia under Admiral Alexander Kolchak, and most dangerously from the south under General Denikin's Volunteer Army, which late in 1919 came within 250 miles of Moscow. However, the Whites lacked coordination, a positive program, and were hopelessly split ideologically, whereas the Reds possessed able leadership, a disciplined Bolshevik Party with worker support, and a flexible policy of national self-determination. Controlling the cities and railways of the central industrial region, the Reds eventually prevailed.

---

[1] V. I. Lenin, *Selected Works*, vol. IX (New York, 1943), p. 258.

MAP 2–1   The Civil War, 1919

Complicating the Russian Civil War but affecting its outcome only marginally was Allied intervention beginning in the summer of 1918. Was the Allied aim, as Soviet spokesmen claimed, to overthrow Bolshevism and divide Russia into spheres of economic and political interest, or to reform an eastern front, deflect German strength, and thus win World War I for the Allies? Soviet propaganda stressed that Allied forces remained on Russian soil long after the end of World War I and aided the Whites significantly. On September 15, 1957, preparing to celebrate forty years of Bolshevism in power, *Pravda* proclaimed:

> The organizer and inspirer of armed struggle against the Soviet Republic was international imperialism. The tremendous revolutionizing effect of the first republic of workers and peasants in world history aroused fear and bitter anger in the ranks of imperialists of all countries. They saw in the victory of the Socialist Revolution a threat to their own parasitical existence, to their profits and their capital, to all their privileges. In the effort to throttle the young Soviet republic, the imperialists, led by the leading circles of England, the U.S.A. and France, organized military campaigns against our country.

The response of Russia's loyal, patriotic masses, continued *Pravda*, had been truly heroic:

> In these difficult circumstances, the Communist Party and the Soviet government summoned the people to a just, revolutionary, and patriotic war against the foreign interventionists and the internal counter-revolutionaries. . . .[2]

As part of the "Cold War," *Pravda* emphasized that the United States had played the chief role in Allied intervention.

On the other hand, George Kennan, an American diplomat who had studied this era carefully, argued that the Allies' paramount concern in 1918 was neither the Soviet regime nor private economic interests but to win World War I. Russia's separate peace in March had dealt a heavy blow to Allied hopes and enabled Germany to shift large forces to the western front. Furthermore, the Allies had shipped into north Russian ports and Vladivostok huge quantities of supplies from barely adequate western stocks for the Russian army—160,000 tons in Archangel alone. Appropriating these, the Bolsheviks refused to pay for them. Allied leaders in Versailles developed a plan for intervention in Siberia and north Russia, using Japanese forces and Czech war prisoners in Russia. In May 1918, as part of this Czech force moved eastward, Trotskii ordered Bolshevik authorities in Siberia to disarm it. However, the Czechs overpowered weak Bolshevik forces, seized control of much of the Trans-Siberian Railroad, and overturned Bolshevik power in most of Siberia. It was this, Kennan argued, that triggered Allied intervention. In July the Allies intervened with small forces in north Russia to safeguard their military supplies and reconstitute an eastern front against Germany. A memorandum of the Supreme Allied War Council argued that if the Allies were to win the war in 1919, they would have to assist the national movement in Russia in order to reform an eastern front. President Woodrow Wilson of the United States, requested by the British to send American forces to occupy Archangel and Murmansk, agreed reluctantly as a loyal ally to send a few troops after Marshal Ferdinand Foch of France, Allied Supreme Commander, affirmed that they were required more urgently in north Russia than in France. The Allied decisions, concluded Kennan, were strictly military ones taken in secret without the knowledge of any "capitalists." Had World War I not been raging, there would have been no Allied intervention in north Russia.[3]

Intervening Allied forces were small except for a Japanese force sent to Vladivostok, which reached 70,000 men. In 1918–1919 British forces in north Russia with a small American contingent retained control there, then yielded command to Russian General E. Miller, who held on until January 1920. Again under intense Allied pressure, President Wilson sent about 7,000 men under

---

[2]Quoted in George Kennan, *Russia and the West Under Lenin and Stalin* (Boston, 1960), p. 65.

[3]Kennan, pp. 70–76.

General William Graves to guard huge stocks of Allied supplies in Vladivostok, not to intervene in the Russian Civil War. Almost never encountering Russians, the Americans were withdrawn belatedly in 1920 by a preoccupied President Wilson. Small British forces were dispatched to the Caucasus and a few French to Ukraine. Great Britain did help equip and supply White armies of Admiral Kolchak in Siberia, General Denikin in south Russia, and General Nicholas Iudenich in Estonia for his attack on Petrograd in 1919.

Did Allied intervention delay or promote Bolshevik victory over the Whites? Moscow's assertions of 1957 that intervention was a major and deliberate effort to overthrow the Soviet regime was simply untrue. American leaders from Wilson on down opposed any such aim and yielded most reluctantly to Allied insistence. Allied proponents of intervention, such as Winston Churchill of Great Britain and Marshal Foch, argued that it prolonged White resistance and stalled the Bolshevik campaign for world revolution by preventing Soviet expansion westward during Europe's maximum vulnerability. However, German occupation of Ukraine and other western borderlands during 1918 contributed far more to that result. Opponents of intervention, including Kennan, stress its ineptitude, arguing that it compromised the Whites and sparked Bolshevik contempt and resentment towards the Western powers. Kennan doubts the Bolsheviks would have prevailed throughout Russia without this ill-conceived, half-hearted Allied intervention.[4] The Allied actions seemed to confirm Soviet propaganda that depicted the Whites as "running dogs of Western imperialism." The intervention's failure appeared to demonstrate that outside powers can rarely determine the outcome of a major civil war.

The Bolshevik Revolution and Allied intervention effectively eliminated Russia as a major factor in Far Eastern affairs. Soon after the November Revolution the Soviet government renounced all unequal treaties that the tsarist regime had concluded with China, including Russia's share of the Boxer indemnity and unequal privileges granted to Russian merchants. Initially, the Soviets pledged to return the Chinese Eastern Railroad to China in order to dissuade the Chinese from aiding Admiral Kolchak. However, after Kolchak was defeated early in 1920, Moscow denied that it had made such an offer and retained control of the railroad until compelled to sell it to Japan in 1935. Soviet weakness allowed the Japanese to replace Russian influence in Manchuria. During the Russian Civil War, Japanese forces occupied Transbaikalia, northern Sakhalin, and the Maritime Province, finally evacuating the latter under American pressure in 1922. In Outer Mongolia, a Russian protectorate before World War I, a renegade White officer, Baron Roman von Ungern-Sternberg, seized control temporarily early in 1921 and utilized it for anti-Soviet raids. After the Red Army defeated the baron that July, the Soviets created a puppet government in Outer Mongolia and restored

---

[4]Kennan, p. 117.

de facto the old tsarist protectorate. This action caused many to doubt Moscow's anti-imperialist rhetoric.

Bolshevik dreams of revolts in the Asiatic and African colonies of imperial powers proved abortive. In September 1920 the Comintern convened a widely heralded "Congress of the Peoples of the East" in Baku. Attending were 1,891 delegates from thirty-seven different nationalities. Comintern spokesmen cited Lenin's calculation that the imperial powers— Britain, France, the United States and Japan—with only 250 million people ruled over countries and colonies with ten times that number. Comintern president Grigorii Zinoviev ended his speech to the delegates dramatically:

> The Communist International turns today to the peoples of the East and says to them: "Brothers, we summon you to a Holy War, first of all against British imperialism."

"Jehad, Jehad! (Holy war)," shouted the delegates, leaping to their feet and unsheathing swords and ripping revolvers from their holsters.[5] However, the Comintern did not envision this as anything more than a propaganda offensive. Supposedly the first annual meeting of oppressed nationalities, the Baku Congress was the only one ever held in Soviet Russia, since Moscow soon abandoned such blatant efforts to revolutionize the East.

THE DECREE ON PEACE AND TREATY OF BREST-LITOVSK, 1917–1918

The Second All-Russian Congress of Soviets, which confirmed Lenin's all-Bolshevik regime on November 7, 1917, also approved his Decree on Land and Decree on Peace overwhelmingly as he sought to redeem the most important Bolshevik promises immediately. Even before returning to Russia in April 1917 Lenin had urged ending Russia's participation in World War I. In his fourth "Letter from Afar" in March Lenin had outlined how the Bolsheviks, once in power, would end the war: The Petrograd Soviet "would declare immediately that it was not bound by any treaties concluded by either the tsarist monarchy or by the bourgeois [Provisional] government. It would publish forthwith all these treaties in order to expose to public obloquy the predatory aims of the tsarist monarchy and of all bourgeois governments without exception." After issuing an armistice proposal, the Soviet "would immediately publish . . . our conditions for peace: the liberation of all colonies; the liberation of all dependent, oppressed, and non-sovereign peoples."[6] Unlike his Russian rivals, Lenin would repudiate completely Russia's treaty obligations and conventional diplomacy.

---

[5]Louis Fischer, *The Soviets in World Affairs: A History of the Relations Between the Soviet Union and the Rest of the World, 1917–1929*, vol. I (Princeton, NJ, 1951), pp. 283–84.

[6]Arno Mayer, *Wilson vs. Lenin: The Political Origins of the New Diplomacy, 1917–1918* (Cleveland, 1959), pp. 247–48.

Lenin's Decree on Peace resembled ideals espoused by American President Wilson, who likewise rejected traditional European secret diplomacy. The new Soviet government, Lenin wrote, "proposes to all warring peoples and their governments to begin immediate negotiations for a just and democratic peace." Mentioning peoples before governments, Lenin appealed directly to the war-weary peoples of Europe. By a just and democratic peace, "the government means an immediate peace without annexations . . . and indemnities." The Decree proposed an immediate armistice to all belligerents to enable their representatives to negotiate a general peace settlement. Lenin explained that these terms were not an ultimatum. The Soviet government would consider other peace terms if stated clearly and openly. The Decree on Peace continued:

> The [Soviet] government abolishes secret diplomacy, and for its part announces its firm intention to conduct all negotiations quite openly in full view of the whole people. It will proceed immediately with the full publication of the secret treaties endorsed or concluded by the government of landowners and capitalists [Provisional Government] . . . The [Soviet] government proclaims the unconditional and immediate annulment of everything contained in these secret treaties insofar as it is aimed . . . at securing advantages and privileges for the Russian landowners and capitalists and at the retention or extension of the annexations made by the Great Russians.[7]

Lenin's advocacy of open diplomacy foreshadowed a similar statement in Point One of Wilson's "Fourteen Points" speech of January 8, 1918: "Open covenants of peace openly arrived at; . . . diplomacy shall proceed always frankly and in the public view."[8]

Fully consistent with Lenin's previous statements on the war, the Decree on Peace inaugurated the new Soviet approach to foreign relations. In the Allied camp many dismissed it as a propaganda stunt, which in part it doubtless was. Nonetheless, Lenin hoped that all belligerents would agree to negotiate thus sparing weak Soviet Russia from facing the victorious Germans alone. Also, Lenin and Trotskii believed sincerely that the Decree would trigger revolutions in Europe.

The Soviet government acted promptly to implement its peace program. On November 21, Foreign Commissar Trotskii wrote all Allied ambassadors in Petrograd asking them to consider a formal immediate armistice on all war fronts and to open peace negotiations immediately. The same message went also to the Central Powers. The next day Trotskii announced publication of inter-Allied secret treaties, which would reveal imperialist Allied war aims. Allied envoys in Petrograd protested that the proposed armistice violated the inter-Allied secret treaty of September 5, 1914, which

---

[7]Robert C. Tucker, ed., *The Lenin Anthology* (New York, 1975), pp. 540–41.
[8]*Congressional Record*, vol. 56 (January 8, 1918), pp. 680–81.

LEV DAVIDOVICH TROTSKII (1879–1940), LEADER IN PETROGRAD SOVIET, 1905, 1917; FOUNDER OF THE RED ARMY; FIRST SOVIET COMMISSAR OF FOREIGN AFFAIRS, 1917–1918

had barred the conclusion of a separate peace with the enemy. There were veiled Allied threats of possible intervention if Russia made a separate peace. Nonetheless, the British ambassador, George Buchanan, recognized that Russia urgently required peace.[9] On November 28, a preliminary cease fire

---

[9]Fischer, pp. 15–22.

was concluded between Russia and the Central Powers, but Petrograd postponed negotiations to give the Allies time to respond.

The Allied reaction revealed confusion and anxiety over the outcome of World War I if Russia made peace. Allied governments and the United States refused to recognize the Bolshevik regime as the government of Russia. Hopelessly divided over any positive approach toward Soviet Russia, the Allies failed to reply to Lenin's appeal and refused to negotiate with the Central Powers. However, the Germans responded favorably. Disregarding Lenin's appeals to German workers, the German High Command discerned great strategic advantages in concluding a separate peace with Soviet Russia. Germany then could shift its troops from the eastern front to France in order to deliver a knockout blow planned for the spring of 1918.

The German–Soviet armistice of early December 1917 allowed negotiations to begin at Brest-Litovsk, the headquarters of Germany's eastern front. On December 22 the first plenary session of the peace conference convened. The Soviet delegation was headed by Adolf Joffe, Lev Kamenev, and Grigorii Sokolnikov, chosen partly for their knowledge of German and because top Soviet leaders were otherwise preoccupied. At Brest-Litovsk German military men headed by Major General Max von Hoffman, an expert on Russia, made the decisions, although Austrians, Turks, and Bulgarians also were present. Joffe's six points, which comprised a basis for negotiations, included no indemnities nor forcible annexation of territories seized during the war; restoration of the independence of nations that had lost it; national self-determination for others; and the protection of minority rights in multinational territories. While accepting the concept of no annexations and indemnities, von Hoffmann explained that the German-occupied borderlands were not ethnically Russian, so their separation from Russia merely reflected the principle of self-determination. The Germans aimed to create satellite states in Poland, the Baltics, and Ukraine. Shocked by this, the Soviet delegates, reacting like nationalists rather than internationalist Bolsheviks, broke off the talks and returned to Petrograd.

In January 1918 the Soviet envoys returned to Brest–Litovsk in a revolutionary mood and led by Foreign Commissar Trotskii. The aim of Soviet Russia, Trotskii explained, was:

> the quickest possible cessation of the criminal war which was murdering Europe and . . . to give every possible aid to the working class of all countries to destroy the rule of capitalism and to seize the government with a view to a democratic peace and the socialist remolding of Europe and all humanity.[10]

Trotskii deliberately dragged out the negotiations in order to prevent imposition of a harsh settlement or renewal of the war until after the

---

[10]Fischer, p. 32.

MAP 2–2   Russian Frontiers, 1914–1918

Frontiers of 1914

— · — Eastern front under the armistice of December 15, 1917

— — — Western frontier between Pruzany and Tarnograd created by the Ukraine-Central Powers Treaty of January 9, 1918

German held front under the Brest-Litovsk Treaty of March 3, 1918. Dotted line in Ukraine is where the German invasion began after Kiev's capture and solid black line depicts the maximum line of German occupation.

— · — · — The "agreed line" with Russia renouncing all territorial rights to the west

——— Principal railroads

Constituent Assembly met January 18. For almost a month the Germans let Trotskii make provocative speeches while they reached a settlement with the disintegrating Ukrainian Rada government to detach all Ukraine from Russia. Trotskii could not prevent that because there were as yet few pro-Bolshevik elements in Ukraine.

Soon after the Soviet delegation returned to Brest-Litovsk, President Wilson, in Point Six of his "Fourteen Points" speech to Congress, urged the evacuation of all Russian territory and the settlement of all issues affecting Russia so that it could determine freely and independently its political future and national policy. Point Thirteen advocated that "an independent Polish state should be erected including the territories inhabited by indisputably Polish populations."[11] Although numerous copies of Wilson's speech were distributed in Russia, the Bolsheviks dismissed it as "empty phrases." Indeed, Wilson's idealistic program had little or no effect on Allied policies towards Soviet Russia.

Completing talks with the Rada, the Germans, on February 8, demanded a quick settlement with Russia. Trotskii broke off negotiations and returned to Petrograd sounding the slogan, "No war, no peace." Russia would not fight an imperialist war, but neither would she sign an imperialist peace pact. That intensified the debate within the Bolshevik Central Committee, where Lenin insisted realistically that the severe German peace terms must be accepted. Soviet Russia, he warned, could not fight and must have a breathing spell; otherwise the revolution in Germany would come too late to save the Soviet regime. Trotskii argued for "no war, no peace," predicting that German workers would rise soon in revolution. At one point his position won a majority in the Central Committee. Left Bolsheviks and Left SR's, led by Nicholas Bukharin, urged revolutionary war, with Russian armies fighting on to promote world revolution. On February 18, the Germans launched an offensive that would soon enable them to dictate peace in Petrograd itself. Only then did the Central Committee authorize Lenin to sue for peace. Meanwhile, the desperate Bolsheviks had turned to Allied representatives for possible aid, contacts that persisted until the Brest-Litovsk treaty was signed. The Soviets accepted a German ultimatum to reopen negotiations, which could last no more than three days.

On March 3, 1918, a new Soviet delegation accepted the Treaty of Brest-Litovsk without even reading its terms, emphasizing that it was a dictated peace. Lenin called it "a Tilsit peace," like that between Napoleon and Alexander I in 1807, and predicted it would not last long. Its terms were more severe than the peace settlements imposed on Germany after two world wars. Russia lost roughly one-third of its population and all the western borderlands of the former Russian Empire including Ukraine, the Baltic provinces, Russian Poland, and Finland. However, those territories were inhabited chiefly by non-Russians, who opposed both Russian and

---

[11]*Congressional Record*, pp. 680–81.

Bolshevik rule. Germany's separate peace with Ukraine was the most damaging blow. Undoing three centuries of Russian expansion in the west, Brest-Litovsk roughly restored Russia's frontiers of 1618. Neither side took the treaty's provisions that seriously and promptly set out to violate them. However, Brest-Litovsk removed Russia from a war she could no longer fight and gave the Bolsheviks the breathing spell they needed desperately in order to preserve the Soviet regime and to concentrate on domestic matters. Brest-Litovsk was nullified de facto by Germany's surrender to the Allies in November 1918 and was abrogated de jure by the Paris Peace Settlement of 1919.

NARKOMINDEL AND COMINTERN: TWO FACES OF SOVIET FOREIGN POLICY, 1917–1919

When the Bolshevik regime was created, a foreign affairs commission was established, subsequently named the People's Commissariat of Foreign Affairs, or *Narkomindel*. Initially, Soviet leaders did not consider diplomacy very important; party militants regarded it as associated irrevocably with old "bourgeois" secret interstate relations. Thus Trotskii stated:

> I have accepted the post of Commissar of Foreign Affairs just because I wanted to have more leisure for party affairs. My job is a small one: to publish the secret documents and to close the shop.[12]

Later, admitting he had exaggerated somewhat, Trotskii added that "the center of gravity then was not in diplomacy."[13]

At first, Narkomindel, lacking its own offices and facilities, operated through the Military-Revolutionary Committee. The old Foreign Ministry remained occupied for weeks by the Provisional Government's officials, most of whom refused to serve the Bolshevik regime. When Trotskii took over Ministry headquarters November 27, only a few minor officials cooperated. The core of Narkomindel consisted of veteran Bolshevik exiles, including such able men as Lev Karakhan and Maxim Litvinov, later to become its chief. Most Russian envoys abroad likewise refused to accept Soviet power, and ambassadors of the former Provisional Government agitated against foreign recognition of the Bolshevik regime. Thus Narkomindel under Trotskii's casual direction performed only minor tasks and focused on propaganda. Major decisions affecting the Brest-Litovsk negotiations were made in the Central Committee, not at Narkomindel. By the end of January 1918 about 200 mostly inexperienced employees had been recruited into Narkomindel.

After Brest-Litovsk Bolshevik leaders provided Narkomindel with greater resources and closer attention. After Trotskii resigned over

---

[12]Quoted in Teddy Uldricks, *Diplomacy and Ideology: The Origins of Soviet Foreign Relations, 1917–1930* (London, 1980), p. 41.

[13]Uldricks, p. 17.

Brest-Litovsk's harsh terms, Grigorii V. Chicherin, a professional diplomat close to Lenin, became foreign commissar and proved an excellent choice. Of aristocratic background and fluent in five languages, the tactful and gentlemanly Chicherin marked a shift from revolutionary amateurism to professional diplomacy. A former Menshevik, he had returned to the Bolshevik fold during World War I but had little standing within the latter party. While Trotskii headed the Soviet delegation at Brest-Litovsk, Chicherin had taken over Narkomindel's daily work, acting as loyal executor of Lenin's course in foreign policy. During 1918 Chicherin built Narkomindel into a solid, competent organ of foreign policy. Through hard work and ability he created a respectable image for Soviet diplomacy, although at first the Allied powers refused to deal with him officially.

Believing firmly in a world revolution whose triumph they viewed as their only salvation, Bolshevik leaders during 1917–1919 sought to exploit war weariness and discontent in Europe, especially in Germany. Representing Lenin's government in Berlin in 1918 was Adolf Joffe, a professional revolutionary. He maintained close ties with German socialists, supplying them with funds and subversive literature. Just before Germany's surrender Joffe and his entire staff were expelled for subversive activities. In November 1918 the collapse of the German imperial regime and its replacement by a democratic socialist government seemingly created a golden opportunity for Bolshevik agitation. Facing the awesome responsibilities of running a defeated country, German socialists split into three groups, the Majority Socialists assuming leadership of what became the Weimar Republic. More radical elements created an Independent Socialist Party. Within it an extreme minority calling itself the Spartacist League emerged, led by the talented revolutionaries, Karl Liebknecht and Rosa Luxemburg; this became the nucleus of a German Communist Party (KPD). Strongly influenced by Lenin's agent, Karl Radek, the Spartacists in January 1919 sought to seize power in Berlin Bolshevik-style. However, the Majority Socialist government, allying itself with the German army, crushed that revolt and Liebknecht and Luxemburg were killed. Lack of mass support for revolution and fear of Bolshevism by German burghers and peasants doomed this attempt to create a Communist Germany.

Lenin had predicted that World War I would surely destroy the Second Socialist International consisting of European democratic socialist parties, but right after the war they sought to reconstitute it as a non-revolutionary alternative to Bolshevism and planned to convene an initial meeting in February 1919. The previous December at large meetings of radical socialists in Moscow and Petrograd predictions abounded of imminent proletarian revolutions in Europe and Asia. On December 24 the Bolshevik Central Committee urged all internationalist socialists to boycott the Second International's scheduled February meeting and announced that there already existed a Third International to spearhead oncoming world

GEORGII V. CHICHERIN (1872–1936), SOVIET COMMISSAR OF FOREIGN AFFAIRS,
1918–1930

revolution. Lenin decided then to establish a Communist International
(Comintern) despite objections of German Spartacists that this would be
premature. "It is for us revolutionary Germans to supply the hyphen
between Russia and the still reformist Socialists of the West," Rosa

KARL RADEK (1885–1939), "OLD BOLSHEVIK"; COMINTERN LEADER

Luxemburg had declared. "We can perform that function better as a Socialist party."[14] Lenin appeared to bow to these Spartacist objections, but then in early March 1919 an internationalist meeting was opened in Moscow with these words: "By order of the Central Committee of the Communist

---

[14]Quoted in B. Lazitch and M. Drachkovitch, *Lenin and the Comintern,*vol. I (Stanford, CA, 1972), p. 60.

Party of Russia I declare this first international Communist *Congress* to be in session."[15]

By no stretch of the imagination could this so-called First Comintern Congress be considered representative even of left-wing socialists. Only thirty-four delegates attended, nearly all in Soviet Russia, then virtually isolated from the outside world. The delegates were mostly chosen by the Bolshevik Central Committee from minority elements of the former Russian Empire. Only five came from abroad, representing Germany, Austria, Holland, Norway, and Sweden. Hugo Eberlein, the German delegate, had to be severely pressured to abstain on the actual vote to create the Comintern. That organization then was created by the Bolsheviks themselves and by four European delegates who did not even represent extant parties. During the four-day meeting Lenin proclaimed repeatedly that world revolution had already begun. Closing the "congress," he trumpeted: "The victory of the proletarian revolution throughout the world is assured. The hour of the founding of an international Soviet republic is near."[16] Bolshevik leaders had reached a peak of optimism about the imminent triumph of their messianic cause.

SOVIET RUSSIA AND THE PARIS PEACE CONFERENCE, 1919

At the end of 1918 Allied statesmen convened in Paris to make peace with the Central Powers and create bases for a new world order. However, the absence of Russia and defeated Germany imperilled that entire process. Earlier, President Wilson had urged a negotiated, not a dictated, peace. Furthermore, his "Fourteen Points" advocated generous treatment of Russia in the hope that the Russian people would ally with the United States against conservative and chauvinistic European governments. However, the severe terms imposed by Germany on a defeated Russia at Brest-Litovsk prompted Wilson to demand Germany's "unconditional surrender."

The "Big Four" (Woodrow Wilson, David Lloyd-George of Great Britain, Georges Clemenceau of France, and Vittorio Orlando of Italy), who dominated the peacemaking process in Paris, were gravely divided on the Russian issue. Wilson wanted Soviet Russia represented in Paris, to end the Russian Civil War, and have Allied troops withdrawn from Russia. British Prime Minister David Lloyd-George tended to agree, convinced that no genuine peace settlement was possible without Russia. However, a "Red Scare" was sweeping both Britain and the United States; conservatives in both countries detested and feared Bolshevism. Declared Lloyd-George before the Paris Conference:

Personally I would have dealt with the Soviets as the *de facto* Government of Russia. So would President Wilson. But we both agreed that we could not carry

---

[15]Lazitch and Drachkovitch, pp. 65–66.
[16]Lazitch and Drachkovitch, p. 60.

to that extent our colleagues at the Congress, nor the public opinion of our countries which was frightened by Bolshevik violence and feared its spread . . .[17]

On the other hand, Premier Georges Clemenceau, the formidable "Tiger of France," stubbornly opposed any Soviet representation in Paris. For him Franco-German rivalry remained the overriding issue at Paris. Russia, argued Clemenceau, had betrayed France by signing a separate peace and therefore could not be invited to the peace conference. He viewed Bolshevism as a menace that needed to be destroyed or at least quarantined. In January 1919 Clemenceau warned the Allied Council of Ten, as its summary noted:

> Bolshevism was spreading. It had invaded the Baltic Provinces and Poland, and that very morning they received very bad news regarding its spread to Budapest and Vienna. Italy also was in danger.

However, Bolshevism, while representing a clear and present danger to Europe, he affirmed, was weak militarily and could easily be crushed by force.[18] France's top soldier, Marshal Foch, urged a quick peace with Germany so the Allies could crush Bolshevism using American troops.[19]

For its part the Soviet government just before the Paris Conference convened stated repeatedly its wish to have Allied intervention ended and establish normal political and commercial relations with Europe; Moscow offered serious concessions to attain this goal. President Wilson found the 1918 Christmas message of Maxim Litvinov, a leading Soviet diplomat, most encouraging. Anxious to follow it up, he sent a personal envoy to confer with Litvinov in Stockholm.

Blocked by Clemenceau over bringing Bolshevik representatives to Paris, Wilson proposed that envoys of all warring Russian factions, provided they agreed to a truce, should attend a conference on Prinkipo Island near Constantinople. The French military sabotaged that idea by failing to transmit the Allied invitation to Moscow. However, a Soviet transmitter picked up news of the planned parley and the Soviet government wired its acceptance, agreeing to most Allied terms. However, White Russian factions, under French pressure, flatly refused to attend the Prinkipo meeting and the idea died.

Wilson then dispatched William C. Bullitt, an American attaché in Paris and subsequently the first American ambassador to Soviet Russia, as his personal envoy to confer with Lenin. In March 1919 Bullitt spoke with Lenin and other Soviet leaders in Moscow and brought back with him a Soviet proposal to end the Civil War on a compromise basis. However, upon his return Bullitt found Wilson and Lloyd-George wholly preoccupied with

---

[17]David Lloyd-George, *The Truth About the Peace Treaties*, vol. I (London, 1938), p. 315.
[18]Fischer, pp. 164–65.
[19]Fischer, p. 160.

the German question. The April 10 deadline of the Soviet government passed without any Allied response. The shortcomings of summit diplomacy helped to negate the Bullitt Mission and destroyed what could have been a favorable basis to conclude a fruitless Allied involvement in the Russian imbroglio.

Surfacing then was a plan of Herbert Hoover, Allied Food Administrator, and Norwegian explorer Fridtjof Nansen to provide food for hungry Russia if the Bolsheviks stopped fighting the Whites. The Allies accepted the proposal, but the Whites protested, and Soviet leaders suspected that this was a plot to deny them victory in the Civil War. The Hoover-Nansen relief proposal, commented French Foreign Minister Stephen Pichon, "would be a moral and material reinforcement of the iniquitous Bolshevik Government." Only non-Soviet controlled areas of Russia should be fed, he concluded.[20]

Both the Bullitt Mission and Hoover-Nansen project were undermined by unwarranted Allied confidence in an impending White victory because Admiral Kolchak was then advancing on Moscow. Wilson, distrusting Kolchak, wished to end American intervention in Russia. However, Lloyd-George and French leaders believed Kolchak was winning, so Wilson yielded reluctantly to their arguments. This prolonged American participation in the Russian intervention for almost a year. Actually, by May 1919 Kolchak was in rapid retreat and soon would be totally defeated. Yet an Allied note of May 26, revealing ignorance of the facts, pledged to aid him with food and munitions provided he pledged support for creating a democratic Russia after his victory. French and British envoys at Kolchak's headquarters drafted his positive reply in order to secure American aid.[21] This was the final Allied action adopted in Paris on the Russian question.

Thus the Paris peace settlement of 1919 concluded without Soviet participation and the Treaty of Versailles dictated to an embittered Germany both rested on precarious foundations. While an alienated Soviet Russia became an anti-Versailles power, the Bolsheviks soon regarded the new League of Nations, which had been written into the Versailles Treaty, as a potential capitalist coalition against Soviet Russia. This helped foster suspicion and hostility between Russia and the West that would long persist. It also would encourage two defeated and outcast former great powers—Weimar Germany and Soviet Russia—to cooperate against the West. Declared Lenin in June 1920:

> The Treaty of Versailles . . . is an even more brutal and foul act of violence against weak nations than was the Treaty of Brest-Litovsk. The League of Nations and the entire postwar policy of the Entente reveal this truth.[22]

---

[20]Fischer, p. 176.

[21]Kennan, pp. 144–46.

[22]Quoted in Tucker, p. 621.

BOLSHEVIK MESSIANISM: EUROPEAN REVOLUTIONS, POLAND, AND THE COMINTERN

Early in 1919, in the immediate aftermath of World War I, occurred a series of radical uprisings that brought left-wing socialist regimes to power briefly in Bavaria and Hungary. In western Europe and the United States these were interpreted as reflecting the sinister machinations of Bolshevik Moscow. In March a mixed Socialist-Communist regime was established in Hungary under a Communist, Bela Kun. Reacting enthusiastically to the news, Lenin wished to provide immediate military aid to Communist Hungary but discovered that Soviet Russia's weakness prevented it. Responding to Kun's urgent request for Soviet aid against Romanian intervention, Lenin wrote: "We are aware of Hungary's difficult and dangerous situation and we are doing our best. But immediate aid is sometimes physically impossible."[23] Indeed, he could do nothing to prevent Kun's defeat.

In April a Bavarian Soviet Republic was established by two Russian Socialist Revolutionaries acting on their own hook. However, it was crushed by nationalist opponents a few weeks later. At this time conservative Poland and Romania effectively isolated Soviet Russia from central Europe. However, the collapse of these socialist experiments in Hungary and Bavaria failed to dispel the firm belief of Lenin and Trotskii that revolution in Europe was imminent. Thus in November 1919 Lenin told the Second All-Russian Congress of Communist Organizations of Eastern Peoples:

> . . . The class struggle in Germany has now intensified, it is getting closer and closer to civil war, to a battle by the German proletariat against Germany's imperialists. . . . Everyone knows that the social revolution is moving forward day by day, hour by hour, in Western Europe, and even in America and England. . . . Only the proletariat of all the world's advanced countries can win final victory.

However, that same month Paul Levi, the top German Communist leader, reported pessimistically: "The proletariat's over-all situation is clear. It has suffered defeat after defeat, and step by step counterrevolution is rising."[24] This latter verdict soon proved correct.

By early 1920, with the defeat of Kolchak and Denikin, the White movement in Russia was withering. This caused the new conservative and nationalistic Polish regime dominated by Marshal Josef Pilsudski to plan an attack on a weak Soviet Russia. After reaching agreement in April 1920 with a tottering White Ukrainian regime, the Poles advanced swiftly and occupied Kiev in May. That led to a powerful Red Army counteroffensive led by General Mikhail Tukhachevskii, who by early July reached the gates of Warsaw, provoking frantic Polish appeals to the Allies. The Red Army's

---

[23]Quoted in Lazitch and Drachkovitch, p. 126.
[24]Quoted in Lazitch and Drachkovitch, p. 127.

advance triggered final Soviet efforts to promote revolutions in Germany and central Europe.

As the Red Army swept forward in Poland, the Second Comintern Congress convened in Moscow. This was the first authentic meeting of its member parties, with over 200 delegates representing the emerging Communist parties of Europe. Believing fervently that 1920 would witness the triumph of Communist revolutions in Europe, Lenin directed all the work of the Congress personally and drafted all its major documents. Among these was "Twenty-One Conditions for Admission" to the Comintern, which ensured Bolshevik domination of that organization. In the hall where the delegates met red flags marking the progress of the Red Army in Poland were moved forward as the delegates cheered what seemed an irresistible Communist tide. Speaking with French socialists Lenin waxed euphoric:

> Yes, the Soviets are in Warsaw. Soon Germany will be ours, Hungary reconquered; the Balkans will revolt against capitalism; Italy will shake. Bourgeois Europe is cracking at every seam in the hurricane.[25]

His enthusiasm and optimism proved contagious. Soviets were being created behind Red Army lines in an apparent effort to communize Poland by force. However, the main Soviet target was Germany, the key to Europe.

Soon after the Second Comintern Congress dispersed these fantastic dreams lay shattered. Encouraged by French advice and moral support, Marshal Pilsudski, exploiting Soviet military mistakes, launched a counteroffensive that forced a hasty Soviet retreat. By the end of August 1920 all ethnically Polish territory had been regained. In September Polish-Soviet peace negotiations began that led to a preliminary Treaty of Riga in October, which provided the Poles with a more favorable frontier than the ethnic line proposed by Britain's Lord George Curzon. The final Treaty of Riga, signed in March 1921, incorporated millions of Belorussians and Ukrainians in postwar Poland. The end of the Polish-Soviet war allowed the Red Army to defeat the last White army under Baron Nicholas Wrangel in November 1920. Russia's Civil War ended with Bolshevik victory and the Ukraine regained. The conclusion of the Civil War coincided with the demise of all real prospects for Communist revolutions in Europe.

Suggested Readings

Borkenau, Franz. *World Communism: A History of the Communist International*. Ann Arbor, MI, 1962.

Bullitt, William C. *The Bullitt Mission to Russia: Testimony before the Committee on Foreign Relations, United States Senate*. New York, 1919.

Bunyan, James, and H. H. Fisher, eds., *The Bolshevik Revolution, 1917–1918: Documents and Materials*. Stanford, CA, 1934.

---

[25]Quoted in Lazitch and Drachkovitch, p. 275.

Davies, Norman. *White Eagle, Red Star—the Polish-Soviet War, 1919–1920.* London, 1972.

Debo, Richard. *Revolution and Survival: The Foreign Policy of Soviet Russia, 1917–18.* Toronto, 1979.

_____. *Survival and Consolidation: The Foreign Policy of Soviet Russia, 1918–21.* Montreal and Buffalo, NY, 1992.

Degras, Jane, ed., *The Communist International 1919–1943: Documents.* vol. 1 (1919–1922). London, 1956.

Filene, Peter. *Americans and the Soviet Experiment, 1917–1933.* Cambridge, MA, 1967.

Fischer, Louis. *The Soviets in World Affairs: A History of the Relations Between the Soviet Union and the Rest of the World, 1917–1929.* 2 vols. 2nd ed. Princeton, NJ, 1951.

Freund, Gerald. *Unholy Alliance: Russo-German Relations from the Treaty of Brest-Litovsk to the Treaty of Berlin.* New York, 1957.

Hulse, James W. *The Forming of the Communist International.* Stanford, CA, 1964.

Johnson, Robert H., ed., *Soviet Foreign Policy, 1918–1945: A Guide to Research and Research Materials.* Wilmington, DE, 1991.

Kennan, George F. *Russia and the West Under Lenin and Stalin.* Boston, MA, 1960.

_____. *American-Soviet Relations, 1917–1920.* 2 vols. New York, 1967.

Lazitch, Branko and M. Drachkovitch. *Lenin and the Comintern.* 2 vols. Stanford, CA, 1972.

Mayer, Arno. *Wilson vs. Lenin: The Political Origins of the New Diplomacy, 1917–1918.* Cleveland and New York, 1959.

Ponomaryov, B., et al. *History of Soviet Foreign Policy, 1917–1945.* Moscow, 1969.

Senn, Alfred. *Diplomacy and Revolution: the Soviet Mission to Switzerland, 1918.* Notre Dame, IN, 1974.

Thompson, John M. *Russia, Bolshevism and the Versailles Peace.* Princeton, NJ, 1966.

Ulam, Adam B. *Expansion and Coexistence: A History of Soviet Foreign Policy, 1917–1973.* 2nd ed. New York, 1974.

Uldricks, Teddy J. *Diplomacy and Ideology: The Origins of Soviet Foreign Relations, 1917–1930.* London, 1980.

Ullman, Richard. *Anglo-Soviet Relations, 1917–1921.* 3 vols. Princeton, NJ, 1961, 1968, and 1973.

Wheeler-Bennett, John W. *Brest-Litovsk: The Forgotten Peace, March 1918.* 2nd ed. London, 1966.

ACCOMMODATION AND RECOVERY, 1920–1927

Even before the Second Comintern Congress with its mood of ebullient optimism about prospects for world revolution, the first halting steps had been taken towards accommodation between Soviet Russia and the capitalist nations of Europe. Interrupted by the Polish-Soviet War (April–October 1920), this trend towards "peaceful coexistence" between Soviet Russia and the West accelerated afterwards and after 1921 brought the normalization of commercial relations and later diplomatic recognition of the USSR by most European countries. During these years there was an increasing Soviet emphasis on diplomacy and a declining effort by Moscow to foster world revolution. These changing Soviet priorities were connected closely with the economic and subsequent political crisis that absorbed Moscow's attention after the defeat of the Whites and the Allied withdrawal.

FIRST STEPS TOWARDS NORMALIZATION, 1920–1921

Both Soviet attitudes towards the West and Allied views about Soviet Russia remained ambivalent during 1920. After May of that year, as a Red victory in the Civil War became probable, Soviet leaders realized the necessity of obtaining Western assistance, or at least toleration, in order to restore the devastated Russian economy. They sought to prevent any further Western intervention by dividing leading capitalist countries and playing one off against the other. Nonetheless, Lenin and Trotskii continued to believe that world revolution was imminent and sought to promote its prospects through the Comintern.

From 1917 to 1922, Lenin coordinated Soviet foreign policy and sought to exploit evident Franco-British contradictions and thus end the perilous isolation of Soviet Russia. In February 1920 the first breach opened in what had been a solid western blockade when Moscow signed the Treaty of Tartu with newly independent Estonia, ending hostilities and pledging non-intervention in each other's affairs. That summer similar agreements were concluded with Latvia and Lithuania. In October Finland recognized Soviet Russia, and an armistice ended the Russo-Polish War. Under the Treaty of Riga (March 1921) Soviet Russia and Poland exchanged diplomats. Thus

MAP 3–1   Soviet Russia and Europe, 1919–1938

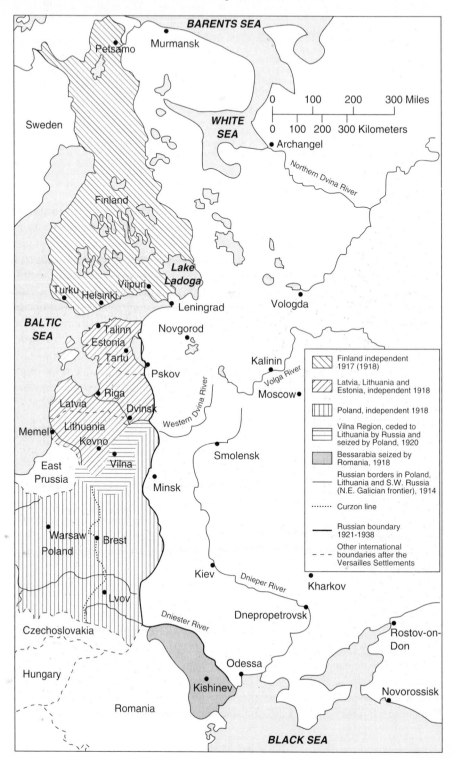

normalization of Soviet Russia's relations with its immediate neighbors was achieved before the compromise New Economic Policy was adopted in Russia.

British Prime Minister David Lloyd-George, a consistent opponent of Allied intervention, was instrumental in ending the Allied blockade against Soviet Russia in January 1920. The following month he advocated reopening commercial ties and basic changes in British policy towards Moscow. Rather naively Lloyd-George told Parliament:

> We have failed . . . to restore Russia to sanity by force. I believe we can save her by trade. Commerce has a sobering influence. . . . Trade, in my opinion, will bring an end to the ferocity, the rapine, and the crudity of Bolshevism surer than any other method.[1]

Successful negotiations led to an exchange of war prisoners between Soviet Russia and the western powers; in May a Soviet trade delegation went to London. Early in July the top Soviet negotiator, L. B. Krassin, took back to Moscow British terms for restoring diplomatic and commercial relations, which the Soviets promptly accepted. However, provoked by the Red Army offensive towards Warsaw, London demanded additionally that Moscow halt the war with Poland and attend a general conference with the Allies, Poland, and the Baltic nations. The Soviet advance reactivated the "Red scare" in Great Britain and a struggle between the pro-Polish Conservatives and pro-Soviet Labour Party. Anglo-Soviet negotiations were put on hold.

The United States had been aiding the Poles with food and war materiel even before the Soviet onslaught began. A note from Secretary of State Bainbridge Colby to the Italian ambassador in August 1920 outlines American policy towards Soviet Russia. Colby states that he "recoils" from recognizing the Bolshevik regime and favors delaying any decision until Russia is no longer "helpless in the grip of a non-representative Government, whose only sanction is brute force." American leaders did not believe that the Soviet regime would survive for long because it had rejected capitalism. The Bolsheviks, affirmed Colby without citing any supporting evidence, "have not the slightest intention of observing undertakings" with foreign powers. Furthermore, the Comintern, heavily subsidized by Moscow, "has for its openly avowed aim the promotion of Bolshevist revolutions through-out the world."[2] Washington had closed the doors to recognition, and they would remain closed during the isolationist and conservative Warren Harding administration that followed.

Once the Red Army retreated hastily from Warsaw, bases were laid for more normal relations with Britain. Lengthy negotiations culminated in the

---

[1] Quoted in George Kennan, *Russia and the West Under Lenin and Stalin* (Boston, 1960), p. 172.

[2] Louis Fischer, *The Soviets in World Affairs: A History of the Relations Between the Soviet Union and the Rest of the World, 1917–1929*, vol. I (Princeton, NJ, 1951), pp. 306–07.

Anglo-Soviet Trade Agreement of March 1921. This did not at first produce much trade between them but established de facto diplomatic relations. Krassin, the chief negotiator, was accredited as the Soviet representative in London, a major triumph for Narkomindel (the foreign commissariat). Other European states swiftly followed Great Britain's lead, and during 1921 the Soviets likewise normalized relations with Turkey, Persia, and Afghanistan.

The Soviet-Persian Treaty of February 1921 laid bases for normal relations and provided for the evacuation of Russian troops if British forces were likewise withdrawn. An offer by the British envoy to Tehran to partition Persia into spheres of influence by Britain and Soviet Russia on the model of 1907 was ignored by Russia's envoy, Theodore Rothstein, who wrote: "Any attempt on our part . . . to start a revolution in any part of Persia would immediately throw it into the arms of the British, who would be received as the saviors of the Fatherland." Both Lenin and Foreign Commissar Georgii Chicherin agreed, preferring to strengthen the Nationalist government in Tehran rather than pursue revolutionary aims.[3]

THE KRONSTADT REVOLT AND THE NEW ECONOMIC POLICY, 1921–1927

Seven years of World War I, Russian Civil War, and Bolshevik experimentation had left Russia in a state of economic crisis unequalled in centuries. Once the Whites had been defeated, the onerous policies of "War Communism," especially forced requisitioning of grain from the peasants, became unbearable for the Russian population. A wave of peasant revolts from Tambov province on the middle Volga to Siberia threatened to destroy the worker-peasant alliance upon which Soviet power rested.

However, it was the Kronstadt Revolt of March 1921, noted Lenin, that "lit up reality better than anything else."[4] Red sailors, the most revolutionary, pro-Bolshevik element in 1917, rose against the Bolshevik regime four years later. Their "Petropavlovsk Resolution" denounced "War Communism," demanded democratic elections to soviets "without Bolsheviks," the end of grain requisitioning, and full freedom of peasants on their land. Bolshevik leaders sought to discredit Kronstadt as a White-émigré plot concocted and manipulated from abroad. However, no aid ever reached the insurgents from Europe, and Kronstadt's leader, S. M. Petrichenko, a Ukrainian sailor, affirmed, "Our revolt . . . was a spontaneous effort to eliminate Bolshevik oppression. . . ."[5] Soon the Kronstadt Revolt was crushed ruthlessly by Trotskii's Red Army. The Bolshevik regime was revealed as a new tyranny relying on military force.

---

[3]Fischer, pp. 429–30.
[4]Paul Avrich, *Kronstadt 1921* (Princeton, NJ, 1970), p. 3.
[5]Avrich, p. 113.

Amidst peasant revolts and the Kronstadt affair the Tenth Communist Party Congress convened in Moscow. At the Congress Lenin argued persuasively that only an immediate agreement with the peasantry could save the Soviet regime and restore the worker-peasant alliance. Over strong opposition from Trotskii and other doctrinaire Bolsheviks, Lenin won approval for a New Economic Policy that included a series of compromises and retreats designed to regain peasant support, promote economic recovery, and consolidate the Soviet regime. Once again Lenin with his realism, insight, and willingness to admit mistakes saved Bolshevik power. Moscow replaced forced requisitioning of grain with a fixed tax in kind per acre of land. The peasant received relative security of tenure, could hire labor, and market his produce as he wished. Temporarily abandoning the Bolshevik goal of socialized agriculture, Lenin stressed that private farming would prevail at least temporarily. Small industries were denationalized and a mixed economy was created that featured small-scale private capitalism; some former owners of firms returned from exile. Lenin characterized these concessions as a step backward towards capitalism in order to prepare the way later for two steps forward towards socialism. The concessions of the New Economic Policy (NEP) promoted the rapid recovery of the Soviet economy, which by 1927 had reached roughly the prewar level in agricultural and industrial output. The policies of NEP made Soviet leaders, in order to stimulate recovery, anxious to secure diplomatic recognition from capitalist powers, restore normal trade and secure credits, long-term if possible.

Even the Third Comintern Congress, held in Moscow in June and July 1921, reflected the compromising spirit of NEP. Attended by 509 delegates from forty-eight countries, it was far larger than the Second Congress a year before. At its meetings were discussed the so-called "March Action" in Germany—an abortive attempt at revolution there—and the Kronstadt Revolt and NEP in Soviet Russia. The Comintern, noted Trotskii, one of its chief leaders, had passed from tactics of assault to those of siege, to infiltration instead of open armed struggle. In a lengthy speech of June 23 to the Congress Trotskii concluded that whereas the international situation remained basically revolutionary, capitalism had nonetheless achieved a temporary equilibrium. Although during 1918–1919 it had seemed "that the working class would in a year or two achieve State power," that had not happened:

> History has given the bourgeoisie a fairly long breathing spell. . . . The revolution is not so obedient, so tame, that it can be led on a leash, as we imagined. It has ups and downs, its crises and booms.[6]

---

[6]Jane Degras, ed., *The Communist International 1919–1943: Documents,* vol. I (London, 1956), pp. 224–25, 229–30.

However, the Comintern continued to defy Western capitalist countries and reiterated its determination to destroy world capitalism. Proclaimed a Comintern resolution of 1922:

> We are the deadly enemies of bourgeois society. Every honest Communist will fight against bourgeois society to his last breath, in word and deed and if necessary with arms in hand. Yes, the propaganda of the Communist International will be pernicious for you, the imperialists. It is the historical mission of the Communist International to be the gravedigger of bourgeois society. . . .[7]

Soviet leaders in 1921 sought diplomatic recognition, security, and economic assistance to enable them at some future date to destroy the West and the entire capitalist order. Surprisingly, the West's response to their overtures was favorable because European countries were then suffering from unemployment and insufficient markets for their products, and Western industrial and political leaders looked longingly to the Russian market to help solve manifold economic problems. Obstacles to normal diplomatic and commercial relations with Soviet Russia included Comintern propaganda in Europe and its colonies, Soviet nationalization of Western properties, and Russia's pre-World War I and wartime debts to Western countries. Allied claims against the Soviet government for these debts totalled some 14 billion rubles. The French Foreign Office estimated in February 1922 that France held 43 percent of all Russian debts followed by Great Britain with 33 percent, Belgium and Germany each with 6 percent, and the United States with 3.4 percent. Whereas most of the debts to Britain were owed to the government, the French debt was held mostly by 1.2 million private owners of Russian bonds, comprising an influential pressure group.[8]

Not to be outdone by the West, the Soviet government submitted huge counterclaims for damage allegedly caused by Allied intervention during 1918–1919. Western governments, generally agreeing that Russia's wartime debts and Soviet counterclaims would roughly cancel each other out, pressed for Soviet repayment of prewar Russian debts and compensation for confiscated Western properties. Refusing to restore foreign properties, as the French and Belgians demanded, Moscow offered to pay something on the prewar debts provided Western governments advanced it major long-term credits. During 1922 negotiations on the debt issue collapsed.

Nevertheless, the outcome of these financial quarrels proved generally favorable to Soviet Russia which persuaded the German, Italian, and Austrian governments to grant Moscow substantial short-term credits. Later, Britain and France concluded trade agreements with Soviet Russia and recognized it de facto without resolving the debt issue.

---

[7]Degras, p. 348.

[8]Stephen White, *The Origins of Détente: The Genoa Conference and Soviet-Western Relations, 1921–1922* (Cambridge, England, 1985), p. 27.

THE NARKOMINDEL AND SOVIET-WESTERN RELATIONS, 1919–1922

Neither for top Bolshevik leaders nor for Foreign Commissar Chicherin did the policy of peaceful coexistence that Moscow adopted during 1921 signify an abandonment of socialist revolution or of efforts to expand socialism in the world. For Chicherin peaceful coexistence meant pursuing peace initiatives abroad in order to protect Soviet Russia while domestic economic reconstruction proceeded. As Bolshevik leaders recognized increasingly the key importance of traditional diplomacy, the authority and prestige of Narkomindel rose significantly during the 1920s.

Narkomindel continued to expand in size as well. In 1918 it possessed some 250 central office employees, but by 1921 that figure had grown to more than 1,300. A decree of June 1921 reorganized its central machinery and created separate departments for relations with the West and East. After the formation of the USSR late in 1922, foreign affairs came entirely under the All-Union government. This ended any independent activity by individual Soviet republics, despite protests by some Ukrainian diplomats. By 1924 Narkomindel employed 804 persons in its central Moscow office, 1,098 in its missions abroad, and 231 more in consulates and missions throughout the USSR. Compared with the British foreign service, Narkomindel was considerably overstaffed and rather bureaucratic. At the top Foreign Commissar Chicherin was often hampered by his relatively low status in the Communist Party. Several of his subordinates outranked him in the Party and in political influence.[9]

After 1919 Soviet decision making became concentrated in the Politburo rather than the larger Central Committee. Thus Lenin reported to the Ninth Party Congress in 1920 that during the previous year the Politburo had decided all domestic and foreign policy issues. Henceforth, it became established practice for the Politburo to formulate the main lines of Soviet foreign policy—until late 1922 with Lenin's close participation. During Lenin's illnesses in 1922–1923 the Politburo reached decisions collectively, transmitting its directives to Chicherin for implementation, confirming the predominance of the Party over state agencies. In foreign affairs Lenin formulated both theoretical and practical concepts. By his fertile political imagination and tactical skill and ingenuity, notes Robert Tucker, Lenin was comparable to Peter the Great. Devoting much time to organizing the Soviet diplomatic service, Lenin was largely responsible for the propagandistic style of Soviet foreign policy pronouncements through 1922.[10]

---

[9]Teddy Uldricks, *Diplomacy and Ideology: The Origins of Soviet Foreign Relations, 1917–1930* (London, 1980), pp. 74–90.

[10]Robert C. Tucker, "Autocrats and Oligarchs," in I. Lederer, ed., *Russian Foreign Policy: Essays in Historical Perspective* (New Haven, CT, 1962), pp. 180–83.

Just after Lenin's death, Foreign Commissar Chicherin provided this interesting, albeit eulogistic, description of Lenin's role in the making of Soviet foreign policy:

> In the first years of the existence of our republic, I spoke with him by telephone several times a day, often at length, and had frequent personal interviews with him. Often I discussed with him all the details of current diplomatic affairs of any importance. Instantly grasping the substance of each issue and giving it the broadest political interpretation, Vladimir Ilich always provided in his conversations the most brilliant analysis of our diplomatic situation and his counsels . . . were models of diplomatic art and flexibility.[11]

Lenin, recalled Chicherin, supervised the details of negotiations with Estonia and Finland in 1919–1920 that led to the establishment of regular diplomatic relations. Lenin directed by telephone the Riga peace talks with Poland in 1921 and the preparations for the Genoa Conference of 1922. This latter conclave represented the true Soviet debut on the European diplomatic stage. In some ways Lenin acted as his own foreign minister, but contrary to the usual autocratic tsarist practice, he relied necessarily on persuasion. Chicherin's position in the 1920s as foreign commissar resembled Alexander M. Gorchakov's as foreign minister in the 1860s. Both acted largely as mouthpieces for foreign policies already determined by the head of state.

During the 1920s Narkomindel had to compete with several other Soviet agencies that executed foreign policy decisions reached by Lenin, and by his successors in the Politburo. In that era Soviet Russia strove to maintain its ambitious role as the spearhead and citadel of world revolution despite obvious military weakness. In compensation it developed a large arsenal of weapons in foreign affairs, including the Comintern, Profintern (trade union international), the Cheka (secret police), and trading and tourist agencies. However, Chicherin competed with increasing success because of his ability and Moscow's evident need for a diplomacy to divide the capitalist West. A strict outward separation was maintained between Narkomindel as an official government agency and the Comintern, theoretically a private organization. Thus the Soviet regime repeatedly denied official responsibility for Comintern propaganda abroad. There was actually considerable friction and jealousy between the two agencies. At times they appeared to be working at cross purposes, such as Narkomindel negotiating with foreign governments that the Comintern sought to subvert and overthrow. However, disputes between them were resolved in the Politburo, where the proper policy would be selected to achieve the Soviet goal. Soviet diplomatic missions abroad, besides regular Narkomindel personnel, included representatives of the Comintern and secret police. Often Chicherin's authority was bypassed or undercut by agencies with a more direct line to top Party authorities.

---

[11]Tucker, p. 183, quoting *Izvestiia*, January 30, 1924.

The Genoa Conference of April 1922 marked Soviet Russia's, and Chicherin's, first actual diplomatic appearance on the European stage. Genoa was the largest and most representative international conference held since the Paris Peace Conference, although an isolationist United States refused to attend. With some exaggeration British Prime Minister Lloyd-George called it "the greatest gathering of European nations which has ever been assembled."[12] Genoa's purpose was to discuss the economic reconstruction of Europe and establish a mutually advantageous relationship between Soviet Russia and the Western powers. In January 1922 Lloyd-George and Premier Aristide Briand of France had decided to invite Soviet participation at Genoa. Supporting this, the Italian government urged Lenin's personal participation. Moscow promptly accepted the invitation with pleasure, naming Lenin to head the Soviet delegation in order to satisfy Lloyd-George's expressed wish that "big men meet big men." Actually, Lenin, already in poor health and concerned with possible White émigré attempts on his life, never intended to come to Genoa.[13] The Western initiators of the Genoa Conference, notably Lloyd-George, envisioned a comprehensive settlement of differences there with the Bolshevik regime. The adoption of the New Economic Policy persuaded many Western leaders that the Thermidor, or turning point, had been reached in the Bolshevik regime and that the Soviets would seek foreign support out of desperation.

Moscow was indeed prepared to make concessions and enter negotiations in order to prevent renewed intervention. Soviet leaders still viewed Great Britain as the greatest world naval and financial power and citadel of world capitalism; an isolationist United States scarcely figured then in their calculations. Traditionally, Russia's raw materials and food exports had gone mainly to Britain; now the Soviet leaders hoped that trade could be revived. Anxious to buy chiefly from the United States and Germany, the Soviets aimed to sell their products primarily to England. Britain, notes American writer George Kennan, remained the chief target in a Soviet campaign for diplomatic equality and normal trade relations.[14] However, departing for Genoa, Soviet delegates headed by Chicherin, while hoping to obtain Western economic aid and credits, faced Franco-Belgian pressure in the form of a threatened international consortium to exact repayment of prewar tsarist Russian debts.

At a preliminary Western meeting in January in Cannes, a so-called coexistence resolution was adopted, which declared:

Nations can claim no right to dictate to each other the principles on which they are to regulate their systems of ownership, internal economy and

---

[12]White, p. vii.

[13]Fischer, p. 319.

[14]Kennan, pp. 224–25.

government. It is for every nation to choose for itself the system that it prefers in this respect.[15]

Suggesting that capitalism and communism could live together peacefully, the Cannes resolution virtually disavowed the entire Allied intervention in Russia as a mistake; perhaps a Red Russia would prove less dangerous than a great and united "White Russia" would have been.

En route to the Genoa Conference, Chicherin and his colleagues stopped in Berlin to confer with leaders of Weimar Germany. Significantly, Lloyd-George had just released to the British press a secret memorandum of his from March 1919, which had stated prophetically:

> The greatest danger that I see in the present situation is that Germany may throw in her lot with Bolshevism and place her resources, her brains, her vast organizing power at the disposal of the revolutionary fanatics whose dream it is to conquer the world for Bolshevism by force of arms.

Lloyd-George seemed to be warning the newly named Premier Raymond Poincaré of France that to treat Soviet Russia severely at Genoa might drive it into Germany's waiting embrace.[16]

Soviet Russia and Weimar Germany were being drawn together by common opposition to a Versailles Treaty they considered unjust and vindictive, by their isolation from the West, and by mutual economic interests. During 1921, as German leaders grew convinced that France sought their economic and political ruin, they resolved to achieve rapprochement with Moscow. Chicherin, anxious to split the capitalist powers, emphasized the numerous economic opportunities available to the Germans in Russia. Moscow needed German industrial skills, efficiency, and experience, and, unlike the Allies, Germany was willing to negotiate on an equal basis. Talks proceeded swiftly, and German and Soviet legal experts drafted a treaty containing the basic elements of the subsequent Rapallo accord. Baron Ago von Maltzan, heading "easterners" in the German foreign office, urged that the treaty be concluded immediately, but the strongly pro-Western Foreign Minister Walter Rathenau demurred because he still hoped to reach a meaningful accord with the Allies at Genoa on German reparations. Chicherin also wished to sign the treaty in Berlin in March 1921 because, as he told the American writer Louis Fischer, he had little hope of a positive outcome in Genoa in the face of French obduracy.[17] However, since the Germans were not ready to sign, the Soviet-German settlement was deferred until after Genoa.

---

[15]British White Paper on the Cannes Conference, quoted in Fischer, p. 321.
[16]Fischer, p. 323.
[17]Fischer, pp. 330–33.

At the Genoa Conference, Foreign Commissar Chicherin in his first international public speech on April 10, 1922, declared that Soviet Russia had come there to achieve peace and European economic reconstruction. Russia, he stressed, with its vast unexploited natural resources was ready to "open its frontiers" and grant all kinds of concessions to Western investors, especially in Siberia. Because reconstruction would be imperiled by "the menace of new wars," Soviet Russia proposed a general limitation of armaments. Chicherin's attempt to introduce the disarmament issue infuriated Louis Barthou, the chief French delegate, who refused to discuss a matter not on the agenda. Lloyd-George salvaged the Genoa Conference by pouring oil on this Soviet-French wrangle. Actually, the chief discussions at Genoa were conducted in secret at Lloyd-George's Villa d'Albertis, where Russian debts and Soviet counterclaims were debated. These talks ended without a final agreement, but an understanding was reached that in a final settlement Soviet counterclaims would largely cancel out Russia's wartime debts.

As these Soviet-Allied pourparlers proceeded, the Germans felt alone and discouraged. No one seemed to want to talk with them, and they realized that a Soviet-Allied accord would leave them permanently isolated. Thus von Maltzan sounded out two Soviet delegates on renewing their recent Berlin treaty talks and found them receptive. At 1 A.M. on Easter Sunday Soviet delegate Adolf Joffe telephoned and awakened von Maltzan to invite the German delegation to come to the Hotel St. Margherite, the Soviet's headquarters in Rapallo, the next morning in order to resume their earlier Berlin talks. Maltzan woke up the entire German delegation that held a famous "pyjama party" to debate the Soviet offer, then German delegates went to the Soviet hotel. At their Sunday conference Chicherin and Rathenau agreed on general principles, then Soviet diplomat Maxim Litvinov and von Maltzan formulated a precise treaty text. The resulting Treaty of Rapallo stated that "Germany and the R.S.F.S.R (Russian Republic) mutually renounce compensation for their war damages" and "for civil damages caused by the forcible measures of the State authorities of the other party." Germany thus recognized the Soviet nationalization of properties in Russia and dropped all claims to compensation. Diplomatic and consular relations were to be restored as well as trade on a most-favored-nation basis. Both delegations were delighted at the outcome, to which they attached great significance.[18]

The Rapallo Treaty was variously interpreted. Western liberals viewed it as a sinister Soviet-German conspiracy against freedom and democracy. Most Germans regarded it as signifying their fortunate escape from military defeat and isolation, and as the beginning of an independent course in foreign affairs. For their part Soviet ideologists considered Rapallo a useful agreement with a bourgeois state and one that had split world capitalism.

---

[18]Fischer, pp. 341–42.

Furthermore, Rapallo scotched the danger of a capitalist consortium or military coalition against Soviet Russia. No longer could the Western Allies, themselves increasingly embroiled, exert pressure on both Soviet Russia and Germany as isolated pariahs; both were restored to the ranks of the major European powers. Finally, the treaty laid foundations for subsequent clandestine Soviet-German military cooperation. The Germans constructed arms factories in the USSR whose produce was shared. Obtaining military bases, they could experiment with advanced military techniques forbidden to them under the Versailles Treaty.

SOVIET SUCCESSES AND REVERSES, 1923–1927

Soviet Russia consistently supported Kemal Pasha (subsequently given the title of Ataturk), who had seized power in Ankara after World War I and established a revolutionary Turkish regime. Although Moscow rejected Kemal's offer of a military alliance, Chicherin established regular diplomatic ties and Soviet Russia supplied Kemal's forces with financial aid, weapons, and military advice. Kemal soon went on to defeat the invading Greeks and nullify the Treaty of Sèvres, most unfavorable to Turkey, concluded in Paris in 1919. After the Greco-Turkish War, a peace conference that included Soviet Russia convened in Lausanne, Switzerland, in December 1922. At Lausanne Chicherin's brilliant performance in behalf of the victorious Turks amazed everyone. He defended Turkish rights of sovereignty over the Straits more forcefully than the chief Turkish delegate, Ismet Pasha. In the battle over the Straits, Chicherin faced the only delegate rivalling him in ability, Lord George Curzon of Britain. Because the Soviet Black Sea Fleet was feeble, Chicherin argued that "the Dardanelles and the Bosphorus must be permanently closed both in peace and war to warships, armed vessels, and military aircraft of all countries except Turkey." To open the Straits to warships would surely allow the dominant seapower, Great Britain, to dominate the Black Sea region. Opposing Lord Curzon's proposal to open the Straits, Chicherin declared:

> Russia is at the beginning of a new era and we wish to start this by creating stable conditions of peace around us, whereas you wish to put us in a situation which will force us to arm.[19]

Nonetheless, the Allies insisted on opening the Straits to warships. Kemal's Turkey found itself compelled to accept this despite Chicherin's advice to reject the Allied terms and force a breach. In case of war, argued Chicherin, France was most unlikely to join with Britain. When the Treaty of Lausanne was finally signed by the Allies and Turkey in July 1923, the USSR refused to ratify it or to participate in the International Commission set up for the Straits.

---

[19] Fischer, pp. 404–05.

After Germany failed to meet its reparation payments, France in January 1923 occupied the industrial Ruhr Valley, bringing Weimar Germany to the brink of collapse and opening revolutionary opportunities for the Comintern. Major worker demonstrations in Moscow protested the French move and the Soviets sent free grain to the people of the Ruhr. Bolshevik leader Nicholas Rukharin denounced Premier Poincaré's resort to force in the Ruhr as an illegal attempt to subvert German independence. "Our sympathy is with Germany, as it is with any oppressed nation," declared Maxim Litvinov.[20] Narkomindel viewed Weimar Germany then as a barrier against possible French aggression. Wrote *Izvestiia*, the Soviet government newspaper, on January 21: "The complete domination of Germany [by France] is a sharp threat to Soviet Russia. It would make French imperialism our immediate neighbor."[21] Soviet warnings to Poland that Moscow would not tolerate any Polish military moves against Germany provided welcome support to a Weimar government supported by Chicherin's Narkomindel. However, deteriorating economic conditions in Germany helped trigger a general strike called by the German Communist Party (KPD). In October 1923 Communists and Left Socialists formed a government in Saxony. In the port of Hamburg Communist-led workers, encouraged and advised by Comintern agents from Moscow, erected barricades and fought the police and the army; soviets were organized and seized control of parts of the city. However, the Soviet Politburo, increasingly divided over the imminent succession to Lenin, made no major attempt to intervene in this German civil strife. War Commissar Trotskii explained:

> We do not interfere in civil wars abroad. . . . We could interfere only by making war on Poland. But we do not want war. We do not hide our sympathies for the German working class in its heroic struggle for its liberation. . . . If we could bring victory to the German revolution without incurring the risk of warlike activities, we would do everything we could. . . .[22]

Circulated throughout Germany, Trotskii's statement helped discourage German workers, whose revolutionary movement was soon crushed.

The defeat of the abortive German revolution of 1923 represented a sharp reverse for the Comintern, although even some of its leaders opposed trying to seize power then. Meanwhile Gustav Stresemann, an able and conservative German politician, won power in August 1923 as chancellor and in November became German foreign minister. Although not opposed to Germany's eastern orientation under Rapallo, Stresemann aimed to balance Germany between Soviet Russia and the West, fulfill some of Germany's obligations under the Versailles Treaty, and persuade the Allies

---

[20] Fischer, p. 450.

[21] Fischer, p. 450.

[22] *Izvestiia*, September 23, 1923.

to abrogate that restrictive treaty. Chicherin warned Stresemann that German membership in the League would mean joining an anti-Soviet coalition. At the same time, however, Stresemann's triumph over revolutionary elements strengthened Chicherin vis-à-vis the Comintern.

Early in 1924 the USSR scored a major diplomatic breakthrough when the British Labour government accorded it full diplomatic recognition. During 1923 the British Foreign Office under Conservative Lord Curzon had pursued a strongly anti-Bolshevik course, but late in the year his party was swept from power and the first Labour cabinet assumed office under Ramsay MacDonald. By recognizing Soviet Russia, MacDonald hoped to alleviate Great Britain's severe unemployment. British recognition was soon followed by similar action by France, Italy, and other European states, but not the United States. The USSR appeared to have reintegrated itself into postwar Europe on an equal basis with other major powers, thus representing a heartening triumph for Chicherin's diplomacy. Although the debt issue had not been finally resolved, on August 10, 1923, an Anglo-Soviet political and commercial treaty was signed. However, opposition to the treaty in Britain remained so strong that MacDonald met defeat in the House of Commons and had to stand for reelection as prime minister.

In October 1923, during MacDonald's reelection campaign, a scandal erupted in Britain over the so-called "Zinoviev Letter," in which the head of the Comintern, Grigorii Zinoviev, supposedly instructed the British Communist Party on tactics for the upcoming election and called for it to subvert the British army "to paralyze all the military preparations of the bourgeoisie." The Conservatives pointed to this letter as allegedly proving MacDonald's folly and naiveté in dealing with Soviet Russia and helped precipitate his defeat in the elections. The Labour press claimed that the "Zinoviev Letter" was a forgery, and Zinoviev himself vehemently denied having written it. Apparently, it was composed by White Russian forgers in Berlin.[23] Restored to power, the Conservatives promptly withdrew the proposed Anglo-Soviet treaty and diplomatic relations between the two nations deteriorated. Truly normal relations were not restored until 1930 when MacDonald returned as prime minister. Thus the false "Zinoviev Letter" blocked the normalization of Anglo-Soviet relations for five years.

Chicherin's normalization campaign suffered another grave reverse with the conclusion of the Locarno Agreement of 1925 between Germany and the Western Allies. Preceding it was the Dawes Plan of September 1924, named after the American Charles G. Dawes, which established belatedly a reasonable basis for German reparations payments and encouraged the German government to apply for membership in the League of Nations. At Locarno, Foreign Minister Stresemann, seeking recognition of German equality, agreed with leaders of Britain, France, and Italy to guarantee

[23]Kennan, pp. 236–37; Gabriel Gorodetsky, *The Precarious Truce: Anglo-Soviet Relations, 1924–27* (Cambridge, England, 1977), p. 45.

Germany's postwar western frontiers thus relinquishing all claims to disputed Alsace-Lorraine. The USSR was pointedly excluded from the Locarno meetings which apparently had reunited the capitalist West. In articles for the Soviet press in the summer and fall of 1925, Chicherin argued that Locarno would turn Germany into a vassal of Great Britain. Moscow received news of that treaty with apprehension and viewed it as a victory for British diplomacy.[24] If Germany were accepted into the League, the danger might arise that German territory could be utilized by western armies for an attack on the USSR. However, Stresemann was careful to assure Chicherin that Germany had not accepted any obligation under the League Covenant to provide transit rights for foreign troops.

The Berlin Treaty of April 1926 allayed some Soviet fears and enhanced relations between Moscow and Weimar Germany. Chicherin seized the initiative to conclude this new treaty aided by two refusals by the League of Nations (March 1925 and March 1926) to admit Germany, rebuffs that aroused bitter German resentment. In October 1925 Chicherin and Stresemann agreed upon the essentials of the new treaty in Berlin just before Locarno. After the League's second rebuff, the Germans quickly accepted Chicherin's terms. The Treaty of Berlin reaffirmed Rapallo as the cornerstone of Soviet-German relations, and both countries pledged mutual neutrality if attacked by another power or powers. The Berlin Treaty represented a limited success for Chicherin but an even greater gain for Stresemann who had achieved his goal of German independence and balance between Russia and the West.

SOVIET RUSSIA AND CHINA, 1921–1927

Lenin never forgot the revolutionary potential of the Orient, where European capitalism appeared most vulnerable, but during "War Communism" Soviet Russia was too feeble in the Far East to exploit its openings. Thus Soviet policies in the East, 1917–1920, amounted to little more than renouncing tsarist privileges and spheres of interest and issuing propagandistic statements. Moscow sought without much success to play up to the United States there in order to frustrate Japanese imperialism in eastern Siberia and the Maritime Province, but the isolationist Harding regime in the United States flatly rejected any diplomatic relations with Moscow.

Soviet policy in China during the 1920s aimed to promote the strength of Chinese nationalism and communism and to expel the Western imperialist powers from their spheres of influence. In 1912 the Chinese Revolution had overthrown the decadent Manchu dynasty but had failed to create a unified national regime. Instead China soon fragmented under the control of warlords and competing local regimes. In the early 1920s a weak national government in Beijing recognized by the major powers faced Sun Yat-sen's

---

[24]Timothy O'Connor, *Diplomacy and Revolution: G. V. Chicherin and Soviet Foreign Affairs, 1918–1930* (Ames, IA, 1988), pp. 103, 108.

MAP 3–2   The Russian Far East, 1898–1945

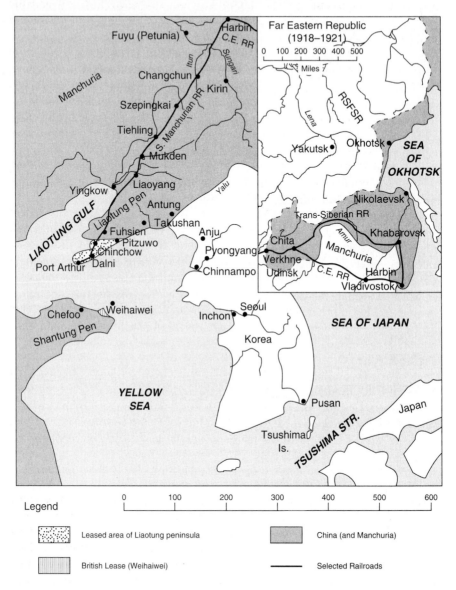

Legend

:::::::: Leased area of Liaotung peninsula   [shaded] China (and Manchuria)

|||||||| British Lease (Weihaiwei)   ——— Selected Railroads

nationalist government in Canton in the south which advocated social reform. The small Chinese Communist Party, founded in 1920 by urban intellectuals but lacking mass support, followed Moscow's direction. Surprisingly, the Soviet government managed for several years to maintain normal relations with all the various Chinese factions although Moscow lacked detailed knowledge of the situation in China. In May 1924 the USSR signed a treaty with the Beijing government, which ruled most of north

China except Manchuria. The Soviets agreed to withdraw their troops from Outer Mongolia and to recognize Chinese sovereignty there; actually Moscow retained its Mongolian protectorate as well as the Chinese Eastern Railroad in Manchuria.

However, Soviet attention during these years focused mostly on Sun Yat-sen's south China regime in Canton and his nationalist Kuomintang Party. In January 1923 the Joffe-Sun declaration, stating that the USSR was not seeking to export Communism to China, pledged to supply advisers and weapons to the Kuomintang. Moscow dispatched able Communist leader Mikhail Borodin to Canton, where he found the Kuomintang disorganized—without structure, program, or even membership cards—and run by Sun Yat-sen. Borodin soon transformed the Kuomintang into a tightly organized, disciplined party modelled after the Russian Communist Party.[25] However, its aims were not revolution but national unity, social reform, and the expulsion of foreign influences from China. Among the young Chinese officers trained in Soviet Russia was Chiang Kai-shek, who upon his return to Canton founded the Whampoa Military Academy and with Soviet backing gradually assumed control over the Kuomintang. Beginning in 1922 the Comintern urged Chinese Communists to join the Kuomintang while simultaneously retaining their own Communist organization.

After Sun Yat-sen died in March 1925, Borodin and Chiang largely determined Kuomintang policies and made that party a strong contender for leadership in all of China. In 1926 the Comintern admitted it to its ranks as a "sympathizing party." During that year the complex Chinese situation was studied by a special Politburo committee led by Trotskii, then still a top Soviet leader. His report in March 1926 stressed China's secondary role in Soviet foreign relations and urged caution there so as not to alienate an aggressive Japan. Until a single Chinese government had been created, wrote Trotskii, Soviet Russia should maintain "loyal relations with the existing regimes in China, the central as well as provincial ones."[26]

Suddenly the Chinese situation escaped Soviet control. In March 1926 Chiang Kai-shek, hitherto apparently an obedient Soviet tool, carried out a coup in Canton, assumed control, arresting some Communists but avoiding a breach with Moscow. Then Chiang launched a northern expedition against the Beijing regime, aided significantly by the Communists, who organized peasant and worker uprisings. After the Kuomintang forces captured Wuhan, Borodin induced some leftish Kuomintang leaders to establish a separate regime there. Moscow's policy in 1927 was to assist Chiang Kai-shek and the Right Kuomintang as long as they proved useful. Joseph Stalin told Moscow Communist workers that spring: "They [Kuomintang] have to be

[25]On Borodin and the Kuomintang see Dan N. Jacobs, *Borodin: Stalin's Man in China* (Cambridge, MA, 1981), pp. 136ff.

[26]Adam Ulam, *Expansion and Coexistence: Soviet Foreign Policy 1917–1973*, 2nd ed. (New York, 1974), pp. 174–75, citing the Trotskii Archive at Harvard University.

utilized to the end, squeezed out like a lemon, and then thrown away."[27] Meanwhile Trotskii still stressed the primacy of the struggle against British influence in China. Then Chiang struck suddenly. Capturing Shanghai with Communist aid, he conducted a massacre of local Communists and virtually destroyed the city-based Chinese Communist Party. The Left Kuomintang regime in Wuhan dissolved, its pro-Soviet leaders fled and the rest joined Chiang Kai-shek. Stalin, then consolidating power within the Russian Communist Party, ordered the Chinese Communists to conduct rural and urban revolts against the Kuomintang. However, by mid-1928 the Communists in the cities had been crushed and only scattered groups remained in the countryside, one led by a peasant Communist, Mao Tse-tung. By then it was evident that Soviet policies had failed dismally. Recriminations were exchanged between Stalin and Trotskii whose left faction had been expelled from its posts in the Russian Communist Party. Chiang appeared on his way to unify China under the nationalist Kuomintang. Returning sadly to Russia, Borodin declared: "When the next Chinese general comes to Moscow and shouts: 'Hail to the world revolution!' better send at once for the OGPU [secret police]."[28] Nonetheless, temporarily the Kuomintang had weakened the hold of the imperial powers in China, although eventually its offensive would trigger the Japanese seizure of Manchuria.

STALIN VS. TROTSKII: "SOCIALISM IN ONE COUNTRY" VERSUS "PERMANENT REVOLUTION"

In May 1922 when Lenin suffered the first of several cerebral strokes, the struggle over the political succession in Soviet Russia began. Lenin named no successor, and his "Letter to the Congress," or "Testament," of December 1922 was critical of all leading contenders, especially Stalin. Unlike the "Old Bolshevik" colleagues of Lenin—Lev Trotskii, Nicholas Bukharin, Lev Kamenev, and Grigorii Zinoviev—who had spent years in European exile hobnobbing with European socialists, Joseph Stalin, born Iosif V. Djugashvili in Gori, Georgia, had remained mostly in Russia and had been exiled repeatedly to Siberia. Beginning in 1919 Stalin had been voted into key positions of power in the Russian Communist Party by colleagues who consistently underestimated this crude but ruthless Georgian. At Lenin's death in January 1924, four major groups formed within the Party: a Stalin "Center," the Trotskyite Left, Bukharin's moderates, and a group in Petrograd led by Zinoviev and Kamenev. Perhaps Stalin's most perilous moment came in May 1924 when Lenin's "Testament," urging Stalin's removal from the post of General Secretary was read, but Zinoviev and Kamenev, then in a ruling triumvirate with Stalin, backed the Georgian out of fear of Trotskii. The latter possessed the most impressive credentials to become Lenin's successor because of his great ideological and practical contributions to the

---

[27]Robert C. North, *Moscow and the Chinese Communists* (Stanford, CA, 1953), p. 96.
[28]Conrad Brandt, *Stalin's Failure in China* (Cambridge, MA, 1958), p. 153.

Bolshevik Revolution and Soviet state. After Lenin's death, Stalin cleverly developed and exploited a cult of Lenin, portraying himself as the founder's truest disciple. Meanwhile he consolidated his stranglehold over the Party machinery.

During the struggle for power within the Russian Communist Party there gradually emerged a major ideological controversy that would affect Soviet foreign policy significantly. Beginning in 1917, Lenin and Trotskii had declared repeatedly that external revolutions in advanced countries were essential to assure the survival and development of the Soviet state. Convinced that the prolonged coexistence of socialism and capitalism was unthinkable, they devoted much effort and attached vast importance to the Comintern as the engine of world revolution. Yet expected socialist revolutions in the West failed to materialize, and by 1924 it was evident that capitalism had stabilized and that prospects for world revolution were slim. This rendered Trotskii's continued emphasis on "permanent revolution" and action through the Comintern appear rather unrealistic. Stalin, on the other hand, had generally emphasized national Russian themes that contrasted with the cosmopolitan, Europe-centered views of Trotskii, Zinoviev, and Kamenev. In August 1917 Stalin had already predicted that Russia, rather than Europe, would lead the world forward to socialism, that capitalism might break first at its weakest link in Russia. Nicholas Bukharin originated the concept of "socialism in one country," arguing that NEP would serve as a means of moving Russia gradually towards that goal. In 1924–1925 Stalin could not afford to quarrel with Bukharin over that interpretation, but he stressed the theme of "one country" in the form of aggressive Soviet Russian nationalism derived from his prediction of August 1917. Until the defeat of the Trotskyist Left in 1927, Stalin had to soft-pedal his interpretation.[29]

Trotskii appeared to be arguing that socialism could be built in the USSR only if the revolution were spread abroad. For him "permanent revolution" remained the precondition for constructing socialism at home. Combating Trotskii's influence within the Party, Stalin argued, at first cautiously, that it would prove possible to build "socialism in one country," that is in Soviet Russia, and that the USSR could pull itself up by its own independent efforts. That argument catered to the nationalist sentiments of younger cadres then entering the Party. In its final demonstration on November 7, 1927, the Trotskyist Left attacked the Stalinists for turning their backs on the world revolutionary cause only to be dispersed and lose their Party posts. After the final defeat of Trotskii, Stalin sounded his nationalist theme more forcefully.

By 1928 Stalin's doctrine of "socialism in one country" had prevailed in the USSR because he had gauged more accurately the prevalent mood

---

[29]On this issue see Robert C. Tucker, *Stalinism* (New York, 1977), pp. 93ff; and Adam Ulam, *Stalin: The Man and His Era* (Boston, 1973), pp. 262ff.

in the Party and because of his tactical skill and ruthless purpose. However, Stalin's dispute with Trotskii was only over means, not about the ultimate goal in foreign affairs. The final objective of both, and indeed of all Russian Communists, was the eventual world triumph of communism. Whereas Trotskii continued to place the emphasis on the Comintern and fomenting revolutions abroad, Stalin stressed the necessity to construct Soviet Russia as an industrial giant *before* turning to the task of spreading revolution to other countries. Building such industrial strength implied constructing powerful military forces which might then be utilized as a threat or even to spread the revolution by force. In any case, by 1928 Stalin had achieved total predominance within the Russian Communist Party and over the Comintern.

Suggested Readings

Angress, Werner T. *Stillborn Revolution: The Communist Bid for Power in Germany, 1921–1923*. Princeton, NJ, 1963.

Brandt, Conrad. *Stalin's Failure in China, 1924–1927*. Cambridge, MA, 1958.

Carr, E. H. *German-Soviet Relations Between the Two World Wars*. Baltimore, 1951.

Calhoun, Daniel. *The United Front!: The TUC and the Russians, 1923–1928*. Cambridge, England, 1976.

Chester, Lewis, et al. *The Zinoviev Letter*. Philadelphia, 1968.

Churchill, Winston S. *The World Crisis—The Aftermath*. London, 1929.

Day, Richard. *Leon Trotsky and the Politics of Economic Isolation*. Cambridge, England, 1973.

Degras, Jane, ed., *Soviet Documents on Foreign Policy*. vol. I, (1917–1924) London, 1951; vol. II, (1925–1923) London, 1952.

———. *The Communist International 1919–1943: Documents*. vol. I, (1919–1922) London, 1956; vol. II, (1923–1928) London, 1960.

Deutscher, Isaac. *The Prophet Unarmed: Trotsky, 1921–1929*. London, 1959.

Draper, Theodore. *American Communism and Soviet Russia*. New York, 1960.

Dyck, Harvey. *Weimar Germany and Soviet Russia: A Study in Diplomatic Instability*. New York, 1966.

Fischer, Louis. *The Soviets in World Affairs, 1917–1929*. 2 vols., Princeton, NJ, 1951.

Fischer, Ruth. *Stalin and German Communism: A Study in the Origins of the State Party*. Cambridge, MA, 1948.

Freund, Gerald. *The Unholy Alliance: Russian-German Relations from the Treaty of Brest-Litovsk to the Treaty of Berlin*. London, 1957.

Gorodetsky, Gabriel. *The Precarious Truce: Anglo-Soviet Relations, 1924–27*. Cambridge, England, 1977.

Jacobs, Dan N. *Borodin: Stalin's Man in China*. Cambridge, MA, 1981.

Kennan, George F. *Russia and the West Under Lenin and Stalin*. Boston, 1960.

Kessler, Harry. *Walter Rathenau—His Life and Work*. London, 1929.

Kochan, Lionel. *Russia and the Weimar Republic*. Cambridge, England, 1954.

Korbel, Josef. *Poland between East and West: Soviet and German Diplomacy toward Poland, 1919–1933*. Princeton, NJ, 1963.

Leong, Sow-theng. *Sino-Soviet Diplomatic Relations, 1917–26*. Honolulu, HI, 1976.

Lloyd-George, David. *The Truth About Reparations and War-Debts*. Garden City, NY, 1932.

North, Robert C. *Moscow and the Chinese Communists.* Stanford, CA, 1953.

O'Connor, Timothy. *Diplomacy and Revolution: G. V. Chicherin and Soviet Foreign Affairs, 1918–1930.* Ames, IA, 1988.

Rosenbaum, Kurt. *Community of Fate: German-Soviet Diplomatic Relations, 1922–1928.* Syracuse, NY, 1965.

Trotskii, Leon. *The Third International After Lenin.* New York, 1936.

Ulam, Adam. *Expansion and Coexistence: Soviet Foreign Policy, 1917–1973.* 2nd ed. New York, 1974.

Uldricks, Teddy. *Diplomacy and Ideology: The Origins of Soviet Foreign Relations, 1917–1930.* London, 1980.

Von Laue, Theodor. "Chicherin," in G. Craig and F. Gilbert, eds., *The Diplomats, 1919–1939.* Princeton, NJ, 1953, pp. 234–81.

White, Stephen. *The Origins of Détente: The Genoa Conference and Soviet-Western Relations, 1921–1922.* Cambridge, England, 1985.

Whiting, Allen. *Soviet Policies in China.* New York, 1954.

"SOCIALIST CONSTRUCTION" AND ISOLATION, 1928–1933

By 1928 Joseph Stalin had consolidated his personal power over the Soviet Communist Party and the world Communist movement and was removing from leading posts opponents who had been V. I. Lenin's principal collaborators. Then Stalin launched what a Soviet poet later called aptly, "A war against the nation.": forced collectivization of agriculture and rapid, state-directed industrialization. Requiring a total effort that left little energy or resources for foreign entanglements, this campaign involved a policy of Soviet isolationism. Because any Soviet involvement in war would doom Stalin's domestic campaign, a pacific foreign policy was demanded. Aiming for total power at home and over foreign Communist parties, Stalin sought to split the working class movement in the West by denouncing as "Social Fascism" democratic socialism linked at least indirectly with his "Old Bolshevik" opponents. Stalin's policy promoted the triumph in Germany of Adolf Hitler and his Nazi Party with traumatic effects for the entire world, especially for the USSR.

STALIN'S "SECOND SOCIALIST OFFENSIVE," 1928–1933

By 1927 Lenin's New Economic Policy had restored the Soviet economy to near pre-World War I levels. In his final years Lenin had favored increasingly policies involving a gradual and non-violent achievement of socialism. On the other hand, Stalin, notes American scholar George Kennan, who observed his rule at first hand, was "a man dominated . . . by an insatiable vanity and love of power . . . ." He possessed "the keenest sense of his own inferiority and a burning jealousy for qualities in others which he did not possess." Stalin exhibited "a most extraordinary talent for political tactics and intrigue," and was "a consummate actor," a master of timing who played people off skillfully against each other.[1]

---

[1] George F. Kennan, *Russia and the West Under Lenin and Stalin* (Boston, 1960), p. 248.

The Fifteenth Congress of the Soviet Communist Party in December 1927 marked the end of the Leninist era of relative diversity and tolerance and confirmed the defeat of the internationalist "Old Bolshevik" opposition led by Lev Trotskii, Lev Kamenev, and Grigorii Zinoviev. In the elections to that congress the opposition garnered less than one percent of the vote. Before the congress met, Adolf Joffe, leader of the initial Bolshevik delegation to Brest-Litovsk, committed suicide after urging his friend, Trotskii, to continue the struggle against Stalin. Kamenev appeared briefly at the congress to plead abjectly for another chance, but he and 121 other oppositionists were expelled summarily from the Party.[2] That Fifteenth Congress approved guidelines for Stalin's grandiose "Second Socialist Offensive" designed to transform the USSR into a fully industrialized socialist country, thus achieving "socialism in one country." The essential foundation for that, declared Stalin, "lies in the transformation of small and scattered peasants' plots into large consolidated farms based on joint cultivation of land using new superior techniques."[3]

Stalin's offensive therefore had twin barrels: forced collectivization of agriculture and intensive state-directed industrialization in order to make the USSR a potent military giant able to foster revolution abroad. Stalin justified forcing millions of resisting peasants into collective farms—a policy condemned specifically by both Marx and Lenin—by citing the selfish refusal of better-off private farmers to market their grain until prices rose. Advocating the destruction of these *kulaks* ("fists") as a class, Stalin aimed to replace Russia's 26 million private farms with about 250,000 collective and state farms. Agriculture would become "socialist," ending Moscow's dependence on the peasantry and guaranteeing adequate food for new industrial cities. Forced collectivization, involving the deportation of more than 3 million persons, as Stalin told Winston Churchill later, provoked a worse struggle than the Nazi invasion of 1941. It resulted in a semi-planned famine in 1931–1932, costing several million lives.

The other barrel of the "Second Socialist Offensive" was rapid industrialization under the First Five Year Plan. Begun in late 1928, the Plan poured huge state resources into constructing mostly heavy industrial plants turning out iron and steel. All industry reverted to state control and management, fulfilling the ideological objective of a fully socialist economy. Initially this campaign stimulated enthusiasm and self-sacrifice by Soviet workers believing they were constructing the foundations of an abundant life. The military aim of the Plan was very important. In a speech to industrial leaders in February 1931 Stalin declared:

To slacken the tempo would mean falling behind. And those who fall behind get beaten. . . . One feature of the history of old Russia was the continual

---

[2] Adam Ulam, *Stalin: The Man and His Era* (Boston, 1973), pp. 285–86.
[3] Ulam, p. 291.

beatings she suffered because of her backwardness. . . . We are fifty or a hundred years behind the advanced countries. We must make good this distance in ten years. Either we do it, or we shall go under.[4]

Ten years and four months later Hitler's Wehrmacht invaded the USSR. Without Stalin's Five Year Plans could the USSR have survived this onslaught? Despite much inefficiency and waste, a major expansion of Soviet heavy industry was achieved by the First Plan while the capitalist West languished in the Great Depression. Rejoicing at the results of the Plan, Stalin in November 1929, soon after the Wall Street crash, declared confidently:

> We are advancing full steam ahead along the path of industrialization to socialism, leaving behind the age-old "Russian" backwardness. We are becoming a country of metal, a country of automobiles, a country of tractors. And when we have put the USSR in a motor-car and the *muzhik* [peasant] upon a tractor . . . , we shall see which countries may then be "classified" as backward and which as advanced.[5]

Simultaneously, Stalin consolidated control over a totalitarian Soviet regime as an all-powerful, ruthless dictator in a Soviet Union that emphasized self-reliance and was virtually quarantined from normal contacts with the capitalist West.

The First Five Year Plan was the key to every aspect of Soviet policy from 1929 to 1933. Fulfilling the Plan meant keeping the country out of war, which Soviet diplomacy, supervised by a cautious Stalin, sought to do. Declared Maxim Litvinov in July 1930: "The larger the scale of our constructive work, the more rapid its tempo, the greater our interest in the preservation of peace."[6] Although the Plan aimed at autarchy, its immediate needs reinforced economic ties with the capitalist West. Obtaining short-term credits, primarily from Germany, to import machinery and capital goods, Moscow saw its external indebtedness rise steadily until after 1932 when an active trade balance and rising gold exports quickly reduced it once again.

THE "WAR SCARE" AND "SOCIAL FASCISM," 1927–1928

Even before the start of the First Five Year Plan, signs of an imminent shift in Soviet foreign policy multiplied. After Great Britain severed diplomatic

---

[4]J. V. Stalin, *Works*, vol. XIII (Moscow, 1955), pp. 40–41.

[5]*Pravda*, November 7, 1929, quoted in Maurice Dobb, *Soviet Economic Development Since 1917* (New York, 1948), p. 245.

[6]Max Beloff, *The Foreign Policy of Soviet Russia, 1929–1941*, vol. I (London, 1947), pp. 27–33.

relations with the USSR, Stalin asserted in July 1927 that London was plotting a new war against Soviet Russia:

> The entire international situation . . . , the British government's "operations" against the Soviet Union, the fact that it organizes a financial blockade of the Soviet Union . . . , that it subsidizes the émigrés' "governments" of the Ukraine, Georgia . . . etc., for the purpose of raising revolts in those states of the Soviet Union . . . proves that the British Tory government has definitely and concertedly undertaken to organize a war against the Soviet Union.[7]

Although there was little basis in fact for this threat of war, it created a panic among Muscovites. Stalin exploited the threat as a means to attack the Trotskii opposition.[8]

During the second half of 1927 official warnings of a shift in Soviet external policies surfaced repeatedly. "At the present moment," declared *Izvestiia* on August 10, "the period of breathing space which our Union has enjoyed since 1921 is clearly coming to an end."[9] That December in his report to the Fifteenth Congress of the Soviet Communist Party, Stalin sounded the same refrain. He asserted that all the talk in the League of Nations about peace and disarmament had led to nothing "except the deception of the masses, except new spurts in armaments." Instead of peace, "stabilization is inevitably giving rise to new imperialist wars." Continued Stalin:

> Whereas a couple of years ago it was possible and necessary to speak of the ebb of the revolutionary tide in Europe, today we have every ground for asserting that *Europe is obviously entering a period of new revolutionary upsurge.*

Although Britain thus far had failed to organize a united front against Soviet Russia, "the threat of war remains in force." What should the USSR do? "The task is to take into account the contradictions in the imperialist camp, to postpone war by 'buying off' the capitalists."[10]

About six months later the Comintern responded to these pointed harbingers of a revised Soviet foreign policy that emphasized intransigence towards the moderate social democracy of Europe. The Sixth Comintern Congress in Moscow (July 17–September 1, 1928) echoed Stalin's declarations at the Fifteenth Congress and confirmed the Comintern's thorough

---

[7]*Izvestiia*, July 28, 1927, quoted in Louis Fischer, *The Soviets in World Affairs: A History of the Relations Between the Soviet Union and the Rest of the World, 1917–1929*, vol. II (New York, 1960), pp. 740–41.

[8]Raymond Sontag, "The War Scare of 1926–27," *Russian Review*, vol. XXXIV, no. 1 (January 1975), pp. 66–77.

[9]*Izvestiia*, August 10, 1927, quoted in Lionel Kochan, *Russia and the Weimar Republic* (Cambridge, England, 1978), p. 129.

[10]J. V. Stalin, *Works*, vol. X (Moscow, 1955), pp. 282ff. (Italics in original.)

Stalinization and subservience. The Congress represented fifty-eight parties all now slavishly dependent on the Soviet host party. Proclaimed the Comintern's Program, the most comprehensive single document that body ever produced:

> The USSR is the base of the world movement of all oppressed classes, the center of international revolution, the greatest factor in world history. . . . She is the international driving force of proletarian revolution that impels the proletariat of all countries to seize power. . . . The USSR is the only fatherland of the international proletariat. . . . [Comintern] must on its part facilitate the success of the work of socialist construction in the USSR and defend her against the attacks of the capitalist powers by all the means in its power. . . .[11]

Henceforth the Comintern, as the USSR's obedient servant, subordinated itself and the international movement it represented to Soviet interests. With France and Britain allegedly preparing renewed armed intervention in Soviet Russia, Stalin declared that the USSR lived in a dangerous capitalist encirclement, a theme he sounded frequently thereafter.

The Sixth Comintern Congress denounced Europe's Social Democrats as "Social Fascists" who allegedly had betrayed the interests of the international working class. This reflected Soviet assertions that the German Social Democrats (SPD), who had reentered the Weimar government in May 1928, were the greatest enemies of the German Communists (KPD) and the Rapallo policy of Soviet-German cooperation. The concept of Social Democrats as "Social Fascists" had been enunciated first by Zinoviev in 1924 because they had supported the pro-Western Foreign Minister Gustav Stresemann rather than the German Communists. Imposing this concept, Stalin now was determined to split the working class movement and to control individual Communist parties, including the KPD, directly and completely.[12]

SOVIET RUSSIA AND THE WEST, 1928–1933

During the First Five Year Plan Soviet foreign policy was predicated on avoiding war or serious foreign complications. Still accusing the West of plotting war against the USSR, Stalin declared in June 1930 at the Sixteenth Soviet Party Congress that through the Soviet policy of improving relations with its neighbors and with European powers:

> We have succeeded in maintaining peace . . . despite a number of provocative acts and adventurist attacks on the part of the warmongers. We will continue to pursue this policy of peace with all our might. . . . We do not want a single

---

[11]Quoted in Alvin Rubinstein, ed., *The Foreign Policy of the Soviet Union* (New York, 1973), pp. 102–06. See Kermit McKenzie, *Comintern and World Revolution, 1928–1943* (New York, 1964), pp. 6ff.

[12]Kochan, pp. 138–40.

foot of foreign territory, but we will not surrender a single inch of our territory to anyone.[13]

That would remain the principal theme in Stalinist foreign policy down to 1939.

Soviet leaders could promote their "policy of peace" after Frank Kellogg, American secretary of state, and French Foreign Minister Aristide Briand concluded a pact to outlaw war as an instrument of national policy. Briand first advocated this idea in April 1927 as a Franco-American agreement, but Kellogg in his reply favored a multilateral pact with all signatories pledging to renounce war. Because Washington, D.C., failed to invite the USSR to join this arrangement, Soviet leaders suspected that it concealed plans for an anti-Soviet bloc. However, the French government then invited Moscow to join and in August 1928 the pact was signed by representatives of fifteen countries in Paris. Whereas Foreign Commisar Grigorii Chicherin criticized the original omission of the USSR, Moscow responded swiftly to the French invitation, and the Soviet Union became the first nation to complete formal adherence to the Kellogg-Briand Pact, then sought to persuade other nations to ratify it. Maxim Litvinov, de facto chief of Narkomindel, proposed to bring Poland and Lithuania into the agreement and accepted the inclusion also of Romania. In February 1929 representatives of the USSR, Poland, Latvia, Estonia, and Romania signed this so-called Litvinov Protocol. Later, Lithuania, Persia, Finland, and Turkey also adhered. Litvinov hailed the protocol as a "link in the long chain" of Soviet efforts towards general peace, in particular in eastern Europe. Emphasizing Moscow's desire for peace, Litvinov strove to prevent the formation of any anti-Soviet bloc, especially one involving its neighbors.[14] The Litvinov Protocol, the first link between the Soviet Union and a worldwide system to preserve peace, represented a significant success for Soviet diplomacy.

By late 1928, with Chicherin's health deteriorating, Litvinov had become the USSR's leading diplomat. His report to the Party's Central Committee at the end of that year was as uncertain in tone as Stalin's report the previous year to the Fifteenth Congress. The Soviet Union, declared Litvinov, wholly absorbed in internal reconstruction, remained aloof from all warlike combinations, but along its western frontiers lurked armed countries (such as Poland) counting upon French military aid. The British Conservatives meanwhile were seeking to complete a Soviet isolation begun in 1925 after the "Zinoviev Letter."

The struggle against our Union has never stopped. It has only taken on different forms according to changing circumstances. Yesterday it was intervention and

---

[13]J. V. Stalin, *Works*, vol. XII (Moscow, 1955), 262ff.

[14]Xenia Eudin and Robert Slusser, *Soviet Foreign Policy 1928–1934. Documents and Materials*, vol. I (University Park, PA, 1966), pp. 5–7.

complete blockade; today it is the attempt at a boycott and isolation; tomorrow it will perhaps again be intervention or war.[15]

Litvinov had achieved preeminence in Narkomindel as the true author of Soviet disarmament policy. Appropriately he was chosen to represent the USSR at the Preparatory Commission for a Disarmament Conference in Geneva, Switzerland, in 1927. In his first speech there he proposed immediate, complete, and general disarmament, a policy reflecting Soviet military weakness and Moscow's desire to undermine French continental hegemony. After Western delegates dismissed this plan as "too simple," Litvinov prepared a detailed draft convention on total disarmament which was presented to the Preparatory Commission in March 1928. His speech defending that idea won support, however, only from the German and Turkish delegates. After the rejection of his proposal, Litvinov advocated partial and gradual disarmament as an initial step towards subsequent total disarmament, but the Commission postponed consideration of that idea. An *Izvestiia* editorial of March 25, 1928, described the Geneva negotiations as a struggle between old and new worlds, represented respectively by the conservative Ronald McNeill, the first Lord Cushendun of Britain and Litvinov of Soviet Russia. In April 1929 Litvinov again urged immediate action on his disarmament proposal, but it was neither discussed nor voted on. The Commission did not even meet again for a year and a half.[16]

In December 1929 Litvinov reported to the Central Committee on the general international situation. Deploring "capitalist sabotage of disarmament," he depicted the USSR as surrounded by enemies. Litvinov described the foreign policies of the capitalist powers as unstable, anarchic, constantly changing, and torn by antagonisms among individual countries; by contrast, Soviet foreign policy was described as unchanging, consistent, and methodical. Its basic aim remained defense of Soviet achievements and to maintain peace. "Further five year plans will follow the first, and for these too conditions of peace will be as necessary as they are for the first."[17]

Until mid-1929 Soviet-German relations remained generally positive and harmonious as both parties benefited from close commercial, military, and political ties. However, late in 1929 occurred another German swing toward the West. The Young Plan of that year finally set the total amount of reparations that Germany owed to the Allies. The Weimar government accepted that plan in return for an Allied pledge to evacuate the Rhineland in 1930, five years before the date prescribed at Versailles. After Berlin, in March 1930, ratified the Young Plan (named after Owen D. Young of the United States) settling the reparations issue, and the Allies agreed

---

[15]Litvinov's Report to the Central Committee of December 1928, quoted in Kochan, pp. 134–36.

[16]Eudin and Slusser, pp. 7–13.

[17]Jane Degras, ed., *Soviet Documents on Foreign Policy, 1917–1941*, vol. II (New York, 1952), p. 409; Eudin and Slusser, pp. 18–19.

to evacuate the Rhineland in June, Germany turned away from the USSR. "Our sovereignty as a great European power is reestablished," commented the German liberal journal, *Der Börsenkurier*, in May 1930. "The time is past when harmony between East and West was necessary. . . ." Reacting to this, leading Soviet newspapers deplored the anti-Soviet wave seemingly pervading the German bourgeoisie.[18]

During 1929–1930 relations with Britain and France remained precarious. Late in 1929 diplomatic ties were restored with London, but negotiations on the difficult Russian debt issue made little progress. Speeches in July by V. M. Molotov and Dmitri Manuilskii, placed in charge of the Comintern in 1930 by Stalin, referred disparagingly to British repression at home and in India showing that Moscow's anti-propaganda pledge had changed little. The show trial of Professor Leonid Ramzin and others at the end of 1930 featured accusations that Britain and France had been involved in a major plot against the Soviet regime; London protested this insinuation officially. Soviet relations with France remained cool with debt and propaganda issues unresolved; Paris accused the USSR of "dumping" its goods in France to undercut world prices.

However, beginning in 1931, in the face of strident German nationalist demands for the return to Germany of the Polish Corridor, Moscow sought rapprochement with both France and Poland. After Molotov, as chairman of the Soviet Council of Ministers, in March 1931 advocated establishing warmer relations with France, negotiations produced a Franco-Soviet non-aggression treaty ready for signature by August; because of French hesitations, Paris only signed it in November 1932. France meanwhile lifted its previous ban on Soviet imports. Simultaneous Soviet-Polish negotiations resulted in a non-aggression treaty that the Germans considered a breach of the spirit of Rapallo. By 1932 therefore the Soviet Union had come close to recognizing the Paris Peace Settlement of 1919.

Stalin's role in bringing Hitler and the Nazis to power in Germany in January 1933 remains disputed. The Great Depression, striking Germany most severely, was an important factor in undermining the democratic Weimar Republic that achieved its peak of success in 1928. To meet the challenge of the depression in March 1930 the Social Democrats turned to a government of economic experts under a decent moderate, Heinrich Brüning. However, as unemployment and desperation grew in Germany, the extreme parties—the Nazis and the Communists (KPD)—won greatly increased electoral support. Nonetheless, as late as the end of 1932 a united left would have overbalanced the Nazis. However, Stalin insisted on implementing his doctrine of "Social Fascism" that excluded any Socialist-Communist cooperation against Hitler. After the November 1932 elections the KPD, at Soviet instruction, redoubled its destructive attacks on the Socialists and the Weimar Republic. Stalin, reluctant to see the unreliable

---

[18]Kochan, pp. 140–44.

KPD achieve power, exploited the German Communists as a weapon to weaken the Socialists, disrupt Germany's relations with the West, and enhance Berlin's waning dependence on Moscow. Apparently not alarmed then at the growth of Nazism in Germany, Stalin believed that it would undermine the Germans' democratic illusions and that eventually the German masses would turn to communism. At Moscow's advice, the KPD spurned Socialist overtures for a common front against Hitler. The KPD's denial of support to Brüning compelled him to rule by decree while the Communists' use of violence created precedents followed by Hitler. Although the evidence does not suggest that Stalin desired a Nazi takeover, he did nothing to prevent one. Thus no one can deny Stalin's responsibility for the failure of the Weimar Republic to surmount the final barriers to stability and permanence.[19]

In this instance Stalin fell victim to his Marxist-Leninist ideology. Believing that the bourgeoisie controlled the Weimar Republic, Stalin did not anticipate that the Nazis, likewise bourgeois, would undertake a revolution against their own class. Soviet leaders viewed the Nazis as no worse than other bourgeois parties, and that by undermining moderate socialism they would foster the eventual triumph of Communism in Germany. Thus when the Socialists (SPD) appealed desperately to the Soviets for aid against the Nazis just before the triumph of Hitler, the secretary of the Soviet embassy in Berlin replied: The USSR believes that the road to a Soviet Germany lies through Hitler. Later, Hitler would launch an invasion of the USSR causing the deaths of about 20 million Soviet citizens. However, World War II led to the creation of a "Soviet" East Germany.

In July 1930 Litvinov assumed formal direction of Narkomindel. At his initial press conference he emphasized that Soviet foreign policy, as before, would defend world peace and create favorable conditions for socialist construction in the Soviet Union despite the capitalist encirclement. Litvinov's close relationship with Stalin was confirmed by his long tenure of office and as one of the few in Narkomindel to survive Stalin's purges. Significantly, Litvinov's favorite diplomat in history was the chameleon-like French Foreign Minister Charles-Maurice de Talleyrand. Attributing all his successes to Stalin's leadership, Litvinov wrote later: "I am chiefly proud of having done my whole party work of forty years under the immediate guidance of our great teachers, Lenin and Stalin."[20]

When President Paul von Hindenburg named Adolf Hitler chancellor of Germany in January 1933, there was no immediate change in Soviet policy. Moscow continued to foster Soviet-German cooperation under Rapallo; overtures to Hitler were combined with efforts to join the Franco-Polish security system. Stalin must have realized that these two

---

[19]Kennan, pp. 279–92.

[20]A. U. Pope, *Maxim Litvinoff* (New York, 1943), p. 191.

MAXIM LITVINOV (1876–1951), SOVIET COMMISSAR OF FOREIGN AFFAIRS, 1930–1939; SOVIET AMBASSADOR TO THE UNITED STATES, 1941–1943

policies were incompatible, but he had to pursue both until he could discern which one would provide a militarily weak USSR with needed security. During 1933, while he waited to see which way Hitler would move, Stalin made no pronouncements on foreign policy. His subordinates—Litvinov, Molotov, and Karl Radek—essentially left the choice of paths up to Hitler. The Nazi leader sought to allay Soviet suspicions that German policy was shifting while rebuffing all direct Soviet overtures. Nevertheless, at Soviet initiative, military contacts between the Reichswehr and the Red Army were dissolved. Gradually Soviet leaders revised their views of the West. In Geneva Litvinov now called France "a great and powerful state"; Radek welcomed warmly the reemergence of Poland.[21] The League of Nations, Stalin suggested, might comprise a desirable force for peace: "If the League is even the tiniest bump somewhat to slow down the drive towards war and help peace, then we are not against the League."[22]

At the end of 1933 Stalin had finally been persuaded by subordinates to undertake a fundamental change in Soviet foreign policy. Since 1919 Soviet spokesmen had attacked the League of Nations and the Versailles system as agents of international imperialism plotting to attack the USSR. However, as the West threatened to crumble in the face of revisionist Germany and Italy and an aggressive Japan, Moscow was faced with rising threats to its security. Soviet leaders had predicted eagerly the downfall of world capitalism only to see the Great Depression strengthen Fascism and Nazism more than international Communism. Although the former major aim of Soviet policy had apparently been partially achieved by the weakening of the capitalist West, that very weakness now threatened not victory but disaster for the Soviet Union. A policy shift was now required not from ideological considerations but from the practical demands of Soviet security which ever since 1918 had been Moscow's paramount concern.

SOVIET FAR EASTERN POLICIES, 1928–1933

After the victorious Chiang Kai-shek had crushed the urban-based Chinese Communists in 1927, Soviet Russia severed most diplomatic relations with his Kuomintang regime in Nanking, which soon became the government of most of China. Nearly all other powers, however, recognized Chiang's regime. Cutting off diplomatic relations with the Kuomintang ended temporarily direct Soviet contacts with most of China. However, in May 1929 Soviet interest in the region revived when the Manchurian authorities, now subservient to Chiang's Nanking government, raided Soviet consulates along the Chinese Eastern Railway, seized documents, and arrested about eighty Soviet officials. Apparently believing that the Soviets were too absorbed by domestic transformations to react, in July Chiang's Manchurian allies seized control of the railway itself. After the Chinese disregarded a Soviet ultimatum to withdraw, Moscow severed the remaining relations with Nanking. In mid-November Red Army troops quickly defeated Manchurian forces and compelled the regime in Mukden to submit. In December 1929 the Soviet position in Manchuria was restored under joint Sino-Soviet administration. Although Soviet attempts then to revive diplomatic ties with Nanking were rebuffed, Moscow regarded Chiang's regime there correctly

---

[21]*Izvestiia*, August 29, 1933, quoted in Kochan, pp. 165–70.
[22]Kochan, p. 170, citing J. V. Stalin et al., *Our Foreign Policy* (Moscow–Leningrad, 1934), p. 9.

as an obstacle to Japanese domination of China and did not seek further gains in Manchuria.[23]

Japan's seizure of Manchuria in 1931 and its transformation the following year into the Japanese puppet state of Manchukuo heralded the eventual coming of World War II and posed a direct challenge to a spineless League of Nations. It also represented a potential Japanese threat to the Soviet protectorate in Outer Mongolia and to the Soviet Far East. Responding with a combination of firmness and conciliation, Moscow reinforced its Far Eastern army, placing it under command of General Vasili Bliukher, a hero of the Russian Civil War. Warning that anti-Soviet statements and actions would no longer be tolerated, an *Izvestiia* editorial of March 4, 1932, reprinted the next day in other leading Soviet newspapers, declared that Soviet Russia had done everything possible to maintain proper relations with Japan despite its violation of Russian interests in Manchuria. Moscow informed Tokyo that it was aware of Japanese plans for aggression against the USSR.

Yet Soviet policy towards Japan combined firmness with conciliation and even appeasement. When the Japanese disregarded Soviet rights on the Chinese Eastern Railway, Moscow initially failed to react realizing that it could no longer intervene effectively in Manchuria. Instead Soviet Russia offered Tokyo a non-aggression pact. The Japanese failed to respond to that offer then, but they realized nonetheless that any move into Outer Mongolia or the Soviet Far East would involve them in a major war with incalculable consequences. In December 1932 Tokyo rejected Moscow's proposed non-aggression treaty on the ground that outstanding disputes had to be resolved first.

In China proper Soviet leaders, while providing moral support to the Chinese Reds under Mao Tse-tung who in 1931 created a rebel government in Kiangsi province in south China, sought to restore diplomatic relations with Chiang's Nationalist regime in Nanking, partly to prevent it from settling up with Japan and thus leave the USSR dangerously isolated. Late in 1932 Moscow and Nanking restored diplomatic ties, although Chiang was seeking unsuccessfully to crush the Chinese Reds. Japan's 1932 attack on the city of Shanghai, chief center of Western commercial interests in China, revealed Tokyo's lust for conquest and worsened its relations with the United States and Great Britain. In early 1933 the Soviet Union, still without a firm ally in the Far East, balanced uneasily between Japan, Nationalist China, and the Chinese Communists.

SOVIET-AMERICAN RELATIONS AND THE ISSUE OF RECOGNITION, 1919–1933

Expanding Soviet-American trade, a growing Japanese threat to the Soviet Far East, and the election of a liberal Democratic president were all factors

---

[23]Beloff, pp. 71–77; Adam Ulam, *Expansion and Coexistence: Soviet Foreign Policy, 1917–1973*, 2nd ed. (New York, 1974), pp. 198–200.

in the belated American decision late in 1933 to recognize the Soviet Union. Since 1917 Soviet leaders had desired American recognition partly because they, especially Stalin, admired American efficiency and enterprise. In 1921 Moscow had hoped that Warren Harding, the new Republican president, might alter U.S. policy towards Soviet Russia. Soon after his inauguration the Soviets sent an appeal to Washington to resume normal relations and urging the regularization of Soviet-American trade. However, Secretary of State Charles Hughes coldly reiterated earlier American refusals. Soviet confiscation of American property in Russia, the repudiation of Russian debts, and Moscow's clear advocacy of world revolution appalled Republican conservatives. In December 1923 President Calvin Coolidge outlined to Congress the requirements for altering American policy towards the Soviet Union:

> Whenever there appears any disposition to compensate our citizens who were despoiled, and to recognize that debt contracted with our government . . . by the newly formed Republic of Russia; whenever the active spirit of enmity to our institutions is abated; whenever appear words meet for repentance, our country ought to be the first to go to the economic and moral aid of Russia.

But when Foreign Commissar Chicherin telegraphed Coolidge that Moscow was ready "to discuss all problems mentioned in your message," Hughes rebuffed his overture: the United States would not "barter away its principles."[24] For almost the next ten years there would be no real change in official American policy towards the USSR.

Nonetheless, even without diplomatic ties trade between Soviet Russia and the United States expanded significantly. After the NEP was introduced in Soviet Russia in 1921, the United States soon was sending more goods to Soviet Russia than it had shipped to tsarist Russia before World War I. By 1924–1925 the United States was in first place among nations supplying the USSR with products, although for the following four years it fell to second behind Germany. Assisting this commercial development was *Amtorg* (American Trading Corporation), created in 1924 as the principal Soviet commercial agency in the United States. The USSR imported primarily cotton, rubber, semi-finished goods, automobiles, and agricultural machinery from the United States, whereas America purchased few Soviet goods. During the First Five Year Plan the Soviets required large quantities of machinery and many technical experts, which the United States could best supply. This upsurge of exports fostered rising support for recognition in American business circles. The deepening of the Great Depression in the United States made Soviet Russia—now the largest purchaser of American industrial and agricultural equipment—highly attractive to market-hungry

---

[24]Quoted in Robert P. Browder, *The Origins of Soviet-American Diplomacy* (Princeton, NJ, 1953), p. 19.

American producers. Broad support to recognize the USSR developed in Congress. Opposing any change in American policy were the American Catholic Church, the American Federation of Labor, and extreme conservative organizations. President Herbert Hoover, too, remained adamant in his opposition. Recognizing the USSR, he argued, would lend respectability to a brutal and oppressive regime and open the way to Communist agitators and Bolshevik propaganda to enter the United States.[25]

During 1932, as its attitude stiffened toward Japanese aggression in Manchuria and China, Moscow became more and more anxious to normalize its relations with the United States. Earlier, Lenin had argued that an eventual conflict between Japan and the United States for hegemony in the Pacific Ocean was inevitable.[26] Bolstering Moscow's hopes was the evident American opposition to Japanese actions in Manchuria. Secretary of State Henry Stimson declared the seizure of Manchuria to be a violation of the Nine Power Agreement, and the United States refused to recognize puppet Manchukuo. In Geneva Litvinov regretted publicly that the United States and the Soviet Union lacked diplomatic relations, thus complicating efforts to preserve peace in the Far East. His remarks became front page copy in leading Soviet newspapers, which exaggerated the degree of American alarm over Japanese actions. As support grew in the U.S. Senate for recognizing Soviet Russia, Senator Hiram Johnson of California declared:

> Some move in the direction of normal relations with Russia at this time would do more to remove the perils from the Far East, and therefore from the world in general, than any other single act.[27]

Recognition of the USSR did not become an issue in the 1932 American presidential election, but the Kremlin sought to reduce opposition to this by cultivating a moderate, respectable image centering around "socialism in one country." Already in the spring of 1933 President Franklin D. Roosevelt had decided upon recognition. Even prior to his inauguration he informed James Farley, the Democratic chairman, that he would actively seek diplomatic relations with Moscow. Continued isolation of both the USSR and the United States, Roosevelt believed, might undermine hopes of preventing a new war. Secretary of State Cordell Hull and Roosevelt concurred that the world was growing more dangerous and that Soviet Russia could help stabilize this perilous situation. Then and later Roosevelt wished to direct talks on recognition personally: "If I could only, myself, talk to one man representing the Russians," he told Henry Morgenthau, Jr., soon to become secretary of the treasury, in mid-summer 1933, "I could straighten out the whole question." Soon Roosevelt realized that William

---

[25]Browder, pp. 24–40.

[26]V. I. Lenin, *Polnoe sobranie sochinenii*, vol. XXVI, 2nd ed. (Moscow, 1930), p. 7.

[27]Browder, pp. 51–57, 71.

Bullitt, who had headed the mission from President Wilson to Moscow in 1919,* was best prepared as the assistant to the secretary of state to handle recognition. Following approval by the president, Bullitt drafted an invitation to open negotiations which Roosevelt sent personally to President Mikhail Kalinin. Success in the negotiations, Bullitt believed, depended on inducing Moscow to dispatch a top diplomat to Washington.[28]

On November 7, 1933, Foreign Commissar Litvinov arrived in Washington, insisting on American recognition first, then negotiations on disputed issues. However, Secretary Hull declared that guarantees on the repayment of Russian debts, protection of Americans in the USSR, and a Soviet pledge against circulating Comintern propaganda in the United States must come first. President Roosevelt helped break a threatened deadlock by assuring Litvinov that the United States only desired a just settlement; Roosevelt resolved most issues personally with the commissar. Litvinov provided reluctant written assurances on Comintern propaganda, and legal protection of Americans, but these pledges, notes Kennan, proved essentially valueless and were based on a profound American misunderstanding of the nature of Soviet Communism.[29]

In November 1933, amidst exaggerated hopes on both sides, Soviet-American relations were inaugurated. The first American ambassador to Moscow was Bullitt, who had maintained his friendship with Soviet Russia since 1919 and was given an extraordinarily warm welcome in Moscow. During an official dinner at Marshal K. E. Voroshilov's apartment, Stalin personally offered the first toast: "To President Roosevelt who in spite of the mute growl of the Fishes [referring to Hamilton Fish, an enemy of recognition] dared to recognize the Soviet Union." Stalin told Bullitt: "I want you to understand that if you want to see me at any time, day or night, you have only to let me know and I will see you at once." Stalin himself explained why Bullitt was being accorded such honors: Stalin believed that a Japanese attack on the USSR that spring was a virtual certainty.[30] Apparently, Soviet leaders believed that if Bullitt were treated generously, he would persuade Roosevelt to conclude a non-aggression pact with the USSR which would protect it against possible Japanese aggression. However, it soon became evident that Roosevelt simply could not undertake any such action because of persisting American isolationism. Nonetheless, by 1933 the Soviet Union had emerged from years of virtual isolation by establishing diplomatic relations with China and the United States and normalizing relations with France and Poland.

---

*See the Bullitt mission, pp. 30–31.

[28]Beatrice Farnsworth, *William C. Bullitt and the Soviet Union* (Bloomington, IN, 1967), pp. 89–95.

[29]Farnsworth, pp. 96–106; Kennan, pp. 298–99.

[30]Farnsworth, pp. 108–11.

Suggested Readings

Baer, George, ed., *A Question of Trust: The Origin of U.S.-Soviet relations. The Memoirs of Loy W. Henderson.* Stanford, CA, 1987.

Beloff, Max. *The Foreign Policy of Soviet Russia, 1929–1941.* vol. I, London, 1947.

Bishop, Donald G. *The Roosevelt-Litvinov Agreements: The American View.* Syracuse, NY, 1965.

Browder, Robert. *The Origins of Soviet-American Diplomacy.* Princeton, NJ, 1953.

Carr, E. H. *Twilight of the Comintern, 1930–1935.* New York, 1983.

Degras, Jane, ed., *Soviet Documents on Foreign Policy.* vol. II, (1925–1932) New York, 1952.

Deutscher, Isaac. *The Prophet Outcast: Trotsky 1929–1940.* New York, 1963.

Draper, Theodore. *American Communism and Soviet Russia.* New York, 1960.

Dyck, Harvey L. *Weimar Germany and Soviet Russia, 1926–1933: A Study in Diplomatic Instability.* New York, 1966.

Eudin, Xenia and Robert Slusser. *Soviet Foreign Policy, 1928–1934: Documents and Materials.* 2 vols. University Park, MD, 1966.

Farnsworth, Beatrice. *William C. Bullitt and the Soviet Union.* Bloomington, IN, 1967.

Filene, Peter G. *Americans and the Soviet Experiment, 1917–1933.* Cambridge, MA, 1967.

Kochan, Lionel. *Russia and the Weimar Republic.* Cambridge, England, 1954.

McKenzie, Kermit E. *Comintern and World Revolution 1928–1943.* London and New York, 1964.

McLane, Charles B. *Soviet Strategies in Southeast Asia: An Exploration of Eastern Policy Under Lenin and Stalin.* Princeton, NJ, 1966.

North, Robert C. *Moscow and the Chinese Communists.* Stanford, CA, 1953.

Schwartz, Benjamin. *Chinese Communism and the Rise of Mao.* Cambridge, MA, 1951.

Tang, Peter S. *Russia and the Soviet Policy in Manchuria, 1911–1931.* Durham, NC, 1959.

Trotsky, Leon. *The Struggle Against Fascism in Germany.* New York, 1971.

Tucker, Robert C. "The Emergence of Stalin's Foreign Policy," *Slavic Review,* vol. XXXVI (December 1977), pp. 563–89.

———. *Stalin in Power.* New York, 1990.

Ulam, Adam. *Stalin. The Man and His Era.* Boston, 1973.

Wandycz, Piotr S. *The Twilight of the French East European Alliances, 1926–36.* Princeton, NJ, 1988.

Whiting, Alan. *Soviet Policies in China.* New York, 1954.

5

THE USSR AND COLLECTIVE SECURITY, 1934–1938

Joseph Stalin, dominant in Soviet Russia after 1928, seemed unconcerned about Hitler's accession to power in January 1933; a full year passed before Soviet policies in Europe showed clear signs of change. However, Moscow hailed the non-aggression pacts it had concluded with its neighbors during 1932 and the normalization of relations with the United States in 1933 as major diplomatic successes. Indeed, the USSR was emerging from several years of virtual isolation from the outside world. Japanese aggressive moves in China beginning in 1931 had warned Soviet leaders that it was urgent to establish firmer and friendlier ties with the democratic West. During 1932–1933 many signs pointed to Soviet acceptance of the Versailles treaty system and the League of Nations as possible deterrents to the rising danger of a new world war. The Polish-German non-aggression pact of January 1934 accelerated Moscow's shift to a new course of "collective security" involving apparent partnership with the Western democracies in Europe and Asia. Tested in 1935 and 1936 and found wanting, collective security was doomed by Nazi expansion during 1938 and was abandoned and repudiated by the Soviet Union in 1939 when it embraced Adolf Hitler's Germany.

SHIFTING COURSE, 1934–1935

During 1933 Moscow made repeated friendly overtures to the new Nazi regime, but the Germans rebuffed these feelers. The Polish-Soviet non-aggression pact of 1932 apparently had consolidated Moscow's friendly relations with Warsaw, but Marshal Josef Pilsudski, Poland's dominant leader, refused to bind his country to the USSR. In December 1933 Pilsudski decided to come to terms with Hitler "as long as the Reich was still weak and ready to pay a good price."[1] In January 1934 a German-Polish non-aggression pact that encouraged Polish designs on the Soviet Ukraine

---

[1]Bohdan Budurowycz, *Polish-Soviet Relations, 1932–1939* (New York and London, 1963), pp. 37–38.

was concluded. This virtually completed Germany's retreat from the warm relationship with the USSR established much earlier at Rapallo. Soviet leaders interpreted Hitler's first major diplomatic move as involving a long-term threat to Soviet security. Although the Soviet government reacted cautiously, the Soviet press expressed concern that "a serious step had been made" towards forming an imperialist Berlin-Warsaw axis against the USSR.[2]

Consequently, Soviet leaders proved receptive to French efforts at this time to create an "eastern Locarno." Its purpose would be to guarantee frontiers in eastern Europe against arbitrary change as had been achieved in the west in 1925. Unofficial talks between Paris and Moscow beginning in October 1933 started this process. In May 1934 Foreign Commissar Maxim Litvinov met with the new French Foreign Minister Louis Barthou, who soon became the chief advocate of an eastern Locarno as a collective mutual assistance pact to include the USSR, Poland, Germany, and Czechoslovakia and to involve guarantees by France. Welcoming this idea, Litvinov urged that the Baltic nations likewise be included. However, Poland rejected that proposal and Polish Foreign Minister Josef Beck's doubts about this scheme were reinforced by his June conversation with Litvinov. The only means of preventing a major war, Foreign Commissar Litvinov told Beck, would be to isolate Germany and Japan through a series of treaties, including an eastern Locarno. However, despite strong French pressure, Poland refused to sign a pact, which Warsaw believed would limit its freedom in foreign affairs and make the USSR into the arbiter of eastern Europe. French warnings that this might compel Paris to conclude a military alliance with the Soviet Union merely alienated the Poles and drove them closer to Germany. Both Marshal Pilsudski and his successor, Beck, sought henceforth to balance between Nazi Germany and the USSR and thus protect Poland's independence.[3] With Poland adamantly opposed, Barthou's death in September 1934 doomed the eastern Locarno idea.

Commissar Litvinov—a Jew, an anti-Nazi, and a sincere Westerner—became the USSR's chief link to the West and embodied the concept of collective security against aggression. Although lacking former Foreign Commissar Georgii Chicherin's vast knowledge, Litvinov was better than his predecessor at establishing friendly contacts with democratic Western leaders. In numerous speeches at the Disarmament Commission in Geneva, sounding the themes of peace and general disarmament, he gained the sympathies of Western delegates if not their actual support. Maintaining a consistently peaceful, conciliatory line, he preserved fruitful connections with Western public opinion. To be sure, he served merely as the loyal executor of the Politburo's policies and played little role in determining Soviet foreign policy. Litvinov also remained dubious about the efficacy of treaties and pacts to ensure international peace. As he told a French journalist

---

[2]*Izvestiia*, January 29, 1934.
[3]Budurowycz, pp. 52–60, 73.

in June 1934: "There is the Kellogg pact and the League of Nations covenant, but since both of these have been violated with impunity, they can no longer satisfy anybody as guarantees of peace."[4] Nor was Litvinov confident that pacts such as an "eastern Locarno" could protect the USSR either.

The entry of the Soviet Union into the League of Nations in September 1934 marked an important milestone on the road to collective security and provided Litvinov with an ideal forum for his speeches on behalf of peace. Moscow's admission to the League had been sponsored vigorously by France. There had been some speculation that Poland might seek to block acceptance of the USSR, but Foreign Minister Beck merely sought assurances that the Soviet Union would adhere to the Polish-Soviet non-aggression treaty of 1932; Moscow readily provided these. Many contemporaries hailed the Soviet entry into the League as a major achievement of Litvinov and of Soviet foreign policy. Underscoring the end of Soviet isolation, it enabled Moscow to utilize the League to promote the security of the USSR from aggression. On occasion of the Soviet entry into the League, September 18, 1934, Litvinov declared in his maiden speech:

> We represent here a new state . . . in its external aspects, its internal political and social structure, and its aspirations and ideals. . . . Today we are happy to be able to state that . . . the advocates of ignoring and isolating the Soviet Union are no longer to be met among broad-minded statesmen.[5]

There was nothing in the League Covenant, explained Litvinov, which the USSR found theoretically unacceptable. Stressing the idea of peaceful coexistence, he advocated increased League activity to preserve the peace in the face of rising militarism. By joining the League the USSR confirmed its abandonment of hostility to the Paris Peace Settlement and its willingness to cooperate with the Versailles powers.

Soviet leaders realized full well that the League of Nations could not ensure the security of the USSR but hoped that it would help restrain aggression. However, the Ethiopian Crisis of 1935 soon revealed such expectations to be unrealistic. Although the Soviet Union joined in the League sanctions imposed on Fascist Italy after it invaded Ethiopia, these proved ineffective. Benito Mussolini conquered that African country and revealed the League as toothless and incapable of keeping the peace.

During 1935 France and the Soviet Union, despite major ideological differences, were driven together by common fear of a revisionist and rearming Nazi Germany, much as tsarist Russia and republican France had forged the Franco-Russian Alliance of 1893. Franco-Soviet negotiations were already proceeding positively when Foreign Minister Barthou was killed in

---

[4]Jane Degras, ed., *Soviet Documents on Foreign Policy*, vol. III (London, 1953), p. 84; Litvinov's interview with Jules Sauerwein, June 23, 1934.

[5]Alvin Rubinstein, ed., *The Foreign Policy of the Soviet Union* (New York, 1973), pp. 130–32.

September 1934. His successor, Pierre Laval, preferred an understanding with Germany, but in April 1935 at Geneva, Litvinov and Laval drafted a Franco-Soviet Pact. Signed in Paris in May, this defensive mutual assistance treaty committed each party to assist the other "in the case of an unprovoked attack by a European state," but it proved much less effective than the Franco-Russian Alliance with its specific military accords. France made its pledge to assist the USSR conditional upon the League of Nations recognizing an attack as an act of aggression. Because Germany and the USSR in 1935 had no common frontier, the Soviets could scarcely assist France unless Poland allowed Soviet troops to cross its territory. Furthermore the treaty did not obligate France to aid the USSR in case it was attacked by Japan. Without any specific military provisions the Franco-Soviet Pact comprised at most a preliminary to an alliance. France was so divided politically then between left and right that an entire year passed before Paris ratified the agreement and only after its wording had been so emasculated that the treaty could not restrain Nazi aggression. V. M. Molotov declared to the Central Executive Committee of the Party on January 10, 1936:

> The Soviet Government would have desired the establishment of better relations with Germany than exist at present. . . . But the realization of such a policy depends not only on us, but also on the German Government.[6]

Likewise at a German embassy reception in Moscow in October 1935 Assistant Defense Commissar Mikhail Tukhachevskii stressed that if Germany and the USSR marched together, they could impose peace on the entire world.[7] Stalin had accepted the need for close ties with France and membership in the League of Nations reluctantly, apparently because of growing German hostility.

In the wake of the Franco-Soviet Pact a mutual assistance treaty was concluded between Soviet Russia and Czechoslovakia on May 16, 1935. It stipulated that the USSR would assist Czechoslovakia in the event of aggression, presumably by Germany, only if France met its obligations first under its pact with the Czechs. The Soviet-Czech Pact extended Moscow's obligations very little, because the USSR lacked a common frontier with Czechoslovakia. Thus the West could not involve Soviet Russia in a war against Hitler while it remained on the sidelines. Nevertheless, the Franco-Soviet and Soviet-Czech pacts enhanced Moscow's reputation as a champion of collective security.

All this required a radical change in Comintern policy and abandonment of the outdated slogan, "Social Fascism." In July 1934 French Socialists and

---

[6]Gustav Hilger and Alfred Meyer, *The Incompatible Allies: A Memoir History of German-Soviet Relations, 1918–1941* (New York, 1953), pp. 269–71.

[7]James McSherry, *Stalin, Hitler and Europe: The Origins of World War II, 1933–1939* (Cleveland and New York, 1968), p. 41.

Communists had agreed to cooperate against Fascism and Nazism, to promote international peace, and defend democratic freedoms. The Seventh—and last—Comintern Congress, an obedient, thoroughly Stalinized conclave, convened in Moscow in July 1935. At this congress the chief slogan was "a united front from above," or a "Popular Front" of all progressive forces to oppose Fascism: workers, peasants, lesser urban bourgeoisie, and intelligentsia. Georgi Dimitrov, a leading Bulgarian Communist, delivered the chief address at the congress. Such a "united front from above," he argued, could pose a threat only to the big bourgeoisie, financiers, and other exploiters. Communists were instructed to support "peaceful" bourgeois powers such as Britain and France, against "aggressive" bourgeois nations such as Germany, Italy, and Japan. However, Moscow viewed the "Popular Front" as a defensive measure to dissuade the West from collaborating with Fascism against the USSR, not to organize a crusade against Fascism. Despite defiant speeches at the congress, few attempts were made to implement them. Communists, Dimitrov emphasized, should retain their identity within the "Popular Front." The Seventh Comintern Congress made it abundantly clear that the Soviet Union had no intention of abandoning the goal of world revolution, ceasing its propaganda efforts, or of embracing socialists too warmly.

COLLECTIVE SECURITY TESTED: THE RHINELAND AND SPAIN, 1936

Only a few days after the French Chamber of Deputies finally ratified the Franco-Soviet Pact early in March 1936, Hitler sent units of the German army into the Rhineland, asserting that the French had violated the Locarno Treaty of 1925. The German Rhineland had been demilitarized under the Treaty of Versailles and Allied troops had evacuated it in 1930 after an agreement with the Weimar government. Hitler's move was in clear violation of Versailles, Locarno, and the Covenant of the League of Nations. Some French leaders wished to resist this Nazi move militarily and France possessed the power to force a German withdrawal, but London dissuaded such action. British leaders argued that inasmuch as the Rhineland was German territory, Hitler was merely moving into his own backyard and that Allied military action would violate the long-held Allied principle of national self-determination. The reoccupation of the Rhineland dealt a heavy blow to the collective security policy pursued by Litvinov and Stalin in order to stiffen the West against Fascist aggression. It revealed Hitler's contempt for the Franco-Soviet Pact and his conviction that the West, still suffering the effects of the Great Depression, would not act forcefully. Actually, Nazi Germany then was in the early stages of rearmament and the French army was far stronger, but France was split between left and right and the government felt too impoverished to act alone.

Once in control of the Rhineland, the Nazis quickly built there the Siegfried Line of fortification. This changed the military balance in Europe significantly, ending an apparent French hegemony in Europe that had persisted since the end of World War I. Once this concrete and steel barrier was completed, French guarantees to Czechoslovakia and Poland, as well as to the USSR, became virtually meaningless because the French army would then have had great difficulty in advancing into Germany.

Soviet leaders were dismayed at Western spinelessness and appeasement of Hitler. In the League of Nations, Litvinov, pointing out that Germany had violated its international obligations, urged the League to act pledging that the Soviet Union would join in any League action. However, a French military advance into the Rhineland would not have obligated the USSR to act under the Franco-Soviet Pact since it was not a clear case of German external aggression. Hitler's success in defying the West, notes George F. Kennan, must have made Stalin look rather foolish for relying on such a weak instrument as the Franco-Soviet Pact. Realizing that Hitler now had achieved his stated goals in the West and was likely in the future to move eastward, Stalin knew that Soviet security would have to be provided by other means. Already he must have envisioned a possible eventual agreement with Hitler to achieve that objective. From the time of the Rhineland reoccupation Stalin must have concluded that it was only a question of time before he either had to fight Hitler or make a deal with him. With Stalin's suspicious and paranoid nature, he apparently concluded that he must eliminate quickly any potential leaders from high positions, especially the "Old Bolshevik" colleagues of Lenin, in case his policies were criticized or attacked at home. Although direct evidence is lacking that foreign policy was a determining factor, only a few days after Hitler's move Stalin issued secret orders to prepare the first great public purge trial of "Old Bolshevik" leaders; his colleagues began to notice the first signs of his abnormal behavior.[8]

The prelude to Stalin's Great Purge was the assassination in December 1934 of Sergei Kirov, a young, popular, and reputedly liberal Leningrad Party leader. Blamed on Trotskyites, Kamenev and Zinoviev, it was actually carried out on orders from Stalin.[9] During 1935 Stalin instructed an expanding secret police (NKVD), comprising virtually a state within a state, to spy on and investigate all other Party leaders. After the Rhineland reoccupation, Stalin moved swiftly to bring Lenin's former colleagues to public trial on charges of conspiracy against him and the USSR on behalf of foreign powers. Despite their confessions to acts of treason that they certainly could not have committed, by 1938 they had all been executed. The Great Purge likewise decimated the leadership of the Soviet armed forces. Marshal Tukhachevskii and other leading generals had been critical of the early public trials. Accused of treasonable collaboration with Germany and Japan, they were arrested and shot. About half the Soviet officer corps was executed

---

[8]George Kennan, *Russia and the West Under Lenin and Stalin* (Boston, 1960), pp. 304–06.

[9]On the Kirov murder see Robert Conquest, *Stalin and the Kirov Murder* (New York and Oxford, England, 1989).

and imprisoned gravely weakening the armed forces. Millions of ordinary Soviet citizens were falsely accused and deported to forced labor camps in Siberia and Central Asia.[10] By this terrible blood purge Stalin consolidated absolute power through fear and now could dictate to a reshaped Politburo, but the USSR paid a high price in weakened defensive capacity and loss of credibility abroad.

Late in July 1936, only a month before the first public trial in Moscow, civil war erupted in Spain. Conservative military officers led by a professed Fascist, General Francisco Franco, revolted against the moderate democratic Spanish Republic. When France and Britain proposed a non-intervention policy, the USSR, Italy and Germany agreed but promptly violated it. Mussolini provided major military aid to Franco almost immediately, and Hitler somewhat less. The Spanish Civil War soon became a struggle between the Left ("Popular Front") and the Right (Fascism), but Stalin reacted with typical caution. Not until October 4 did Stalin telegraph the head of the Spanish Communist Party to express his support for the Spanish Republic.[11] When Mussolini and Hitler blatantly violated the non-intervention accord, the Soviet Politburo decided in early September to intervene in Spain secretly through the Comintern. Stalin could not tolerate a swift triumph of Fascism in Spain since it might spread to France and provoke the collapse of the anti-Fascist Popular Front throughout Europe. That would leave Hitler free to move east against the USSR. Thus Moscow carried out a swift and efficient rescue operation: Soviet officers took charge of military operations and security in the Madrid region and saved the Spanish capital from capture by Franco's forces. The Soviets did not seek to bring the weak Spanish Communists to power in Spain because Stalin realized that would alienate the West, with which he still sought to cooperate. Thus Moscow insisted that the Spanish Communists adhere to the Popular Front line and cooperate fully with the Republic.[12] The Comintern recruited "volunteers" to fight for Republican Spain from all over the world, including the Lincoln Brigade from the United States, but no Soviet army units were engaged. Stalin carefully avoided any open confrontation with the Fascist powers that might have involved the USSR in war with them while the West sat on the sidelines.

In February 1937 Moscow's policy shifted again. Soviet military aid to the Republic virtually ceased while modest economic assistance continued. By then Stalin knew that a Republican victory over Franco only would be possible with a massive Soviet military commitment that Moscow was unwilling to make and which might involve the USSR in a major war during

---

[10]On Stalin's purges see Robert Conquest, *The Great Terror* (New York, 1968); and David Dallin and Boris Nicolaevsky, *Forced Labor in Soviet Russia* (New Haven, CT, 1947).

[11]Adam Ulam, *Expansion and Coexistence: Soviet Foreign Policy, 1917–1973*, 2nd ed. (New York, 1974), p. 244.

[12]Kennan, pp. 308–310; David Cattell, *Communism and the Spanish Civil War* (Berkeley, CA, 1955).

the purges. To prevent their possible triumph within the Republican camp, Stalin ordered strong action, including assassinations, against Trotskyite elements in Spain. However, the Republic's final defeat in 1939 resulted primarily from the overwhelming military superiority of General Franco and his Italian and German allies. Idealistic Western and Soviet volunteers and officials active in Spain became victims of the Stalin purge. Declared Stalin's security chief, Walter Krivitskii: "We cannot allow Spain to be turned into a field of free activity of anti-Soviet forces coming here from all over the world." Hundreds of volunteers of the International Brigade were killed secretly in Spain, and most of the few hundred Soviet volunteers were eliminated when they returned home.[13]

Why had Moscow undertaken its limited and relatively brief intervention in Spain? The claim of Fascists and many conservatives that Stalin aimed to establish a Soviet republic in Spain can be dismissed for lack of evidence. Liberals in the West viewed Soviet intervention as an effort to draw the hesitant, appeasement-minded Western powers into a war against Fascism and thus prevent a Nazi move eastward. Comintern and pro-Communist spokesmen emphasized that Moscow's intervention was an attempt to put teeth in collective security and halt the spread of Fascism. These latter explanations appear to have much validity.

In Ethiopia in 1935, the Rhineland crisis in 1936, and Spain in 1936–1937, Stalin had pursued, albeit unenthusiastically, a policy of collective security to block the spread of Fascism. Discovering that the West was unwilling to make sacrifices or even to defend its own interests and treaty commitments, Stalin purged all those in the USSR who might replace him or criticize a shift in his policies. Western appeasement and the purge of the Red Army officer corps doomed the collective security idea and frustrated attempts to form a Western-Soviet alliance against Nazi expansion.

THE DECLINE OF COLLECTIVE SECURITY, 1937–1938

As the Comintern began channeling major assistance to the Spanish Republic, Hitler and Mussolini in October 1936 concluded a Rome-Berlin Axis that was dominated increasingly by a rapidly rearming Nazi Germany. In November Germany, Italy, and Japan—subsequently partners in World War II—concluded the Anti-Comintern Pact, apparently directed against the USSR. Actually, in the short run that agreement probably reduced the danger of either Germany or Japan attacking the Soviet Union, because each partner assumed that the other would block Soviet intervention in its sphere of interest. Under the Anti-Comintern Pact the partners merely pledged to remain neutral if the USSR attacked one of them. They also promised not to conclude an agreement with the Soviet Union, although both Germany and Japan did so subsequently.

[13]Quoted in V. A. Kumanev, "Imperskie traditsii Rossii vo vneshnei politike Stalina" (unpublished article).

During 1937 Stalin pursued cautious external policies as the Great Purge raged in the Soviet Union. Already he was distancing himself gradually from collective security and sharply reduced Soviet aid to the Spanish Republic. While the Axis powers remained tied down in Spain, the danger of their attacking the USSR remained remote. Officially the Soviet Union continued to champion collective security. Litvinov, probably the only leading Soviet diplomat to still believe in it, continued to advocate common resistance to aggression. "We cannot preserve the League of Nations . . . ," he declared, "if we turn a blind eye to breaches of those treaties [Versailles, League Covenant] or confine ourselves to verbal protests." In September 1937 in a speech to the League Assembly, the foreign commissar reiterated:

> We have had four aggressions in the course of five years. We see how aggression, when it meets with no check, passes from one continent to another, assuming larger and larger dimensions every time. Yet I am convinced that a resolute policy pursued by the League of Nations in one case of aggression would rid us of all the other cases.[14]

Late in 1937 Nazi Germany shifted its emphasis menacingly towards the east. On November 5 Hitler told his generals and diplomats assembled at a secret conclave that Germany had rearmed sufficiently to undertake the aim expounded in *Mein Kampf* (1925) of bringing all Germans of central and eastern Europe into a Greater Germany before the West could rearm fully. Soon the Germans withdrew most of their personnel from Spain, leaving Mussolini to shoulder the burden of ensuring a Fascist victory. In February 1938 Hitler purged the German High Command in order to ensure its utter loyalty to him, thus removing a final restraint on forceful action. Simultaneously, Anthony Eden, advocating resistance to Fascist aggression, resigned as British Foreign Secretary, and Lord Halifax, a supporter of appeasement, replaced him. The previous November Halifax for the Neville Chamberlain government, had offered Hitler "a kind of alliance . . . and a free hand in Central and Eastern Europe." Thus when Eden resigned, Hitler had good reason to decide the time had come to carry out his planned program of aggression.[15]

In March 1938, to prevent the Austrians from voting on the issue of annexation to Germany, Hitler ordered the Nazi Wehrmacht into Austria and announced the *Anschluss* (annexation) of that country to Greater Germany. When the Western powers limited themselves to polite protests over this blatant violation of the Versailles Treaty, Stalin must have concluded that the West would do nothing to halt Hitler's advance in central Europe. The Anschluss coincided with the final public purge trial in Moscow

---

[14]Quoted in McSherry, pp. 49–50.

[15]Ivan Maisky, *Who Helped Hitler?* Trans. Andrew Rothstein (London, 1964), p. 73. (Maisky served as Soviet ambassador in London, 1932–1943.)

featuring Nicholas Bukharin. Reacting to Hitler's move, Litvinov told American Ambassador Joseph E. Davies that the acquiescent attitude of the Chamberlain government had encouraged Hitler to act. If Germany next attacked Czechoslovakia, he declared, France must aid the Czechs, "otherwise it would also be the end of France." And Britain, Litvinov predicted, would in turn be compelled to assist France.[16] Contrasting the Anschluss with earlier acts of aggression, Litvinov warned journalists on March 17 that it had occurred in the heart of Europe. Moscow still stood ready, he affirmed, "to participate in collective actions" to prevent further aggression. Late in March the foreign commissar reiterated that the USSR would aid Czechoslovakia provided France did, but he did not specify how.[17]

After Hitler's seizure of Austria, partly because of a Soviet-Japanese clash on the Manchurian border, signs multiplied that Moscow would welcome improved relations with Nazi Germany. As Hitler turned up the rhetoric and military preparations that summer against Czechoslovakia, Soviet spokesmen still affirmed that a strong Western-Soviet stand in support of the Czechs could halt Hitler. In Stalin's name Ivan Maisky, Soviet ambassador to Britain, assured the Czech minister to London that the USSR would fulfill all its obligations to Prague as soon as France did.[18] However, the Soviet government newspaper, *Izvestiia*, warned that Prime Minister Neville Chamberlain of Britain planned to sacrifice the interests of small east European states and France in order to turn the latter into London's junior partner.[19] Moscow evidently wanted the West to stand by Czechoslovakia but refused to aid the Czechs militarily alone.

Hitler's chief demand to the Czechs was to cede the Sudetenland in western Czechoslovakia, containing a German majority, the principal Czech mountain barriers and defenses to Germany. A London *Times* editorial, echoing the appeasement-minded Chamberlain government, urged Prague to yield the Sudetenland. This foreshadowed the Franco-British agreement to pressure the Czechs to surrender that territory at the infamous Munich Conference of September 29, 1938, from which the Soviet Union was excluded. Thereby the West drove the final nail into the coffin of collective security and rendered Czechoslovakia indefensible and helpless. Chamberlain returned to London sporting his famous umbrella and rejoicing in "peace in our time." Moscow emerged from the Czech crisis as apparently the only power to have upheld its commitments. However, in practice it would have been extremely difficult without a common frontier for the Soviets to have provided effective military aid to Czechoslovakia within

---

[16]*The Foreign Relations of the United States, The Soviet Union, 1933–1939* (Washington, DC, 1952), pp. 533–34. (These works are commonly referred to as *FRUS*.)

[17]Degras, pp. 276–77; McSherry, pp. 59–64.

[18]*The Foreign Relations of the United States, 1938*, vol. I (Washington, DC, 1952), pp. 546, 548.

[19]*Izvestiia*, July 17, 1938, cited in McSherry, p. 63.

a reasonable time. Soviet assertions of loyal fulfillment of their pledges thus cost them nothing. Thus the statement of V. P. Potemkin, a Soviet diplomat, "The Soviet Union proved to be the only government which kept faith with its international obligations in relations with Czechoslovakia," means little.[20]

After the Munich Agreement had wholly discredited Litvinov's collective security approach, Soviet foreign policy late in 1938 again reached a turning point. Stalin now was prepared to follow Lenin's course at Brest-Litovsk: reach timely accommodation with a more powerful foe— Germany in both cases. Stalin's control over Soviet foreign policy only became complete, affirms Robert Slusser, an American scholar, with the destruction of the Bukharin faction, thus ending a deep split over both domestic and foreign policy at the summit of the Soviet Communist Party. During that temporary deadlock at the top, Litvinov had enjoyed considerable latitude to maneuver and both Politburo factions had supported collective security.[21] Hitler's clear turn towards the east in 1938 compelled Stalin to begin moving toward him since the West neither sought to stop the Nazis nor to collaborate meaningfully with the Soviet Union.

MOSCOW'S RELATIONS WITH THE FAR EAST AND THE UNITED STATES, 1934–1938

During 1935 Soviet leaders displayed deep concern about the dangerous situation facing them in the Far East. Following its recognition by the United States, the USSR had failed to enlist American support to halt Japanese expansion in north China. After the Japanese seizure of Manchuria and their attack on Shanghai, Chiang Kai-shek's Nationalist government reached accommodation with Tokyo and concentrated its military efforts against Mao Tse-tung's Chinese Communists. In 1934 Chiang compelled the Communists to abandon their base in south China and undertake their difficult "Long March," followed by their creation of a Chinese Red state centered in Sian in northwest China. Moscow realized the danger that Japan, without military involvement in China proper, might turn against the Soviet sphere of interest in Mongolia or against the Soviet Far East. Seeking to prevent that, Moscow early in 1935 agreed to sell the Chinese Eastern Railroad to Japan. It became in the Soviet interest to encourage the outbreak of a Sino-Japanese war, and it seems scarcely accidental that the Red Chinese delegate at the Seventh Comintern Congress in July affirmed "the earnest desire of the Chinese people to take up arms against the Japanese oppressors."[22] To that end Mao Tse-tung's Chinese Reds sought accommodation with Chiang so that both could oppose the Japanese. However,

---

[20]V. P. Potemkin, ed., *Istoriia diplomatii*, vol. III (Moscow, 1945), p. 644.

[21]Robert Slusser, "The Role of the Foreign Ministry," in Ivo Lederer, ed., *Russian Foreign Policy: Essays in Historical Perspective* (New Haven, CT, 1962), pp. 227–28.

[22]Quoted in Ulam, p. 233.

Chiang Kai-shek, during 1936, continued to aim to destroy the Chinese Communists and to unify China.

Chiang's policies toward the Communists and Japan changed following the bizarre "Sian Incident" of December 1936 when he was detained at the headquarters of the Manchurian warlord, Chang Hsueh-liang, where they had been planning another campaign against the Chinese Reds. Chiang's release was arranged by the shrewd Chou En-lai, the top Chinese Red diplomat, after the Nationalist leader promised to abandon that campaign and adopt a firm anti-Japanese position. A united front of the Kuomintang and Chinese Communists against Japanese imperialism was worked out in further negotiations.

Meanwhile the Japanese during the summer of 1935 had pushed deeper into Inner Mongolia; that winter minor Soviet-Japanese clashes occurred on the border of Soviet-controlled Outer Mongolia. In February 1936 Litvinov told American Ambassador William Bullitt that a major Japanese attack there was unlikely because Tokyo was having much trouble controlling Manchuria and Inner Mongolia. On March 4 when asked by Roy Howard, an American journalist, how Moscow would react to a Japanese attack on Outer Mongolia, Stalin replied: "If Japan ventures to attack the Mongolian People's Republic, seeking to destroy its independence, we will have to assist [it]."[23] That same month Moscow countered this Japanese threat with a mutual assistance treaty with Outer Mongolia while reaffirming Chinese sovereignty there. In Nanking the Soviet ambassador told an American journalist that Soviet policy toward Japan was "one of defiance based on the theory that a strong attitude would be more likely to prevent Japanese aggression and resultant war than a weak one."[24] Moscow's new tough line reflected increased Red Army strength in the Far East and better relations with the West.

With its relations with Nanking deteriorating, Japan on July 7, 1937, attacked Nationalist China and soon controlled most coastal regions. That induced the Chinese Communists to tighten their alliance with Nanking and subordinate themselves at least nominally to the Nationalist government. *Izvestiia* compared the Japanese assault on China to the seizure of Manchuria in 1931 and called it "the beginning of the second stage of the conquest of China, long and thoroughly prepared by the Japanese imperialists."[25] Japan's invasion of China caused rejoicing in Moscow since apparently this provided the Soviet Far East with greater security and made a Japanese attack on Soviet areas unlikely. In August 1937 Moscow concluded a friendship treaty with Nanking and began sending arms, credits, and military instructors to Nationalist China. In October Litvinov told Vice

---

[23]Degras, p. 164.

[24]*FRUS*, 1936, vol. IV, pp. 100–02.

[25]*Izvestiia*, July 22, 1937, quoted in Harriet Moore, *Soviet Far Eastern Policy, 1931–1945* (Princeton, NJ, 1945), p. 84.

Premier Leon Blum of France that he was delighted at the Japanese attack on China that assured the Soviet Union of many years of peace in the Far East.[26]

However, the Sino-Japanese War did not prevent serious hostile incidents between the Japanese and the Soviets. In June 1937 the Soviets had occupied several islands in the Amur River, provoking Japanese artillery to sink a Soviet gunboat. Litvinov agreed to withdraw the Soviet troops, and soon the Japanese occupied the disputed islands, causing only a mild protest from Moscow. Once Japan invaded China, Soviet policy in the region stiffened. On July 6, 1938, a Soviet patrol occupied Changkufeng Hill on the Soviet-Manchurian border near Vladivostok and later fortified it. Following a July 31 Japanese attack that threw the Soviets off that hill, a major Soviet counteroffensive accompanied by air attacks on various Japanese targets induced Tokyo to offer to restore the situation before hostilities began. On August 11 Litvinov accepted a ceasefire; four days later Japanese forces withdrew from contested ground. Considerable casualties were suffered on both sides.[27] Clearly both sides wished to avoid a major conflict, but Stalin had served notice that despite the Great Purge, Tokyo could not infringe with impunity upon Soviet interests in the Far East.

Meanwhile Soviet-American relations, inaugurated with such optimism in November 1933, soon cooled as both sides became disillusioned. Moscow soon realized that it could not conclude a non-aggression pact with a United States only slowly emerging from decades of isolation nor forge real cooperation with Washington to halt Japanese aggression. By mid-1935 Ambassador Bullitt, abandoning his friendship for the USSR, stood appalled at Stalin's brutal police state. The Soviet Russia of 1934, Bullitt reported, had no more freedom than tsarist Russia and was ruled by fanatics prepared to sacrifice themselves and others for the sake of international Communism. Pledges made at the Seventh Comintern Congress for cooperation with the West against Fascism left Bullitt unimpressed since the Comintern continued to sponsor Communist agitation in the United States. Slightly earlier to Bullitt's statement that the United States had desired truly friendly relations with the Soviet Union, Foreign Commissar Litvinov had replied bluntly that there was no such thing as "really friendly relations" between nations.[28] Bullitt's return to the United States in June 1936 marked the final failure of efforts of the Franklin Roosevelt administration to establish truly warm Soviet-American relations. The time had not yet come for Washington to play an active role in European or Asian affairs.

---

[26]*FRUS*, 1937, vol. III, pp. 635–36.

[27]*FRUS*, 1938, vol. III, pp. 455–85; McSherry, pp. 16–18.

[28]Beatrice Farnsworth, *William C. Bullitt and the Soviet Union* (Bloomington, IN, 1967), pp. 140–50.

Suggested Readings

Beck, Josef. *Final Report.* New York, 1957.

Budurowycz, Bohdan. *Polish-Soviet Relations, 1932–1939.* New York and London, 1963.

Cattell, David. *Communism and the Spanish Civil War.* Berkeley, CA, 1955.

_____. *Soviet Diplomacy and the Spanish Civil War.* Berkeley, CA, 1957.

Churchill, Winston S. *The Gathering Storm.* London, 1948.

Clarke, J. Calvitt III. *Russia and Italy Against Hitler. The Bolshevik Fascist Rapprochement of the 1930s.* Westport, CT, 1991.

Coulondre, Robert. *From Stalin to Hitler.* Paris, 1950.

Davies, Joseph E. *Mission to Moscow.* New York, 1941.

Degras, Jane, ed., *Soviet Documents on Foreign Policy.* vol. III, (1933–1941) London, 1953.

Dimitroff, Georgi. *The United Front.* New York, 1938.

Eden, Anthony. *Facing the Dictators.* Boston, 1962.

Fischer, Louis. *Men and Politics, an Autobiography.* New York, 1941.

The Foreign Relations of the United States, the Soviet Union, 1933–1939. Washington, DC, 1952.

Haslam, Jonathan. *The Soviet Union and the Threat from the East, 1933–41.* Pittsburgh, PA, 1992.

Hilger, Gustav and Alfred Meyer. *The Incompatible Allies: A Memoir History of German-Soviet Relations, 1918–1941.* New York, 1953.

Hochman, Jiri. *The Soviet Union and the Failure of Collective Security, 1934–1938.* Ithaca, NY, 1984.

Krivitsky, Walter. *In Stalin's Secret Service.* New York, 1939.

Litvinov, Maxim. *Against Aggression.* New York, 1939.

Maisky, Ivan. *Memoirs of a Soviet Ambassador.* New York, 1968.

_____. *Who Helped Hitler?* Trans. A. Rothstein. London, 1964.

McSherry, James E. *Stalin, Hitler and Europe: The Origins of World War II 1933–1939.* Cleveland and New York, 1968.

Moore, Harriet. *Soviet Far Eastern Policy, 1931–1945.* Princeton, NJ, 1945.

Scott, William E. *Alliance Against Hitler: The Origins of the Franco-Soviet Pact.* Durham, NC, 1962.

Taylor, A. J. P. *The Origins of the Second World War.* London, 1962.

Wheeler-Bennett, John. *The Nemesis of Power.* London, 1953.

6

THE NAZI-SOVIET ALLIANCE, 1939–1941

Stalin the realist, after Czechoslovakia's dismemberment at the Munich Conference, recognized the likelihood of an eventual accommodation with Nazi Germany. Nonetheless, he remained open to Western proposals and authorized Maxim Litvinov to make some of his own. However, V. M. Molotov's replacement of Litvinov as foreign commissar in May 1939 reflected a major shift in Soviet foreign policy despite persisting suspicions between Moscow and Berlin. Stalin interpreted the subsequent Nazi-Soviet Pact of August 1939 as a great triumph for Soviet diplomacy that provided the USSR with security. However, when Stalin moved to exploit the pact by building an eastern European buffer zone, frictions and suspicions multiplied between the new allies, notably after the Molotov-Ribbentrop talks in November 1940. Why did Stalin sign an alliance with Hitler rather than with the West? Why did Hitler decide subsequently to invade the Soviet Union?

MOSCOW IS WOOED BY BOTH SIDES, JANUARY–JULY 1939

After Munich, Joseph Stalin, having completed the purge of his rivals and ideological enemies, could dictate to an obedient Politburo. His successor, Nikita S. Khrushchev, wrote:

> Stalin thought that now he could decide all things alone and all he needed were statisticians; he treated all others in such a way that they could only listen to and praise him.[1]

However, until the Eighteenth Party Congress of March 1939 a transition period persisted. According to Max Jakobson, a leading Finnish diplomat, the Soviet-Finnish negotiations at that time revealed a startling administrative chaos in Moscow. Individual Politburo members formulated foreign

---

[1]Nikita S. Khrushchev, "The Crimes of the Stalin Era," *The New Leader*, Annotated by Boris I. Nicolaevsky (New York, 1956), p. 21.

policies without coordinating their actions with Litvinov's supposedly official course.[2]

Early in 1939 even pacific Western statesmen realized that Hitler would not be satisfied just with the Sudetenland. In January Nazi Foreign Minister Joachim von Ribbentrop pressed the diplomatic offensive against Poland with claims on the city of Danzig. Meanwhile in Britain optimism prevailed that an age of peace had dawned. Such dreams were rudely dispelled by Hitler's March 14 invasion of Czechoslovakia, whose western portions were incorporated summarily into the German Reich while Slovakia received "independence" as a German satellite. Prime Minister Neville Chamberlain, discarding his failed appeasement policy, pledged British aid to Poland if attacked by Germany; France followed suit. Their guarantees, however, were militarily worthless without a Western-Soviet alliance.

Subsequent negotiations that spring for such an accord foundered on mutual suspicion and doubts that either side would implement it militarily. Thus when, on March 21, Litvinov proposed a Six Power Conference (USSR, Britain, France, Poland, Romania, and Finland), Chamberlain wrote privately:

> I must confess to the most profound distrust of Russia. I have no belief whatever in her ability to maintain an effective offensive, even if she wanted to. And I distrust her motives, which seem to me to have little connection with our ideas of liberty. . . . Moreover, she is both hated and suspected by many of the smaller states, notably by Poland, Rumania, and Finland.[3]

Thus London received Litvinov's proposal coldly and allowed it to languish.

Stalin's speech of March 10, 1939, to the Eighteenth Party Congress heralded a major change in Soviet foreign policy. A "new imperialist war" was raging, Stalin asserted, as aggressive imperialist states infringed upon the interests of "non-aggressive" England, France, and the United States. "The non-aggressive, democratic states [combined] are unquestionably stronger than the fascist states, both economically and militarily," affirmed Stalin. However, the West feared that a new imperialist war would provoke revolution in one or more countries. As the danger of general war grew, Stalin concluded, "our country is unswervingly pursuing a policy of preserving peace." Moscow simultaneously was building up its armed forces.[4] Stalin's speech suggested that only differing ideologies still separated Moscow and Berlin.

---

[2]Max Jakobson, *The Diplomacy of the Winter War: An Account of the Russo-Finnish War, 1939–1940* (Cambridge, MA, 1961), pp. 9ff.

[3]Quoted in Winston Churchill, *The Gathering Storm* (Boston, 1948), p. 349.

[4]"Report to the Eighteenth Party Congress," in Myron Rush, ed., *The International Situation and Soviet Foreign Policy* (Columbus, OH, 1970), pp. 94–95.

On April 15 negotiations began in Moscow between the British Ambassador and Foreign Commissar Litvinov. The next day Litvinov made a formal offer of a Soviet-British-French mutual assistance pact of five to ten years' duration. The three powers, together with Poland if possible, were to guarantee all eastern European countries threatened by Nazi aggression. However, Polish leaders feared Soviet "protection" as much as they did Nazi Germany. Later, Churchill regretted that the West had not accepted Litvinov's final effort because such a pact might well have averted war. When no response came from London, in Moscow Litvinov's initiative was considered a failure.[5]

On May 3 Moscow announced suddenly that Litvinov had resigned as foreign commissar at his own request. Replacing him was Viacheslav M. Molotov, long an intimate colleague of Stalin, who remained also chairman of the Council of Ministers. The Soviet press greeted Molotov with great fanfare while Litvinov's dismissal was contained in a miniscule notice.[6] Gustav Hilger, counsellor in the German embassy, had observed Molotov closely and considered him an efficient administrator and executor of Stalin's policies who "never showed any personal initiative, but seemed to keep strictly to the rules laid down by Stalin." Whenever anything unforseen arose, Molotov declared he must consult his "government," that is, Stalin. As the war danger grew, Stalin wanted a devoted servant. Nevertheless, Molotov possessed an amazing memory and vast energy that enabled him to handle a wide variety of issues.[7] Much later Molotov confided: "I viewed my task as foreign minister to expand the frontiers of our fatherland as much as possible. And it seems that Stalin and I accomplished that task well."[8] Molotov, according to Winston Churchill, had always favored an arrangement with Adolf Hitler and as foreign commissar aimed to achieve this at Poland's expense.[9] Heading a Politburo group that formulated foreign policy, Molotov was the first foreign commissar since Lev Trotskii to possess real power within the Party.

Molotov wasted little time in purging the Narkomindel of independent-minded cosmopolitans from Lenin's time. He surrounded himself mostly with Great Russians from a new generation of Soviet civil servants and bureaucrats. The innovative, pro-Western diplomats who had served with Litvinov soon were gone. Their replacements had little knowledge of foreign languages or the outside world. Under Molotov

---

[5]Churchill, pp. 362–65.

[6]General Kurt von Tippelskirch to German Foreign Office, May 4, 1939, in Raymond J. Sontag and James S. Beddie, eds., *Nazi-Soviet Relations: Documents from the Archives of the German Foreign Office* (Washington, DC, 1948, reprint Westport, CT, 1976), p. 2.

[7]Gustav Hilger and Alfred Meyer, *The Incompatible Allies: A Memoir History of German-Soviet Relations, 1918–1941* (New York, 1953), pp. 290–91.

[8]*Sto sorok besed s Molotovym. Iz dnevnika Feliks Chueva* (Moscow, 1991), p. 14.

[9]Churchill, pp. 366–68.

the Narkomindel lost the flexibility and sensitivity of a first-rate dip-lomatic service.

On May 8 London responded belatedly to Litvinov's April 16 proposal. *Izvestiia* complained on May 10 that Britain had not pledged to aid the Soviet Union if it were attacked while meeting its obligations towards an eastern European country. However, that same day Chamberlain declared that if Moscow wished to make its intervention "contingent on that of Great Britain and France," London would not object. Had this assurance been made two weeks earlier, according to Churchill, Litvinov's collective security policy might still have prevailed. Instead Anglo-Soviet negotiations limped along. When David Lloyd-George, Anthony Eden and Churchill all pressed the government to commit itself immediately to fundamental agreements with the USSR, Prime Minister Chamberlain became cool and disdainful toward Moscow's offer.[10]

Litvinov's abrupt removal reassured Hitler, although mutual suspicions still clouded Soviet-German relations. Only two days after Berlin learned of Litvinov's fall, Counsellor Hilger for the first time was summoned to meet with Foreign Minister von Ribbentrop. Hilger, a professional diplomat, was unimpressed by Ribbentrop, a former wine salesman:

> He was a man who occupied a responsible position for which he had neither talent, knowledge, nor experience, and he himself knew or sensed this very well. As a consequence, he made himself abjectly dependent on a vast staff of expert and not so expert advisers. . . . He sought to hide his feelings of inferiority by an arrogance that often seemed unbearable. . . . He was under a morbid compulsion to put his own person in the foreground all the time and to live in the grandest possible style.[11]

Hitler asked Hilger why he thought Stalin had dismissed Litvinov. Litvinov had sought an understanding with Britain and France, replied Hilger, but Stalin had concluded that the West wanted to have Moscow pull its chestnuts from the fire. Might Stalin be prepared to reach an understanding with Germany?, Hitler queried. Hilger cited Stalin's March 10 declaration that he saw no reason for a Soviet-German conflict. Hilger's emphasis on the success of Soviet industrialization and a new Soviet patriotism impressed Hitler. If Hilger were correct, Hitler told Ribbentrop, "then we have no time to lose in taking measures to prevent any further consolidation of Soviet power."[12]

In June 1939 France and Britain made a final but indecisive effort to reach a political agreement with Moscow. Former Undersecretary Anthony

---

[10]Churchill, pp. 370–73.

[11]Hilger and Meyer, p. 293.

[12]Hilger and Meyer, pp. 296–97.

Eden, an experienced diplomat who had visited Stalin in 1935, offered to go to Moscow, but instead Chamberlain sent a subordinate Foreign Office official, William Strang, which the Soviets interpreted as a deliberate snub. Strang's negotiations in Moscow continued through July without real results. Finally, the Soviets proposed holding military talks. France and Britain sent ranking military officers, but the negotiations foundered over refusals by Poland and Romania to allow Soviet troops to cross their territory. The Polish attitude was: "With the Germans we risk losing our liberty; with the Russians our soul."[13]

Later, in August 1942, Stalin told Churchill that he had placed little faith in the Western offers:

> We formed the impression that the British and French governments were not resolved to go to war if Poland were attacked, but that they hoped the diplomatic line-up of Britain, France, and Russia would deter Hitler. We were sure it would not.[14]

However, he and Molotov believed it essential for bargaining purposes to conceal their actual intent to sign with Germany until the last moment. Thus as late as August 4 German Ambassador to Soviet Russia Friedrich von der Schulenburg telegraphed from Moscow: "My overall impression is that the Soviet Government is at present determined to sign with England and France if they fulfill all Soviet wishes."[15]

In the summer of 1939 Nazi-Soviet negotiations intensified. Berlin informed Schulenburg on May 30 that the German government had decided to undertake definite negotiations with the Soviet Union.[16] By mid-June trade talks were progressing well. Late in July Hitler, anxious to guarantee Soviet neutrality during his planned invasion of Poland, decided to seize the initiative. At Hitler's instruction Ribbentrop on August 15 telegraphed his eagerness to visit Moscow to discuss a treaty of friendship. Delaying matters a bit, Molotov objected that elaborate preparations would be required for such an important visitor. Would Germany agree, countered Molotov slyly, to a non-aggression pact and use its influence to improve Soviet-Japanese relations? Would Germany confirm that the Baltic countries lay in the Soviet sphere of interest? Stalin, grasping quickly what Ribbentrop was offering, instructed Molotov to hand Ambassador Schulenburg on the next day a draft of a non-aggression pact and to inform Berlin that Ribbentrop would be received one week after the commercial treaty was signed, or about August 27.[17] The groundwork had been laid for a Nazi-Soviet alliance.

---

[13]Churchill, pp. 389–91, quoting Paul Reynaud, *Memoirs,* vol. I, p. 587.

[14]Churchill, p. 391.

[15]Sontag and Beddie, p. 41.

[16]Sontag and Beddie, p. 15.

[17]Hilger and Meyer, pp. 298–300.

THE NAZI-SOVIET PACT AND SUPPLEMENTARY PROTOCOL, AUGUST–SEPTEMBER 1939

Hitler was dissatisfied with Stalin's proposed negotiating schedule. He wanted German-Soviet relations clarified before his invasion of Poland, scheduled for September 1, 1939. Thus he instructed Ambassador Schulenburg to transmit his personal telegram to Stalin: Foreign Minister Ribbentrop must be received at the Kremlin by August 23. The commercial treaty had been signed, so a non-aggression pact and a supplementary secret protocol on spheres of influence that Moscow desired could be settled swiftly when Ribbentrop arrived in Moscow.[18]

Hitler's hints in a proposed secret protocol that Germany was willing to share the spoils of war and that a Nazi attack on Poland was imminent convinced Stalin to act promptly; he agreed to receive Ribbentrop on August 23. Hitler, Hilger later learned, received Stalin's invitation to Ribbentrop with exaltation: "Now I have the world in my pocket!"[19] Later, Ribbentrop claimed that he had originated the idea of a pact with the USSR and had urged it on Hitler.

Right until Ribbentrop's trip to Moscow, Hilger asserted, Moscow continued to consider a possible alliance with the West. However, the unfavorable outcome of talks with British and French envoys that summer and the broader prospects opened by an accord with Germany had caused Stalin to opt for the pact with Hitler. Believing in an eventual conflict among the capitalist powers, Stalin concluded that if the USSR remained on the sidelines, it could reap major benefits. Stalin was confident Britain and France would aid Poland, thus involving them in what he believed would be a lengthy and exhausting struggle while the Soviet Union rearmed.[20]

Ribbentrop arrived in Moscow at noon on August 23. The crucial discussions in the Kremlin continued until well after midnight, but the non-aggression pact and secret protocol nonetheless were dated August 23. Molotov recalled in 1974 that when he asked Ribbentrop what he proposed, the latter replied: "Let's divide up the world. You need to advance southward to the warm seas."[21] After a twenty-four hour stay, Ribbentrop left Moscow in exaltation. For the first time Stalin had directed negotiations with a foreign power personally because theoretically until May 1941 he remained legally only a Party official. Stalin's presence suggested strongly that the pact must be concluded then or not at all. When Stalin tried to induce Molotov to conduct the final negotiations with Ribbentrop, Molotov had objected: "No, Joe, you do the talking; I'm sure you will do a better job than I." Stalin then had outlined the Soviet viewpoint concisely and clearly. Stalin, Hilger noted, often surprised the Germans by his detailed

---

[18]Hilger and Meyer, p. 300; Sontag and Beddie, p. 66.

[19]Hilger and Meyer, p. 300.

[20]Hilger and Meyer, pp. 306–07.

[21]*Sto sorok besed*, p. 26.

FOREIGN COMMISSAR VIACHESLAV M. MOLOTOV SIGNS THE NAZI-SOVIET PACT. JOACHIM VON RIBBENTROP, JOSEPH STALIN, V. N. PAVLOV, AND MOLOTOV'S INTERPRETER WATCH.

knowledge of technical issues and by his self-confident decisionmaking, even on matters of style.[22]

The public Soviet-German non-aggression pact aimed allegedly to strengthen the "cause of peace" between them and stemmed from their Neutrality Agreement of April 1926. It provided:

> *Article I*—Both High Contracting Parties obligate themselves to desist from any act of violence, any aggressive action, and any attack on each other, either individually or jointly with other powers.

> *Article II*—Should one of the High Contracting Parties become the object of belligerent action by a third power, the other High Contracting Party shall in no manner lend its support to this third power.

Both sides would "maintain continual contact," consult one another, and exchange information on common problems (Article III). Honored at first, that article would frequently be violated later by both parties.

---

[22]Hilger and Meyer, pp. 301–02.

Joachim von Ribbentrop and Joseph Stalin are all smiles at the signing of the Nazi-Soviet Pact on August 23, 1939.

Article IV—Neither of the two Contracting Parties shall participate in any grouping of powers whatsoever that is directly or indirectly aimed at the other party.

Disputes between them were to be settled through "friendly exchange of opinion" or arbitration (Article V). The treaty was to run for ten years, and if not denounced a year before its scheduled expiration, it would be extended automatically for another five years (Article VI). The pact was to be ratified "within the shortest possible time" but would take effect as soon as it was signed (Article VII). Ribbentrop signed for Germany and Molotov for the Soviet Union.[23]

A Secret Additional Protocol, also dated August 23, was appended to the Non-Aggression Pact at Stalin's insistence, setting the boundaries of Soviet and German spheres of influence in eastern Europe. It provided:

1. In the event of a territorial and political rearrangement in the areas belonging to the Baltic States (Finland, Estonia, Latvia, Lithuania), the northern boundary of Lithuania shall represent the boundary of the spheres of Germany and the USSR. In this connection the interest of Lithuania in the Vilna area is recognized by each party.

2. In the event of a territorial and political rearrangement of the areas belonging to the Polish state the sphere of influence of Germany and the USSR shall be bounded approximately by the line of the rivers Narew, Vistula, and San. The question of whether the interests of both parties make desirable the maintenance of an independent Polish state and how such a state should be bounded can only be definitely determined in the course of further political developments.

The two parties would resolve that issue by a subsequent agreement.

3. With regard to Southeastern Europe attention is called by the Soviet side to its interest in Bessarabia. The German side declares its complete disinterestedness in these areas.

4. This protocol shall be treated by both parties as strictly secret.

This was signed likewise by Ribbentrop and Molotov.[24]

After the pact and secret protocol had been signed, noted Hilger, Ribbentrop presented a flowery, bombastic draft of a joint communiqué extolling the new Soviet-German friendship. Smiling, Stalin turned to Ribbentrop:

Don't you think that we have to a pay a little more attention to public opinion in our countries? For many years now we have been pouring buckets of slop over each other's heads . . . and now all of a sudden . . . all is forgiven and forgotten? Things don't work so fast.

---

[23]Sontag and Beddie, pp. 76–77.
[24]Sontag and Beddie, p. 78.

MAP 6–1   Territorial changes, 1939–1941

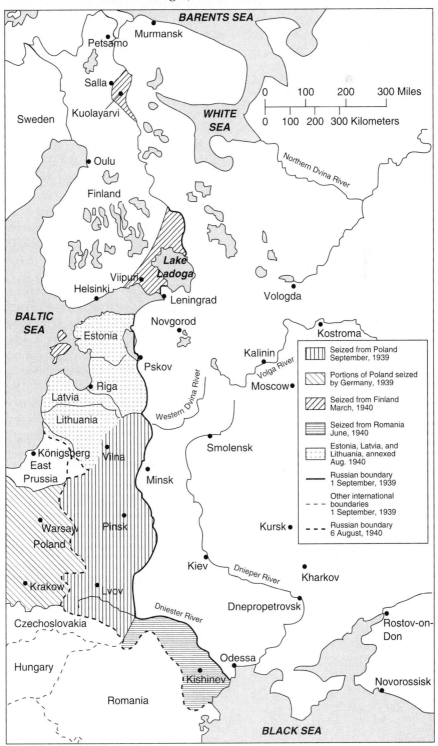

BARENTS SEA

Murmansk
Petsamo

Salla

Kuolayarvi

Sweden

WHITE
SEA

0   100   200   300 Miles

0   100 200 300 Kilometers

Northern Dvina River

Oulu

Finland

Lake
Ladoga

Viipuri

Helsinki

Leningrad

Vologda

BALTIC
SEA

Novgorod

Kostroma

Estonia

Kalinin

Volga River

Pskov

Moscow

Riga

Latvia

Western Dvina River

Lithuania

Smolensk

Königsberg

Vilna

East
Prussia

Minsk

Warsaw

Pinsk

Kursk

Poland

Krakow

Lvov

Kiev

Dnieper River

Kharkov

Czechoslovakia

Dniester River

Dnepropetrovsk

Rostov-on-
Don

Hungary

Odessa

Kishinev

Novorossisk

Romania

BLACK SEA

	Seized from Poland September, 1939
	Portions of Poland seized by Germany, 1939
	Seized from Finland March, 1940
	Seized from Romania June, 1940
	Estonia, Latvia, and Lithuania, annexed Aug. 1940
	Russian boundary 1 September, 1939
	Other international boundaries 1 September, 1939
	Russian boundary 6 August, 1940

Stalin instead suggested a more moderately worded draft, which was readily adopted.[25]

Following the signings the four men (Stalin, Molotov, Ribbentrop, and Hilger) were served a simple supper. Stalin then rose and delivered a short speech, describing Hitler as a man he had always greatly admired. Considering the pact his personal achievement, Ribbentrop now believed that he had become a great foreign minister. Stalin proposed a toast to Hitler; Ribbentrop offered one to Stalin. Before the Germans left, Stalin emphasized to them that he considered the pact with the utmost seriousness and guaranteed that the USSR would not betray its partner.[26]

Both dictators considered the Nazi-Soviet Alliance highly advantageous. For the first time during his tenure as Soviet leader, the prospect opened to Stalin for major territorial expansion without apparent cost or risk. For Hitler the division of eastern Europe created advantageous conditions for the invasion of Poland. For that reason he had made extensive concessions to the Soviet Union. For several months after its conclusion Hitler appeared to believe that the Nazi-Soviet Pact provided a basis for a lasting and beneficial relationship for both sides.

Launched September 1, as scheduled, the Nazi invasion of Poland within a week had destroyed much of the Polish army. That lightning campaign *(Blitzkrieg)* must have shocked Stalin out of any complacency. Despite German urgings, he refused to undertake hasty action to claim the Soviet sphere in eastern Poland. Ambassador Schulenburg reported on September 10 that Moscow had been surprised at the speed of the German advance, and that the Red Army was not yet ready to move in.[27] Then on September 17 Stalin gave the Germans only four hours' notice of the Soviet advance into eastern Poland. The Soviet communiqué noted the need "to protect the interests" of the Ukrainian and Belorussian populations there. Against whom, the Germans must have asked. However, the Red Army occupation caused only a few initial incidents with the Germans and encountered no significant Polish resistance.

Moscow now opposed the creation of a rump Polish state, which the pact had suggested as a possibility. On September 19 Stalin proposed to Schulenburg to revise the two spheres of interest by ceding Lithuania to the Soviet sphere in return for extending German control in Poland up to the ethnic Curzon Line. Telegraphing his consent, Ribbentrop gladly agreed to return to Moscow. Leaving a rump Poland, Stalin argued, might create Soviet-German friction. The result was a Secret Supplementary Protocol of September 28 that amended the territorial provisions of the August 23 protocol as follows:

---

[25]Hilger and Meyer, p. 304.
[26]Sontag and Beddie, pp. 75–76.
[27]Sontag and Beddie, p. 91.

... The territory of the Lithuanian state falls to the sphere of influence of the USSR, while, on the other hand, the province of Lublin and part of the province of Warsaw fall to the sphere of influence of Germany. As soon as the Government of the USSR shall take special measures on Lithuanian territory to protect its interests, the present German-Lithuanian border ... shall be rectified in such a way that the Lithuanian territory situated to the southwest of the line marked on the attached map should fall to Germany....[28]

Speaking to the Supreme Soviet on August 31, 1939, Foreign Commissar Molotov emphasized the "tremendous positive value" to the USSR of the Nazi-Soviet Pact by "eliminating the danger of war between Germany and the Soviet Union." By contrast, the preceding negotiations with the West had encountered insuperable obstacles, notably that Poland had rejected any Soviet military assistance.[29]

The Nazi-Soviet Pact has often been compared with the Tilsit Accords of 1807 between Napoleon and Tsar Alexander I. Once again a Russian ruler was giving an aggressive western dictator a free hand to deal with Great Britain and the European continent in return for peace and a free hand in eastern Europe. However, in 1939 the Russians stood to gain economically from collaboration with Germany whereas joining Napoleon's Continental System had imposed severe sacrifices on the Russia of Alexander I. In drawing up the pact, Stalin, like Alexander I, had made the crucial decisions at every step of negotiations, even helping to draft memoranda. This marked another return to tsarist methods in foreign affairs.

THE SOVIET UNION EXPLOITS THE PACT, 1939–1940

Stalin wasted no time in exploiting his agreements with Hitler. On September 24, 1939, Estonia's foreign minister was summoned to Moscow and compelled to sign a mutual assistance pact, which gave Moscow the right to garrison key bases on its territory. This same procedure was followed with Latvia and Lithuania. Abandoned by Germany to the Soviet sphere, the Baltic countries could not resist militarily. There followed large-scale deportations of anti-Communists and ordinary citizens from all three countries, especially Estonia, to Siberia and Central Asia. Subsequent "elections" in all three returned a virtually unanimous vote in favor of joining the Soviet Union. In June 1940, acting with a brusqueness that surprised even the Nazis, Stalin without consulting Berlin annexed the three Baltic countries to the USSR. This cynical destruction of Baltic independence was never recognized by the United States nor by the Western powers.

---

[28]Sontag and Beddie, p. 107.

[29]V. M. Molotov, "The Meaning of the Soviet-German Non-Aggression Pact," in Alvin Rubinstein, ed., *The Foreign Policy of the Soviet Union* (New York, 1960), pp. 145–51.

Finland, the other key to the eastern Baltic, proved a much tougher nut for Stalin to crack. In October 1939 Moscow demanded that the Finnish frontier on the Karelian Isthmus, then only about twenty miles from Leningrad, be moved considerably northwards, and that the Soviets be granted leases of the Finnish ports of Petsamo and Hangö as naval and air bases. In return Moscow agreed to cede to Finland some of desolate Soviet Karelia. Some Finnish leaders favored accepting this Soviet offer, but the Helsinki government found unacceptable the demand for Hangö, the key to the Gulf of Finland, as destroying Finland's security. After negotiations had broken down, on November 28 Molotov denounced the Soviet-Finnish non-aggression treaty. Two days later Soviet troops attacked Finland along its thousand-mile frontier and bombed its capital, Helsinki.[30]

Moscow counted on a swift, easy victory over Finland, but initial Soviet attacks were repelled by a 200,000-man Finnish army that outfought Soviet troops poorly prepared for severe winter conditions. Moscow recognized and signed a treaty with the "Government of the Democratic Republic of Finland," a handful of Finnish Communists residing in the USSR headed by Otto Kuusinen, a veteran Comintern official. Indignation over this blatant Soviet aggression against a small, peaceloving country rose steadily in the West and especially in the United States. On December 14 the Soviet Union was expelled from the League of Nations as an aggressor. Molotov denounced American protests, but Stalin realized the importance of maintaining normal relations with the United States.

After the valiant Finns had held their own during January 1940, the Soviets launched a massive offensive in February against the Mannerheim Line, the Finnish defenses on the Karelian Isthmus, breaching it by the end of that month. Meanwhile France and Britain had made plans to send an expeditionary force across Scandinavia to aid Finland and to bomb the Baku oil fields. If carried out, that certainly would have provoked war between the West and the Soviet Union. With the international situation deteriorating and Soviet prestige at a low ebb, Stalin disbanded the Finnish Communist shadow regime and hastily concluded a rather lenient peace with Helsinki. Peace terms adhered closely to the original Soviet demands of 1939. Most of the Karelian Isthmus and naval and military bases in Finland went to the USSR.

Addressing the Supreme Soviet on March 29, 1940, about the meaning of the Winter War, Molotov asserted groundlessly that Finland had been incited "by certain third States to adopt a hostile policy toward the USSR. . . ." "Forces hostile to the Soviet Union" had created military bases in Finland for the benefit of unspecified foreign powers. "It was not merely Finnish troops whom our troops encountered here," he

---

[30]Churchill, p. 539; Adam Ulam, *Expansion and Coexistence: Soviet Foreign Policy, 1917–1973*, 2nd ed. (New York, 1974), p. 289.

MAP 6–2   Finnish frontiers, 1939–1940

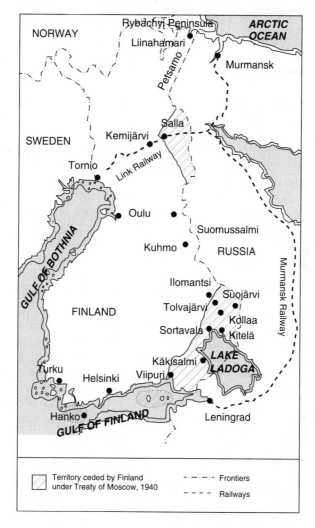

Territory ceded by Finland
under Treaty of Moscow, 1940

– · – · – · –   Frontiers

– – – –   Railways

claimed, "but the combined forces of the imperialists of a number of countries, including British, and French. . . ."[31] That allegation turned out to be totally false.

The Winter War cost the Red Army heavy losses. Molotov admitted the Soviets had suffered more than 200,000 casualties, including about 50,000 dead. The Red Army's highly dubious showing convinced Western leaders that Soviet Russia would make an unfit partner. Hitler and many

---

[31]Rubinstein, pp. 152–53.

other German leaders waxed overconfident. In January 1940 the German
minister in Helsinki wrote to Berlin:

> The Red Army has such shortcomings that it cannot even dispose of a small
> country. . . . It might now be possible to adopt an entirely different tone toward
> the gentlemen in the Kremlin from that of August and September.[32]

The Winter War doubtless figured in Hitler's decision later that year to
attack the USSR in expectation of an easy victory.

German attacks in northern and western Europe in 1940 first relieved
then alarmed Moscow. In April Nazi troops quickly seized control of Denmark
and Norway thus blocking any prospective Western move against the USSR in
the Baltic. However, the overwhelming German Blitzkrieg against the Low
Countries and France causing their surrender by mid-June 1940 left Stalin
shaken. Having greatly overestimated Western military power, he now faced
the dismal prospect of confronting Hitler's juggernaut alone since Britain
seemed unlikely to resist for long. On June 18 Molotov nonetheless congratulated Ambassador Schulenburg on the "splendid success" of German arms.[33]

Forming a new National Government in Britain in May 1940 after
Chamberlain's resignation, Winston Churchill sought to establish friendlier
relations with Moscow. On June 25, writing Stalin for the first time,
Churchill requested him to receive the new British ambassador, Sir Stafford
Cripps, a socialist excluded from the Labor Party for urging cooperation
with the Communists. The new factor that might stimulate warmer
Soviet-British relations was "the prospect of Germany establishing a
hegemony over the Continent." Churchill urged Stalin to discuss this issue
with Cripps. However, the latter's initial interview with Stalin, noted
Churchill, bore "a formal and frigid character."[34]

Stalin hastened to collect the final territorial spoils outlined in the
Nazi-Soviet Pact, then went one step further. On June 26 the Romanian
minister in Moscow received abrupt Soviet demands to cede Bessarabia and
northern Bukovina to the USSR, although in 1939 the latter territory had
not been included in the Soviet sphere. Moscow's claim to Bukovina,
designed to protect the vulnerable Ukraine, came as a disagreeable surprise
to Hitler; Ribbentrop had to remind him that they had stated in August
1939 that "Germany is politically disinterested . . . in the southeast of
Europe."[35] Now dominant on the European continent and exalted by
German military victories, Hitler was disinclined to view Soviet aspirations
in the Balkans so leniently.

---

[32]*Documents on German Foreign Policy, 1918–45*, Series D, vol. VIII (Washington, DC,
1956), p. 651.

[33]Sontag and Beddie, p. 154.

[34]Winston Churchill, *Their Finest Hour* (Boston, 1949), pp. 135–36.

[35]Sontag and Beddie, p. 158.

THE DETERIORATION OF
NAZI-SOVIET RELATIONS, 1940–1941

The first few months of the Nazi-Soviet Alliance constituted a honeymoon period in their relations, but disturbing signs of eventual conflict appeared quite early. Addressing the chiefs of the German armed forces on November 23, 1939, Hitler stated:

> At the present time Russia presents no danger. . . . Besides, we have the pact with Russia. But treaties are kept only as long as they are expedient. . . . Now Russia still has far-reaching aims, particularly the strengthening of her position on the shores of the Baltic Sea. We can oppose her only if we are free in the West. In addition, Russia strives to strengthen her influence on the Balkan peninsula and aims toward the Persian Gulf. But those are also aims of our own foreign policy.[36]

Early in 1940, as Soviet friendship for Germany cooled, many minor problems in their relationship emerged. However, after Hitler's occupation of Denmark and Norway came a sudden renewal of Soviet friendliness and cooperation. German sympathies during the Winter War lay with Finland, but officially Berlin supported the Soviets. Stalin's demands on Romania for Bessarabia and northern Bukovina induced Berlin reluctantly to persuade Bucharest to yield those lands. When Hungary also raised claims to Romanian territory, the Axis mediated their dispute. The Vienna Award, granting considerable Romanian territory to Hungary, infuriated Stalin whose appetite for Balkan territory was increasing. Stalin claimed that Romania and Bulgaria both lay in the Soviet sphere.[37]

After crushing France, Hitler believed there were no limits to what he could achieve. Destiny had summoned him to end Bolshevism, and he could not rest until he had supplied the German people with necessary living space *(Lebensraum)*. Late in July 1940 Hitler apparently decided tentatively to invade the Soviet Union during 1941. General Franz Halder, chief of the German General Staff, noted in his diary that on July 31, 1940, Hitler told his military chiefs of his intention to attack the USSR in May 1941 and "smash" it in five months.[38] By the end of August the High Command's operations division had drawn up a tentative plan of attack; by December the General Staff completed the actual plans. On December 18 Hitler signed the directive for "Operation Barbarossa" for an invasion of the USSR.[39]

In September 1940 the Three Power Pact (Germany, Italy, and Japan) was concluded partly to discourage the United States from entering the war. "This alliance," Ribbentrop told Molotov, "is directed exclusively against

---

[36]Heinz Holldack, *Was wirklich geschah* (Munich, 1949), p. 460.

[37]George Kennan, *Russia and the West Under Lenin and Stalin* (Boston, 1960), pp. 340–41.

[38]*Documents on German Foreign Policy, 1918–1945*, Series D, vol. X (Washington, DC, 1956), p. 373.

[39]Ulam, p. 302.

Foreign Commissar V. M. Molotov is greeted in Berlin by Nazi Foreign Minister Joachim von Ribbentrop on November 11, 1940. Gustav Hilger, the German Counselor, interprets.

the American warmongers . . . to bring the elements pressing for America's entry into the war to their senses" by showing Washington that it would have to face all three of these powers. Ribbentrop considered bringing the USSR into what would become a Four Power Pact to prevent Moscow from defecting to the other side in the war. Therefore on October 13 Ribbentrop sent Stalin a lengthy letter summarizing German policies on all matters concerning the Soviet Union and noting "the historical mission of the Four Powers—the Soviet Union, Italy, Japan, and Germany—to adopt a long-range policy and to direct the future development of their peoples into the right channels by delimitation of their interests on a world-wide scale."[40] Stalin soon agreed that Molotov should proceed to Berlin for discussions.

Molotov remained in Berlin for two days, the first visit ever abroad of the head of the Soviet government on official business. Molotov and Ribbentrop spent those two days in tense discussions. Hitler was present at some of the talks. Greeting Molotov warmly, Hitler outlined plans to divide up the world among the four powers, virtually writing off Britain. But a British air-raid compelled Ribbentrop and Molotov to complete their talks in a deep, sumptuously furnished shelter. When Ribbentrop proposed dividing up the world, Molotov reportedly inquired: "What will England

---

[40]Sontag and Beddie, p. 213.

say?" "England," replied Ribbentrop, "is finished." "If that is so," remarked Molotov, "why are we in this shelter and whose are these bombs which fall?"[41] Molotov indicated possible Soviet interest in joining the Three Power Pact provided Soviet interests were taken into account, especially in the Balkans. Hitler evidently wished to push the USSR southward toward the Persian Gulf but refused to recognize Soviet Balkan interests.

Two weeks later, after discussing Ribbentrop's proposals, the Soviet government informed Ambassador Schulenburg that Moscow would accept the draft of a Four Power Pact that Ribbentrop had outlined on November 13:

Moscows provisions:

1. Provided that the German troops are immediately withdrawn from Finland, which under the compact of 1939, belongs to the Soviet Union's sphere of influence. . . .
2. Provided that within the next few months the security of the Soviet Union in the Straits is assured by the conclusion of a mutual assistance pact between the Soviet Union and Bulgaria . . . , and by the establishment of a base for land and naval forces of the USSR within range of the Bosporus and the Dardanelles by means of a long-term lease.
3. Provided that the area south of Batum and Baku in the general direction of the Persian Gulf is recognized as the center of the aspirations of the Soviet Union.

Japan was also to renounce its rights to coal and oil concessions on northern Sakhalin Island.[42] This marked a clear return to traditional tsarist objectives; Nazi-Soviet friction over Finland, the Balkans, and the Straits recalled that between Napoleon and Tsar Alexander I prior to the French invasion of Russia in 1812.

Moscow never received a reply to Molotov's memorandum. That document merely confirmed Hitler's belief that the Soviets would assert their own aspirations and resist German aims. It was no accident that the Führer issued his "Barbarossa" order only three weeks later. Nevertheless, German-Soviet trade negotiations produced the treaty of January 10, 1941, by which Moscow consented to continue delivering large quantities of raw materials to Germany. However, Nazi-Soviet relations deteriorated further after Berlin sent strong military forces into Romania on the pretext of countering alleged British operations planned in Greece. Moscow had referred repeatedly to Bulgaria and the Straits as Soviet security zones, so when Bulgaria joined the Three Power Pact in March 1941 and German troops marched into it, the Soviets protested strongly.

That same month Yugoslavia became a focal point in Nazi-Soviet relations. On March 25, succumbing to German pressure, the Yugoslav regime, headed by Prince Paul Karadjordjević, joined the Three Power Pact

---

[41]Stalin's account to Churchill, quoted in Churchill, *Their Finest Hour,* p. 584.

[42]Friedrich von der Schulenburg to German Foreign Office, November 26, 1940, in Sontag and Beddie, pp. 258–59.

touching off massive protest demonstrations in Yugoslav cities. During the night of March 26–27 a military coup led by General Dušan Simović elevated the boy king, Peter II, to the throne. Yugoslavia promptly repudiated the Three Power Pact. On April 5 a Soviet-Yugoslav friendship and non-aggression treaty was signed in Moscow. The very next day Hitler's armies invaded Yugoslavia, which soon collapsed. Stalin had sought to strengthen the Yugoslav will to resist the Axis and deflect Hitler away from the Soviet Union. Once again he had underestimated Nazi military strength. Nothing that Moscow did between 1939 and 1941 angered Hitler more than this Soviet-Yugoslav treaty, which contributed much to the final German-Soviet breach. After Yugoslavia and Greece had fallen, Stalin, realizing his mistake, sought desperately to appease Hitler, but the latter remained committed to "Barbarossa." Thus Moscow faithfully delivered everything promised under the commercial treaty, although the Germans had fallen far behind in their deliveries. In May 1941 the USSR even broke relations with Yugoslavia, Norway, Greece, and Belgium on the pretext that they had lost their sovereignty under German occupation. However, Stalin's appeasement merely convinced Hitler that he had a golden opportunity to crush Soviet Russia and provide the German people with promised *Lebensraum*.[43]

During the spring of 1941 rumors multiplied about major German troop movements eastward toward the Soviet frontier. Ambassador Schulenburg and other German diplomats warned Hitler against attacking the Soviet Union to no avail. Stalin apparently believed that Hitler was merely increasing pressure on Moscow in order to extort economic and possibly territorial concessions. He did realize, however, that the Red Army then was no match for the German Wehrmacht. Stalin remained convinced that, if the USSR observed loyally all its obligations under the Nazi-Soviet Pact, Hitler would not attack. Strangely, Stalin appears to have trusted Hitler more than he did other people.

THE SOVIET-JAPANESE NON-AGGRESSION PACT, APRIL 1941

Tokyo did not find the Nazi-Soviet Pact of August 1939 acceptable and protested to Berlin that it conflicted with the Anti-Comintern Pact of 1936. The Japanese had been engaged in a serious conflict with Soviet troops in Nomonhan district on the Mongolian-Manchurian border. Beginning as skirmishes in May 1939, it took on major dimensions in June. Moscow viewed this affair as a diplomatic move and probing action by Japan. On September 16 a truce was reached and a commission was set up to establish a mutually acceptable frontier. Nomonhan represented a severe localized Japanese defeat that Tokyo ascribed to highly mechanized Soviet forces. Tokyo was confirmed in its decision to strike against the European imperial

---

[43]Hilger and Meyer, pp. 326–27.

powers in southeast Asia, not against the USSR. By the end of October Molotov could report that signs pointed to improving Soviet-Japanese relations and noted that developing Soviet-Japanese trade lay in the interest of both countries.[44]

The outbreak of the European war in September 1939 caused no immediate change in Moscow's view of the Far Eastern scene. The Soviets continued to view Nationalist China's resistance to Japan as a "just" war of national liberation that merited Moscow's support. The USSR supplied considerable aid to China which the latter acknowledged gratefully and often. The Chinese Communists continued to support Chiang Kai-shek's resistance to Japan.

The conclusion of the Soviet-Japanese Neutrality Pact on April 13, 1941, represented a major triumph for Stalin's diplomacy and had far-reaching consequences. It was a product of Foreign Minister Yosuke Matsuoka's visits to various European capitals that spring. In Berlin Matsuoka heard hints of a possible German move against the USSR, but Nazi leaders emphasized their desire that Japan strike against the British in Asia. Thus Hitler unwisely failed to press Tokyo to make a simultaneous attack on the USSR that almost certainly would have caused its collapse. In Moscow Stalin was most attentive and flattering to Matsuoka, and the Japanese diplomat responded by urging Tokyo to authorize signature of a five-year neutrality pact that provided the USSR with enhanced security in the Far East. Both sides pledged to maintain peaceful and friendly relations and to respect each other's spheres of interest and satellites in Mongolia and Manchukuo. If one party were attacked, the other promised to remain neutral.[45] Welcoming the Japanese desire to end frictions with the Soviet Union, *Izvestiia* called the pact "an historic reversal in Japanese-Soviet relations."[46]

Suggested Readings

Ansell, Walter. *Hitler Confronts England*. Durham, NC, 1960.

Bethell, Nicholas. *The War Hitler Won: The Fall of Poland September 1939*. New York, 1972.

Bullock, Alan. *Hitler: A Study in Tyranny*. New York, 1962.

Churchill, Winston S. *The Gathering Storm*. Boston, 1948.

———. *Their Finest Hour*. Boston, 1949.

Degras, Jane, ed., *Soviet Documents on Foreign Policy III: 1933–41*. London and New York, 1953.

Documents on German Foreign Policy, 1918–45, Series D, vol. X , Washington, DC, 1957.

Gafencu, Grigoire. *Prelude to the Russian Campaign*. London, 1945.

---

[44]V. M. Molotov, *The Foreign Policy of the Soviet Union* (Moscow, 1939), p. 27, cited in Harriet Moore, *Soviet Far Eastern Policy, 1931–1945* (Princeton, NJ, 1945), pp. 113–15.

[45]Ulam, pp. 308–09; Moore, p. 122; and text of the treaty, Moore, pp. 200–01.

[46]*Izvestiia*, April 15, 1941.

Gordetsky, Gabriel. *Stafford Cripps; Mission to Moscow, 1940–42.* Cambridge, England, 1984.

Higgins, Trumbull. *Hitler and Russia.* New York, 1966.

Hilger, Gustav and Alfred Meyer. *The Incompatible Allies: A Memoir History of German-Soviet Relations, 1918–1941.* New York, 1953.

Irving, David. *Hitler's War.* New York, 1977.

Jakobson, Max. *The Diplomacy of the Winter War: An Account of the Russo-Finnish War, 1939–1940.* Cambridge, MA, 1961.

Jones, F. C. *Japan's New Order in East Asia: Its Rise and Fall, 1937–1945.* New York, 1954.

Miner, Steven. *Between Churchill and Stalin: The Soviet Union, Great Britain, and the Origins of the Grand Alliance.* Chapel Hill, NC, 1988.

Moore, Harriet. *Soviet Far Eastern Policy, 1931–45.* Princeton, NJ, 1945.

Molotov, V. M. *Soviet Foreign Policy: The Meaning of the War in Finland.* New York, 1940.

Ribbentrop, Joachim von. *The Ribbentrop Memoirs.* London, 1953.

Roberts, Geoffrey. *The Unholy Alliance: Stalin's Pact with Hitler.* Bloomington, IN, 1989.

Rossi, Angelo. *The Russo-German Alliance, 1939–1941.* Boston, 1951.

Sontag, Raymond J. and James S. Beddie, eds., *Nazi-Soviet Relations: Documents from the Archives of the German Foreign Office.* Washington, DC, 1948; reprint, Westport, CT, 1976.

Tanner, Väinö. *The Winter War: Finland Against Russia, 1939–1940.* Stanford, CA, 1950.

Weinberg, Gerhard L. *Germany and the Soviet Union, 1939–1941.* Leiden, Netherlands, 1954.

THE GRAND ALLIANCE, 1941–1945

Before dawn on June 22, 1941, more than three million German and satellite troops stormed across Soviet borders in a sudden and wholly unprovoked assault on the Soviet Union, unleashing the greatest land conflict in world history. Adolf Hitler's invasion of the USSR and Japan's subsequent attack on Pearl Harbor transformed a limited European war into genuine world conflict. After December 1941 an aggressive Germany, Italy, and Japan stood against Great Britain, the United States, the Soviet Union, Nationalist China, and, later, liberated France. This Grand Alliance—created by Axis aggression, not voluntary cooperation—was soon plagued by numerous disagreements and a profound divergence over war aims that reflected national differences in institutions and outlooks. Although Western leaders hoped for, and even believed in, a long-term partnership with Soviet Russia, Joseph Stalin apparently entertained no such illusions.

THE ALLIANCE IS FORMED, 1941
Originally, Hitler intended to attack the USSR in mid-May 1941, but the Italian initiated Balkan campaign forced a five-week delay that may have saved Moscow from capture. Despite the massive German military buildup on Soviet frontiers in the spring of 1941, Stalin apparently believed Hitler was bluffing and wished to extract economic and perhaps territorial concessions from Moscow. Stalin dismissed numerous Western warnings of impending invasion as efforts to embroil the USSR with the Nazis while the West sat on the sidelines.*

The initial Nazi drive found the Soviet defenders disorganized. Soviet forces, forbidden by Stalin to maneuver in frontier areas, were mostly surprised and overwhelmed; much of the Soviet airforce was destroyed on the ground. Nonetheless, Moscow ordered frontier units to attack and shift operations to enemy territory. Temporary confusion, even panic, ensued in Moscow as Stalin in nervous shock remained secluded until July 3. Ordered to the Kremlin just after the attack began, Ambassador Friedrich von der

---

*For these warnings see Barton Whaley, *Codeword Barbarossa* (Cambridge, MA, 1973).

Schulenburg delivered the German message breaking relations to Foreign Commissar V. M. Molotov, who, calling the German action a breach of confidence unprecedented in history, added: "Surely we have not deserved that."[1]

Prime Minister Winston Churchill of Great Britain, a staunch and uncompromising foe of Communism during 1918–1919, pledged that same evening in a famous speech:

> We shall give whatever help we can to Russia and the Russian people. We shall appeal to all our friends and allies in every part of the world to take the same course and pursue it, as we shall, steadfastly to the end.[2]

Churchill's speech was excerpted in *Pravda* and in other Soviet newspapers. When Moscow failed to respond officially to the prime minister's pledge, Churchill wrote Stalin on July 7 praising the Russians' strong resistance "to the utterly unprovoked and merciless invasion of the Nazis." "We shall do everything to help you that time, geography, and our growing resources allow," he wrote.[3] Three days later Churchill proposed that the British and Soviet governments pledge that they would "render each other assistance of all kinds in the present war against Germany," and that they would "neither negotiate nor conclude an armistice or treaty of peace except by mutual agreement."[4] A formal alliance to that effect was signed by Molotov and British Ambassador Sir Stafford Cripps in Moscow on July 13.

Stalin's message to Churchill of July 18 revealed his desperation in the face of the Nazi onslaught and initial Soviet defeats. Because they were now allied against Hitlerite Germany, ". . . The military situation of the Soviet Union, as well as of Great Britain, would be considerably improved if there could be established a front against Hitler in the West—northern France—and in the north—the Arctic." Soviet pressure for a "second front" began at the outset and recurred in Stalin's letters "with monotonous disregard . . . for physical facts," Churchill noted. Explaining the manifold difficulties that barred a second front then, Churchill promised "anything sensible and effective that we can do to help."[5]

Harry Hopkins, longtime confidant of American President Franklin Roosevelt, played a key role in consolidating ties among leaders of the Grand Alliance. On his own initiative he sought Roosevelt's permission to fly to Moscow and confer with Soviet leaders when most Western military men believed Soviet Russia would collapse soon in the face of German attacks. As the president's personal envoy Hopkins, on July 29, told Stalin in the

---

[1]Gustav Hilger and Alfred Meyer, *The Incompatible Allies: A Memoir History of German-Soviet Relations, 1918–1941* (New York, 1953), p. 336.

[2]Winston Churchill, *The Grand Alliance* (Boston, 1950), p. 370.

[3]Churchill, p. 380.

[4]Churchill, p. 382.

[5]Churchill, pp. 383–84.

MAP 7–1   USSR in World War II

Allied supply line from Britain & U.S.

Murmansk
Kandalaksha
Archangel
N. Dvina R.
Kotlas
Kirov

NORWAY
FINLAND
SWEDEN
Helsinki
DENMARK
Leningrad
Tikhvin
Vologda
ESTONIA
Volga R.
Kazan
Riga
LATVIA
BALTIC SEA
LITHUANIA
Mozhaisk
Moscow
Gorkii
Danzig
Vilna
Smolensk
Tula
Kuibyshev
Berlin
EAST
PRUSSIA
Minsk
Torgau
Oder R.
Bialystok
Brest-Litovsk
Orel
Warsaw
POLAND
BELORUSSIA
Kursk
Voronezh
Volga R.
CZECHO-
Lvov
Kiev
Kharkov
Don R.
Stalingrad
SLOVAKIA
UKRAINE
Vienna
AUSTRIA
Budapest
Dnepropetrovsk
HUNGARY
Dneiper R.
Rostov-on-Don
Kuban R.
Belgrade
ROMANIA
Kerch
Novorossiisk
Mozdok
YUGOSLAVIA
Bucharest
Sevastopol
Yalta
Terek R.
ITALY
BLACK SEA
Caucasus
Sofia
Batum
Tiflis
ALBANIA
BULGARIA
Erivan
Istanbul
Allied supply line from Persian Gulf
GREECE
Ankara
IRAN
Izmir
TURKEY
Athens
IRAQ
Crete
SYRIA

Axis and occupied areas, June 22, 1941	Front lines in Russia	Russian and allied drives 1941-1945
1938 boundaries	–·–·– 1941 – ··· – 1942	
Russian boundary, 1941	– – – – 1943 – ·· – 1944	

Kremlin that Roosevelt considered Hitler the enemy of mankind and thus wished to aid the USSR in every possible way against Germany. What aid did Soviet Russia require immediately and also during a lengthy war? Responded Stalin: "Give us anti-aircraft guns and aluminum and we can fight for three or four years."[6] Asked how the supplies should be sent, Stalin preferred the route around the North Cape to Archangel. In two days of talks Hopkins obtained more information from Stalin about Soviet strength and military prospects than had ever been provided to another outsider. Later, Hopkins described the Soviet dictator for the *American* magazine:

> Not once did he repeat himself. He talked as he knew his troops were shooting—straight and hard. . . . There was no waste of word, gesture, nor mannerism. . . . Joseph Stalin knew what he wanted, knew what Russia wanted. . . . The questions he asked were clear, concise, direct. . . . His answers were ready, unequivocal. . . .

And as Hopkins prepared to depart, Stalin stood, an "austere, rugged, determined figure in boots that shone like mirrors, stout baggy trousers, and snug-fitting blouse." Said Hopkins:

> He's built close to the ground, like a football coach's dream of a tackle. . . . He curries no favor with you. He seems to have no doubts. He assures you that Russia will stand against the onslaughts of the German army. He takes it for granted that you have no doubts either. . . .[7]

After Hopkins' return President Roosevelt predicted boldly that the Russian front would hold and that Moscow would not fall. Still officially neutral, the United States pledged major Lend-Lease aid to the Soviet Union.

However, during August and September Soviet armies suffered severe defeats including the fall of Kiev and the capture of hundreds of thousands of Russian soldiers. In near desperation Stalin, on September 4, wrote Churchill, pleading for an immediate second front in the Balkans or France and for at least 400 aircraft and 500 tanks monthly. Otherwise, he said, "the Soviet Union will be defeated or be much weakened." Churchill replied with regret that no such British actions could be undertaken in 1941. On September 15 Stalin amazed Churchill: "It seems to me that Great Britain could without risk land in Archangel 25–30 divisions or transport them across Iran to the southern reaches of the USSR."[8] Since the British did not have that many troops in the entire British Isles, Churchill considered this request absurd. Soon afterwards, in Moscow, the British envoy William Aitken, Lord Beaverbrook, and U.S. Ambassador William Averell Harriman

---

[6]Robert Sherwood, *Roosevelt and Hopkins: An Intimate History* (New York, 1950), pp. 327–28.

[7]Sherwood, pp. 343–44.

[8]Churchill, p. 462.

concluded an agreement to ship large amounts of supplies to Russia starting in October 1941. U.S. President Franklin Roosevelt, claiming Russia was a "threatened power," circumvented the neutrality laws to extend such aid before the United States entered World War II. Although very little aid could arrive until early 1942, morale in Moscow nonetheless rose considerably.

Early in October 1941, after the capture of Kiev, Hitler finally authorized Nazi tank forces to resume their offensive towards Moscow from Smolensk. As Soviet forces fell back within forty miles of Moscow, the government and diplomatic corps were evacuated eastward to Kuibyshev on the Volga. Irritated by Soviet surliness, Churchill wrote Ambassador Cripps on October 28: "They certainly have no right to reproach us. They brought their own fate upon themselves when, by their pact with [Nazi Foreign Minister Joachim von] Ribbentrop, they let Hitler loose on Poland and so started the war."[9] On November 13 Hitler ordered a final drive on Moscow, but it bogged down in heavy mud succeeded by intense early winter cold that caught the thinly clad German troops unprepared. Reinforcements from the Soviet Far Eastern army helped Marshal Georgii Zhukov turn the tide before Moscow. On December 8, as the United States entered the war against them, the Germans announced that their 1941 Russian campaign had ended.

Meanwhile Polish-Soviet relations, severed in September 1939, were restored. In talks held under British auspices in July 1941 between General Wladyslaw Sikorski, heading the expatriate Polish regime in London, and Soviet Ambassador Ivan Maiskii the Soviets agreed to amnesty Polish prisoners and deportees in the USSR and allow Polish army units to form there. At the beginning of December 1941 Stalin implied to the visiting General Sikorski that a compromise frontier somewhere between those of 1921 and 1939 could be worked out. However, after the Soviet victory before Moscow, Stalin's attitude hardened toward the London Poles foreshadowing subsequent tension and recriminations.

When British Foreign Secretary Anthony Eden met with Stalin in Moscow on December 16, the latter handed him draft treaties for a Soviet-British alliance against Germany stipulating that neither side would conclude a separate peace. In an attached secret protocol Stalin sought British recognition as Soviet territory of all lands acquired by the USSR under the Nazi-Soviet alliance. Germany was to be dismembered with the Rhineland and possibly Bavaria becoming separate states; Austria would regain its independence. Poland's western frontier was to be moved to the Oder River. During the next four years Stalin would adhere to these objectives with great consistency. Citing President Roosevelt's opposition to such secret agreements, Eden refused to make any territorial commitments without consulting Churchill, Roosevelt, and the British Dominion

---

[9]Churchill, p. 472.

countries.[10] The aims of Stalin's diplomacy in Europe thus remained simple and clear: to retain the eastern European buffer zone and all that Molotov had demanded of Hitler in November 1940. Stalin could achieve this either through Red Army occupation or by persuading his allies to promise these territories to him.[11]

By invading the USSR, Hitler's objective had been to end the war in eight to ten weeks by capturing Leningrad, Moscow, occupying Ukraine, and advancing to a line roughly from Astrakhan on the Caspian to Archangel. The main Soviet armies and their airpower were to be destroyed and a defense line set up against a weakened Asiatic Russia, thus providing Germany with the territory and resources for Hitler's "new order." Despite striking early victories, those aims could not be achieved. Soviet forces had rallied and halted the Germans short of all their main objectives. Whereas the populace in frontier areas had mostly welcomed the Germans as liberators from Stalinist tyranny, Hitler's brutal *Ostpolitik* (eastern policy), resulting from Nazi fanaticism and absolute confidence in victory, had compelled Russians to choose between Hitler and Stalin. Mass murder by German Waffen *Schutzstaffel* (SS) detachments, notably in Ukraine, contrasting with Stalin's concessions to nationalism and religion persuaded most Soviet citizens to fight to defend their country. Their resolve and Stalin's crucial decision in October 1941 to remain in Moscow and lead its defense had denied a swift victory to the Nazis.

THE CRUCIAL YEAR, 1942

During the winter of 1941–1942 Soviet counteroffensives forced the Germans back somewhat from Moscow. However, in the spring of 1942 the Germans retained the potential to deal Soviet Russia a knockout blow, but Hitler aimed primarily to obtain Ukrainian grain and Caucasus oil rather than capture Moscow and disorganize the Soviet regime. During that campaign Western Lend-Lease supplies and the rugged Caucasus mountain range helped stiffen Soviet resistance.

Until the spring of 1942, Western equipment reached Soviet Russia with little Nazi interference. Although in August 1941 Soviet and British troops had occupied Iran primarily to provide a supply route to Russia, the northern route around Norway remained the major one. A few Soviet ships were used, but soon British and American vessels carried about three-fourths of the supplies. Starting in March 1942 German aircraft, submarines, and surface vessels based in Norway began inflicting serious damage on Western convoys, while President Roosevelt pressured Churchill constantly to maximize deliveries. Finally, Churchill wrote the president on May 2, 1942: "I beg you not to press us beyond our judgment in this operation, which

---

[10]Robert Beitzell, *The Uneasy Alliance: America, Britain, and Russia, 1941–1943* (New York, 1972), pp. 7–10.

[11]George Kennan, *Russia and the West Under Lenin and Stalin* (Boston, 1960), pp. 350–51.

we have studied most intently. . . . We are absolutely extended, and I could not press the Admiralty further." A week later Churchill, explaining the great dangers to the convoys from German surface ships, wrote Stalin: "We are resolved to fight our way through to you with the maximum amount of war materials. . . . We shall continue to do our utmost."[12]

In convoy P. Q. 17, sent from Iceland in July 1942, twenty-three of thirty-four merchant ships were sunk and only about one-third of the convoy's cargo was delivered. The next scheduled convoy thus was not sent off; Stalin concluded that London was refusing to dispatch further war materials by the northern route. Soviet naval experts found British arguments justifying halting the convoys to northern ports "unconvincing wholly."[13] Not until September was another convoy, this time with a powerful naval escort, dispatched by this route. Twelve merchant vessels were lost but twenty-seven arrived safely. In the succeeding convoy of December 1942 only one ship was lost.[14]

Following America's entry into the war in December 1941, President Roosevelt sought to establish a close personal relationship with Stalin and to convince Soviet leaders to trust the West. Counting on his personal charm and persuasiveness, the president regrettably avoided reliance on Russian experts, such as Charles Bohlen and George Kennan. Roosevelt once told former ambassador William Bullitt, who sought to enlighten him about Stalinist totalitarianism:

> I think that if I give him [Stalin] everything I possibly can and ask nothing in return, *noblesse oblige*, he won't try to annex anything and will work with me for a world of peace and democracy.[15]

President Roosevelt's March 18, 1942, letter to Churchill indicates his naive approach towards Stalin and the Soviet Union during the war:

> I know that you will not mind my being brutally frank when I tell you that I think I can personally handle Stalin better than either your Foreign Office or my State Department. Stalin hates the guts of all your top people. He thinks he likes me better, and I hope he will continue to.[16]

In May 1942 Foreign Commissar Molotov had gone to London to remove remaining obstacles to Soviet-British agreements discussed during Eden's mission to Moscow. He demanded again that London confirm Soviet possession of all territories acquired in 1939 and 1940. Nonetheless, on May

---

[12]Winston Churchill, *The Hinge of Fate* (Boston, 1950), pp. 259–61.

[13]Churchill, *The Hinge of Fate*, pp. 264–70.

[14]Churchill, *The Hinge of Fate*, p. 273.

[15]Robert Nisbet, *Roosevelt and Stalin: The Failed Courtship* (Washington, DC, 1988), pp. 3–6.

[16]Quoted in Nisbet, p. 15.

26 he signed a twenty-year alliance containing no territorial provisions. Pressed once again by Molotov on a second front, Churchill warned that even with the best efforts, it was unlikely that any British move in 1942, could draw off major enemy land forces from the Eastern Front. The British, noted Churchill, then were engaging forty-four German divisions compared with forty that Molotov urged that a second front divert from the east. In order to mislead the Germans, London agreed to issue a communiqué stating "full understanding was reached with regard to the urgent task of creating a second front in Europe in 1942." However, Churchill refused to promise Molotov that a second front in France could be launched in 1942.[17]

Between visits to London Molotov conferred with President Roosevelt and warned him that without a second front in France Soviet resistance might collapse. Although American military leaders gave a very guarded approval of a second front, Roosevelt blithely authorized Molotov to inform Stalin: "We expect the formation of a second front this year."[18] The president thus disregarded the considered views of top British military leaders that a cross-channel invasion could not be undertaken before 1943, if then. By the fall of 1942 only five American divisions would be ready, so clearly Britain would bear the brunt of such an invasion. Churchill and the British military chiefs sought vainly to persuade Roosevelt and General George Marshall to abandon such plans; they concluded correctly that senior American generals still lacked strategic field competence.[19]

To Churchill's alarm Molotov returned from Washington with a Soviet–American draft communiqué stating the urgency of launching a second front in Europe during 1942. Roosevelt informed Molotov he was prepared to sacrifice 120,000 men if need be to accomplish this, most of them British. Churchill flatly rejected the communiqué. Later that year it became clear that the United States could not then provide the required troops. Confirming the dismal prospects then facing a second front was the August 1942 British commando raid against Dieppe, France, which suffered 70 percent casualties.

When Churchill and Ambassador Harriman flew to Moscow in August 1942 the Germans were sweeping onward inexorably toward Stalingrad on the Volga River and the oilfields of the Caucasus. When Churchill gave Stalin the bad news about a second front in 1942 and the necessary curtailment of Western convoys to northern Russia, Stalin declared insultingly: "This is the first time in history that the British navy has ever turned tail without fighting." According to Harriman, Churchill angrily reminded Stalin that Britain had fought Hitler alone all during the Nazi-Soviet Alliance. After Churchill's brilliant performance, Stalin was

---

[17]Churchill, *The Hinge of Fate*, pp. 336–42.

[18]Sherwood, pp. 562–63.

[19]Mark Stoler, *The Politics of the Second Front* (New York, 1977), pp. 42ff.

careful not to insult him again.[20] When Stalin handed Churchill an aide-memoire deploring London's refusal to create a second front and noting that most German forces had been moved to the eastern front, Churchill retorted that the best second front then would be the forthcoming Anglo-American "Torch" operation in North Africa:

> If this can be effected in October it will give more aid to Russia than any other plan. . . . Compared with "Torch," the attack with six or eight Anglo-American divisions on the Cherbourg peninsula and the Channel Islands would be a hazardous and foolish operation.[21]

Showing immediate interest in and grasp of "Torch," Stalin then assured Churchill that the Russians would stop the Germans in the Caucasus Mountains.

Until 1943 all President Roosevelt's efforts to arrange a personal meeting with Stalin were rebuffed. Stalin asserted that given his largely personal command of the Red Army, he had to remain in Moscow to direct the war. According to Marshal Josip Tito of Yugoslavia, however, Stalin trusted neither Churchill nor Roosevelt and wanted from them only unlimited supplies and a second front.[22]

Soviet wartime memoirs testify to Stalin's complete control over political, economic, and military aspects of the Soviet war effort. He personally made every important wartime decision and wholly dominated his civilian associates. Stalin impressed Western military men with his organizational skill, his grasp of overall strategy, and his knowledge of tactical detail. Often intervening in the conduct of combat operations to change petty details, Stalin demanded very detailed information about the situation at the front, but when he intervened in large-scale military operations, he contributed little. Nonetheless, he selected able commanders and allowed them latitude to plan operations while reserving for himself the ultimate power of decision. His leadership improved during the war partly because of the enhanced operational skill of Soviet professionals. Soviet generals clearly feared Stalin more than they did the Germans.[23]

In the fighting on the German-Soviet front in the summer of 1942 the Germans had the advantage in men and fighter planes, the Soviet forces in artillery and tanks. The German summer offensive began on June 28 east of Kursk, and only a month later fighting occurred near Stalingrad. On July 28 Stalin issued a desperate order: "It is time to put an end to retreats. . . . Not a single step backwards. . . . Each position, each meter of

---

[20] W. Averell Harriman and Elie Abel, *Special Envoy to Churchill and Stalin, 1941–1946* (New York, 1975), p. 157.

[21] Churchill, *The Hinge of Fate*, pp. 481–82.

[22] Nisbet, p. 39.

[23] Seweryn Bialer, ed., *Stalin and His Generals: Soviet Military Memoirs of World War II* (New York, 1969), pp. 34–43.

Soviet territory must be stubbornly defended."[24] On August 5 the Germans captured Stavropol, and four days later they secured Krasnodar in the north Caucasus. Halted near Grozny, they failed to reach Transcaucasia, but by fall 1942 German armies had advanced deeper into Russia than had any invading army from the west. The epic Battle of Stalingrad started in late July when the Germans reached its western suburbs. During August and September the Nazis advanced slowly in stubborn street fighting. The city's fall might have enabled the Germans to create a solid frontier on the Volga River, end the war, and set up a collaborationist regime. However, Stalingrad's defenders under Marshal Zhukov, victor at Moscow the previous year, repelled all German assaults. By mid-October the Germans went over to the defensive at Stalingrad.

The Soviet counteroffensive on the Stalingrad front began November 19, and within four days the German Sixth Army of General Friedrich von Paulus was surrounded. Denying him permission to break out, Hitler ordered him to await relief, but by mid-December the German relief force had to withdraw. On February 2, 1943, von Paulus and 90,000 demoralized Germans surrendered. The Soviet victory at Stalingrad was accompanied by offensives along the entire front that cleared the Caucasus and partially lifted the siege of Leningrad.

SOVIET COUNTEROFFENSIVE AND SOVIET-WESTERN FRICTION, 1943

Stalingrad constituted the true turning point of the Nazi-Soviet war. Despite a few local offensives, the Germans thereafter never held the initiative on the eastern front. With growing Soviet superiority in manpower and materiel, after mid-1943 an eventual Soviet victory appeared virtually certain. The war then assumed an increasingly political character as Stalin sought to ensure Soviet expansion and control of an eastern European buffer zone.

The Casablanca Conference (January 1943) of Roosevelt and Churchill coincided with the Soviet counteroffensive at Stalingrad, giving Stalin an excellent pretext to stay home. His absence contributed to Anglo-American decisions to concentrate on Mediterranean operations for the balance of 1943 and to postpone a cross-channel invasion. Stalin, however, did not view the North African and Italian campaigns as a genuine second front. At Casablanca Roosevelt apparently first suggested insisting that the Axis powers surrender unconditionally. Churchill, taken by surprise when Roosevelt announced this at a news conference in Casablanca, disliked that idea as involving a likely prolongation of the war.[25]

On January 26 Roosevelt and Churchill informed Stalin about proposed Anglo-American operations during 1943:

---

[24]Quoted in Mikhail Heller and Aleksandr Nekrich, *Utopia in Power: The History of the Soviet Union from 1917 to the Present* (New York, 1986), pp. 391–92.

[25]Nisbet, pp. 43–44.

Our main desire has been to divert strong German land and air forces from the Russian front and to send to Russia the maximum flow of supplies. . . . We are also pushing preparations to the limit of our resources for a cross-Channel invasion in August in which both British and American forces would participate.

Limiting factors that might delay such an operation, they cautioned, were shipping resources and assault landing-craft.[26] Alleging that since December the Germans had shifted twenty-seven divisions from west to east, Stalin on February 16 urged moving up the date of a second front to spring or early summer.

During the dark months—January-early March 1943—two additional Western convoys totalling forty-eight merchant ships were sent northward, forty of which arrived safely. Then the return of daylight facilitated German attacks. With the Battle of the Atlantic against German submarines at a crisis, the proposed March convoy to north Russia was postponed; in April the British Admiralty proposed, and Churchill agreed, that northern convoys to Russia should be suspended until autumn darkness.[27]

In April 1943 Moscow abruptly severed all relations with the Polish exile government in London. General Sikorski had just informed Churchill that he had proof that in April 1940 Moscow had ordered the murder of 15,000 Polish officers and other prisoners, then had buried them in mass graves in Katyn Forest near Smolensk. In September 1939 the Soviets had arrested and deported all Polish officers and intellectuals they could locate. Incarcerated in three detention camps, nothing had been heard from any of them after April 1940. Occupying German troops had discovered their graves and the Berlin government had asked the International Red Cross to investigate. The London Poles joined this effort without informing the British government. When the Red Cross refused to investigate without a Soviet invitation, the Germans conducted their own investigation, then accused the Soviets of responsibility. Reacting violently, Moscow accused the Germans of murdering the Poles in January 1944. Churchill proved unable to prevent a breach between Moscow and the London Poles. Thereafter, Moscow, combating the London Poles at every turn, built the nucleus of a postwar Polish Communist regime.[28]

During the spring of 1943 the nature of Soviet wartime diplomacy changed significantly. The role of professional diplomats like Ambassador Harriman became secondary. Henceforth most disputed issues in Soviet-Western relations were settled by the "Big Three" leaders and their trusted envoys. During 1943 the old school ambassadors Maiskii and Maxim Litvinov were recalled from London and Washington, respectively, suggesting that Stalin no longer relied so heavily on Western goodwill.

---

[26]Churchill, *The Hinge of Fate*, pp. 743–44.

[27]Winston Churchill, *Closing the Ring* (Boston, 1951), pp. 256–58.

[28]Churchill, *The Hinge of Fate*, pp. 757–61; Kennan, pp. 359–60.

After an Anglo-American meeting at Quebec, Roosevelt and Churchill agreed that the Big Three needed to meet to discuss wartime strategy and postwar frontiers. On September 25 Churchill wrote Stalin about convening a secret meeting at Teheran, Iran; all three leaders finally agreed to go there in November.

At the front the Red Army by then had gained the upper hand over the Germans. The Nazis had launched a summer offensive July 5 near Kursk, south of Moscow, provoking the greatest tank battle in history. In August Soviet forces counterattacked and retook Kharkov for good after that key city had changed hands a number of times. The Battle of Kursk shattered the Wehrmacht's offensive power and was followed by Soviet advances all along the line. The eastern Ukraine and Kiev were recaptured as were parts of central Russia and Belorussia.

In October 1943 a Big Three foreign ministers' conference convened in Moscow. The Soviets demanded a cross-channel invasion, now code-named "Overlord," by spring 1944. Writing Eden in Moscow, Churchill retained reservations about such an invasion and opposed any commitment to invade in the spring of 1944 if that meant denuding the Italian front. "I will not allow, while I am responsible, the great and fruitful campaign in Italy . . . to be cast away and end in a frightful disaster for the sake of [Overlord] in May."[29] However, after Molotov secured the release of two detained British sailors, the conferees sensed that a more friendly atmosphere prevailed than had been evident previously. Churchill, though, opposed Roosevelt's idea that Russian military representatives attend Anglo-American staff meetings asserting that they would merely demand an earlier second front and block other discussion. "Considering they tell us nothing of their own movements," he said, "I do not think we should open this door to them."[30]

At the Teheran Conference (late November 1943) President Roosevelt accepted Stalin's offer of a house inside the Soviet legation compound. Molotov explained that Soviet security in Teheran had uncovered a German plot to assassinate President Roosevelt. Ambassador Harriman later denied that any such plot had existed and affirmed that Stalin had aimed to keep the American president under Soviet surveillance. From Roosevelt's perspective it was a perfect solution enabling him to hold three private meetings with Stalin before the plenary sessions. At these meetings Poland and its postwar boundaries were discussed, and Stalin stressed that he would demand all territory acquired by the USSR under the Nazi-Soviet Pact. At their third private talk Roosevelt, in regard to the Polish question, alluded to the problem of his reelection campaign. With over six million people of Polish background in the United States, "as a practical man, [he] did not want to lose their votes." The president agreed with Stalin about

---

[29]Churchill, *Closing the Ring*, pp. 284–99.
[30]Churchill, *Closing the Ring*, p. 315.

restoring a Polish state but wished to see its eastern frontier moved westward and the western boundary advanced to the Oder River. The Baltic peoples, Roosevelt believed, would vote voluntarily to join the Soviet Union. Thus he revealed his abyssmal ignorance about brutal Soviet policies in those lands after 1939. Stalin must have rejoiced at receiving pledges from Roosevelt in an hour of what he had sought for years in Poland and the Baltics merely in return for honoring the president's reelection wishes. At these private meetings was discussed almost everything later dealt with in the plenary sessions of the Big Three. Roosevelt supported strongly Stalin's insistence that Overlord begin as early in 1944 as possible. The president outlined his plan for a postwar international organization headed by "the Four Policemen"—the Big Three and China. They agreed that France did not deserve membership and should lose its colonies.[31]

These private Roosevelt-Stalin talks undermined Churchill's position at Teheran and turned the plenary sessions mostly into arguments between Stalin and Churchill. Noted Charles Bohlen, Roosevelt's translator at those meetings:

> I did not like the attitude of the President who not only backed Stalin but seemed to enjoy the Churchill-Stalin exchange. Roosevelt should have come to the aid of a close friend and ally, who was really put upon by Stalin.[32]

From these secret conversations and Roosevelt's open support for him at the plenary sessions Stalin realized that apparent Anglo-American unity concealed genuine divisions of interest, notably over British imperial policies. Roosevelt's aim to weaken France stemmed from his constant courtship of Stalin and his personal dislike of the French leader, General Charles de Gaulle. Thus the president agreed with Stalin that postwar Germany should be dismembered and France denied any major role there.

Stalin, backed by President Roosevelt, mostly prevailed at the plenary sessions. However, Churchill also aided Stalin's plans to dominate Poland, stating: "Personally, I thought Poland might move westward. . . ." Thus at Teheran the Big Three determined basically Poland's postwar frontiers, without Polish participation, by moving the country westward to the Oder and prescribing the ethnic Curzon Line in the east. Continuing to emphasize the key importance of Overlord, Stalin dismissed as secondary the Mediterranean campaigns that Churchill favored.[33]

Believing Stalin was getting an incorrect impression of British policies from Roosevelt, Churchill sought a personal meeting with the Soviet leader. Stalin believed that London was seeking to undercut Overlord in favor of an invasion of the Balkans. Churchill informed Stalin that the British had

---

[31]Nisbet, pp. 44–47.

[32]Charles E. Bohlen, *Witness to History, 1929–1969* (New York, 1973), pp. 141, 146.

[33]Churchill, *Closing the Ring*, pp. 359ff.

two or three times as many troops as the United States in the Mediterranean theater. He wished to employ them, induce Turkey to join the Allies, and achieve victory over the Germans in Italy. Unless the Germans concentrated superior forces in France, Overlord would go forward as planned, Churchill declared. At a Big Three luncheon Roosevelt informed a pleased and relieved Stalin that Overlord would be launched in May 1944. Churchill stressed that the Anglo-American command must remain in closest touch with the Soviets on all operations in the east, west, and the Mediterranean. Concurring, Stalin promised a major Soviet offensive for June 1944 to prevent the Germans from reinforcing their western front.[34]

At the British sponsored dinner in Teheran, Churchill rejoiced over a "memorable occasion in [his] life," with the American president on his right and Russia's dictator to his left: "Together we controlled practically all the naval and three-quarters of all the air forces in the world, and could direct armies of nearly twenty millions of men, engaged in the most terrible of wars that had yet occurred in human history." Churchill rejoiced at the great progress they had made toward victory.[35] Later, Stalin rejected Roosevelt's suggestion that Moscow resume relations with the Polish London government because it had "slandered Russia." Churchill then asked about Soviet views on Polish frontiers. Once again seeking the Curzon Line frontier in the east, Stalin added that Lvov should also go to Russia but opposed annexing any Polish-inhabited districts. The Poles, noted Churchill, should accept Big Three advice on frontiers. Stalin agreed to Roosevelt's expressed desire that Finland be encouraged to leave the war on a reasonable basis. As to Germany, Stalin and Roosevelt urged that it be dismembered; Churchill did not object to this in principle but warned that a fragmented Germany would inevitably seek to reunite. Stalin stressed that the Big Three must remain strong enough to defeat Germany if it reunited and became aggressive.[36]

At Teheran the Big Three reached a basic agreement on their strategy for the balance of the war in Europe and laid the bases for European peace, initialling a document summarizing their agreements. Most important was their accord that Overlord should begin in May or June 1944 in conjunction with an operation in southern France. Finally, Stalin agreed that the USSR should enter the Far Eastern war soon after Germany's defeat. As 1943 ended the Grand Alliance appeared on course for war and peace.

DEFEATING GERMANY, 1944–1945

As 1944 began, while the Western allies prepared for Overlord, the Red Army's winter offensive completely freed Leningrad and liberated the western Ukraine and Crimea; that spring the prewar Soviet frontier was

---

[34]Churchill, *Closing the Ring*, pp. 376–83.
[35]Churchill, *Closing the Ring*, pp. 384–85.
[36]Churchill, *Closing the Ring*, pp. 393–403.

reached. The Germans, no longer able to meet Soviet forces on an equal basis, were retreating constantly despite Hitler's pleas to stand fast. An Allied offensive in Italy beginning in mid-May liberated Rome on June 4, bringing warm congratulations from Stalin.

Polish issues continued to poison inter-Allied relations, however. At Teheran the West had conceded all essential Soviet territorial claims. In January 1944 a Moscow communiqué stated that Poland's eastern frontier would be the Curzon Line. Churchill sought to get this approved by the London Poles now headed by Stanislas Mikolajczyk, a Peasant Party leader, while the Soviets continued to denounce his government over the Katyn Forest affair.

These clouds were dispelled temporarily by the great cross-channel invasion of June 6, 1944, which took the Germans by surprise. Churchill informed Stalin immediately, and Stalin sent congratulations and revealed that the Soviet summer offensive would begin in mid-June. As these operations unfolded, the two leaders remained in close contact.

In July 1944 the Red Army entered Poland and advanced swiftly to the Vistula River near Warsaw. In Lublin a Soviet-sponsored Polish Committee of National Liberation was created that was clearly opposed to the London Polish government. The latter had authorized its Polish Home Army under General Bor-Komorowski to launch a general insurrection in Warsaw against the German occupiers whenever it seemed opportune. On August 1, after Soviet troops crossed the Vistula near Warsaw, General Tadeusz Bor-Komorowski ordered a general rising. The Red Army promptly halted "to regroup," and Soviet air activity near Warsaw suddenly ceased. As British and American aircraft dropped supplies to the Polish insurgents, Stalin claimed that Polish reports had greatly exaggerated the uprising and objected to Western planes utilizing Soviet bases. Churchill and Roosevelt made a joint appeal to Stalin: "We believe that all three of us should do the utmost to save as many of the patriots there [in Warsaw] as possible." Retorted Stalin cynically: "Sooner or later the truth about the group of criminals who have embarked on the Warsaw adventure in order to seize power will become known to everybody." By the time the Soviets occupied devastated Warsaw in December, the Polish insurrection had been wholly crushed.[37] Stalin happily allowed the Nazis to perform his dirty work to destroy the Polish Home Army.

Simultaneously, talks between Premier Mikolajczyk of the London Poles failed to reach agreement with Stalin on frontiers or on a postwar Polish government. Stalin insisted on the Curzon Line and a Polish government that would accept Soviet policies unconditionally. On the other hand, the London Poles favored restoring Poland's pre-1939 frontiers. By then Stalin had granted authority in most of Poland to his puppet Lublin regime.

---

[37]Winston Churchill, *Triumph and Tragedy* (Boston, 1953), pp. 128–45.

In late September 1944, when Churchill proposed to meet with Stalin in Moscow, Roosevelt supported the idea and instructed Ambassador Harriman to participate as an observer. Arriving in the Soviet capital October 9, Churchill was greeted by Molotov and others at the airport. That evening, seizing a propitious moment, Churchill told Stalin:

> Let us settle about our affairs in the Balkans. Your armies are in Rumania and Bulgaria. We have interests, missions, and agents there. Don't let us get at cross-purposes in small ways. So far as Britain and Russia are concerned, how would it do for you to have ninety percent predominance in Rumania, for us to have ninety percent of the say in Greece, and go fifty-fifty about Yugoslavia?

While that was being translated, Churchill wrote out the percentages of influence in Balkan countries on a half-sheet of paper and pushed it across the table. Stalin took his blue pencil and made a large tick upon it and passed it back. "It was all settled in no more time than it takes to set down," according to Churchill. Then Churchill remarked: "Might it not be thought rather cynical if it seemed we had disposed of these issues, so fateful to millions of people, in such an offhand manner? Let us burn the paper." Replied Stalin: "No, you keep it."[38] Writing President Roosevelt, Churchill reported: "We have found an extraordinary atmosphere of goodwill here." He and Stalin would not commit Roosevelt to anything, but "we should try to get a common mind about the Balkans so that we may prevent civil war breaking out in several countries. . . ."[39]

While in Moscow Churchill met with leaders of the so-called Polish National Committee. He soon realized they were mere Soviet puppets. Thus Boleslaw Bierut, Lublin's premier, declared: "We are here to demand on behalf of Poland that Lvov shall belong to Russia. This is the will of the Polish people." Churchill looked at Stalin; the twinkle in Stalin's eye seemed to say: "What about that for our Soviet teaching?" As Churchill wrote King George VI of Britain about the Poles: "Our lot from London are . . . decent but feeble, but the delegates from Lublin . . . appeared to me to be purely tools, and recited their parts with well-drilled accuracy." Despite differences over Poland, Churchill concluded a profitable two weeks "in which we got closer to our Soviet Allies than ever before or since."[40]

The months between this Moscow meeting and the Big Three summit at Yalta in February 1945 marked the high point in wartime Anglo-Soviet relations. Stalin's cordial and cooperative messages to Churchill reflected Soviet appreciation over reduced German military pressure after the Normandy invasion. Meanwhile the Red Army was busily occupying eastern Europe. Liberating Belgrade, Yugoslavia, in October 1944, the Russians

---

[38]Churchill, *Triumph and Tragedy*, pp. 226–28.
[39]Churchill, *Triumph and Tragedy*, pp. 228–29.
[40]Churchill, *Triumph and Tragedy*, pp. 235–42.

advanced up the Danube River and had surrounded the Hungarian capital, Budapest, by late December. In January 1945 the Soviets crossed into eastern Germany from Poland and occupied east Prussia. By the end of January, except for Hungary and northern Italy, Hitler was virtually confined to Germany. Romania and Bulgaria were under Soviet occupation; Poland had exchanged one conqueror—Germany—for another—Russia—when over Western objections Moscow recognized the Lublin Committee as the Provisional Government of the country. In the West the German Ardennes counteroffensive in December halted the Allied advance and provoked pleas to Stalin to launch a new Soviet offensive.

With German defeat fast approaching, the Big Three in February 1945 convened at Yalta in the Crimea since Stalin insisted on meeting on Soviet territory. This was the Big Three's most controversial meeting: subsequently American conservatives blamed Western concessions at Yalta for Soviet control of eastern Europe. President Roosevelt, advised by leftists like Alger Hiss, allegedly had sold Poland and China "down the river." Actually, the crucial decisions on Poland had been made at Teheran and only resolute Anglo-American unity at Yalta could have salvaged any Polish independence. By the time of Yalta Stalin controlled Poland, Romania, and Bulgaria and would scarcely have agreed to evacuate them. However, Yalta gave moral legitimacy to what Stalin had obtained through Red Army victories and earlier Western weakness. Once again Roosevelt spurned genuine Russian experts and continued to play up to Stalin.[41]

At the initial plenary session of February 5 the three leaders discussed the German question at the splendid Livadia palace. Stalin asked how Germany should be divided. Churchill responded that all three powers agreed that Germany should be dismembered, but that such a complex issue could not well be settled in a few days at Yalta. The Big Three agreed to submit that question to their foreign ministers who were to produce a definite plan within a month. Largely because of Churchill's intercession, France would receive an occupation zone in Germany carved from the British and American sectors. For Churchill a major postwar role for France became more urgent once Roosevelt declared that the United States could not maintain an army in Europe for more than two years after the war. Churchill objected to extravagant Soviet reparations claims against Germany pointing to the sad experience of the Allies with reparations after World War I.[42]

Debate ensued over the American proposal to form a United Nations organization and about voting within it. Molotov accepted the basic American proposals provided the Big Three remained unanimous. Dropping his earlier demand for sixteen Soviet votes in the General Assembly—one for each Soviet republic—Stalin agreed to accept three Soviet seats provided

---

[41]Nisbet, pp. 70–72.
[42]Churchill, *Triumph and Tragedy*, pp. 349–56.

THE "BIG THREE": GREAT BRITAIN'S WINSTON CHURCHILL, UNITED STATES' FRANKLIN D. ROOSEVELT, AND SOVIET UNION'S JOSEPH STALIN POSE WITH THEIR AIDES AT THE YALTA CONFERENCE IN FEBRUARY 1945.

*move
Yalta
Decisions*

Ukraine and Belorussia were accepted as members. The USSR and the United States both insisted that the great powers be granted the power to veto any important UN decision. The Big Three debated the future of Poland at great length during seven of Yalta's plenary sessions. After tense discussion by them, by their foreign ministers, and subordinates, the Curzon Line was accepted as Poland's eastern frontier. Despite Western pleas, Stalin refused to concede Lvov or the nearby oilfields to Poland. On the west Stalin declared that the Western Neisse and Oder rivers should comprise the frontier with Germany. While agreeing that Poland should be moved westward, Churchill warned: "It would be a great pity to stuff the Polish goose so full of German food that it died of indigestion."[43] Moving Poland to the Western Neisse, he objected, would require more than six million Germans to migrate westward into Germany. As to a permanent Polish government, Roosevelt noted that most American opinion opposed recognizing the unrepresentative Lublin regime. He proposed to Stalin that in its place a new all-Polish government should be formed containing representatives of Poles abroad and within Poland. Churchill backed this

---

[43]Churchill, *Triumph and Tragedy*, p. 374.

idea, affirming that if eight to ten Polish leaders like Mikolajczyk entered the Lublin government, the Western powers should recognize it. But Molotov asserted stubbornly that Lublin, unlike the London regime, was supported by most Poles and urged enlarging the Lublin Committee. Subsequently, Molotov proposed reorganizing Lublin on a wider democratic basis with the inclusion of democratic leaders from Poland itself and also from those living abroad. The foreign ministers of Britain, the United States, and the Soviet Union were to consult in Moscow on how to achieve that goal. Once reorganized, the Lublin government was to pledge to hold free elections as soon as possible. Roosevelt and Churchill insisted that these elections be truly fair and free.[44] To be implemented these schemes for a new Polish government clearly would depend upon Soviet good faith and willingness to permit a truly free and independent Poland.

[handwritten margin note: Debately on Poland.]

However, it soon grew evident that the USSR was not implementing the three-power accords formulated at Yalta to broaden the Lublin regime to include all parties and promote democracy in eastern Europe. With Poland under Soviet occupation, time was on the side of Moscow and its Polish allies. Molotov refused to accept any views other his own concerning Poland, barred most Western-sponsored candidates, and refused to allow foreign observers to supervise the elections. Churchill proposed sending a sharp note to Stalin, writing Roosevelt on March 13:

> Poland has lost her frontier. Is she now to lose her freedom? . . . We are in the presence of a great failure and an utter breakdown of what was settled at Yalta. . . . I believe that combined dogged pressure . . . would very likely succeed.[45]

However, Roosevelt, already in failing health which his intimates concealed carefully, was unable and unwilling to exert such pressure, and the West could only watch the progressive communization of Poland and other eastern European countries such as Romania. Early in March Soviet Deputy Minister Andrei Vyshinskii had engineered a coup in Romania, followed by the forcible installation of a Communist minority regime.

As the Red Army besieged Berlin, Western Allied commander General Dwight David Eisenhower, moving against a reputed Nazi redoubt in Bavaria, abandoned any attempt to advance on Berlin or to occupy Prague in Czechoslovakia. On May 8 the war in Europe ended with Germany's surrender. The Soviet Union stood wholly predominant in eastern Europe.

THE USSR AND THE WAR AGAINST JAPAN, 1943–1945

At Teheran in late 1943 Stalin had agreed in secret talks with the Western allies to bring the Soviet Union into the Far Eastern war against Japan after the war against Germany ended. In the meantime he was careful to preserve

---

[44]Churchill, *Triumph and Tragedy*, pp. 386–87.
[45]Churchill, *Triumph and Tragedy*, p. 426.

complete Soviet neutrality in the Pacific conflict. At Yalta, in rigid secrecy, Stalin informed Churchill and Roosevelt that Moscow would agree to enter the Pacific war two to three months after Germany's surrender on the following conditions: preservation of the status quo in Outer Mongolia (as a Soviet protectorate) and restoration of Russian rights lost to Japan in 1905. Those rights would include a). the recovery of southern Sakhalin and adjacent islands; b). internationalization of Dairen, a commercial port in southern Manchuria, and restoration of the Russian lease of the naval base of Port Arthur; c). joint operation by a Sino-Soviet company of the Chinese Eastern and South Manchurian railways, ensuring Soviet predominance in Manchuria; and d). Soviet acquisition of the Kurile Islands. This agreement would require the concurrence of Nationalist China, which President Roosevelt, at Stalin's request, undertook to secure. Churchill emphasized later that while he had approved of this he had played no part in reaching that accord.

Only in late 1943, when Stalin realized that Japan's defeat would allow the Soviet Union to recover all of Russia's losses in the Russo-Japanese War and become the dominant east Asian power, would he discuss entering the Pacific war. Throughout the war with Japan, American leaders were most anxious to have the USSR enter and had few objections to having some Japanese possessions go to Russia. At the Cairo Conference, just before Teheran, Roosevelt and Hopkins met with Chiang Kai-shek, the Chinese Nationalist leader, and drew up the Cairo Declaration, pledging that all territories seized by Japan since 1931 would be returned to China, including Manchuria.

At the Quebec Conference of September 1944 the Anglo-American combined chiefs of staff estimated that roughly eighteen months after Germany's surrender would be required to defeat Japan. To save American lives it became vitally important for Roosevelt to bring the Soviet Union into the Pacific war. In October 1944 the question of Russia's participation was put to Stalin once again during Churchill's visit. General John Deane, the American military attaché, emphasized that United States military plans in the Pacific would depend partly on Soviet actions. Surprisingly, Stalin asked whether the United States really wished the USSR to participate rather than handling the Japanese alone. The American response was that the United States command wanted the Soviets to join the Pacific war as soon as possible, particularly to destroy the Japanese army in Manchuria.[46] Presumably that would give the Russians a free hand in that region. Asked by Ambassador Harriman in December 1944 what the "political considerations" were that Stalin had mentioned, Stalin listed most of the concessions demanded formally two months later at Yalta. Of these only the Kurile Islands had not been held by Russia in 1904.

---

[46]Kennan, p. 380.

On August 8, 1945—two days after the first American atomic bomb was dropped on Hiroshima—the Soviet Union declared war on Japan. To justify this action Stalin cited the "treacherous Japanese attack" on Russia in 1904 and the latter's humiliating defeat. For forty years he, as a member of the older generation, had awaited this day, Stalin declared. On August 14 Japan surrendered, largely in response to American atomic attacks. However, Soviet historiography claimed that Japan's defeat was ensured by the Soviet offensive in Manchuria. Soviet operations continued there until August 19, when the Japanese commander surrendered. Soviet forces continued to occupy Manchurian territory and advanced into Korea as far south as the thirty-eighth parallel, the demarcation line agreed upon with the United States. Other Soviet troops occupied southern Sakhalin and the Kuriles. At minimal cost the Soviet Union regained, temporarily, Russia's pre-1904 position in the Far East.

Suggested Readings

Beitzell, Robert. *The Uneasy Alliance: America, Britain and Russia, 1941–1943.* New York, 1972.

Bennett, Edward. *Franklin D. Roosevelt and the Search for Victory: American-Soviet Relations, 1939–1945.*Wilmington, DE, 1990.

Bialer, Seweryn, ed., *Stalin and His Generals: Soviet Military Memoirs of World War II.* New York, 1969.

Bohlen, Charles E. *Witness to History.* New York, 1973.

Bor-Komorowski, Tadeusz. *The Secret Army.* New York, 1951.

Churchill, Winston S. *The Second World War.* 6 vols. London and Boston, 1948–53.

Ciechanowski, Jan. *Defeat in Victory.* Garden City, NY, 1947.

Clark, Alan. *Barbarossa: The Russian-German Conflict, 1941–45.* New York, 1965.

Dawson, Raymond H. *The Decision to Aid Russia, 1941.* Chapel Hill, NC, 1959.

Deane, John R. *The Strange Alliance: The Story of Our Efforts at Wartime Cooperation with Russia.* New York, 1957.

Djilas, Milovan. *Conversations with Stalin.* Trans. M. Petrovich. New York, 1962.

Erickson, John. *The Road to Stalingrad. Stalin's War With Germany.* vol. I. New York, 1975.

_____. *The Road to Berlin.* Boulder, CO, 1983.

Feis, Herbert. *Churchill–Roosevelt–Stalin: The War They Waged and the Peace They Sought.* Princeton, NJ, 1957.

Fischer, George. *Soviet Opposition to Stalin: A Case Study in World War II.* Cambridge, MA, 1952.

Gilbert, Martin. *Winston S. Churchill: Road to Victory, 1941–1945.* Boston, 1986.

Great Patriotic War of the Soviet Union, 1941–1945. A General Outline. Moscow, 1970.

Harriman, W. Averell and E. Abel. *Special Envoy to Churchill and Stalin, 1941–1946.* New York, 1975.

Hull, Cordell. *The Memoirs of Cordell Hull.* 2 vols. New York, 1948.

Martel, Leon. *Lend-Lease, Loans, and the Coming of the Cold War.* Boulder, CO, 1979.

Mastny, Vojtech. *Russia's Road to the Cold War: Diplomacy, Warfare, and the Politics of Communism, 1941–1945.* New York, 1979.

McNeill, William H. *America, Britain and Russia: Their Cooperation and Conflict, 1941–1946*. London, 1953.

Motter, T. H. Vail. *The Persian Corridor and Aid to Russia*. Washington, DC, 1952.

Nisbet, Robert A. *Roosevelt and Stalin: The Failed Courtship*. Washington, DC, 1988.

Rozek, Edward J. *Allied Wartime Diplomacy: A Pattern in Poland*. New York, 1958.

Sherwin, Martin. *A World Destroyed: The Atomic Bomb and the Grand Alliance*. New York, 1975.

Sherwood, Robert. *Roosevelt and Hopkins: An Intimate History*. New York, 1950.

Snell, John L. *Illusion and Necessity: The Diplomacy of Global War, 1939–1945*. Boston, 1963.

_____, ed., *The Meaning of Yalta*. Baton Rouge, LA, 1956.

Stalin's Correspondence with Churchill, Attlee, Roosevelt, and Truman 1941–45. 2 vols. Moscow, 1957.

Standley, William and A. Ageton. *Admiral Ambassador to Russia*. Chicago, 1955.

Stoler, Mark A. *The Politics of the Second Front*. New York, 1977.

Whaley, Barton. *Codeword Barbarossa*. Cambridge, MA, 1973.

Zawodny, Janusz. *Death in the Forest: The Story of the Katyn Forest Massacre*. Notre Dame, IN, 1962.

Ziemke, Earl F. *Stalingrad to Berlin: The German Defeat in the East*. Washington, DC, 1968.

THE COLD WAR AND SOVIET BLOC, 1945–1953

The end of World War II in Europe found the Soviet Union occupying or controlling most of eastern Europe after suffering losses of some twenty million dead and about one-fourth of its capital resources. About three million Soviet citizens remained outside Moscow's control and few of them wished to return home. Britain and France had been weakened, but the USSR faced a powerful United States that had lost few men and boasted a monopoly of atomic weapons. Disputes between the Soviets and their Western allies had surfaced repeatedly during the war. Now, with peace restored, these disputes soon deepened into the so-called "Cold War," a political and military rivalry for predominance in the postwar world. Joseph Stalin exploited an eastern European power vacuum to seize control there while the Chinese Reds were defeating Chiang Kai-shek's Nationalists and conquering mainland China. What caused the Cold War? Which side was primarily responsible? What impact did the Red Chinese triumph have on the Soviet position in Asia?

SOVIET-WESTERN TENSIONS AND PEACEMAKING, 1945–1946

An official Soviet account of the mid-1970s claims that the USSR emerged from World War II much strengthened politically, with the world's greatest military forces, and with enhanced international authority, whereas "the imperialist camp," except for the United States, had been much weakened. Soviet victory triggered a powerful revolutionary surge, fostering the collapse of capitalism in many countries in Europe and Asia and the birth of a worldwide system of socialist states.[1]

Becoming American president in mid-April 1945 upon Roosevelt's sudden death, Harry Truman, without much knowledge of foreign affairs, vacillated between Winston Churchill, who exhorted him to adopt a firm

---

[1]A. A. Gromyko and B. N. Ponomarev, eds., *Istoriia vneshnei politiki SSSR, 1945–1975*, vol. I (Moscow, 1976), pp. 5–6.

line towards the USSR, and advisers such as former ambassador Joseph
Davies, who urged placating Stalin. Truman's initial policies proved ineffective in halting Soviet predominance in eastern Europe and even promoted
it. Rejecting Churchill's advice, in May 1945 Truman sought to smooth over
tensions with Stalin by removing American troops from advanced positions
there despite his realization that the Soviets were violating their Yalta
commitments. He dispatched the pro-Soviet Harry Hopkins to Moscow to
resolve disputes over the future of Poland. Urged by Hopkins to suggest
a solution of the wrangle over the postwar Polish regime, Stalin offered
four or five of twenty ministries to non-Lublin Poles. Early in June Truman
accepted this formula, although it was far less than previous Anglo-American
demands. This marked the end of a post-Yalta crisis brought on by the Polish
question and the abrupt cessation by the United States in May 1945 of
lend-lease shipments to Britain and Soviet Russia on the grounds that such
aid was only to be provided during the war in Europe. A strong opponent
of British imperialism, Truman sought to act as mediator between Britain
and the USSR.

As Stanislas Mikolajczyk, the former leader of the London-based Polish
expatriates, and a few other non-Communist Poles entered a Polish
Communist-dominated regime, Churchill was describing Soviet advances
into central Europe as "one of the most melancholy in history" and vainly
urged a showdown with Stalin before the Americans withdrew. In mid-May
Churchill complained that the Soviets had dropped "an iron screen across
Europe from Lübeck to Trieste behind which we had no knowledge of what
was going on." As Moscow busily erected puppet governments in its zone,
Churchill found the Soviet attitude "incomprehensible and intolerable."[2]

Thus revisionist American scholars—such as Gar Alperowitz, Walter
LaFeber and Daniel Yergin—who asserted Truman's primary responsibility
for the coming of the Cold War by arbitrarily ending lend-lease, rejecting
Soviet loan requests, and making intemperate objections over violations of
the Yalta agreements, appear to overlook his willingness to withdraw
American troops promptly from the Soviet sphere and to allow Stalin to
resolve the Polish question largely in accordance with his desires.[3]

The Potsdam Conference (July 1945), although reaching limited accords
on Poland and Germany, generally widened Soviet-Western differences. At
Potsdam, President Truman and his new secretary of state, James F. Byrnes,
aimed to resolve remaining wartime issues in order to terminate American
military and political responsibilities in Europe as quickly as possible.
Despite a United States monopoly of the atomic bomb, the Western allies

---

[2]Winston Churchill, *Triumph and Tragedy* (Boston, 1953), pp. 601–09; Fraser Harbutt,
The Iron Curtain: Churchill, America, and the Origins of the Cold War (New York, 1986), pp.
102–03.

[3]Lawrence Aronsen and Martin Kitchen, *The Origins of the Cold War in Comparative
Perspective: American, British and Canadian Relations with the Soviet Union, 1941–48* (New
York, 1988), pp. 32–33.

SOVIET AND U.S. LEADERS POSE AT THE POTSDAM (GERMANY) CONFERENCE IN JULY 1945. LEADING THEIR DELEGATIONS WERE (L-R) SOVIET FOREIGN COMMISSAR V. M. MOLOTOV, U.S. SECRETARY OF STATE JAMES F. BYRNES, PRESIDENT HARRY S TRUMAN, AND PREMIER JOSEPH STALIN.

obtained no real satisfaction over Soviet violations of Yalta. Soviet leaders did not appear unduly concerned over this new weapon. Truman refused to recognize the Soviet-sponsored puppet regimes in Romania and Bulgaria. Meanwhile, Churchill strove to halt the growth of Soviet power in eastern Europe by offering Stalin the prospect of easier Soviet access to the Turkish Straits and Baltic Sea. Happy at Churchill's welcoming the USSR as a naval power, Stalin refused to make any sacrifices on land in his sphere of interest. When Churchill expressed anxiety over the Soviet advance westward, Stalin denied any such intention and added that he was busily withdrawing and demobilizing Soviet troops. Stalin delighted Truman by pledging once again to enter the Pacific war very soon and agreeing to set up a Council of Foreign Ministers including France and China to conclude peace with Italy and lesser Axis satellites. Defeated in British elections, Churchill and his foreign secretary, Anthony Eden, hastily left Potsdam; later Churchill told his physician, Lord Moran: "After I left, Joe [Stalin] did what he liked."[4]

---

[4]Harbutt, p. 111.

After Churchill's departure, the Big Three—now Truman (U.S.), Stalin (USSR), and Clement Attlee (Britain)—reached decisions on occupation zones in Germany and on Polish frontiers. In return for the West's provisional acceptance of the Oder-Western Neisse River boundary for Poland, Stalin dropped his earlier demand for $20 billion in reparations from Germany. Each power would obtain reparations from its own occupation zone with the USSR and Poland getting 10 percent of surplus capital equipment from the western zones. At Potsdam there was not only a noticeable increase in coolness between the Soviets and Western leaders but also between Truman and the British. While the British resisted Soviet arbitrary actions in eastern Europe, the Americans remained passive. In the light of their deteriorating relations, the Big Three held no more such summits after Potsdam.

Why did the generally friendly wartime relations among the former allies come to such a quick end? Once common enemies had been defeated, no ideological links remained, and Soviet expansion brought their security interests into increasing conflict. Stalin and Foreign Commissar V. M. Molotov were strongly xenophobic and suspicious about the West. Even before the war ended, an ideological campaign against capitalism began inside the Soviet Union. Internal factors may well have been decisive in moving the USSR away from postwar collaboration with the West. Stalin insisted on reimposing tight dictatorial control over the Soviet people, isolating them once again from "dangerous" Western ideas, and imposing heavy new sacrifices upon them in order to rebuild the shattered USSR. The swift postwar reduction of the Soviet armed forces suggests that military fear of Western intentions did not then explain Soviet actions. According to Soviet figures, the Soviet armed forces were reduced from more than 11 million in 1945 to less than 3 million in 1948; in the same period the United States cut its forces even more drastically. The atomic bomb dropped on Hiroshima, Japan, in August, while enhancing American confidence, did not seem to worry Stalin unduly but heightened his determination to obtain such an obviously powerful weapon for the USSR.

After Potsdam the Soviets challenged Britain increasingly, while American attitudes towards both countries became rather detached. In January 1946 an Anglo-Soviet "cold war" developed featuring thinly concealed Soviet threats against Turkey and encouraging separatism in northern Iran. American leaders meanwhile still aimed to withdraw U.S. troops from Europe while promoting its economic recovery.

The former World War II allies were able to achieve basic agreement over the peace treaties with the lesser Axis states. Modest progress on those questions was scored during negotiations in Paris in the summer and fall of 1946. Foreign ministers of the "Big Five" (United States, USSR, Britain, France, and China) agreed to internationalize the port of Trieste, grant the USSR modest reparations from Italy, and approve drafts of the peace treaties. Although the widening East-West rift complicated matters somewhat, in February 1947 treaties were signed with Italy, Romania, Bulgaria, Hungary, and Finland. All of them had to agree to pay reparations to the USSR and to make certain territorial concessions. The outbreak of the Cold War, however, prevented peace treaties from being drawn up with Germany and Austria, both of which remained under Allied occupation.

THE COLD WAR BEGINS, 1946–1949

Within a year after the end of the European war the Grand Alliance had yielded to a Cold War between the Western powers and the Soviet Union. Important speeches by Stalin in February and Churchill in March 1946 heralded a confrontation that grew more intense and dangerous until mid-1949. On February 9 in a "pre-election" speech in Moscow, Stalin asserted that World War II had been "the inevitable result of the development of world economic and political forces on the basis of modern monopoly capitalism." The uneven development of capitalism, Stalin predicted, would soon split the capitalist West into warring factions. He exhorted the Soviet people to fulfill the Fourth Five Year Plan in order to rebuild the country and prepare it for an eventual showdown with the West. Stalin was openly pessimistic about chances of developing friendly postwar relations with the capitalist powers.[5] Justifiably, American Supreme Court Justice William O. Douglas noted that Stalin's speech amounted to a declaration of World War III. As harsh Soviet domestic policies cut off the USSR from normal contacts with the West, General Lucius Clay, American commander in Germany, in late February warned Washington that Moscow might seek soon to unify Germany by force. From Moscow the American diplomat, George Kennan, in a "long telegram" widely circulated in Washington, argued that the Soviets were motivated by deeply rooted suspicions of the West reinforced by Marxist-Leninist ideology.[6]

In a major address at Fulton, Missouri, on March 5 Winston Churchill echoed Stalin's pessimistic appraisal. Sponsoring Churchill's carefully prepared peroration was President Truman, who introduced him ominously: "We are either headed for complete destruction or we are facing the greatest age in history."[7] Truman, Byrnes, and Admiral William D. Leahy—Churchill's American backers—greeted his speech enthusiastically, though not his key assertion that an Anglo-American alliance was required to combat Soviet expansionism. Noting growing Soviet control over eastern Europe, Churchill coined a phrase in this famous passage:

> From Stettin on the Baltic to Trieste in the Adriatic, an iron curtain has descended across the Continent. Behind that line lie all the capitals of the ancient states of central and eastern Europe. Warsaw, Berlin, Prague, Vienna,

---

[5]Joseph Stalin, "Pre-Election Speech," quoted in Alvin Rubinstein, *The Foreign Policy of the Soviet Union* (New York, 1973) pp. 221–23.

[6]Aronsen and Kitchen, pp. 40–41.

[7]Quoted in Harbutt, p. 188.

Budapest, Belgrade, Bucharest and Sofia, all these famous cities and the populations around them lie in the Soviet sphere and all are subject in one form or another, not only to Soviet influence but to a very high and increasing measure of control from Moscow. . . . The Communist parties, which were very small in all these eastern states of Europe, have been raised to preeminence and power far beyond their numbers and are seeking everywhere to obtain totalitarian control.[8]

Churchill sought to dispel the notion hitherto prevalent among American leaders that accommodation or appeasement would produce agreement with the USSR. He outlined the basis for a vast alliance of countries around the Soviet Union including the British Empire, North America, and Britain's Near Eastern clients. Only through a special Anglo-American relationship, Churchill argued, could Soviet expansionism be halted and the United Nations reach its full potential as a peacekeeping organization.

The Fulton speech, producing dramatic headlines, was recognized almost everywhere as a harbinger of change. Conservatives in Britain, Europe, and the United States generally hailed it; leftists and Communists denounced it. Soviet leaders were dismayed at Churchill's apparent success in forging so quickly a major anti-Soviet coalition. Churchill was instigating war, Stalin told American ambassador Walter B. Smith. Moscow concluded that Churchill, although not then in power, was speaking for the British government. "Ever since Churchill gave his speech in Fulton calling for the capitalist countries of the world to encircle the Soviet Union," recalled N. S. Khrushchev years later, "our relations with the West had been strained."[9]

Early Cold War clashes occurred in the Near East where Britain and the United States remained the chief obstacles to Soviet expansionism. In the summer of 1945 Stalin conducted a diplomatic and propaganda war against Turkey, demanding bases near the Turkish Straits and the return of Ardahan and Kars, former Russian territories, and massing Soviet troops on the Turkish frontier. Washington supported the Turks diplomatically and reinforced its naval forces in the eastern Mediterranean. Truman explained later that his "get tough" policy sought to test Moscow's intentions: "We might as well find out whether the Russians are bent on world conflict now as in five or ten years."[10] The Turks resolutely rejected the Soviet demands, and by the fall Soviet pressure had eased.

The first skirmish, won decisively by the West, was in Iran, occupied by the Allies during World War II to ensure the flow of supplies to the USSR. At Teheran in late 1943 the Big Three had agreed to withdraw their troops soon after the end of the war. However, in northern Iran the Soviets built up the Tudeh Party (Communist), which demanded an autonomous

---

[8]*New York Times*, March 6, 1946, p. 4.

[9]Nikita S. Khrushchev, *Khrushchev Remembers* (Boston, 1970), p. 339.

[10]Quoted in Aronsen and Kitchen, p. 45.

Azerbaijani state. After the war ended, Moscow sought to fragment northern Iran, barred Iranian troops, and kept Soviet troops there, apparently preparing to annex the region to the USSR.

In January 1946, accusing the Soviets of interfering in its domestic affairs, Iran appealed to the United Nations. Withdrawing their troops by the March 2 deadline, the United States and Britain supported Teheran diplomatically. Iran was the first place where Moscow imperilled American strategic and economic interests, notably access to Middle Eastern oil. Concluding that Soviet moves in Iran were aggressive, the Truman administration sought to mobilize world opinion against the Soviets through the United Nations. Unaware of secret American encouragement to Iran, Stalin apparently believed Teheran would cave in to Soviet pressure tactics. The Western powers encouraged Iran to take the issue to the Security Council on March 25. After a brief war scare, Moscow and Teheran then agreed on April 4 that a Soviet troop withdrawal would be coupled with an accord to exploit jointly northern Iranian oilfields. Soon Soviet troops withdrew, the Iranian army suppressed separatism in the north, and, to Moscow's dismay, the Iranian parliament refused to ratify the agreements with the USSR. In Iran Stalin backed down, although it was contiguous to the USSR and historically had been under Russian influence, avoiding a confrontation with an Anglo-American coalition with atomic weapons. The Iranian and Turkish cases foreshadowed the containment strategy; the West succeeded when both Britain and the United States took timely action.

The United States and Soviet Russia disagreed over the control of atomic weapons. In March 1946, Washington released the Acheson-Lilienthal Plan—named after Undersecretary of State Dean Acheson and David Lilienthal—to place atomic weapons under international control in a series of stages. Bernard Baruch, the U.S. delegate to the United Nations Atomic Energy Commission, proposed in June the control of atomic energy by an international agency with a virtual monopoly through international inspection and sanctions; the veto power would not apply. Andrei Gromyko, the Soviet delegate, on the other hand, advocated destroying all atomic weapons, ending their production, and obtaining pledges from all powers not to utilize them. The Soviets refused flatly to abandon the veto power or to permit international inspection of their facilities.

As economic conditions in western Europe deteriorated and civil war raged between Communist and conservative elements in Greece, London informed Washington in February 1947 that Britain would have to withdraw its troops from Greece and cease economic support to threatened Turkey. Reacted Secretary of State George C. Marshall: "It was tantamount to British abdication from the Middle East with obvious implications as to their successor."[11] Truman's closest advisors urged that the United States provide economic and military aid before the Soviets won the region by default.

---

[11]Walter Millis, ed., *The Forrestal Diaries* (New York, 1951), p. 245.

Since Washington was already assisting British efforts in Greece, the State Department swiftly drew up a detailed aid proposal. On March 12, 1947, President Truman proposed to Congress a $400 million program of economic and military assistance to Greece and Turkey designed to defeat Communist insurgents in Greece and block Soviet expansion against Turkey. Although in itself the aid proposal did not represent a radical departure in American foreign policy, its justification certainly was new. Amounting to Truman's declaration of Cold War, it urged Americans to enter a global struggle against Communism. Greece and Turkey, Truman emphasized, represented democratic forces resisting the Communist way of life "based upon the will of a minority forcibly imposed upon the majority. It relies upon terror and oppression, a controlled press and radio, fixed elections, and the suppression of personal freedoms," he said.[12] Emphasizing the concept of a struggle by the "free world" against totalitarianism, Truman conveniently overlooked American support for authoritarian regimes in Europe and Asia. "The anti-communism of the Truman Doctrine," noted Senator William Fulbright, "has been the guiding spirit of American foreign policy since World War II."[13] By stressing this anti-communist theme, Marshall and Dean Acheson persuaded a reluctant, Republican-controlled Congress to vote the necessary money.

Moscow reacted immediately and sharply. In Greece, declared *Izvestiia*, the United States was supporting reactionary, anti-democratic forces, as the British had done, as a smokescreen for expansion: "American claims to leadership in international affairs grow along with the appetite of the American quarters concerned."[14] *New Times* of Moscow viewed the Truman Doctrine as an attempt to convert the United Nations into a tool of American policy: "The only lawful and sensible way to assist Greece and Turkey . . . is by action undertaken through the UNO."[15]

The Marshall Plan of June 1947, logically following up the Truman Doctrine, involved a far-reaching, long-term American commitment to European stability. Returning from a foreign ministers' meeting in Moscow, Marshall warned that western Europe required immediate economic aid to avoid collapse. At Harvard University on June 5 Marshall announced American willingness to help reconstruct Europe's shattered economies provided Europeans could compile their needs and set up machinery to utilize the aid. This offer was issued to all European nations, including the USSR and eastern Europe. However, the proviso that participants' economic records must be open to American inspection made Soviet acceptance unlikely. Under Franco-British leadership a conference of European states

---

[12]Quoted in Adam Ulam, *Expansion and Coexistence: Soviet Foreign Policy, 1917–1973*, 2nd ed. (New York, 1974), p. 432.

[13]Quoted in Walter LaFeber, *America, Russia and the Cold War, 1945–1980*, 4th ed. (New York, 1980), p. 50.

[14]*Izvestiia*, March 13, 1947.

[15]"American Foreign Policy," *New Times*, March 21, 1947, p. 3.

including the Soviet Union convened in Paris on June 27. Foreign Minister Molotov,* bringing a large staff of economic experts to Paris, conferred the next three days at length with Moscow. Whereas France and Britain proposed that a joint European proposal be worked up, Molotov urged that each country draw up its own individual recovery program.

On June 29 Moscow abruptly denounced the Marshall Plan as a scheme to expand American investments and markets in light of an approaching crisis of capitalism. Molotov left angrily, warning that the plan would undermine the participants' national sovereignty, revive German power, divide Europe, and allow the United States to dominate the European continent. Addressing the United Nations, Andrei Vyshinskii denounced the Truman Doctrine and Marshall Plan for ignoring the UN and violating its principles. "The United States also counted on making all these countries directly dependent on the interests of American monopolies, which are striving to avert the approaching depression by an accelerated export of commodities and capital to Europe . . . ," Vyshinskii said.[16] Soon Poland and Czechoslovakia, which initially wished to participate, announced they could not do so because it "might be construed as an action against the Soviet Union."[17] The American Congress approved the European request for a four-year aid program totalling $17 billion in order to prevent the USSR from dominating Europe. Exceeding all expectations, the Marshall Plan fostered an economic recovery that brought European countries ahead of their prewar levels of industrial production.

The Soviet response to the Marshall Plan was the so-called "Molotov Plan" of July 1947, which began linking eastern European countries with the USSR economically. In January 1949 this was further developed in COMECON (Council for Economic Cooperation), a centralized agency under Moscow's control intended to stimulate and control eastern Europe's economic development. Thus Soviet trade with bloc countries grew from about $380 million in 1947 to more than $2,500 million in 1952. Moscow's political response was to create the Cominform (Communist Information Bureau) to link together the Soviet Communist Party with those of eastern Europe, France, and Italy. Concerned by the uncoordinated eastern European response to the Marshall Plan, Stalin felt it essential to establish a formal, but not a worldwide, Communist organization to enhance his control.

The Cominform had its seat in Belgrade, not Moscow, and supposedly was not under Soviet control. It issued a periodical journal, which Stalin insisted on calling *For a Lasting Peace, For a People's Democracy*. At its opening conference in September 1947, Andrei Zhdanov, heir apparent to Stalin,

---

*Molotov's title was changed from foreign commissar to foreign minister in 1946 confirming the decline in ideology in the formulation of foreign policy, but the new title did not change the foreign minister's role.

[16]Vyshinskii speech of September 18, 1947, excerpted in Rubinstein, pp. 234–35.

[17]Quoted in LaFeber, p. 61.

delivered a speech that comprised the most significant statement of postwar Soviet foreign policy. Soviet-Western collaboration of the wartime era was irrevocably over, warned Zhdanov. Of the six great imperial powers in the capitalist world before the war, military defeat had eliminated three and gravely weakened France and Britain. By aggravating "the crisis of the colonial system," World War II had created a new situation:

> ... The division of the political forces operating on the international arena into two major camps; the imperialist and antidemocratic camp, on the one hand, and the anti-imperialist and democratic camp on the other. The principal driving force of the imperialist camp is the USA. ... The cardinal purpose of the imperialist camp is to strengthen imperialism, to hatch a new imperialist war, to combat Socialism and democracy, and to support reactionary and anti-democratic pro-fascist regimes and movements everywhere. The anti-fascist forces comprise the second camp ... based on the USSR and the new [people's] democracies.

The "democratic" and "Socialist" forces, despite imperialist efforts, were growing steadily stronger, Zhdanov claimed.

> Soviet foreign policy proceeds from the fact of the coexistence for a long period of the two systems—capitalism and socialism. ... Cooperation between the USSR and countries with other systems is possible, provided that the principle of reciprocity is observed.

However, warned Zhdanov, America and Britain, by seeking to isolate the USSR, were violating their commitments and trampling the rights of "democratic" nations:

> The strategical plans of the United States envisage the creation in peacetime of numerous bases and vantage grounds situated at great distances from the American continent and designed to be used for aggressive purposes against the USSR and the countries of the new democracy.[18]

Zhdanov's hardline two-camp thesis, prevailing until Stalin's death, was reflected in orders to foreign Communist parties to foster strikes and disorder in the West.

A key feature in this deepening Cold War was the American containment doctrine outlined anonymously in his famous "X" article by George Kennan, a State Department analyst. Kennan ascribed Soviet behavior to a combination of Marxist-Leninist doctrine and Stalin's determination to preserve his own absolute power. Soviet diplomacy, wrote Kennan, "moves along the prescribed path like a persistent toy automobile wound up and

---

[18] Andrei Zhdanov, *The International Situation* (Moscow, 1947); for excerpts see Rubinstein, pp. 236–39.

headed in a given direction, stopping only when it meets some unanswerable force." Endemic Soviet aggressiveness could be contained "by the adroit and vigilant application of counterforce at a series of constantly shifting geographical and political points." If the United States executed such a strategy, eventually the Kremlin would have to abandon its efforts at world domination:

> For no mystical Messianic movement—and particularly not that of the Kremlin—can face frustration indefinitely without eventually adjusting itself in one way or another to the logic of that state of affairs.

The result would be "the break-up or the gradual mellowing of Soviet power."[19] Kennan's prophetic message was that the United States should be patient, purposeful, and unprovocative.

The "X" article provoked a debate with Walter Lippmann, dean of American political commentators, who argued that Soviet foreign policy reflected traditional tsarist Russian expansionism more than Communist ideology, that Stalin was "not only the heir of Marx and Lenin but of Peter the Great." With the Soviet advance into central Europe, Stalin could achieve the tsarist dream of guaranteeing Russia's national security interests. The Soviets, argued Lippmann, were likely to accept an offer to withdraw American and Russian power from central Europe, thus defusing Soviet-American tensions. On the other hand, Lippmann argued, the "X-Truman Doctrine policy" would mean "unending involvement in all the countries that are supposed to 'contain' the Soviet Union," leading to destruction or emasculation of the UN and imposing tremendous strains on the American economy.[20]

The next year, 1948, brought a worsening of the Cold War in Europe with the Communist takeover in Czechoslovakia, the Soviet blockade of West Berlin, and the Tito-Stalin split. Post-World War II Czechoslovakia, governed by a coalition regime of Communists and non-Communists under democratic president Eduard Beneš, had seemed to be a viable bridge between eastern Communism and Western democracy. However, early in 1948 the efforts of the Communist interior minister to pack the police with Communists caused non-Communist ministers to resign. Under intense Soviet pressure, President Beneš reluctantly accepted an all-Communist government, then resigned. Completing the Sovietization of eastern Europe, this "coup" spread shock waves through western Europe. The U.S. Congress promptly approved $5,200 million for the first year of the European Recovery Program.

June 1948 constituted a key month in the developing Cold War as Moscow blockaded West Berlin and Josip Tito's Yugoslavia was

---

[19] "X," "The Sources of Soviet Conduct," *Foreign Affairs* (July, 1947), pp. 566–82.
[20] Walter Lippmann, *The Cold War: A Study in U.S. Foreign Policy* (New York, 1947); see LaFeber, pp. 65–66.

excommunicated from the Soviet bloc.* Both moves amounted to major Stalin miscalculations of Western responses that soon halted postwar Soviet expansion in Europe. Soviet-Western relations concerning Germany had been deteriorating since 1946. When the Soviets refused to keep the Western powers informed of reparations being taken from eastern Germany to promote Soviet economic recovery, the West halted deliveries of industrial equipment from their zones. Early in 1948 the three Western allies agreed to unify their occupation zones and to form a West German federal government. In June a currency reform was carried out in those zones aimed to prevent the Soviets from blocking western Germany's economic recovery. The Soviet decision to impose a blockade on West Berlin was their response to the currency reform's extension to West Berlin. Moscow demanded the right to examine freight and passengers on Western military trains entering the Soviet zone. When the West refused, on June 24 the Soviets cut all land traffic from the western zones into Berlin. President Truman reacted defiantly: "We are going to stay, period."[21] General Clay, the U.S. commander, urged calling Moscow's bluff by forcing the blockade with an armored train, but Washington decided on the less provocative response of a counter-blockade and a massive American airlift to fly in all necessary food and supplies.

The effective American response in Berlin and Marshal Tito's successful defiance of the Cominform, leading to Yugoslavia's expulsion from that body in June 1948, compelled Stalin to question Zhdanov's hard-line foreign policy. In late July Zhdanov either was poisoned or died of a heart attack after violent arguments with Stalin. A Western counterblockade, tightened early in 1949, had serious effects on eastern Germany. When the Soviet blockade's failure grew evident, it was ended after secret negotiations with the West. Two separate German regimes were established in the aftermath of this Berlin crisis: the Federal Republic in the west, and the German Democratic Republic, a Soviet-occupied satellite, in the east. At a subsequent foreign ministers meeting Vyshinskii argued unsuccessfully for restoring four-power control over Germany. The conference reached no agreements on Germany or Austria. Confirmed was the Soviet failure to prevent a shift in the European balance of power against the USSR as most of Germany became integrated into the West.

Western unity and determination in opposing threatening Soviet moves were not yet reflected in adequate conventional military strength in Europe. Whereas the Soviet Union in 1948, according to a Western estimate, had fifty to sixty divisions poised to sweep westward to the Atlantic, western Europe could counter this with only six divisions.[22] The impression of militant Soviet policies and overwhelming military strength spurred Western

---

*On the Tito-Stalin split see pp. 145–47.

[21] LaFeber, p. 78.

[22] *New York Times*, February 13, 1949, p. 16.

rearmament and demands for a multinational collective security system to deter possible Soviet aggression. The North Atlantic Treaty Organization (NATO) of 1949, composed of most of the western European countries, the United States, and Canada, represented the Western response to Soviet conventional military superiority and the communization of eastern Europe. A key provision (Article 5) declared: "The Parties agree that an armed attack against one or more of them in Europe or North America shall be considered an attack against them all."[23] The United States monopoly of atomic weapons protected NATO which at first did not include West Germany. If NATO were not approved and funded by the U.S. Congress, warned W. Averell Harriman, former U.S. ambassador to Moscow, appeasement and neutrality would grow unchecked in western Europe. After the Soviets exploded an atomic device in September 1949, Congress swiftly approved funds for NATO, and the Pentagon decided to build up large conventional European and American forces and include German units. NATO's formation confirmed the complete division of Europe into two hostile power blocs.

CONSTRUCTING A SOVIET BLOC AND FIRST RIFT, 1945–1953

Soviet military victory over Germany in World War II foreshadowed the establishment of Soviet control over eastern and southeastern Europe. Immediate postwar Soviet objectives in Germany apparently included: 1) building a security belt against a resurgent Germany or a Western "capitalist" invasion of the USSR (President Roosevelt had recognized that goal of Stalin as legitimate); 2) ensuring control there to elements "sympathetic" to the USSR—that is, Communists ("capitalist" governments, the Soviets believed, were bound to be hostile); 3) utilizing eastern European resources to rebuild devastated western portions of the USSR, especially through reparations from ex-Axis states; and 4) setting up military bases there to influence events in western Europe.

A later official Soviet view attributed the postwar events in eastern Europe to powerful revolutionary and national liberation movements unleashed by Soviet victory. "That victory," wrote Leonid I. Brezhnev in May 1965, "opened the way for the rise of a revolutionary struggle of the working class, the unprecedented scope of the national liberation movement, and the collapse of a shameful colonial system."[24]

After World War II, recalled Nikita S. Khrushchev, Stalin's successor:

> Stalin took an active personal interest in the affairs of [Poland and Hungary] as well as of Czechoslovakia, Bulgaria and Romania. The rest of us in the

---

[23]Quoted in LaFeber, p. 83.

[24]A. A. Gromyko and B. N. Ponomarev, eds., *Istoriia vneshnei politiki SSSR, 1917–1976,* vol. II (Moscow, 1976), p. 48.

leadership were careful not to poke our noses into eastern Europe unless Stalin himself pushed our noses in that direction.[25]

Worker and peasant revolutions in eastern Europe, stressed Soviet accounts, overturned prewar rule by capitalists and landowners and moved the new "people's democracies" along a Soviet path towards socialism.

Western accounts, by contrast, emphasize Soviet use of force and pressure to transform eastern Europe by 1948 into obedient satellite states. Soviet methods differed somewhat by country but were fundamentally similar in approach. In all cases military "liberation" and occupation by the Red Army was a factor although relatively unimportant in Czechoslovakia and Yugoslavia. After military "liberation," local Communist parties in eastern Europe were rebuilt, in some cases virtually from scratch. Eastern European Communist leaders, residing in Moscow during the war, returned to their homelands as Stalin's agents. Soviet direction of Communist parties was especially close in Poland, Hungary, and Bulgaria, whereas the Czech and Yugoslav parties were much more independent. For local Communists Moscow secured the chief levers of power: control over the army, police, and ministry of information. Coalition governments were formed composed initially supposedly of all "democratic" and anti-Fascist political parties. Local actions, supported from Moscow, disorganized political opposition and conservative groups, accused of collaboration with the Nazi occupiers, were banned. Socialist parties were split, then merged with the Communists. Able non-Communist leaders were removed by arrest, exile, or intimidation. Wherever possible elections were delayed until a majority was assured for a Communist-Socialist leftist bloc.

Poland was the key eastern European country for the USSR by size, population, and previous history. A hostile Poland would effectively exclude the Soviets from central Europe and complicate their control over eastern Germany. During the war Nazi and Soviet extermination of much of its intelligentsia, officer class, and huge wartime losses had left Poland gravely weakened. Decimating the Polish Communist leadership in his 1938 purges, Stalin revived the Communists in 1945 as the Polish Workers' Party. They dominated a Provisional Government consisting mostly of loyal Communists. From the start they held key ministries; opponents like Stanislaw Mikolajczyk were politically powerless. Very popular among Polish peasants, democrats, and conservatives, Mikolajczyk probably would have won a free election, but terror was applied against him and his Peasant Party forcing him to flee into exile.* Single-slate elections in 1947 brought a leftist coalition to power, which created a Communist regime.

The Soviets found it easier to communize Bulgaria and Romania, former Axis satellites. In Bulgaria the leftist Fatherland Front seized power in a

---

[25]Khrushchev, p. 361.
*See Stanislaw Mikolajczyk, *The Rape of Poland* (New York, 1948).

Map 8–1   USSR and Eastern Europe, 1945–1989

Soviet occupied zones in Austria (evacuated in 1955) and Germany	Former German and Czechoslovak territory annexed by USSR in 1945
British, French, and American occupied zones	Area annexed by the USSR in 1939–1940 and reincorporated as part of the USSR in 1945

The "Iron Curtain" in 1948

Principal areas of anti-Soviet protest and revolt 1953–1968 crushed by Soviet military intervention (East Germany, Hungary, Czechoslovakia) and by strong political pressure (Poland)

coup in September 1944. During 1945, under Soviet pressure, the Agrarian Party was split and opposition leaders were barred from the Bulgarian government. After a rigged plebiscite in September 1946, the monarchy was ended and the king exiled. Late in 1947 a fully Communist regime was set up and the chief anti-Communist Agrarian leader, Nikola Petkov, was hanged. However, only a week later, the United States recognized the Bulgarian government.

In Romania, despite an anti-Russian sentiment left over from the war, the Communists succeeded in gradually gaining power. Under strong pressure from Soviet Foreign Minister Andrei Vyshinskii, Romanian King Michael appointed a Communist as interior minister in the Petru Groza cabinet. At Western request Moscow advised the king to bring two opposition members into the government, then Britain and the United States recognized it. The Communists then delayed national elections until the opposition had been weakened by arrests and intimidation. The elections of November 1946 were rigged in favor of the Communists. Western protests were ignored. Moscow then compelled the popular King Michael to abdicate in December 1947. In March 1948 new elections gave nearly all parliamentary seats to the leftist government, and a new constitution created the People's Republic of Romania. In four years a tiny, unpopular Romanian Communist Party with constant Soviet support destroyed the opposition and shifted Romania from monarchy to "republic."

In Hungary, bordering on Allied-occupied Austria, the Communist party was weak. In relatively free elections in 1945 the Communists received only 17 percent of the vote while the Smallholders, a peasant party, obtained 57 percent and formed a government under Ferenc Nagy. The Communists soon formed a leftist bloc with two other left parties. When Nagy left on a foreign trip in 1947, the Communists forced his resignation and altered the electoral law in their favor. In August 1947 elections the Left received 60 percent, though the Communists still polled only 22 percent. By late 1947 a Communist-dominated government took power.[26]

The Yugoslav case differed radically from the others from the start. During World War II the Communist-led Partisans of Josip Broz Tito defeated the Chetniks of General Draža Mihajlović, loyal to the London exile regime of King Peter II and liberated most of Yugoslavia before the Red Army captured Belgrade late in 1944. The Partisan-controlled National Liberation Committee established a provisional government. Under the Tito-Šubašić Agreement of November 1944, endorsed by the Big Three, a regency was to act for King Peter pending a plebiscite. In March 1945 a Communist-led cabinet was formed headed by Tito as premier and war minister and Ivan Šubašić as foreign minister, but non-Communists held only five of 28 cabinet posts. As the Communists utilized intimidation and

---

[26]See Zbigniew Brzezinski, *The Soviet Bloc: Unity and Conflict* (New York, 1960), pp. 9–18, and Hugh Seton-Watson, *The East European Revolution* (New York, 1956), pp. 49–70.

secret police terror, opposition leaders including Šubašić resigned, and their parties boycotted elections to a constituent assembly. Thus even Tito's Partisans with greater popular support than other eastern European Communist parties did not risk a free election and thus could not claim a true public mandate. The constituent assembly in November 1945 proclaimed Yugoslavia a federal people's republic, and Yugoslavia's 1946 Constitution closely resembled Stalin's 1936 Soviet constitution. The Tito regime followed more closely in Soviet footsteps than others in eastern Europe with rapid industrialization and agricultural collectivization but without Soviet domination. In neighboring Albania Communists seized control by 1945, and it became a Yugoslav satellite.

On June 28, 1948, the Soviet-dominated Cominform expelled Tito's Yugoslavia, in effect excommunicating the regime and its leaders. Coming as a terrible shock to Yugoslavs and Russians, this step provoked amazement in the West, where Yugoslavia had been considered the most loyal member of the Soviet bloc. Why did this breach occur and what did it portend? During World War II, Stalin, finding Tito and his colleagues too independent-minded, had provided little ideological or material support to the Partisans. During a mission to Moscow in January 1948 to settle Soviet-Yugoslav differences over Albania, Milovan Djilas, then close to Tito, was shocked by Stalin's casual declaration: "We have no special interest in Albania. We agree to Yugoslavia swallowing Albania!" And Stalin pretended to swallow his fingers.[27] Only in Yugoslavia did the Soviets encounter resistance to their "joint companies" formed to exploit satellite economies on behalf of the USSR. The Yugoslavs resented Soviet penetration of their party, army, police, and economic agencies. Stalin did manage to recruit a few highly placed Yugoslav party and army leaders. Meanwhile, disparaging Yugoslav wartime military achievements, Moscow claimed that the Red Army had liberated Yugoslavia and affirmed that the Partisans had done no more than the Bulgarians. All this roused Yugoslav national pride against overblown Soviet claims.

Early in 1948, notes Vladimir Dedijer, Tito's biographer, signs appeared that Stalin aimed to annex all of eastern Europe directly to the USSR. Having to subjugate Yugoslavia to achieve this, Stalin anticipated an easy victory.[28] In February, Yugoslav and Bulgarian leaders were summoned to an urgent meeting in Moscow. Stalin was furious that Tito, pleading ill health, had refused to come. Yugoslav delegates, including Edvard Kardelj and Djilas, were subjected to an angry monologue by Stalin. His chief target, though, was Georgi Dimitrov of Bulgaria, for allegedly concluding a Yugoslav-Bulgarian accord without consulting Moscow. When Stalin refused to conclude a promised commercial treaty with Yugoslavia in March, the

---

[27] Milovan Djilas, *Conversations with Stalin* (New York, 1962), p. 143.

[28] Vladimir Dedijer, *The Battle Stalin Lost: Memoirs of Yugoslavia, 1948–1953* (New York, 1970), pp. 33–34.

Yugoslav Central Committee rejected a Stalin-sponsored "federation" with Bulgaria. On March 18, citing Yugoslav "hostility," the Soviets withdrew their military and civilian advisors. Stalin reputedly then declared: "As soon as I move my little finger, Tito will be thrown out."[29] On March 27 Stalin and Molotov wrote the Yugoslav Central Committee in a tone of brutal superiority, speaking as if to their servants. Claiming that the Yugoslav Party had secretly slandered the Soviet Party, they asserted it contained no democracy and was not truly Marxist-Leninist. Added were ominous charges of Menshevism, Trotskyism, revisionism and even imperialism.[30] These charges boiled down to the Yugoslav refusal to accept Soviet dictation and close supervision.

When the Yugoslav Central Committee convened to discuss the Soviet charges, those criticized offered to resign, but Tito refused their offer declaring that Moscow was seeking to wreck the Central Committee. All of its members except Sreten Žujović, serving as finance minister, supported Tito's draft reply; Žujović was then expelled. Tito's reply of April 13 was conciliatory but dignified. He attributed false Soviet allegations to Žujović and Andrija Hebrang (a Croatian partisan leader), attacked Soviet efforts to penetrate Yugoslav agencies, defended the Yugoslav party, and invited Moscow to send members of its Central Committee to investigate. A key Yugoslav statement went:

> No matter how much each of us loves the land of socialism, the USSR, he can, in no case, love his country less, . . . the Federal Republic of Yugoslavia for which so many thousands of its most progressive people fell.[31]

A second Soviet letter in May claimed that the Red Army had liberated Yugoslavia and that the Soviet ambassador had the right to investigate the Yugoslav party. These supposedly secret letters were circulated to all the Soviet satellites, which slavishly supported Stalin.

Stalin then demanded that Tito and his colleagues attend a meeting of the Cominform in Bucharest to discuss their differences. On June 20 the Yugoslavs rejected Stalin's final telegram of the 19th, noting that they could not accept the meeting's agenda and would not meet on an unequal basis. The Cominform on June 28 then expelled the Yugoslav Communist Party; "sound elements loyal to Marxism-Leninism" were called upon to remove "the Tito clique" from power.[32] Andrei Zhdanov even stated: "We possess information that Tito is a foreign spy."[33] The Yugoslav reply the

---

[29] Djilas, pp. 171–74.

[30] Royal Institute of International Affairs, *The Soviet-Yugoslav Dispute* (London, 1948), pp. 12–17.

[31] Royal Institute, p. 19.

[32] Dedijer, p. 131. Dedijer notes that six of the obedient eastern European delegates, who voted for the June 28 resolution, were later purged by Stalin.

[33] Vladimir Dedijer, *Tito* (New York, 1953), p. 361.

next day, composed by Djilas, refuted the Soviet charges and justified Belgrade's actions.

Expelling the Yugoslav Party proved to be a major Stalin miscalculation. Instead of removing Tito as he had anticipated, the Yugoslav Party and people rallied behind Tito; Cominformists were imprisoned. Whereas Tito promptly published the entire Soviet-Yugoslav correspondence, Moscow kept it strictly secret in the USSR. At the Fifth Yugoslav Party Congress in July Tito denounced the Cominform attacks as untrue and un-Marxist, but neither he nor other speakers attacked either Stalin or the USSR. Stalin also revealed his basic caution by avoiding a Soviet military invasion of Yugoslavia although it lacked foreign allies and an invasion probably would have succeeded quickly. Stalin apparently feared that such a move might trigger war with the United States. Instead, Moscow resorted to half-measures of blockade by Soviet satellites, border incidents, and subversion. Such pressure tactics compelled Tito to turn to the West for economic and military aid. Soon Tito's Yugoslavia was evolving a distinctive form of national Communism with considerable economic freedom, important ties with non-aligned countries, and a drastically decentralized state structure. Yugoslavia closed its borders to Greek Communist guerrillas contributing significantly to a Greek government victory by 1949.

While Yugoslavia set out on its own road toward socialism, Stalin, to prevent the emergence of other nationalist leaders like Tito, cracked down harshly on eastern European satellite regimes. In 1949 Wladyslaw Gomulka, already being labeled the "Polish Tito," was removed as head of the Polish Workers' Party for refusing to follow the Soviet model closely. This began a massive purge of all satellite governments and Communist parties, featuring treason trials resembling those in the USSR during the 1930s. After 1948 an elaborate system of controls evolved in the satellites to link them indissolubly with the Soviet Union. Stalinism as an interstate system, notes Zbigniew Brezezinski, a prominent American political scientist of Polish origin, featured autocratic regimes and the absolute priority of Soviet interests. Formal ties included bilateral state agreements between each "People's Democracy" and the USSR, under which Moscow could exploit its resources and insure its obedience. Reinforcing this system were Soviet troops, military "advisors," economic experts, and diplomats. The satellites were effectively isolated from the West by the "Iron Curtain." Stalin's prestige and omnipotence cemented this entire apparatus of power.[34] Between 1949 and Stalin's death in March 1953 a monolithic Soviet bloc was created, with satellites reduced to utter conformity and national interests and differences suppressed.

Meanwhile world Communism seemed immeasurably strengthened by the Red Chinese triumph over Chiang Kai-shek's Nationalists in 1949. At the end of the Pacific War in August 1945 the Chinese Reds controlled

---

[34]On this power system see Brzezinski, pp. 104ff.

roughly one-fifth of China and were outnumbered about five to one by Nationalist troops. However, the corrupt Nationalist regime wasted most American aid and drove much of the Chinese peasantry into the hands of fellow peasant, Mao Tse-tung. Stalin, however, clearly preferred a divided China to one united under either Chiang or Mao. The Truman administration, seeking to prevent renewed Chinese civil war, sent George Marshall in 1945 as an impartial mediator to arrange a coalition government. Marshall appeared to be succeeding until the Soviets withdrew from Manchuria in April 1946 taking billions of dollars worth of industrial equipment but leaving huge stocks of military equipment to the Chinese Reds. Late in 1946 open civil war resumed after Chiang attempted to occupy Manchuria with United States support.

Victorious in Manchuria, Chinese Communist forces by late 1948 were winning the civil war. Distancing his administration gradually from Chiang, President Truman sought in vain to divide the Red Chinese from Moscow. Meanwhile the Soviet press largely ignored the Chinese civil war, and as late as early 1949 Moscow apparently advised Mao to halt at the Yangtse River and accept a partition of China with the Nationalists. After the fall of Nanking the Soviet ambassador followed the Nationalists south to Canton. Only in October 1949 when the People's Republic of China was proclaimed did the Red Chinese make *Pravda*'s front page as Moscow recognized the new regime. In China, as elsewhere, Stalin subordinated the interests of local Communists to Soviet aims and interests.[35] While the United States continued some support to Chiang's Nationalist regime on Taiwan, Britain and several smaller European countries promptly recognized the new Beijing government.

In mid-December 1949 Mao arrived in Moscow by train from Beijing to conclude military and economic agreements and celebrate Stalin's seventieth birthday. The Sino-Soviet Treaty of February 1950, finalized after two months of tough bargaining between Stalin and Mao, included a mutual assistance pact by which they pledged to aid one another if either were attacked by Japan or states allied with Japan (meaning the United States). Retaining its special privileges and sphere of interest in Manchuria, Moscow advanced a stingy $300 million in economic aid to China. The Chinese accepted Outer Mongolia's continued dependence on the USSR. At the signing of these accords Foreign Minister Chou En-lai declared that the Sino-Soviet treaty had utterly defeated American imperialism's attempt "to foster divisions between our two countries."[36] However, even in 1950 it was evident that Red China was not a Soviet satellite. Like Tito, the Red Chinese had achieved power almost wholly by their own efforts.

---

[35]Gordon Chang, *Friends and Enemies: The United States, China and the Soviet Union, 1948–1972* (Stanford, CA, 1990), pp. 28–29.

[36]Chang, p. 64.

Communism likewise scored advances in other parts of eastern Asia. Occupied by Soviet forces from Manchuria in 1945, North Korea received a Communist regime. Communist influence was strong in the Vietminh movement of Vietnam under a Moscow-trained Communist, Ho Chih-minh. As Western colonialism weakened and receded, the prospects for further gains by the huge Communist bloc appeared excellent.

THE KOREAN WAR, 1950–1953

By 1950 the American containment policy featuring the construction of U.S. air bases around the western and southern periphery of the Soviet Union and the formation of NATO had significantly reduced Moscow's prestige and halted Soviet advances in Europe and the Near East. Soviet foreign policy, 1949–1953, was more than ever Stalin's personal policy. Increasingly divorced from reality, the Soviet dictator believed he was infallible and that intra-capitalist conflicts involved a greater danger of war than did tensions between the USSR and the imperialist camp. Seeing French reluctance to admit the new West German Federal Republic to NATO, Stalin was not very worried about that organization without German participation. In 1950 a united, neutral Germany might still have been achieved; after that German membership in NATO and its rearmament eliminated that option.

The North Korean frontal invasion of South Korea on June 25, 1950, provoked a major crisis in the Cold War. Until 1949 Korea, divided at the thirty-eighth parallel, remained under occupation by Soviet troops in the north and American forces in the south. After the Soviet withdrawal, the North Korean army, much larger than that of the south, remained Soviet-equipped and supplied. The North Korean dictator, Kim Il-sung, according to Khrushchev, was wholly confident of victory:

> I remember Stalin had his doubts. He was worried that the Americans would jump in, but we were inclined to think that if the war were fought swiftly—then intervention by the USA could be avoided. . . . I must stress that the war wasn't Stalin's idea, but Kim Il-sung's. . . . Stalin, of course, didn't try to dissuade him.[37]

In the United States the view prevailed that the North Korean attack marked a new militant Communist worldwide policy, with Moscow accepting the risk of a general conflict. Probably Stalin saw an opportunity to prevent the United States from creating a firm military base in Japan. The Korean move, according to the American scholar, Marshall Shulman, had been planned during Sino-Soviet meetings in Moscow earlier that year. Moscow may have interpreted statements by American Far East Commander General Douglas MacArthur and Secretary of State Acheson in December 1949 and January 1950 that Korea did not lie within the

---

[37]Khrushchev, p. 368.

American defense perimeter in the Pacific as signifying a renunciation of American interests there.[38]

Responding to an American request, the UN Security Council convened the very day of the North Korean invasion. The Soviet Union, boycotting the UN over the admission of Red China, thus could not block a unanimous resolution demanding an immediate North Korean withdrawal and requesting aid from all UN members. Thus President Truman could justify American intervention as a legitimate UN operation. Truman assured Stalin (on June 27) that American aims were limited. He hoped Moscow would help restore the prewar situation. The Soviets accused South Korea of aggression and denounced the United States for intervening in a Korean civil war. Returning to the Security Council August 1, the Soviet delegate sought to weaken the virtual unanimity in the UN against North Korea.

After their initial offensive brought them to Korea's southern coast at Pusan, the North Koreans were thrown back into North Korea. On October 7, 1950, the UN General Assembly authorized its forces to enter North Korea. However, as General MacArthur's armies approached their Yalu River frontier, the Chinese first dispatched "volunteers," then intervened massively on behalf of North Korea and pushed the UN forces south of the thirty-eighth parallel. After a final Chinese offensive was repelled in May 1951, UN forces resumed the offensive and secured approximately the line of the 38th parallel, or prewar frontier. As stalemate ensued, truce talks began in July 1951, dragging on for two years. The Korean War triggered a major American military buildup that left the USSR's relative world position weakened. That was confirmed by the Japanese peace settlement of September 1951 by the United States and forty-eight other nations (but not the USSR) and by the beginning of West German rearmament. Once again Stalin had miscalculated.

The Nineteenth Party Congress in Moscow (autumn 1952), marking Stalin's last major appearance and pronouncements, confirmed his shift to a basically defensive foreign policy that sought to play upon Western "contradictions." Increasingly Stalin accepted that the proletariat in advanced capitalist countries was non-revolutionary. Stalin predicted at the congress that western Europe and Japan would soon "try to tear loose from American bondage and take the path of independent development."[39] Reaffirming Zhdanov's rigid two-camp thesis, Stalin considered war between the United States and other industrial countries as more likely than between them and the USSR. Georgii Malenkov, Stalin's new heir apparent, foresaw a peaceful victory of socialism in economic competition with capitalism and declared that the Soviet Union would not seek to force its system on anyone. "The

---

[38]Marshall Shulman, *Stalin's Foreign Policy Reappraised* (Cambridge, MA, 1963), pp. 140–44.

[39]J. V. Stalin, *Economic Problems of Socialism in the USSR* (New York, 1952), p. 28; Shulman, p. 242.

export of revolution," stated Malenkov quoting Stalin, "is nonsense."[40] This approach anticipated the theme of "peaceful coexistence" that was to be stressed under Nikita S. Khrushchev.

Suggested Readings

Aronsen, Lawrence and Martin Kitchen. *The Origins of the Cold War in Comparative Perspective: American, British and Canadian Relations with the Soviet Union, 1941–48.* New York, 1988.

Bialer, Seweryn. *The Soviet Paradox: External Expansion, Internal Decline.* New York, 1986.

Blum, Robert M. *Drawing the Line: The Origin of the American Containment Policy in East Asia.* New York, 1982.

Bohlen, Charles E. *Witness to History, 1929–1969.* New York, 1973.

Borisov, O. B. and B. T. Koloskov. *Soviet-Chinese Relations, 1945–1970.* Ed. and Trans. Vladimir Petrov. Bloomington, IN, 1975.

Byrnes, James F. *Speaking Frankly.* New York, 1947.

Chang, Gordon H. *Friends and Enemies: The United States, China, and the Soviet Union, 1948–1972.* Stanford, CA, 1990.

Cumings, Bruce. *The Origins of the Korean War.* Princeton, NJ, 1981.

Dedijer, Vladimir. *Tito.* New York, 1953.

Djilas, Milovan. *Conversations with Stalin.* Trans. M. Petrovich. New York, 1962.

Feis, Herbert. *From Trust to Terror: The Onset of the Cold War, 1945–1950.* New York, 1970.

Fleming, D. F. *The Cold War and Its Origins, 1917–1960.* 2 vols. New York, 1961.

Gaddis, John L. *The United States and the Origins of the Cold War.* New York, 1972.

Harbutt, Fraser J. *The Iron Curtain: Churchill, America and the Origins of the Cold War.* New York, 1986.

Kaplan, Morton. *The Life and Death of the Cold War: Selected Studies in Postwar Statecraft.* Chicago, 1976.

Kennan, George F. *Memoirs, 1925–1950.* Boston, 1967.

Khrushchev, Nikita S. *Khrushchev Remembers.* Ed. and Trans. Strobe Talbott. Boston, 1970.

LaFeber, Walter. *America, Russia and the Cold War, 1945–1980.* 4th ed. New York, 1980.

Lippmann, Walter. *The Cold War: A Study in U.S. Foreign Policy.* New York, 1947.

Mee, Charles. *Meeting at Potsdam.* New York, 1975.

Millis, Walter, ed., *The Forrestal Diaries.* New York, 1951.

Paterson, Thomas. *Soviet-American Confrontation: Postwar Reconstruction and the Origins of the Cold War.* Baltimore, 1973.

Ra'anan, Gavriel. *International Policy Formulation in the USSR: Factional "Debates" during the Zhdanovshchina.* Hamden, CO, 1983.

Shulman, Marshall D. *Stalin's Foreign Policy Reappraised.* Cambridge, MA, 1963.

Smith, Walter Bedell. *My Three Years in Moscow.* New York, 1950.

The Soviet-Yugoslav Dispute: Text of the Published Correspondence. London, 1948.

---

[40]Malenkov's Report to the Nineteenth Congress, pp. 105–06, quoted in Shulman, pp. 242–46.

Ulam, Adam. *Titoism and the Cominform.* Cambridge, MA, 1952.

Wheeler-Bennett, John and Anthony Nicholls. *The Semblance of Peace: The Political Settlement after the Second World War.* New York, 1972.

Wolfe, Thomas. *Soviet Power and Europe, 1945–1970.* Baltimore, 1970.

Yergin, Daniel. *Shattered Peace: The Origins of the Cold War and the National Security State.* Boston, 1977.

THE POST-STALIN TRANSITION, 1953–1957

Joseph Stalin's death in March 1953 touched off a struggle in the Soviet Union among its leading power centers—Party, state, security police, and army—and among the individual leaders who utilized them, especially Nikita S. Khrushchev, Georgii Malenkov, Lavrentii Beria, and V. M. Molotov. As this power struggle unfolded, Stalin's heirs sought with mixed success to present a facade of unity to the world as a collective leadership. The perilous transition from the brutal dictatorship of Stalin to the modified authoritarianism of Khrushchev, achieved without a bloody purge, nonetheless encouraged some countries in the Soviet bloc to seek autonomy or independence, producing, during 1956, a crisis in intrabloc relations. Meanwhile the collective leadership sought to normalize Soviet relations with the West and to place its relations with bloc countries on a basis of greater equality. That involved the renunciation of certain aspects of Stalin's legacy in both domestic and foreign relations.

THE MALENKOV ERA, MARCH 1953–FEBRUARY 1955

On March 5, 1953, *Pravda* announced the death of Stalin from natural causes and his replacement by a collective leadership headed by Malenkov as premier and, initially, as Party chief; Beria as head of the security police; Molotov as foreign minister; and Khrushchev, who soon assumed the top Party post. The new leaders nervously warned the Soviet populace to avoid panic, but at first the Soviet power apparatus was badly disorganized. Soon induced to relinquish the position of first party secretary, which Khrushchev acquired formally that September, Malenkov retained the top governmental post until 1955 and appeared to be the chief Soviet leader.

Stalin's death had a major and almost immediate impact on the formulation and implementation of Soviet foreign policy. His demise ended abruptly the era of monolithic unity of the Communist bloc under an omnipotent ruler as well as unquestioned Soviet preeminence within it. None of Stalin's successors ever achieved his prestige or dictatorial powers; instead factional and pressure politics prevailed. Whereas on his own Stalin had initiated sudden and major shifts in domestic and foreign policy, the

Stalin Able to make decisions on his own

collective lead— must make collective decisions. difficult

collective leadership and its successors had to produce a consensus by negotiating with major power elements. Soviet and bloc politics grew steadily more complex. The International Department of the Soviet Communist Party acquired more influence over formulating foreign policy decisions than the Foreign Ministry itself. Important matters were often decided within the ID or Secretariat before reaching the Politburo for final discussion. From the early 1960s the ID relied increasingly on research institutes of the Soviet Academy of Sciences, notably the Institute for Study of the USA and Canada. The views of the Foreign Ministry, therefore, comprised only part of the information utilized by the Politburo to reach decisions. The role of the foreign minister, as before, depended largely on his position within the Party. As ideological considerations waned in importance, increasing reliance was placed on professionally trained diplomats.

trouble →

Stalin's death at the time "seemed like a terrible tragedy," recalled Khrushchev, but he "feared that the worst was still to come" because the ruthless and exultant Beria clearly sought to seize full power: "I already sensed that Beria would start bossing everyone around and that could be the beginning of the end."[1] Khrushchev played a key role in blocking this power drive and arranging for Beria's arrest in July 1953. With Beria removed, the secret police was promptly subordinated to Party control, and the climate of fear began to dissipate both in the USSR and in eastern Europe. Even before that a major challenge to Soviet authority in the bloc had occurred. In June 1953, made desperate by poverty and increased work norms, thousands of workers struck and demonstrated against the Communist regime in east Berlin, then in other major eastern German cities. This genuine proletarian uprising was swiftly crushed by Soviet tanks, confirming that Moscow's domination over eastern Europe was maintained by force; it revealed that even an uncertain collective leadership was resolved to preserve Soviet rule.

—workers revolution crushed

New leaders try to restore old contacts

At Stalin's death, after failure of his major policies in Europe and Asia, the Soviet Union was in virtual isolation. The new leadership moved quickly to restore some of the contacts needlessly severed during Stalin's final years and to reduce tension with the West. Initial signs of more flexible Soviet foreign policies were the appointment of a moderate, V. N. Kuznetsov, as ambassador to Beijing and the conclusion of economic assistance agreements with China on March 26. These began several years of Soviet contributions to Chinese industrial and military development. On April 25 *Pravda* published a speech by recently inaugurated U.S. President Dwight Eisenhower without the usual abusive language. Diplomatic ties were restored with Israel, and Moscow sought to forge some links with Tito's Yugoslavia. As the Soviet press campaign against Yugoslavia ceased, other Cominform countries obediently followed Moscow's example. On May 30 the Soviets

USSR helps china

---

[1]Nikita S. Khrushchev, *Khrushchev Remembers* (Boston, 1970) pp. 322–23.

withdrew all territorial claims against Turkey and advocated a new approach toward the Straits problem. A joint Sino-Soviet initiative revived armistice talks in Panmunjon, Korea, and it soon became evident that both Communist powers wished to end the Korean War. On July 27 an armistice was signed ending the fighting.[2]

Thus when Premier Malenkov delivered a major address to the Supreme Soviet on August 8, 1953, Moscow had already partly escaped Stalinist isolation. Malenkov hailed the Korean armistice, but he intimated that the West had organized the East German workers' revolt "to suppress Germany's democratic forces, to destroy the German Democratic Republic . . . and to recreate a hotbed of war in the heart of Europe." The speech disavowed important aspects of Stalinist foreign policy and advocated significant steps to improve Soviet-Western relations. Confirming that Soviet external policies were changing, Malenkov declared: "We firmly stand by the belief that there are no disputed or outstanding issues today that cannot be settled peacefully by mutual agreement between the parties concerned."[3]

In the West, initial overtures were made even earlier in the speeches of April 20 and May 11, 1953, by Prime Minister Winston Churchill, urging direct contact with the new Soviet leaders. Initially, such a course was opposed in Washington by the new secretary of state, John Foster Dulles, who refused to believe that the Soviet Union had changed or could change. On April 23 this "cold warrior" told European leaders:

> The Soviet leaders are to a very large extent the prisoners of their own doctrine which is intensively held by their followers, who are fanatics. The Soviets look upon anybody who is not for them as against them; and . . . as we know, the leaders of Soviet Russia are not subject to any moral inhibitions against the use of violence where it will serve their purpose.[4]

Nonetheless, on July 10 Western leaders invited the Soviets to discuss outstanding problems at a September conference. Despite the apparent rebuff contained in Malenkov's August 8 speech, they persisted until Moscow agreed to hold a foreign ministers' conference in January 1954 in Berlin. At that conclave, however, Foreign Minister Molotov presented the Soviet position in familiar hard-line terms. In March appeared signs of ideological differences between Malenkov and the other new Soviet leaders. Malenkov declared that nuclear war would cause the destruction of world civilization, not merely the downfall of capitalism, as Stalin had claimed. Other leaders remained true to the old line. Although Malenkov soon had to modify his stand, once Khrushchev became premier it became

---

[2]J. M. Macintosh, *Strategy and Tactics of Soviet Foreign Policy* (London, 1962), pp. 73–75.

[3]Malenkov's Report to the Supreme Soviet in Myron Rush, ed., *The International Situation and Soviet Foreign Policy: Reports of Soviet Leaders* (Columbus, OH, 1970), pp. 155–65.

[4]Quoted from the Dulles Papers in Walter LaFeber, *America, Russia and the Cold War, 1945–1980*, 4th ed. (New York, 1980), p. 155.

established doctrine that war between capitalism and socialism was not inevitable.[5]

The new Soviet leadership sought in vain to prevent West Germany from rearming and entering NATO. After Churchill's May 1953 speech, Moscow proposed a conference of east and west Germans to draw up a peace treaty for a neutral Germany, after which free elections could be held. In July, Secretary Dulles, rejecting the procedure suggested by the Soviets, insisted that free elections be held first, which Moscow in turn rejected. Soviet leaders sought to torpedo the European Defense Community, reacting happily when the French Assembly in August 1954 refused to ratify it. However, in October the Paris agreements were concluded bringing West Germany into NATO and authorizing its rearmament. In vain Moscow proposed a new four-power conference to arrange for German reunification and all-German elections. Molotov warned: "If it comes to the point of ratification and implementation of the Paris Agreements . . . , a new situation will arise in Europe which will only aggravate the threat of a new war."[6] However, only Soviet bloc countries attended a Moscow sponsored European security conference whose communiqué of December 2 stated their willingness to participate in a Europe-wide security organization provided the Paris agreements were scrapped. Otherwise, they would have to create their own body to insure their security. With Moscow refusing to abandon its East German regime in order to keep West Germany disarmed, Soviet policies towards Germany under Malenkov ended in total failure.

The collective leadership's policies in the Far East proved more successful. At the Berlin foreign ministers' conference Moscow proposed that a conference dealing with Korea and the war in Indochina against the French be convened in Geneva, Switzerland. At a preliminary meeting among Soviet, Chinese, and Vietminh leaders they worked out their strategy for Geneva. At that time the military situation seemed unfavorable for the Vietminh, and their leader, Ho Chih-minh, warned that unless a ceasefire were concluded soon, the French would triumph. However, by the time the delegates reached Geneva, the Vietminh had captured the key French fortress of Dienbienphu. To Soviet delight, the French proposed the seventeenth parallel to demarcate non-Communist South Vietnam from a new pro-Communist North Vietnam. After haggling briefly, the Soviets accepted this French offer and a peace treaty was signed. Recalled Khrushchev: "We had succeeded in consolidating the conquests of the Vietnamese Communists."[7]

In September 1954 a high-powered Soviet delegation journeyed to Beijing to consolidate warmer Sino-Soviet relations. Included were Marshal Nikolai Bulganin, Anastas Mikoyan, and Alexander Shelepin, who became a rival of Khrushchev. Heading the delegation was Khrushchev, still without

---

[5]Charles E. Bohlen, *Witness to History, 1929–1969* (New York, 1973), p. 363.

[6]*Pravda*, November 20, 1954.

[7]Khrushchev, pp. 481–83.

a government post and inexperienced in diplomacy. Then largely ignorant of the external world, Khrushchev learned very fast as his determination and much practice soon turned this rough peasant into a world statesman. Warmly received by the Chinese, the Russians agreed to assist China's industrial development and to send them military experts and weapons "in a common effort against the USA." Moscow's weakened position vis-à-vis Mao Tse-tung's China was revealed by its voluntary renunciation of Port Arthur, Darien, and the Chinese Eastern Railroad, tsarist concessions recovered by the USSR at the end of the Pacific War in 1945. These Sino-Soviet accords of October 11, 1954, declared:

> Taking into consideration the change in the international situation in the Far East in connection with the ending of the war in Korea and the establishment of peace in Indochina . . . [and] the strengthening of the defense potential of the Chinese People's Republic, the governments of the Soviet Union and the Chinese People's Republic have agreed that Soviet military units are to be evacuated from the jointly used naval base of Port Arthur and the installations in the area are to be transferred to the government of the Chinese People's Republic without compensation.[8]

The Soviets agreed to complete their evacuation by May 1955, and joint companies that had exploited the resources of Sinkiang would cease operating that January. The Soviet agreement to deliver considerable quantities of capital goods to China constituted an attempt by Moscow to bring it into the Soviet economic orbit.

The decisions of the Malenkov government to end the wars in Korea and Indochina undoubtedly helped to end those conflicts. Abandoning many of Stalin's counterproductive tactics and adopting more reasonable policies toward the non-Communist world, the collective leadership nonetheless remained rather inflexible on the future of Germany and Austria and over the political reunification of Korea. However, it had presided over the post-Stalin transition without making any major concessions to the West.

KHRUSHCHEV'S RISE AND THE TWENTIETH PARTY CONGRESS, 1955–1956

In February 1955, admitting mistakes and pleading "inexperience," Malenkov resigned as premier and became a deputy of the new premier and Khrushchev ally, Marshal Nikolai Bulganin. Malenkov's weakening position had been revealed after he had stated on January 1, 1955, that the Soviet possession of the hydrogen bomb made peaceful coexistence "necessary and possible." Khrushchev had immediately accused him of seeking to undermine the cause of proletarian revolution with atomic weapons.[9] After his

---

[8]Quoted in Alvin Rubinstein, ed., *The Foreign Policy of the Soviet Union* (New York, 1973), pp. 294–95.

[9]Arnold Horelick and Myron Rush, *Strategic Power and Soviet Foreign Policy* (Chicago, 1966), pp. 17–30.

resignation Malenkov retained his position in the Presidium, but Khrushchev now emerged as clearly the most powerful Soviet leader. During 1955 he asserted a preeminent role in foreign policy as well. On a series of foreign trips he was usually accompanied by Bulganin acting as his front man.

In response to West Germany's entry into NATO, the Warsaw Treaty Organization was established in May 1955, with a joint military command under Soviet Marshal Ivan Konev. The Warsaw Treaty linked eastern European countries—except for Yugoslavia—firmly with the USSR in a supposedly defensive alliance, called the Warsaw Pact, to ensure the security of socialist states against possible aggression from the capitalist West. Moscow exploited widespread fears in Czechoslovakia and Poland of a resurgent, militaristic Germany in order to integrate eastern European military forces under firm Soviet control. The pact legitimized the stationing of Soviet troops in the satellites. Ironically, Article 8 required pact members to respect the independence and sovereignty of other members and non-intervention in their internal affairs. These provisions were soon to be grossly violated in Hungary. Membership in the Warsaw Pact was soon equated with loyalty to the Soviet Union as head of the socialist bloc; Moscow regarded subsequently any attempt to leave it as a betrayal of socialism.

In Khrushchev's emerging policy of peaceful coexistence with the West the first concrete step was the signature of an Austrian peace treaty on May 15, 1955. That was made possible when Moscow abandoned its former insistence on its right to reintroduce Soviet troops into Austria if the peace treaty were violated. Under this settlement Austria was compelled to become a neutral country forbidden to join either power bloc. All foreign troops were to be withdrawn, the first instance of a Soviet military and political withdrawal from an area in central Europe under their control. The Austrian treaty further undermined the position of Foreign Minister Molotov who continued to advocate a hard-line foreign policy. John Foster Dulles, his fellow hard-liner in the United States, noting that "the wolf has put on a new set of sheep's clothing," advocated that American policy remain unchanged.[10]

An even more remarkable turnaround was reflected in Khrushchev's visit to Belgrade in late May to arrange reconciliation with Marshal Josip Tito. Preceding Soviet economic and political overtures to Yugoslavia during 1954 had brought Tito to declare in October 1954: "This beginning of normalization [with the USSR] fills us with hope that the process will continue to develop" and thus free Tito from excessive dependence on the West. Tito concluded that the times when the Soviet Union could be considered "a highly menacing, aggressive power are now over."[11] However, Tito made it clear that rapprochement with Moscow would not mean any loss of Yugoslavia's independence or severing its friendly ties with the West.

---

[10]Dulles' news conference of May 15, 1955, cited by LaFeber, p. 183.

[11]George Hoffman and Fred Neal, *Yugoslavia and the New Communism* (New York, 1962), pp. 423–24.

Nikita Sergeevich Khrushchev (1894–1971), Party first secretary, 1953–1964; premier, 1958–1964.

On May 27, 1955, Khrushchev accompanied by Bulganin, Mikoyan, and Dmitrii Shepilov, being prepared to replace Molotov as foreign minister, landed in Belgrade and were greeted cordially but without warmth by Yugoslav leaders. Khrushchev admitted that he had been disappointed at their reception, but actually he was furious. In his airport speech Khrushchev

Khrushchev furious w/ yugo greeting

[margin note: A little like yeltsin]

angered Tito by blaming the USSR's contemptuous treatment of Yugoslavia in 1948 on Beria, not Stalin. At this time Khrushchev was still drinking heavily and had to be restrained repeatedly from extreme outbursts by the watchful Mikoyan. Whereas Khrushchev sought a reconciliation of the two Communist parties, Tito insisted that their discussions remain government to government. Khrushchev's rather humiliating "trip to Canossa" nonetheless marked a major shift in Soviet policy since he accepted at least tacitly the Titoist position that each socialist country could pursue its own independent road to socialism. A *Pravda* editorial expressly approved that idea in general and not just for Yugoslavia.[12] That foreshadowed significant changes in Soviet relations with other bloc countries.

[margin note: USSR - yugo end negotiations]

The Geneva Conference of July 1955, designed as the culmination of Khrushchev's initial détente with the West, failed to achieve meaningful agreements although it did create a pleasanter atmosphere. Geneva marked Khrushchev's first meeting with Western leaders, and he faced President Eisenhower and British Prime Minister Anthony Eden with profound feelings of inferiority. Also at the conference was French Premier Edgar Faure. Right up to his death, recalled Khrushchev, Stalin had told those around him: "You'll see, when I'm gone the imperialistic powers will wring your necks like chickens." Thus after Stalin's death, "it was an interesting challenge for us to try to deal with the foreign powers by ourselves. . . . The Geneva meeting was a crucial test for us: Would we be able to represent our country competently?" Khrushchev's self-confidence was not enhanced by his arrival in a small, primitive, two-engined Iliushin airplane. The Soviet delegation included Premier Bulganin, Foreign Minister Molotov, and Marshal Georgii Zhukov. The Western leaders at Geneva, recalled Khrushchev, aimed "to restore capitalism in the countries liberated by the Soviet army after World War II," especially Poland. Their primary objective though remained reunification of Germany, "meaning expulsion of socialist forces from the German Democratic Republic." Predictably, the two sides soon deadlocked on the German question. Overruling a wavering Bulganin, Khrushchev refused to permit free elections in East Germany until after West Germany had disarmed. He likewise rejected President Eisenhower's rather ingenuous "open skies" proposal to allow planes to photograph the other side's territory in order to prevent a surprise attack. Khrushchev argued that this would infringe upon the USSR's territorial integrity. Although he apparently realized that the Geneva Summit would produce no major agreements, Khrushchev declared: "It was still useful. . . : it gave the leaders of the four great powers an opportunity to see each other at close quarters and to exchange views informally."[13]

[margin note: Khrushchev Nervous - untried diplomate]

---

[12]*Pravda*, June 3, 1955. The text of the Belgrade accords was published in *Borba* (Belgrade) and the *New York Times* of June 3, 1955, p. 3.

[13]Khrushchev, pp. 392–95.

Khrushchev was not much impressed by President Eisenhower. "Our people considered him a mediocre general and a weak president," Khrushchev later said. "He was much too dependent on his advisors." Actually determining American policy, he believed, was Secretary of State Dulles who "seemed obsessed with the idea of encirclement. . . . Dulles knew how far he could push us, and he never pushed us too far."[14] Dulles' formula was "to reach the brink of war but never overstep it. We considered him our number one ideological enemy. . . ."[15] However, Geneva also featured friendly talks between Eisenhower and Marshal Zhukov, his World War II counterpart, and the meetings did help to relax tensions between the two superpowers.

Dulles seems to run the show

Unable at Geneva to obtain an all-European security pact, the Soviets settled for establishing formal diplomatic relations with West Germany during a visit to Moscow by Chancellor Konrad Adenauer in September 1955. A week later the USSR granted sovereign powers in foreign relations to East Germany thus confirming the division of Germany. In January 1956 the East German army entered the Warsaw Pact.

During 1955, breaking sharply with Stalinist doctrine and methods, Khrushchev rejected former Party leader Andrei Zhdanov's two-camp thesis and sought to cooperate with leading national leaders in uncommitted countries in Asia and Africa. Thus Moscow supported a Chinese proclamation in April 1955 on peaceful coexistence at the Bandung Conference of non-aligned countries in Indonesia. Khrushchev and Bulganin made a state visit to India where they established friendly ties with Premier Jawaharlal Nehru, and Moscow began loaning money to India to help it build up its industry. On their way home the Soviet leaders stopped in Afghanistan, a neutral country now being courted by both the Soviet Union and the United States. "It was clear to us," noted Khrushchev, "that the Americans were penetrating Afghanistan with the obvious purpose of setting up a military base."[16] By the end of 1956 Moscow had concluded fourteen economic and military assistance agreements with Asian and Middle Eastern countries and was competing actively with the United States for the allegiance of the Third World.

At the crucial Twentieth Congress of the Soviet Communist Party—the first held since Stalin's death—Khrushchev dominated the proceedings. On February 14, 1956, he delivered the chief report outlining the international situation in optimistic terms and revising some Stalinist doctrines. While emphasizing the increasing strength economically and politically of the socialist world, he denied that Moscow had any desire to export revolution to capitalist countries. Denying that war was inevitable as long as capitalism

---

[14]Khrushchev, pp. 395–98; LaFeber, pp. 183–84.

[15]Nikita S. Khrushchev, *Khrushchev Remembers: The Last Testament* (Boston, 1974), pp. 362–63.

[16]Khrushchev, *Khrushchev Remembers*, pp. 507–08.

existed, Khrushchev proclaimed: "The Leninist principle of peaceful co-existence of states with different social systems has always been and remains the general line of our country's foreign policy."[17] He stressed the steps taken recently by the Soviet Union to relax tensions and normalize relations with the Western powers.

[margin note: Khrushcev Trying to overcome stalin]

Ten days later, on the night of February 24, Khrushchev gave a lengthy "secret speech" to a closed session of the congress seeking to enhance his personal power by undermining the still massive figure of Joseph Stalin. To a rapt audience he denounced the crimes of the Stalin era while reaffirming the correctness of Stalin's emphasis on heavy industry in the Five Year plans and forced collectivization of Soviet agriculture, as well as the correctness of one party dictatorship. Khrushchev denounced the cult of Stalin's person "which became . . . the source of a whole series of exceedingly serious and grave perversions of party principles, of party democracy, of revolutionary legality."[18]

Khrushchev had won reluctant approval from his colleagues to deliver this speech. He and his fellow leaders had found it most difficult to free themselves from Stalin's deadly hand:

> For three years we were unable to break with the past . . . [or] lift the curtain . . . [covering] arbitrary rule and executions . . . of Stalin's reign. . . . We persisted in believing the delusion perpetrated by Stalin that we were surrounded by enemies.

[margin note: khrush gives speech denouncing Stalin practices speech published in NYT]

They had blamed everything bad on Beria. "I sensed the falsity of our position in 1955 when we talked with Tito," recalled Khrushchev.[19] His colleagues warned correctly that Khrushchev would not be able to keep his revelations secret. Indeed, copies of the speech were circulated to satellite Communist parties and "our document fell into the hands of some Polish comrades who were hostile toward the Soviet Union."[20] Soon the *New York Times* published the entire text which was issued in Russia only in 1992. Nonetheless, Khrushchev concluded that he had acted correctly to reveal Stalin's reign of terror.

After the Twentieth Congress, Soviet spokesmen blamed the Soviet-Yugoslav quarrel of 1948 squarely on Stalin. Two months later Moscow dissolved the Cominform which had excommunicated Tito. Also, foreign Communist parties were urged to cooperate "at their own discretion and

---

[17]Khrushchev's report to the Twentieth Party Congress, February 14, 1956, cited in Rush, pp. 166–85.

[18]Nikita S. Khrushchev, "The Crimes of the Stalin Era: Special Report to the 20th Congress of the Communist Party of the Soviet Union," *The New Leader*, Annotated by Boris I. Nicolaevsky (New York, 1956), p. 57.

[19]Khrushchev, *Khrushchev Remembers*, pp. 343ff; LaFeber, p. 185.

[20]Khrushchev, *Khrushchev Remembers*, p. 351.

taking into account specific conditions of their work."[21] Tito's victory seemed virtually complete. Indeed, the trend toward true Soviet-Yugoslav cooperation reached its peak on June 2, 1956, when Tito arrived in Moscow on a state visit. The previous day his old foe, Molotov, had been ousted as Soviet foreign minister. Khrushchev now pulled out all the stops for Tito who traveled around the Soviet Union like a conquering hero as Russian crowds chanted "Ti-to, Ti-to!" Normal links between the Soviet and Yugoslav Communist parties were restored. Hailing "the Leninist policy of the Soviet Communist Party," Tito declared that Yugoslavia and the USSR were "marching shoulder to shoulder along the path of Marx, Engels and Lenin."[22] The Yugoslav dictator told Khrushchev: "We are part of the same family— the family of socialism. . . . Never again will anything come between us."[23] Nonetheless, Tito and his colleagues continued to stress Yugoslavia's independence. They realized that there was a serious rift in the Kremlin between "Stalinists," apparently led by Molotov, and reformers headed by Khrushchev. Tito apparently believed that he could promote victory by the reformers.[24]

CRISIS IN THE SOVIET BLOC AND ITS AFTERMATH, 1956–1957

Khrushchev's revelations in his so-called "secret speech" had devastating effects on bloc countries other than China. They destroyed a vital unifying force in the bloc: the giant figure of an omnipotent and omniscient Stalin. During the era of collective leadership, without a clearly dominant Soviet leader, the satellite regimes, which lacked real popular roots, were plunged into turmoil and confusion. Some adhered rigidly to Stalinism while others instituted mild liberal changes that merely provoked widespread demands for genuine freedom and independence.

In Poland Stalinist controls eroded gradually in the years after Stalin's death. In December 1953 Colonel J. Swiatlo, a leading secret police officer, defected to the West. His revelations about his organization's misdeeds and Soviet manipulation of it when broadcast back into Poland shook up the Polish Workers' Party. In December 1954 Wladyslaw Gomulka, purged as a Titoist in 1949, was released from confinement. In the spring of 1955 the first discussion clubs of intellectuals formed in Warsaw; a year later over sixty of these were eagerly debating key issues of reform. The revelations in Khrushchev's "secret speech" intensified these discussions. As younger Party members sought "a Polish road to socialism," conservatives were forced onto the defensive and the Warsaw regime's ideological underpinnings disintegrated. When Boleslaw Bierut, the Stalinist party chief, died suddenly

[handwritten margin note: devastating effects of Khrush. speech]

---

[21] *Pravda*, April 18, 1956.

[22] *Pravda*, June 3, 1956.

[23] *New York Times*, June 20, 1956, pp. 1, 4.

[24] Hoffman and Neal, pp. 432–34.

*Poland
manipulated*

in March 1956, Khrushchev flew immediately to Warsaw and helped engineer the selection of a conservative successor, Eduard Ochab.

The process of gradual liberalization in Poland ended after a workers' uprising in Poznan in June 1956 was finally suppressed by the Polish army. That action, however, undermined the army's morale. In late July Soviet leaders Bulganin and Zhukov, attending a special plenum of the Polish Central Committee, emphasized the need for socialist unity in light of alleged Western efforts to exploit the Poznan riots. Warned Bulganin: "Every country should go its own way to socialism, but we cannot permit this to be used to break up the solidarity of the peace camp. . . ."[25] But the Workers' Party leadership was splitting into Stalinist (Natolin) and reformist wings. Adopting a precarious middle position at the recent Seventh Plenum, Ochab flew right afterwards to confer with Khrushchev in Yalta. Gomulka's future role remained unresolved. Soon after Ochab returned to Warsaw, the Soviet ambassador there informed Khrushchev that "tumultuous dem-onstrations and general turmoil" had exploded at factories in some Polish cities with distinct anti-Soviet overtones. Demonstrators demanded the

*Pols
fight back*

withdrawal of Soviet troops from Poland. "We had every right to have troops in Poland," recalled Khrushchev. ". . . It looked to us as if Polish events were rushing forward on the crest of a giant anti-Soviet wave. . . . We were afraid Poland might break away from us at any moment."[26]

The Eighth Plenum of the Polish Central Committee convened on October 19, 1956, to select a new Politburo. A powerful Soviet delegation, including Khrushchev, Mikoyan, Molotov, and Lazar Kaganovich (earlier Khrushchev's Party patron), arrived in Warsaw that same day without any invitation and against the recommendations of Polish leaders. As the Soviet leaders proceeded to the meeting straight from the airport, Soviet tank forces from their bases in Wroclaw began advancing towards Warsaw. Coopted onto the Polish Central Committee, Gomulka was among the Polish leaders who conferred with the Soviets. Khrushchev recalled:

> It was a very stormy meeting, conducted in the most venomous, acrimonious atmosphere. . . . We added oil to the fire. . . . Our only worry was that Gomulka's elevation to the First Secretaryship* was partly achieved as a result of political machinations by certain anti-Soviet forces.

*Possible
conflict
Pols- USSR*

Gomulka declared: "Comrade Khrushchev, I've just received a report that some of your forces are moving toward Warsaw. I ask—*I demand*—that you order them to stop and return to their bases."[27] As the people and armed workers of Warsaw prepared to resist Soviet troops, a bloody and potentially catastrophic conflict loomed.

---

[25] Quoted in Zbigniew Brzezinski, *The Soviet Bloc: Unity and Conflict* (New York, 1960), p. 246.

[26] Khrushchev, *The Last Testament*, pp. 196–99.

*His election occurred at the end of this meeting.

[27] Khrushchev, *The Last Testament* pp. 203–04.

It was Khrushchev who blinked and issued orders to Soviet forces to halt. Polish unity and coolness and the moderation of leaders like Gomulka helped dissuade the Soviets from military intervention. The Soviet delegation returned to Moscow as a new Polish Politburo was elected with Gomulka as first secretary. The Polish-born Marshal Konstantin Rokossovskii, commanding Soviet forces in Poland, was ordered by Moscow to run for a seat on the Polish Politburo, but he failed to be elected and returned to the USSR. A Soviet-Polish compromise was achieved. Poland obtained full domestic autonomy while proclaiming loyalty to Soviet foreign policy and remaining firmly within the Warsaw Treaty Organization. That November Gomulka was warmly received in Moscow and stressed Soviet-Polish friendship and reliance upon the USSR, statements which reassured Khrushchev. Most Polish debts to the Soviet Union were then cancelled. Poland's "domesticism" became the model for treaties with other satellites. Preserving the substance of Soviet influence, it freed Moscow from the need for detailed supervision. That solution worked successfully in Poland because Gomulka, viewed as a martyr of Stalinist persecution, had enough prestige to contain popular discontent but was a moderate loyal to the USSR.

Such a course only succeeded in Hungary belatedly after a bloody popular revolution and Soviet armed intervention in November 1956. In June 1953 the Hungarian Stalinist leader, Matyas Rakosi, after meeting with Soviet leaders in Moscow, was forced to resign as premier (but remained Party first secretary), and was succeeded by a reformer, Imre Nagy. Nagy followed in Malenkov's wake by stressing legality and consumer industry and closing internment camps. However, in the spring of 1955, simultaneous with Malenkov's fall, Nagy was forced from the premiership, Rakosi recovered full power, and Nagy was expelled from the Politburo. Rakosi's return stimulated a powerful opposition movement that compelled him to make concessions, including rehabilitating those purged in Hungary after 1948. His Stalinist policies became an increasing liability for Moscow, and after Mikoyan visited Budapest in July 1956, Rakosi resigned "for health reasons." Ernö Gerö, Rakosi's successor as Party first secretary, followed a middle course between Stalinism and genuine reform, relying on the Hungarian army, secret police, and Soviet occupation forces. Meanwhile the intellectual opposition won over many workers and passive peasant support.

Early in October 1956, with public pressure mounting, Gerö and Janos Kadar, a subordinate, conferred in Moscow with Soviet leaders Mikoyan and Mikhail Suslov, the Politburo's ideological chief. Soon, Nagy was restored to Party membership and was supported by reformist elements.

The unpopular Gerö's refusal to step down as Party chief sparked a popular revolt in Budapest on October 23 that restored Imre Nagy as premier without any consultation with Moscow. That same evening G. Marosan of the Hungarian Politburo appealed in that body's name for Soviet military assistance and Soviet troops entered Budapest. Two days later Mikoyan and Suslov flew to Budapest, forced Gerö out as Party first secretary and had Kadar named to that position. On October 27 several leading non-Communists joined the Nagy government. The following day, Nagy concluded a ceasefire with the insurgents, and on the 29th Soviet troops began leaving Budapest. "Completely independently of Imre Nagy's demands," claimed Khrushchev, "we decided to pull our troops out of Budapest and to station them at the airfield outside the city."[28] By this time much of the Hungarian army had defected to the revolutionaries. On October 30, as Nagy was pushed toward fundamental political changes, a multiparty system was restored. The next day Nagy announced that Hungary intended to withdraw from the Warsaw Pact, and on November 1 he proclaimed the country's neutrality.

These latter moves, threatening to bring down Communism in Hungary and to disintegrate the Soviet bloc, finally forced Moscow's hand. Until November 1 Nagy had retained Soviet backing, but the decisions to leave the pact and make Hungary neutral were reached without consulting Moscow. Khrushchev suggests great indecision in the Kremlin whether to reintroduce Soviet troops into Budapest. Soviet leaders consulted the Chinese leadership on this and obtained reluctant support from Yugoslavia's Marshal Tito. After long deliberation the Soviet Presidium decided on November 1 that "it would be unforgivable, simply unforgivable, if we stood by and refused to assist our Hungarian comrades." Khrushchev recalled asking Marshal Konev, commanding Soviet troops in Hungary, how long it would take him to restore order there. "Three days, no longer," replied Konev. "We were all thinking about the well-being of the Hungarian working class and about the future of the Hungarian people," claimed Khrushchev piously.[29] The Anglo-French attack on Egypt then facilitated the Soviet military intervention. Party chief Kadar had split with the Nagy regime and literally went over to the Soviet camp in Uzhgorod. From there he formally requested Soviet intervention. On November 4 the Soviets sent 250,000 troops and 5,000 tanks against the Hungarian revolutionaries and crushed their resistance within a few days despite United Nations' demands for them to withdraw. Premier Nagy, who sought refuge in the Yugoslav embassy, was later turned over to the Soviet-installed Kadar government, tried, and shot.

Soviet armed suppression of the Hungarian Revolution showed that Moscow would not tolerate a non-Communist regime or even genuine national Communism, except in Yugoslavia, making Titoism somewhat less attractive in eastern Europe. It revealed that, because of the atomic standoff, the Soviet Union could act at will in its own sphere of interest without fear of Western intervention. Soviet action in Hungary proved that Moscow's domination of eastern Europe was based solely on military might that even a collective leadership could employ. The virtual dissolution within days of Communist power in Hungary revealed the fragility and unreliability of satellite armies and regimes. Khrushchev realized that the USSR must

---

[28] Khrushchev, *Khrushchev Remembers*, p. 417.

[29] Khrushchev, *Khrushchev Remembers*, pp. 418–20.

place its relations with eastern European countries on a more equitable basis by moving toward what he termed "a socialist commonwealth" and thus to liquidate one-sided, unfair economic arrangements. Since the West remained passive, Soviet intervention also discredited John F. Dulles' announced resolve to "roll back" Soviet control over eastern Europe. Communism had survived its year of crisis, but 1956 marked a rebirth of national differences artificially suppressed under Stalinism. In Hungary the Kadar regime moved gradually to implement some of Nagy's policies representing a marked liberalization and autonomy for Hungary.

Coinciding with Soviet intervention in Budapest, the Suez Crisis allowed Moscow to cover its brutal suppression of the Hungarian Revolution and to enhance its influence in an increasingly nationalist Arab world. Whereas in 1952 Stalin had criticized Egyptian leaders Muhammed Najib and Gamel Nasser as "bourgeois nationalists" and "stooges of Western imperialists," Khrushchev courted them actively urging them to reject ties with the West. American preoccupation with containing the USSR by building multinational alliances along its frontiers gave Moscow an opening to the Arab world in 1955–1956. Early in 1955 General Nasser had requested major Soviet military aid, and that October an Egyptian-Czechoslovak agreement (Prague covered for Moscow) promised to provide Egypt with major arms shipments and economic and technical assistance. Moscow's new warm relationship with Egypt enabled it to expand contacts with other Arab states, notably Syria.[30]

Although not a satellite, Egypt became dependent on Soviet aid. In July 1956, when the United States and Britain refused to finance the Aswan High Dam, Egypt's key modernization project, Cairo promptly announced the nationalization of the Suez Canal Company. Defending Nasser's right to nationalize the canal, Foreign Minister Dmitrii Shepilov warned the West that resort to force might provoke "a serious conflict which would encompass the whole of the Near and Middle East and perhaps go even further."[31] In late September, France and Britain, unable to obtain action from a London conference of canal users, took the issue to the UN Security Council. In the midst of negotiations Israel, on October 29, suddenly attacked Egypt. Then, on November 5, France and Britain supported Israel by invading Egypt. This allowed Khrushchev to stride forth as the protector of the Arabs. Moscow accused the Western powers and Israel of premeditated aggression to "crush the national-liberation movement of the Arab peoples" and "to restore the colonial system throughout the Middle East and North Africa." Foreign Minister Shepilov cabled the Security Council's president demanding a cease-fire and, without consulting Washington, threatened Soviet-American military intervention. Premier Bulganin stated that Moscow was "fully resolved to use force to crush the aggressors and

[30] Oles Smolansky, *The Soviet Union and the Arab East Under Khrushchev* (Lewisburg, PA, 1974), pp. 23–32.

[31] *Pravda*, August 22, 1956.

to restore peace in the Middle East."[32] The Soviets threatened to annihilate Israel and employ missiles against London and Paris unless they accepted a cease-fire. Because both Washington and Moscow opposed their military actions, France and Britain complied reluctantly and the crisis ended. Each Soviet move during the Suez Crisis, notes the American scholar, Oles Smolansky, was calculated to win Arab support. However, Moscow's failure to act at the decisive moment showed Arab leaders that the USSR dared not challenge American nuclear preeminence. Thus afterwards occurred a slow deterioration in Soviet-Egyptian relations.[33]

Khrushchev leadership threatened

Khrushchev emerged weakened domestically from the Hungarian and Suez events. To be sure, the Chinese strongly supported Soviet foreign policy as revealed by Chou En-lai's January 1957 visits to Moscow, Budapest, and Warsaw as he recognized the USSR as the leader of the socialist world. Beijing's loyalty was rewarded with economic and technical assistance later that year. However, at home Khrushchev faced major opposition from Stalinists who almost removed him from power. To reinforce his position Khrushchev in February 1957 proposed creating regional economic councils that would undermine the central economic ministries controlled by his opponents. The implementation of these reforms in May 1957 caused the Stalinists to take desperate counteraction. In June, after Khrushchev and Bulganin returned from a visit to Finland, his rivals in the Presidium voted out Khrushchev as General Secretary. Refusing to accept this, Khrushchev, securing the key support of the army under Marshal Zhukov, insisted that this issue be resolved by the entire Central Committee where he commanded majority support. After Zhukov arranged for Khrushchev's provincial supporters to be flown into Moscow, the Central Committee reversed the Presidium's action and expelled his chief rivals—Malenkov, Molotov, Kaganovich, and Shepilov—dubbed the "anti-Party group." Instead of being physically purged, they were assigned to obscure posts far from Moscow. (Molotov was named ambassador to Mongolia.) In March 1958 Bulganin was forced to resign as premier and Khrushchev assumed that post too. Marshal Zhukov was removed from the Presidium and accused of building a personality cult in the army. These moves formally ended the era of collective leadership and post-Stalin power struggle by reuniting top Party and State positions in Khrushchev's hands.

Khrushchev takes more power

Collective leadership Ends

Suggested Readings

Behbehani, Hashim. *The Soviet Union and Arab Nationalism, 1917–1966.* London and New York, 1986.

Bohlen, Charles E. *Witness to History, 1929–1969.* New York, 1973.

Brant, Stefan. *The East German Rising.* New York, 1957.

Brzezinski, Zbigniew. *The Soviet Bloc; Unity and Conflict.* Revised and enlarged. Cambridge, MA, 1967.

---

[32] *Pravda*, November 6, 1956.

[33] Smolansky, pp. 51–54.

Dallin, David J. *Soviet Foreign Policy After Stalin.* Philadelphia, 1961.

Gati, Charles. *Hungary and the Soviet Bloc.* Durham, NC, 1986.

Gehlen, Michael. *The Politics of Coexistence: Soviet Methods and Motives.* Bloomington, IN, 1967.

Hoffman, George W. and Fred W. Neal. *Yugoslavia and the New Communism.* New York, 1962.

Horelick, Arnold L. and Myron Rush, *Strategic Power and Soviet Foreign Policy.* Chicago, 1966.

Khrushchev, Nikita S. *Khrushchev Remembers.* Ed. and Trans. Strobe Talbott. Boston, 1970.

_____. *Khrushchev Remembers: The Last Testament.* Ed. and Trans. Strobe Talbott. Boston, 1974.

LaFeber, Walter. *America, Russia and the Cold War, 1945–1980.* 4th ed. New York, 1980.

Leonhard, W. *The Kremlin Since Stalin.* New York, 1962.

Linden, C. A. *Khrushchev and the Soviet Leadership, 1957–1964.* London, 1967.

Macintosh, J. M. *Strategy and Tactics of Soviet Foreign Policy.* London, 1962.

Nogee, Joseph L. and Robert Donaldson. *Soviet Foreign Policy Since World War II.* 4th ed. New York, 1992.

Rakowska-Harmstone, Teresa and Andrew Gyorgy, eds., *Communism in Eastern Europe.* Bloomington, IN, 1979.

Rush, Myron, ed., *The International Situation and Soviet Foreign Policy: Reports of Soviet Leaders.* Columbus, OH, 1970.

Smolansky, Oles M. *The Soviet Union and the Arab East Under Khrushchev.* Lewisburg, PA, 1974.

Syrop, K. *Spring in October: The Polish Revolution of 1956.* New York, 1958.

Tatu, Michel. *Power in the Kremlin: From Khrushchev to Kosygin.* New York, 1969.

Ulam, Adam B. *Titoism and the Cominform.* Cambridge, MA, 1952.

Wolfe, Bertram. *Khrushchev and Stalin's Ghost.* New York, 1957.

Zinner, Paul, ed., *National Communism and Popular Revolt in Eastern Europe.* New York, 1956.

_____. *Revolution in Hungary.* Cambridge, MA, 1961.

CHAPTER

10

KHRUSHCHEV AND PEACEFUL COEXISTENCE, 1957–1964

After defeating the "anti-Party group" in 1957 and assuming the premiership the next spring, Nikita S. Khrushchev emerged as the dominant Soviet leader. However, his opponents were scattered, not destroyed, and his position remained precarious throughout his seven years of personal power. Pressure on him mounted to score major successes abroad as his domestic policies faltered. Combined with his gambler's nature, those pressures triggered sudden gyrations in his foreign policy, notably towards the West. Officially, Soviet foreign policy remained based on the concept of peaceful coexistence between capitalism and the socialist world. On the crucial German question, despite repeated ultimatums to the Western powers, Khrushchev achieved little success. Meanwhile dissension grew within the Communist world, merely papered over by world conferences of Communist leaders in Moscow in 1957 and 1960. A second Soviet-Yugoslav dispute, followed by a growing rift with Red China, confirmed the rise of polycentrism within what had seemed to be a monolithic Communist bloc. The open schism with China after 1960 encouraged eastern European countries to assert greater autonomy or even to defy the USSR. Finally, the Cuban Missile Crisis of 1962 undermined Khrushchev's position fatally and contributed significantly to his removal from power in October 1964.

THE SECOND SOVIET-YUGOSLAV DISPUTE, 1957–1958

Belgrade hailed Khrushchev's victory over the conservative "anti-Party group" in June 1957. With Khrushchev's support, Marshal Josip Tito moved promptly towards full rapprochement with Moscow. On August 4 Radio Moscow declared: "Our views are identical in the majority of cases. . . . Every possibility exists for even broader and more fruitful cooperation between our countries."[1] Tito sought to meet with Khrushchev, hoping to confirm

---

[1]Quoted in Zbigniew Brzezinski, *The Soviet Bloc: Unity and Conflict* (Cambridge, MA, 1967), p. 310.

Yugoslav independence and win approval for greater diversity in eastern Europe. At a meeting in Bucharest in August the two leaders reached limited agreement. Khrushchev secured Yugoslav support for his foreign policy in Europe and the Middle East, and Tito agreed to participate in a November conference of Communist parties in Moscow.

However, it soon became evident that Khrushchev and Tito viewed the world very differently. Moscow's draft resolutions for the November conference, reiterating the Soviet cold war view of a world divided between two hostile blocs, disputed Yugoslav claims to neutrality. Moscow's denunciation of revisionism implied criticism of Yugoslav domestic policies. Sending Aleksandar Ranković and Edvard Kardelj to Moscow, Tito refused to attend the conference in person. In Moscow his colleagues faced demands considerably exceeding the draft. Chairman Mao Tse-tung of China insisted on a recognition of Soviet hegemony over the Communist world. The Yugoslav refusal to sign the final conference communiqué caused anger in Moscow, but no other Communist leader gave any support to the Yugoslav position.

Afterwards Belgrade and Moscow diverged rapidly. In the draft program of March 1958 for their Seventh Party Congress in Ljubljana, Slovenia, the Yugoslavs asserted that both the USSR and the United States were to blame for the Cold War; that each Communist state should determine its own road to socialism; and that the Soviet regime had departed from true Marxism-Leninism. When Soviet leaders objected to this and claimed that the Yugoslav draft exaggerated the evils of Stalinism, Tito toned down wording offensive to Moscow, but the Soviets remained dissatisfied and insisted that the entire Soviet bloc boycott the Ljubljana congress in April. When Ranković and Kardelj in Ljubljana sharply criticized Soviet actions, Moscow's ambassador walked out of the congress. Nonetheless, Belgrade still sought to prevent an open breach.

However, on May 5, 1958, *Jen Min Jih Pao*, an official Beijing organ, asserted that Titoism aimed at "splitting the international Communist movement and undermining the solidarity of the socialist countries." The Ljubljana communiqué, it declared, was "an anti-Marxist, anti-Leninist, out-and-out revisionist program."[2] The next day *Pravda* of Moscow confirmed Kremlin approval by reprinting this Chinese diatribe in full. Almost daily denunciations of the Yugoslav Communists followed, provoking this defiant response from *Borba*, the Yugoslav party organ: "If anybody thinks the Communists of Yugoslavia and the people of Yugoslavia can be shaken in their beliefs through unprincipled attacks, these are sheer illusions."[3] On June 3, Khrushchev, visiting Bulgaria, denounced Tito as a "Trojan horse" and denied that Yugoslavia was truly socialist. Tito retorted that Khrushchev had personally plotted the assault on Yugoslavia and denounced the Chinese as "warmongers." When even Poland's Wladyslaw Gomulka attacked Yu-

---

[2] *New York Times*, May 11, 1958.
[3] *Borba* (Belgrade), May 15, 1958.

goslav "revisionism," Belgrade, as in 1948, stood totally isolated from the Communist world.[4]

However, the new Soviet-Yugoslav breach was not as complete as that of 1948: there was no blockade nor threats of invasion. Belgrade's leaders realized that Khrushchev's foreign policy was basically pacific and that he had not reverted to Stalinism. Even in 1958–1959 on specific foreign policy issues Yugoslavia sided more often with Moscow than with the West. As the Yugoslavs reaffirmed their independence and concept of national Communism, Tito collaborated closely with non-aligned countries and hastened to restore good relations with the West.

SOVIET-WESTERN RELATIONS, 1957–1960

During the second term of U.S. President Dwight D. Eisenhower's presidency, Khrushchev's policies toward the West alternated between angry ultimatums and efforts to achieve accommodation with the United States. To Khrushchev, peaceful coexistence meant avoiding nuclear war and preventing West Germany from obtaining atomic weapons. Even a few bombs in the hands of West German militarists, he feared, might be used to blackmail the satellites or even the Soviet Union. Khrushchev supported strongly the Rapacki Plan of October 1957 (named after the Polish foreign minister Adam Rapacki) to create a nuclear-free zone in central Europe, including the two Germanies, Poland, and Czechoslovakia.

The successful launching of the world's first manmade satellite, Sputnik, on October 4, 1957, enhanced Soviet prestige in the Third World and caused great worry in the United States. Furthermore, the Soviet economy between 1950 and 1958 had grown more than 7 percent annually, almost 50 percent more than the American rate. Thus Khrushchev boasted that the Soviet Union was rapidly overtaking the United States as the most productive society. The USSR was no longer besieged by the West, argued Khrushchev, but was challenging it throughout the world on an increasingly equal basis.

Khrushchev's penchant for gambling was reflected in moves that touched off a second Berlin crisis. On November 27, 1958, he issued the Cold War's first ultimatum, demanding that the Western powers evacuate their 10,000 troops from Berlin within six months. Berlin would become a "free city," then the West would have to negotiate for continued access with an East German regime it did not recognize. With full NATO support, U.S. Secretary of State John Foster Dulles rejected Khrushchev's demands, refused to recognize East Germany, and threatened military retaliation if the West were denied access to Berlin. When Khrushchev produced a draft peace treaty to create a neutral Germany in March 1959, the West began to negotiate largely on Soviet terms. Alarmed by Khrushchev's threats, Prime Minister Harold MacMillan of Britain went to Moscow and made major concessions in order to have the Soviet ultimatum set aside. At a foreign

---

[4]George Hoffmann and Fred Neal, *Yugoslavia and the New Communism* (New York, 1962), pp. 448–51.

ministers' conference convened to solve the German dispute, the West was confronted with unacceptable Soviet demands. In order to prevent a breakdown of the talks and a breach with Moscow, American negotiators, appealing to Khrushchev's ego and apparently without consulting Eisenhower, invited him to visit the United States later that year. Khrushchev's acceptance temporarily defused the Berlin dispute.

In January 1959, in the midst of the Berlin crisis, Khrushchev delivered the main report to the Soviet Twenty-First Party Congress in a tone of aggressive optimism: the USSR within slightly over a decade would surpass the United States in per capita output. Warning that West Germany, aided by the Western powers, "is being turned into the main atomic and rocket base of NATO," Khrushchev urged swift conclusion of a German peace treaty. Denouncing Yugoslav "revisionism," he asserted that "the socialist camp . . . is a community of equal nations fighting for peace and a better life for the working people." Noting Politburo member Anastas Mikoyan's warm reception in the United States on a mission to establish contacts with American business leaders, Khrushchev sounded a positive note on Soviet-American relations:

> The Soviet Union . . . has more than once expressed its sincere desire to normalize relations with the United States, and has backed its words with deeds. . . . Our two countries have never had any territorial claims on each other, nor have they any today. There are no grounds for clashes between our two peoples. . . . We welcome the efforts of all Americans who advocate an end to the "cold war" and support peaceful coexistence and cooperation between all countries.[5]

Proposing atomic-free zones for the Far East and central Europe, Khrushchev clearly sought to block China and West Germany from acquiring nuclear weapons.

Over strong Chinese objections, Khrushchev in September 1959 visited the United States at President Eisenhower's invitation. "I'll admit I was curious to have a look at America . . . ," recalled Khrushchev. "America occupied a special position in our thinking and view of the world." At Mikoyan's suggestion, and in a sharp break with Stalinist traditions, he took along his wife, Nina Petrovna Khrushcheva. With his curiosity and openness Khrushchev made a strong and generally favorable impression on Americans. Because no Russian ruler had ever visited the United States, he regarded the trip as a personal triumph. Also, it was for him another sign of Soviet-American equality: "We were proud we had finally forced the United States to recognize the need for closer contact with us." Khrushchev attributed this to growing Soviet economic and military strength. His talks with President Eisenhower at Camp David outside Washington, D.C.,

---

[5]"Khrushchev's Report to the XXI Congress," in Myron Rush, ed., *The International Situation and Soviet Foreign Policy: Reports of Soviet Leaders* (Columbus, OH, 1970), pp. 187–97.

convinced him that the United States would risk war only under extreme provocation and induced him to press for major concessions on Berlin while advocating détente. He also visited Iowa to view American farming methods. The "spirit of Camp David," though amiable, produced few concrete agreements. However, the two leaders agreed to hold a great power summit in Geneva, Switzerland, the following spring, then Eisenhower was to visit the USSR. On the results of his American visit Khrushchev commented:

> We were plowing virgin soil . . . ; we broke the ice which had held our relations in a paralyzing grip. Now it remained for our diplomats to remove the stubborn chunks of ice from our path and clear the way for further improvement in relations. . . . My talks with Eisenhower represented a colossal moral victory.[6]

Addressing the Supreme Soviet in January 1960 Khrushchev declared that the international situation had definitely improved: "The clouds of war menace have begun to disperse. . . . International tensions are beginning to relax and the 'cold war' champions are suffering defeat." Revealing the plans for a summit meeting in Paris in mid-May, Khrushchev predicted that "a spirit of realism, frankness, and cooperation will prevail. . . ."[7] Prior to the Geneva summit, Khrushchev spent eleven days in France at the invitation of its independent-minded president, Charles de Gaulle.

However, by late April hopes of resolving Soviet-Western differences had dwindled in the face of sharp statements from Moscow and Washington. During his early spring trips to Indonesia and France, Khrushchev warned that unless a German settlement based on previous Soviet proposals was reached, Western occupation rights in West Berlin would be ended by a Soviet peace treaty with East Germany. On April 20, criticizing Khrushchev's pronouncements on Berlin, U.S. Undersecretary of State Douglas Dillon added that "the so-called German Democratic Republic [East Germany] is one of the outstanding myths in a vast Communist web of prodigious mythology"; he reaffirmed American support for West Berlin. Reiterating Soviet policy on Berlin, Khrushchev interpreted Dillon's statement as changing the American position outlined at the Camp David talks and warned that when "such hotheads [as Dillon] start invoking force and not right and justice, it is but natural that this force will be countered with the force of the other side."[8]

On May 5, 1960—just before the scheduled Paris summit—Khrushchev suddenly announced that the Soviets had downed a U-2 spy plane near Sverdlovsk after it had violated Soviet air space. The State Department claimed erroneously that it was only a "weather research" plane. When

---

[6] Nikita S. Khrushchev, *Khrushchev Remembers: The Last Testament* (Boston, 1974), pp. 368–415.

[7] Khrushchev to the Supreme Soviet, January 14, 1960, in Rush, pp. 209–10.

[8] Quoted in Walter LaFeber, *America, Russia and the Cold War, 1945–1980*, 4th ed. (New York, 1980), pp. 210–11.

Khrushchev produced film from the plane and revealed that its pilot, Francis Gary Powers, was in Soviet custody, President Eisenhower assumed full responsibility for overflights that had occurred since 1956. "The time had come to pin down the Americans and expose their lies," noted Khrushchev. Having portrayed Eisenhower as a peaceloving moderate, Khrushchev now had to react violently to the U-2 affair in order to cover himself before his colleagues. Eisenhower, commented Khrushchev graphically, "had, so to speak, offered us his rear end, and we obliged him by kicking it as hard as we could."[9] En route to Paris, Khrushchev insisted that Eisenhower apologize for this incident. When the president refused, the Geneva Summit, already undermined by the Sino-Soviet quarrel and the Berlin dispute, was cancelled. Khrushchev also withdrew his invitation to Eisenhower to visit the Soviet Union. The U-2 affair made true entente between the two superpowers impossible during the rest of the Eisenhower presidency. "I'm still convinced we handled the [U-2] matter correctly," later wrote Khrushchev. "I'm proud we gave a sharp but fully justified rebuff to the world's mightiest state, that we put the Americans in their place when they violated our sovereignty."[10]

Khrushchev's final visit to the United States in the fall of 1960 was scarcely triumphant. Without invitation by President Eisenhower, Khrushchev appeared before the United Nations during the Congo crisis to propose that the office of Secretary General (he was then feuding with Secretary General Dag Hammarskjöld) be replaced by a three-man commission representing socialist, Western, and neutralist countries. Discomfited by lack of support for his "troika" scheme, during a speech by Britain's Harold MacMillan Khrushchev removed his shoe and banged it boorishly on his desk; other Communist representatives followed suit. That incident helped convince some of his colleagues that it was time to retire Khrushchev.

THE SINO-SOVIET QUARREL AND ITS IMPACT, 1957–1964

In 1960 the long-simmering quarrel between the two Communist giants–the Soviet Union and China–erupted publicly. Since Mao's first visit to Moscow in 1949–1950 it had been evident that he was no Soviet stooge and that Sino-Soviet relations would differ basically from those with the satellites. Mao and the Chinese first reacted negatively to Khrushchev's attacks on Stalin at the Twentieth Party Congress because they were good Stalinists. Meeting Mao at the international Communist conference in Moscow in 1957, Khrushchev recalls: "I was struck by how much he sounded like Stalin."[11]

At issue throughout the early years of the Sino-Soviet dispute was whether Moscow would aid the Chinese develop a thermonuclear capacity

---

[9]Khrushchev, pp. 446–51.
[10]Khrushchev, p. 461.
[11]Khrushchev, p. 252.

and perhaps even supply China with a sample atomic bomb. An initial Soviet pledge to do so in October 1957 temporarily improved Sino-Soviet relations and prevented serious friction at the November Moscow conference. Afterwards Khrushchev's efforts to promote détente with the United States alienated Beijing, which then had adopted an ultra-leftist course at home and abroad. The Chinese were also antagonized by Khrushchev's refusal to assist them militarily against the United States during the Sino-American crisis in 1958 over a threatened Chinese attack on Taiwan and the offshore islands. Deteriorating Sino-Soviet relations then induced Khrushchev in June 1959 to cancel his offer to help Beijing develop atomic weapons.

Which basic factors underlay the momentous Sino-Soviet quarrel? One was clearly geopolitical. The emergence after 1949 of a unified Communist China constituted an increasingly formidable challenge to Soviet domination of Asia and represented a potential threat to underpopulated Soviet Siberia. Whereas Moscow aimed to employ Chinese bases to develop a major new naval role in the Pacific, a unified Maoist China had compelled the Soviets in 1954 to relinquish their naval base at Port Arthur, regained from Nationalist China in 1945. The Chinese suspected Khrushchev of seeking to bring China under Soviet military control. For their part, the Soviets viewed Chinese obduracy as obstructing the Communist bloc's strategic advantages.

Ideological differences contributed significantly to the outbreak and deepening of the dispute. The two countries were in different phases of their revolutions, and their Communist parties relied upon different social elements: primarily workers in Russia and peasants in China. Whereas during Stalin's lifetime, Mao Tse-tung deferred to him as the senior world Communist leader, afterwards Mao claimed that honor for himself and refused to accept tutelage from a Soviet collective leadership or from Khrushchev. Adopting a militant line of promoting revolutions in Africa and Asia, Beijing began accusing Khrushchev's USSR of revisionism for avoiding conflict with the capitalist world and for seeking warmer relations with the West. Radical Chinese domestic policies drew sharpening Soviet criticism after Mao claimed that his "great leap forward" might well bring China to the goal of Communism before the Soviet Union could reach it. Ideological differences were revealed also in sharp exchanges over Khrushchev's 1957 reconciliation with Tito's Yugoslavia. Moscow and Beijing engaged in an intense competition to control the world Communist movement and to determine its policies.

Economic issues played a subordinate yet contributory role in the Sino-Soviet rift. The Chinese nursed a number of real and imagined economic grievances against the USSR. In 1946 when Soviet troops left Manchuria, they moved several billions of dollars worth of industrial equipment into the USSR. Subsequently, the Soviets supplied considerable sums in economic aid to China, but as loans at interest, not as grants. Soviet economic assistance was niggardly, complained the Chinese, as the USSR proved far more generous to neutralist India than to them. Then in 1959

Moscow, citing Chinese mistreatment of Soviet technicians, withdrew them from China and halted all economic and technical assistance.

Territorial frictions and disputes became important only after the dispute became public. Many portions of their common 4,000-mile frontier had never been delimited and provided a basis for subsequent conflict. Only in 1963 did Beijing assert that Russia's acquisition of the Maritime Province with Vladivostok and the Ili district of Sinkiang had been the unfair product of European nineteenth-century imperialism and demanded these territories back. Continued Soviet domination of Mongolia, formerly a Chinese dependency, also sparked friction between the two powers.

Looking at the dispute chronologically, between 1956 and 1960 sporadic but increasing tension occurred between China and the USSR, but it was carefully concealed by both sides, so that as late as early 1960 President Eisenhower did not realize its significance. Destalinization in the USSR provoked initial Chinese dissatisfaction with Khrushchev in 1956, but the two large Communist powers cooperated fairly closely during the crisis in eastern Europe later that year. Apparent unity prevailed at the November 1957 Communist party meetings in Moscow. Mao catered to his Soviet hosts by declaring: "The Communist Party of the Soviet Union should be the one and only center of the international Communist movement, and the rest of us should be united around that center." Also, just before the conference in a speech at Moscow University, Mao provided the most complete endorsement of Soviet hegemony over world Communism of any delegate, stating, "The socialist camp must have one head, and that head can only be the USSR." Khrushchev claimed he had reacted skeptically to these words. He later said, "We had the unsettling feeling that sooner or later, friction was bound to develop between our countries and our parties."[12] On the issue of nuclear war Mao even then diverged in a major way from Khrushchev's position. He shocked Soviet leaders by proclaiming: "No matter what kind of war breaks out, we will win. If the imperialists attack China, we may lose 300 million, but we'll get to work and produce more babies."[13]

Following serious Sino-Soviet friction during the crisis over Taiwan in 1958 a brief but partial détente in their relations ensued, but it soon was undermined by the extreme policies of the so-called Chinese "Cultural Revolution." By mid-1959, as he sought accommodation with the United States, Khrushchev strove to induce Beijing to abandon its aggressive ideological and political strategy for the Communist world. Their relations deteriorated rapidly after Khrushchev's refusal in June 1959 to supply China with further atomic technology. By August both sides were convinced that a breach in relations was imminent.[14]

---

[12]Khrushchev, p. 254.

[13]Khrushchev, p. 255.

[14]William Griffith, *The Sino-Soviet Rift* (Cambridge, MA, 1964), pp. 16–18.

By the time of his third visit to Beijing in mid-1959, Khrushchev sensed upon his arrival the growing chill in Sino-Soviet relations. The Chinese, he claims, were doing everything to discredit Soviet specialists sent to help them build new industrial plants. Instead of thanking Moscow for its help, the Chinese resented the presence of Soviet experts in China. According to Khrushchev, "They smeared everything Soviet." Meanwhile Chinese students in the USSR were allegedly circulating anti-Soviet leaflets and organizing anti-Soviet demonstrations on Soviet trains. In China gangs of drunken Red Guards abused Soviet advisors and ransacked their homes. "That was the thanks we got for building whole plants for the Chinese and for giving credits at 2–2½ percent," recalled Khrushchev.[15] Finally, Moscow decided to recall all its advisors and to expel Chinese students from the USSR. Khrushchev did not attribute such hostility to the Chinese people but mostly to Mao and his colleagues: "He's acting like a lunatic on a throne and is turning this country [China] upside down."[16]

It was Mao who brought the long-smouldering Sino-Soviet quarrel into the open. In April 1960, *Red Flag* of Beijing published an article entitled "Long Live Leninism!"—later attributed to Mao personally—castigating Khrushchev's peaceful coexistence with capitalism, especially with the United States. Without referring to the USSR directly, it attacked "revisionists" and "Yugoslav deviationists." Clearly this referred to Khrushchev's efforts at détente with the West. A nuclear war, proclaimed the article, would destroy imperialism but not the socialist camp: "The victorious people would create very swiftly a civilization thousands of times higher than the capitalist system and a truly beautiful system for themselves."[17]

In June, Khrushchev counterattacked at the Romanian Party Congress in Bucharest. Recently an Albanian delegation had gone to Beijing and had adopted its anti-Soviet position. In Bucharest the Albanians, advocating a strong pro-Chinese position, spoke out openly against the USSR. Khrushchev had bitter written attacks on Chinese leaders circulated at the Congress, accusing them of being nationalists, adventurers, and "madmen" seeking to unleash nuclear war. He also argued violently with the Chinese delegate, Peng Chen. At Bucharest, noted Khrushchev, only the Chinese and Albanians disagreed with the majority about the development of the world Communist movement.[18]

That summer Khrushchev, seeking to restore unity in the Communist movement, convened a world congress in Moscow. Eighty-one Communist parties attended, and the Soviets achieved surface agreement with a compromise statement on peaceful coexistence while denouncing Yugoslav revisionism. However, behind the scenes a violent quarrel erupted between

---

[15] Khrushchev, pp. 263–64.

[16] Khrushchev, pp. 265, 279.

[17] "Long Live Leninism!" *Red Flag* (Beijing), April 16, 1960, *Documents on International Affairs, 1960* (London, 1964), pp. 197–207.

[18] Khrushchev, pp. 266–67.

Khrushchev and the chief Chinese delegate who attacked Khrushchev personally for criticizing Chairman Mao, being "soft on capitalism," and allegedly favoring India over China.

During the brief lull that ensued, Moscow increased pressure on Albania to accept Soviet policies. That deceptive calm was shattered at the Twenty-Second Soviet Party Congress in October 1961, which the Albanians refused to attend. Their leader, Enver Hoxha, praised Stalin and denounced Khrushchev. At the Congress Khrushchev excoriated Hoxha. In December the USSR severed relations with Albania, now firmly in China's camp. During the next year, with China the true target, Moscow denounced Albania; the Chinese attacked Yugoslav revisionism when they really meant the USSR. By mid-1963 the Chinese were attacking Khrushchev's chief domestic and foreign policies. In July Beijing issued maps showing the Maritime Province of the USSR as Chinese territory seized illegally by imperial Russia in the 1850s. This territorial dispute completed the breach between Moscow and Beijing.

The Sino-Soviet breach had a major impact on intrabloc relations in eastern Europe. Albania's defiance frustrated Khrushchev since the country was shielded territorially by Yugoslavia. Subsidized by China, Albania continued to denounce Khrushchev and his successors with impunity as it continued ultra-Stalinist domestic policies.

Romania exploited Sino-Soviet differences to play between the giants and win Soviet concessions. Rumors kept reaching Moscow, noted Khrushchev, that Romanian Communist leaders were criticizing the USSR at closed Party meetings. By 1963 streets in Bucharest named after Russians were being renamed. Soviet leaders, noted Khrushchev, wrote the Romanians: "Even if you don't like us, the fact remains that history has made us neighbors, and you're stuck with us. . . . Now that Romania is a socialist country, there is no reason for us not to have fraternal relations."[19]

At official Soviet-Romanian party discussions Khrushchev discerned no divergence over China, but Moscow's relations with Romania continued to deteriorate. Bucharest's dissatisfaction was partly territorial: Bessarabia and Moldavia, Romanian until World War II, had been reincorporated in the USSR in 1945. More important were a hitherto repressed and now resurgent nationalism and economic factors. As Romania sought greater freedom to trade with western Europe and develop its economy independently, Bucharest objected increasingly to planning in Comecon dominated by the Soviet Union. The Soviet refusal to allow Romania to build a proposed steel mill at Galati convinced Bucharest that Moscow aimed to relegate Romania to being a colony producing raw materials and food for the Soviet Union. At the June 1962 Comecon meeting Bucharest rejected Soviet demands to abandon its plans for heavy industrial construction and refused to yield its economic sovereignty. During 1963 Romania proclaimed neutrality between the USSR and China, its ambassador returned to Albania,

---

[19]Khrushchev, pp. 230–31.

and Romania began voting against the USSR in the United Nations. Thus a formerly obedient satellite emancipated itself partially from Soviet control revealing the Soviet bloc's fragility.

The Sino-Soviet quarrel was a potent factor in promoting polycentrism in the bloc. The emergence of a disaffected and powerful China encouraged smaller Communist states to broaden their autonomy. The USSR remained as suzerain in most of eastern Europe, but its socialist partners no longer jumped in unison obediently as under Stalin. Western Europe's growing prosperity and increasing contacts with bloc countries complicated maintaining Soviet control. East European nationalism was reborn, stimulated by a West idealized by much of the youth. Clearly uncertain how to handle the bloc's growing complexities, Khrushchev tried to govern it and the USSR by consent rather than force. Yet Marxist-Leninist ideology, which Khrushchev genuinely believed in and sought to use as a common language, had largely atrophied, while attempted economic integration through Comecon sparked nationalist resistance. Khrushchev's concept of a "socialist commonwealth" based on equality met multiple challenges. Nonetheless, Moscow still coordinated bloc countries' foreign and military policies, except for defiant Albania.

KHRUSHCHEV, KENNEDY, AND THE CUBAN MISSILE CRISIS, 1961–1962

John F. Kennedy's election as United States president in November 1960 encouraged Khrushchev to seek a striking victory against a young and inexperienced leader. Khrushchev desperately needed successes abroad to salvage his precarious position in the Politburo and to handle growing economic problems. Opportunity beckoned in January 1959 after the triumph in Cuba of Fidel Castro over the unpopular Batista dictatorship. At first Castro's victory was welcomed in the United States as a triumph of democracy, but soon it grew evident he was relying on Communists for personnel and on Communism to defy the United States. Castro's emergence posed a dilemma for Moscow. Should it embrace a political adventurer and become involved close to American shores? Would Castro prove reliable and controllable? After the abortive Geneva summit of May 1960, Soviet-Cuban relations tightened as they deteriorated with the United States. As Castro acted as a full-fledged Communist, Moscow supplied Cuba with arms and technology and bought Cuban sugar. Khrushchev warned Washington that the United States was no longer immune to Soviet rockets. If need be Soviet artillerymen would support the Cuban people if the United States intervened militarily in Cuba. The Monroe Doctrine, he added, was a thing of the past. For the next two years Cuba became the key problem in Soviet-American relations.

In April 1961 Cuban exiles, supported by the American Central Intelligence Agency, invaded Cuba at the Bay of Pigs in an operation planned under Eisenhower and authorized by President Kennedy against his better judgment. Although the Soviets knew about the CIA preparations, Moscow did not warn the United States against undertaking an invasion. Poorly planned and inadequately supported from Washington, the Bay of Pigs operation met swift and humiliating defeat by Castro's forces, enhancing his and Khrushchev's confidence.

Two months later Khrushchev and Kennedy held a summit meeting in Vienna, Austria, a neutral site. They discussed issues that Khrushchev and Eisenhower had failed to resolve, notably Germany's future. Kennedy's position on that differed little from Eisenhower's, but Kennedy, noted Khrushchev, appeared to grasp better the concept of peaceful coexistence and had already advocated it publicly. Although they reached no significant agreements, Khrushchev developed a respect and liking for Kennedy that would prove most important the following year:

> John Kennedy and I met man to man, as the two principal representatives of our countries. He felt perfectly confident to answer questions and make points on his own. This was to his credit, and he rose in my estimation at once. He was, so to speak, both my partner and my adversary. . . . He wouldn't make any hasty decisions which might lead to military conflict. A man like this I could respect.[20]

However, Khrushchev in Vienna sought to frighten Kennedy with harsh ideological diatribes and threatened to sign an accord with East Germany by December 1961 if no all-German peace treaty had been concluded by then. Khrushchev has confirmed that he felt sorry for a youthful, apparently weak Kennedy and regretted that their Vienna meeting deepened the Cold War.

Another Berlin crisis heated up soon afterwards. Showing American resolve to resist Khrushchev's ultimatum, Kennedy sent to Berlin General Lucius Clay, who had been involved in the 1948 airlift. Khrushchev countered with Marshal Ivan Konev and described Berlin as the sore blister on America's foot in Europe. In August 1961 East Germany with Moscow's blessing suddenly constructed the Berlin Wall sealing off West Berlin from East Germany. It halted abruptly an alarming tide of refugees to West Germany from the east that was undermining the East German regime. In Berlin Soviet and American tank forces confronted each other in an incident that could have provoked serious trouble but fortunately did not. Soviet belligerence over Berlin aimed to prevent West Germany from obtaining nuclear weapons and to give Khrushchev leverage over China and Kremlin conservatives.

Khrushchev sounded warmer themes at the Twenty-Second Party Congress in Moscow in October 1961. Reporting to the Congress, he noted

---

[20] Khrushchev, pp. 497–98.

that Foreign Minister Andrei Gromyko had reported that Western leaders wished to solve the German question in a mutually acceptable fashion.

> If the Western Powers show readiness to settle the German problem, the issue of a time limit for the signing of a German peace treaty will no longer be so important; in that case, we shall not insist that a peace treaty absolutely must be signed before December 31, 1961.[21]

Khrushchev again urged the creation of atomic-free zones in central Europe and the Far East. After the chief Chinese delegate, Chou En-lai, had denounced the United States as the chief enemy of peace, Foreign Minister Gromyko praised the Vienna Summit as a momentous event and made what sounded like a plea for a Soviet-American alliance:

> Our country places special importance on the character of the relations between the two giants—the Soviet Union and the United States. If those two countries united their efforts in the cause of peace, who would dare and who would be in a position to threaten peace? Nobody. There is no such power in the world.[22]

Gromyko's statement implied a Soviet-American accord against Beijing. The Twenty-Second Congress, apparently marking the zenith of Khrushchev's power, saw further denunciations of Stalin, but the increasingly open Chinese challenge revealed his vulnerability.

As 1962 began Khrushchev's priorities in foreign affairs remained to somehow prevent China from becoming a nuclear power, or at least to control its nuclear role; keep West Germany from obtaining atomic weapons; and to sign a German peace treaty to perpetuate the division of Germany. Moscow's interest in atomic disarmament and nuclear free zones now appeared genuine as it sought to persuade the Chinese that they needed no atomic weapons because the USSR would protect them. Anyway, what good were only a few atomic bombs? However, Soviet-American negotiations in Geneva on nuclear disarmament in July 1962 proved inconclusive.

The Soviet decision to install nuclear missiles in Cuba was reached in June or July 1962. For some time Khrushchev had been preoccupied as to how to prevent another American invasion of Cuba:

> It was during my visit to Bulgaria that I had the idea of installing missiles with nuclear warheads in Cuba without letting the United States find out they were there until it was too late to do anything about them.[23]

---

[21] Rush, pp. 264–65.

[22] Quoted in Adam Ulam, *Expansion and Coexistence: Soviet Foreign Policy, 1917–1973,* 2nd ed. (New York, 1974), pp. 656–57.

[23] Nikita S. Khrushchev, *Khrushchev Remembers* (Boston, 1970), p. 493.

He knew he must first inform Castro and secure his consent. If the Soviets could install the missiles secretly, Washington could not destroy them without exposing the American east coast to devastating attack. Khrushchev emphasized:

> When we put our ballistic missiles in Cuba, we had no desire to start a war. On the contrary, our principal aim was only to deter America from starting a war. We were well aware that a war which started over Cuba would quickly expand into a world war. . . . We wanted to keep the Americans from invading Cuba . . . by confronting them with our missiles.[24]

Khrushchev failed to admit to the broader economic and strategic motives for his Cuban adventure. By the summer of 1962 he needed a bold stroke to redress a strategic balance that had tilted radically in favor of the United States in nuclear arms. At home he faced a rising criticism for alleged economic failures and political blunders. By April he had raised the question of deploying missiles in Cuba in the Politburo but found some of his colleagues dubious; Gromyko and apparently Politburo leader Mikoyan warned of the American response. However, by June a decision was reached and orders were issued to prepare medium- and intermediate-range missiles and a force of 40,000 Soviet troops to be sent to Cuba. By restoring rough nuclear parity with the United States, this move would balance off American nuclear missiles in Turkey. Once installed in Cuba, Soviet missiles could be utilized, believed Khrushchev, as bargaining chips to obtain a German peace treaty, block nuclear weapons for West Germany, and secure an atom-free zone in the Far East.

While visiting Moscow in July, Raul Castro, Fidel's brother, learned that the Soviets would install missiles in Cuba, but was not given the details. In August, Che Guevara, a leading Cuban Communist, went to Moscow to discover the precise Soviet intentions. At the end of that visit a Soviet communiqué stated vaguely that to protect Cuba from "aggressive imperialist threats," the USSR would send arms and technicians to train Cubans in their use. In August and September large Soviet shipments to Cuba roused American suspicions. On September 4 President Kennedy warned Moscow that if nuclear missiles were being installed in Cuba, "the gravest issues would arise."[25] Meanwhile the Soviets sought to lull Kennedy into complacency with assurances that no action would be taken on the German question until after the November congressional elections.

On October 14 a routine American reconnaissance overflight of Cuba revealed that the Soviets were constructing twenty-four launching pads for

---

[24]Khrushchev, *Khrushchev Remembers*, pp. 495–96.
[25]Quoted in Ulam, p. 667.

medium-range missiles and sixteen for intermediate-range missiles.[26] Had they been completed much of the American east coast would have been exposed to atomic attack from Cuba. American leaders then debated how to counter this threat. A "war faction" of Dean Acheson, General Maxwell Taylor and the Joint Chiefs of Staff urged an air strike against the missile sites even if Soviet technicians there were killed. Undersecretary of State George Ball gradually built support for a sea blockade to prevent further Soviet ships from reaching Cuba. Supporting this, Defense Secretary Robert MacNamara argued that an air strike could be launched if naval action failed. Attorney General Robert Kennedy, the president's brother, backed this idea, which was adopted. Apparently Khrushchev believed that the United States was basically peaceloving and would not undertake a nuclear strike against the USSR when it discovered the missile emplacements despite its major lead in intercontinental missiles.

In a dramatic speech on October 22 President Kennedy, announcing the discovery of the Soviet missiles, declared a naval blockade of Cuba. Initially, this triggered an alert of Soviet rocket, submarine, and air forces and of the Warsaw Pact. However, the next day Moscow, deciding wisely not to force the sea blockade, sought to salvage something through correspondence. Khrushchev and Kennedy exchanged letters that soon produced an acceptable compromise. Recalled Khrushchev:

> I dictated the messages and conducted the exchange from our side. I spent one of the most dangerous nights at the Council of Ministers office in the Kremlin. I slept on a couch in my office—and I kept my clothes on. . . . I was ready for alarming news to come any moment, and I wanted to be ready to react immediately.[27]

By October 26 Khrushchev had decided to withdraw the Soviet missiles from Cuba if Kennedy would pledge not to invade the island. A second Khrushchev note suggested swapping the Cuban missile bases for similar American bases in Turkey, but Kennedy accepted the initial Khrushchev offer, and the crisis ended to the enormous relief of all concerned. The world had stood on the brink of nuclear war. Declared a *Pravda* writer and Khrushchev confidant: "We have lived through the most difficult week since World War II."[28]

Putting the best possible interpretation on the outcome in order to save face, Khrushchev affirmed that resolution of the Cuban crisis represented an historic landmark: "For the first time in history, the United States pledged publicly not to invade one of their neighbors and not to interfere in its internal affairs." He claimed he had saved Cuba from an American invasion and produced de facto American recognition of Castro's Cuba. However, the Cuban venture actually was a disaster for Khrushchev, one from which

---

[26]Arthur Schlesinger, Jr., *A Thousand Days: John Kennedy in the White House* (Boston, 1965), p. 796.

[27]Khrushchev, *Khrushchev Remembers*, p. 497.

[28]Quoted in Ulam, p. 675.

he never made a full political recovery. It discredited his foreign policy approach in the Politburo, which viewed the crisis as typical of his "hairbrained schemes." Khrushchev's bold attempt to solve his major foreign policy problems had failed. Soviet weakness in the missile race with the United States was clearly revealed.

The Chinese rejoiced maliciously at Khrushchev's discomfiture. During the crisis Beijing had backed Moscow with bellicose statements. But once it ended, they rubbed salt in Khrushchev's wounds by questioning his recklessness in placing missiles in Cuba, then capitulating in cowardly fashion to the demands of American imperialism. Chinese leaders conspicuously absented themselves from the November 7 celebrations of the anniversary of the Bolshevik Revolution.

THE AFTERMATH OF CUBA AND THE FALL OF KHRUSHCHEV, 1962–1964

Following the Cuban affair Khrushchev's declining authority was reflected in the intensifying Sino-Soviet quarrel and Moscow's loosening hold over eastern Europe. China was preempting the earlier Soviet role in the Third World where Moscow now appeared conservative and defensive. Kennedy's enhanced prestige after Cuba helped induce Khrushchev to seek limited agreements with the United States in order to reduce dangers of accidental nuclear war. Symptomatic of his weakened position, many of Khrushchev's domestic plans were reversed or blocked in the Politburo. Between December 1962 and March 1963 Khrushchev acquiesced in a partial rehabilitation of Stalin.

On December 12, 1962, Khrushchev sought to justify his policies concerning the Cuban Missile Crisis in a speech to the Supreme Soviet. Blaming the crisis on aggressive American efforts to destroy Castro's Cuba, he justified installing the missiles by citing "exclusively humanitarian motives—Cuba needed weapons as a means of deterring the aggressors." Moscow, he claimed, had proposed the solution and thus had saved the peace: "The Soviet Union and the forces of peace and socialism have proved that they are in a position to impose peace on the advocates of war." It had been reason, the security of peoples, and world peace that had triumphed, Khrushchev asserted.[29]

By mid-1963 Khrushchev seemingly had regained the political initiative, although his room for maneuver was narrowed by Chinese hostility. At a Central Committee plenum in June, Khrushchev renewed his assaults on Stalin and the "anti-Party group." Again seeking support from the West, Khrushchev's diplomats concluded an accord on July 25, 1963, with the United States and Great Britain to end tests of nuclear weapons in the atmosphere, outer space, and under water. However, the powers failed to agree to ban underground tests because Moscow refused to allow the

---

[29]Rush, pp. 277–81.

essential on-site inspections. Nor was there a non-proliferation agreement, because Khrushchev realized that Beijing would oppose that adamantly. Such restraint by Khrushchev did not prevent angry rhetoric from Beijing after the test ban treaty that made the Sino-Soviet quarrel seemingly insoluble. However, that may have facilitated other Soviet accords with the United States. That summer a "hot line" was established between Moscow and Washington to allow immediate communication in order to prevent misunderstandings that might escalate into nuclear war.

At a special plenum of the Soviet Central Committee on February 14–15, 1964, whose documents were made public two months later, Moscow responded sharply to Chinese attacks. The main report by Mikhail Suslov, the top Soviet ideologist, depicted Mao Tse-tung as another Stalin aiming to extend his personal dictatorship over the world Communist movement. Mao allegedly sought to "tower god-like over all the Marxist-Leninist parties and would decide all questions of their policy and activity according to his whim." Closing ranks, the plenum stressed Soviet party unity behind Khrushchev, glorified as "a passionate revolutionary . . . , an indefatigable fighter for peace and Communism. . . ."[30] The personal Mao–Khrushchev feud blocked any Sino-Soviet settlement during their tenure of office.

In August 1964 the Japanese press published a Mao interview with several Japanese socialists; *Pravda* issued a summary with commentary September 2. Mao denounced the USSR as an imperialist country that had seized parts of Romania and Poland after expelling "the local inhabitants." Accusing Russia of appropriating the Amur region and Mongolia from China in the nineteenth century, Mao claimed large parts of Soviet Siberia. He also demanded that the USSR return the Kurile Islands to Japan. *Pravda*'s response to all this abuse was remarkably mild.

Khrushchev's sudden fall from power in mid-October 1964 resulted from long-standing failures in foreign and domestic policy and from moves that alienated key Party and army leaders. An embarrassing political "testament" by the Italian Communist leader, Palmiro Togliatti, who died in August 1964 while on vacation in the USSR, sharply criticized Khrushchev's domestic and foreign policies and revealed that the Soviet leader's prestige was gravely impaired. A coalition of most of his Politburo colleagues, backed by the KGB, prepared to remove Khrushchev while he was vacationing in the Crimea. The powerful Politburo leader, Mikhail Suslov, summoned Khrushchev back to Moscow where he was removed from office and isolated.*

Why was Khrushchev removed in mid-October 1964? One factor was a worsening agricultural situation that required large grain imports; another

---

[30]Quoted in Ulam, pp. 689–90.

*On Khrushchev's fall see especially Sergei Khrushchev, *Khrushchev on Khrushchev: An Inside Account of the Man and His Era*. Trans. and ed. William Taubman (Boston, 1990).

was abortive efforts to foster industrial growth and efficiency by numerous bureaucratic reorganizations. Khrushchev's insistence on reshaping and redirecting the Communist Party by splitting its regional and provincial bodies into agricultural and industrial hierarchies alienated Party secretaries who had supported him loyally in 1957. Khrushchev had alienated military leaders with sizable cuts in the Soviet ground forces. Abroad he had scored few successes since 1959. Repeated ultimatums had produced no results in Berlin or progress toward a German peace treaty. The clear deterioration of the Communist bloc and feud with China probably proved as important as the Cuban fiasco in convincing his colleagues that it was time to change leaders. Without significant political or military support, a depressed Khrushchev accepted retirement. His mistakes had drawn his opponents together, but in retrospect his basic policies appear to have been sensible and moderate. These included de-Stalinization, reducing the terror apparatus, normalizing relations and increasing contacts with the West, establishing friendly ties with the Third World, and promoting peaceful coexistence. Could a new and younger leadership perform better?

Suggested Readings

Adomeit, Hannes. *Soviet Risk-Taking and Crisis Behavior: A Theoretical and Empirical Analysis.* London and Boston, 1982.

Adzhubei, Alexei, ed., *Face to Face with America—The Story of the Voyage of N. S. Khrushchev to the United States.* Moscow, 1959.

Beschloss, Michael R. *The Crisis Years: Kennedy and Khrushchev, 1960–1963.* New York, 1991.

Bloomfield, Lincoln, et al. *Khrushchev and the Arms Race: Soviet Interest in Arms Control and Disarmament, 1954–1964.* Cambridge, MA, 1966.

Borisov, O. B. and B. T. Koloskov. *Soviet-Chinese Relations, 1945–1970.* Ed. and Trans. Vladimir Petrov. Bloomington, IN, 1975.

Brzezinski, Zbigniew. *The Soviet Bloc: Unity and Conflict.* Revised and enlarged. Cambridge, MA, 1967.

Caldwell, Dan. *American-Soviet Relations: From 1947 to the Nixon-Kissinger Grand Design.* Westport, CO, 1981.

Chang, Gordon. *Friends and Enemies: The United States, China, and the Soviet Union, 1948–1972.* Stanford, CA, 1990.

Clemens, Walter. *The Arms Race and Sino-Soviet Relations.* Stanford, CA, 1968.

Clubb, O. Edmund. *China and Russia: The "Great Game."* New York, 1971.

Crankshaw, Edward. *Khrushchev: A Career.* New York, 1966.

Cousins, Norman. *The Improbable Triumvirate: John F. Kennedy, Pope John and Nikita Khrushchev.* New York, 1972.

Dinerstein, Herbert S. *The Making of a Missile Crisis: October 1962.* Baltimore, 1976.

Eisenhower, Dwight. *Waging Peace, 1956–1961.* New York, 1965.

Garthoff, Ray. *Reflections on the Cuban Missile Crisis.* Washington, DC, 1987.

Griffith, William. *Albania and the Sino-Soviet Rift.* Cambridge, MA, 1963.

————. *The Sino-Soviet Rift.* Cambridge, MA, 1964.

Hoffman, George W. and Fred W. Neal. *Yugoslavia and the New Communism.* New York, 1962.

Hyland, William and R. W. Shryock. *The Fall of Khrushchev.* New York, 1968.

Khrushchev, Nikita S. *Khrushchev Remembers.* Ed. and Trans. Strobe Talbott. Boston, 1970.

————. *Khrushchev Remembers: The Last Testament.* Ed. and Trans. Strobe Talbott. Boston, 1974.

————. *Khrushchev Remembers: The Glasnost Tapes.* Boston, 1990.

Laqueur, Walter. *The Soviet Union and the Middle East.* New York, 1959.

Linden, Carl A. *Khrushchev and the Soviet Leadership.* Baltimore, 1966.

Medvedev, Roy. *China and the Superpowers.* Trans. Harold Shukman. Oxford, England, 1986.

Reeves, Richard. *President Kennedy.* New York, 1993.

Rush, Myron, ed., *The International Situation and Soviet Foreign Policy: Reports of Soviet Leaders.* Columbus, OH, 1970.

Saran, Vimla. *Sino-Soviet Schism: A Bibliography, 1956–1964.* London, 1971.

Schlesinger, Arthur, Jr., *A Thousand Days: John Kennedy in the White House.* Boston, 1965.

Seaborg, Glenn T. *Kennedy, Khrushchev, and the Test Ban.* Berkeley, CA, 1981.

Smolansky, Oles. *The Soviet Union and the Arab East under Khrushchev.* Lewisburg, PA, 1974.

Sodaro, Michael. *Moscow, Germany and the West from Khrushchev to Gorbachev.* Ithaca, NY, 1990.

Sorensen, Theodore C. *Kennedy.* New York, 1965.

Tatu, Michel. *The Great Power Triangle: Washington-Moscow-Peking.* Paris, 1970.

Ulam, Adam. *Expansion and Coexistence: Soviet Foreign Policy 1917–73.* 2nd ed. New York, 1974.

Zagoria, Donald S. *The Sino-Soviet Conflict 1956–1961.* Princeton, NJ, 1962.

THE BREZHNEV ASCENDANCY, 1964–1974

The sudden fall of Nikita Khrushchev in October 1964 brought a new collective leadership into power in the USSR. Headed by Leonid I. Brezhnev as first party secretary and Aleksei N. Kosygin as premier, the new leadership appeared prudent, cautious, and rather colorless. Both top leaders were engineers, representing the Soviet technocracy that had emerged under Khrushchev. The new chiefs were primarily concerned not with ideology nor world revolution, but with making the Soviet system work more effectively and eliminating the risk and uncertainty prevalent under Khrushchev. Confounding predictions at the time that these were interim leaders, the Brezhnev-Kosygin team ruled Soviet Russia for sixteen years, with Brezhnev gradually becoming the dominant figure. Initially lacking in self-confidence, they overcame a major crisis in Czechoslovakia in 1968. Once the USSR achieved nuclear parity with the United States with a huge arms buildup and having preserved the Soviet bloc by military force, Brezhnev pursued agreements and détente with the West, especially the United States. During his initial decade in power, Brezhnev, the consensus politician, appeared to be highly successful because the United States was bogged down in the treacherous jungles of Vietnam. However, the continuing Sino-Soviet quarrel, rising nationalism in the bloc, and increasing domestic economic problems cast deepening shadows over the Brezhnev regime.

THE COLLECTIVE LEADERSHIP
FEELS ITS WAY, 1964–1967

Initially the new leaders, uncertain in their foreign policy, blamed Khrushchev for both internal problems and external complications with China. When Khrushchev fell, the USSR's international position appeared unfavorable. Sino-Soviet tension was severe, eastern Europe stirred restively, and U.S.-Soviet relations remained cool. The new leaders, promptly halting polemics with China, sought unsuccessfully to resolve their differences with Beijing. Deteriorating relations with China and the United States stemmed partly from the deepening crisis over Vietnam as Washington escalated its military aid to South Vietnam. Beijing and Moscow disagreed sharply over their policies there; China accused the Soviets of providing only niggardly aid to North Vietnam. Also in October 1964 Moscow stood virtually isolated within the Communist world, but soon wild and extreme Chinese attacks improved Soviet relations with other Communist parties.[1]

Still heading the Soviet Foreign Ministry was Andrei Gromyko, an experienced career diplomat. Although the Politburo framed basic decisions in foreign affairs, Gromyko, in office since 1957, acquired more authority under Brezhnev than he had enjoyed under Khrushchev. His ministry's initial approach was: we are not angry with anyone and wish to improve relations. Still inferior to the United States in nuclear strength, Moscow emphasized continued peaceful coexistence with capitalism in foreign affairs, not in ideology. Under the new leadership the trend was toward developing a career diplomatic service recruited from Russia's Georgetown—the Institute of International Relations. Greater emphasis was placed on obtaining and utilizing objective information to reach pragmatic foreign policy decisions. At first eschewing dramatic changes or initiatives, Soviet foreign policy responded to events with quiet diplomacy. Regarding proletarian revolutions abroad as unlikely and probably undesirable, Moscow urged foreign Communist leaders to work for practical gains within the capitalist system.

During Brezhnev's initial years polycentrism grew within the Soviet bloc, fostered by the intensifying quarrel with China. During 1965 Romania's autonomy was confirmed in its unique position as an ally of the USSR, a friend of China, and on good terms with the West. Romania's 1965 constitution stipulated that the country could be involved in war only by its own decision. Bucharest's dominant and autocratic leader, Nicolae Ceausescu, in May 1966 denounced both hostile military blocs, urged changes in the Warsaw Treaty Organization to reduce Soviet hegemony, and angered Moscow by referring to Bessarabia and Northern Bukovina, annexed to the USSR in 1940, as "lost provinces." Romania, the first bloc country to establish diplomatic ties with West Germany, maintained relations with Israel despite the Arab-Israeli conflict of 1967. Romania's role in the Soviet bloc resembled that of Charles de Gaulle's France in the Western alliance. (In 1966, before visiting Moscow, de Gaulle withdrew France from the NATO command.) Because the Romanian Communist Party ruled the country strictly, Moscow tolerated this broadened Romanian autonomy.

Meanwhile Moscow sought to loosen the West European-United States alliance. In January 1965 the opposition Social Democratic leader in West Germany, Willy Brandt, outlined his subsequent *Ostpolitik* (eastern policy) by advocating closer economic and cultural ties with East Germany. With Moscow's support, Poland's Foreign Minister Adam Rapacki suggested holding an all-European security conference. In April 1967 at a conference

---

[1]Isaac Deutscher, *Russia, China, and the West* (London, 1970), pp. 320–22.

in Karlovy Vary, Czechoslovakia, European Communist leaders declared that European security depended upon the:

> inviolability of the existing frontiers in Europe, especially the Oder-Neisse frontier and the frontier between the two German states . . . , the existence of two sovereign German states with equal rights . . . , [and] denying the Federal German Republic access to nuclear weapons. . . .[2]

As West German foreign minister, Brandt continued to develop his concept of *Ostpolitik*, and Moscow negotiated with Bonn during 1967 and early 1968, foreshadowing the agreements of 1971–1972.

Strongly influencing Moscow's evolving approach to the West on security was an intensifying Sino-Soviet quarrel. Soviet overtures to Beijing in 1964–1965 were rebuffed as they competed for influence over North Vietnam and the proper policy to pursue there. As China began building testing facilities for intercontinental ballistic missiles (ICBMs), Moscow began to view it as a major potential military threat. The USSR reinforced its armies near the Chinese frontier and introduced forces into the Mongolian People's Republic, a Soviet satellite. By then Beijing considered the Soviet Union, not the United States, as China's primary enemy. Rejecting an invitation to attend the Soviet Twenty-third Party Congress, Beijing declared: "Russia . . . used to be the center of the international working-class movement [but now] . . . the leadership of the CPSU has become the center of modern revisionism."[3] In 1966 in China began the extremist Cultural Revolution that undermined orthodox Soviet-style Leninism. Russians in China were beaten up by fanatical and ignorant Red Guards, Sino-Soviet trade shrank to near zero, and Chinese students left the USSR. Soviet spokesmen now portrayed China as ultra-nationalist and described Maoism as "a great power adventurist policy based on a petty bourgeois nationalistic ideology alien to Marxism-Leninism."[4]

Friction mounted along the 4,000-mile Sino-Soviet frontier, with numerous violent incidents in 1968–1969, including bloody skirmishes on the frozen Ussuri River in March 1969. A leading Soviet writer, Evgenii Yevtushenko, likened the Chinese to the thirteenth century Mongol invaders of Russia. Moscow supported a dissident group in China led by Liu Shao-chi until the Mao Tse-tung regime purged it during the Cultural Revolution, just as the Chinese had supported the Soviet "anti-Party group" against Khrushchev. To Beijing's dismay, during 1969 Moscow implemented a massive military buildup along the Chinese frontier and pressured the Chinese to discuss their disputed borders. During 1969–1970 there seemed

---

[2]Quoted in Robin Edmonds, *Soviet Foreign Policy 1962–73: The Paradox of Super Power* (London, 1975), p. 66.

[3]Quoted in Joseph L. Nogee and Robert Donaldson, *Soviet Foreign Policy Since World War II*, 4th ed. (New York, 1992), p. 260.

[4]*Pravda*, January 11, 1969.

imminent danger of war between the Communist giants, especially that the Russians might seek to destroy the Chinese nuclear center at Lop Nor before a major Chinese atomic strike force could be created. Evidently intimidated by the Soviet invasion of Czechoslovakia and the buildup on their frontiers, Beijing halted provocative frontier incidents late in 1969 and tension gradually subsided. Nonetheless, during the 1970s the two countries maintained huge military forces on their common frontier.

THE PRAGUE SPRING AND SOVIET INVASION OF CZECHOSLOVAKIA, 1968

The disintegration of Soviet control over eastern Europe under the impact of polycentrism seemed irreversible until the Brezhnev-Kosygin regime in August 1968 employed overwhelming military force to crush the reformist Dubček regime in Czechoslovakia. During the 1960s, as the Czechoslovak government faced growing criticism, the gap widened steadily between intellectuals and the Communist leadership. In November 1967 a protest march by Prague university students was met with brutal police suppression. Grievous economic decline in a country that had been the most advanced in central Europe before World War II undermined the hold on absolute power of Czechoslovak Party chief and premier, Antonin Novotny. After the Slovak Party revolted against dictation from Prague and allied with Czech Party progressives, in January 1968 Novotny was removed as party first secretary at an unprecedentedly free Central Committee plenum. He was replaced by Alexander Dubček, the first Slovak to hold that top position. Brezhnev's decision to allow Novotny's replacement with the supposedly reliable, pro-Soviet Dubček left Brezhnev vulnerable later to criticism by his Politburo colleagues.

During the next six months Dubček, pushed swiftly along the road of internal reform, sought to achieve a so-called "socialism with a human face" (suggesting that Soviet socialism was inhuman). His reforms included establishing intra-party democracy, abolishing censorship over the Czech media, restoring normal ties with West Germany, and granting the right to travel freely abroad. Much of the rigid, overcentralized Stalinist economic system of Czechoslovakia was dismantled. Through the reforms Dubček sought to rehabilitate Czechoslovak Communism while preserving three conditions that he believed would prevent Soviet intervention: maintaining Prague's alliance and cooperation with Moscow, retaining state control of industry, and keeping the Communist Party in control of Czechoslovak society.

Internal change in Czechoslovakia itself might not have provoked Soviet intervention. Dubček pledged to confine the reforms to his country, and initially the USSR seemed to accept his assurances. However, as the reform process deepened, Moscow concluded that Dubček had let things get out of control and that the Leninist model was being destroyed in Czechoslovakia. Dubček could not prevent the liberal contagion from spreading to neighboring East Germany, Poland, and Ukraine. Poland's Wladyslaw

Gomulka and East Germany's Walther Ulbricht feared that unchecked democracy in Prague would undermine their regimes and lead to an independent Czech foreign policy, especially a rapprochement with West Germany. After Novotny was ousted also as president in April, Prague's foreign policy grew bolder and more unacceptable to Moscow. Reports appeared of alleged Soviet complicity in Foreign Minister Jan Masaryk's mysterious death in February 1948. A prominent Czech general questioned Soviet hegemony over the Warsaw Pact's command.

Soviet leaders initially were divided and hesitant over how to deal with a liberalizing Czechoslovakia. At first Brezhnev appeared to support Dubček's appointment as Party first secretary, surprising Czech leaders with his flexible attitude. Only after April when Ukrainian Party leaders grew alarmed did Brezhnev adopt a harder public line, although he was somewhat reassured that Dubček did not directly challenge Soviet national security interests and did not advocate having Czechoslovakia leave the Warsaw Pact. Nonetheless, in early spring a Soviet and Warsaw Pact military buildup began near the Czech frontiers; by June Soviet divisions in East Germany and Poland were camped on the Czech border. Most worried among Soviet leaders were P. E. Shelest, first secretary of Ukraine, and P. M. Masherov, a Belorussian party leader. Such hard-liners there, and in Moscow, by April viewed the Czech situation as "counterrevolutionary" and considered military intervention as the only proper policy. Typically, Brezhnev sought to build a consensus in the Politburo. Only when that had been achieved in favor of intervention did he act.

Also, what would be the American reaction to military intervention? During Dubček's first months in power, despite a few sympathetic statements, Washington remained mostly silent. Soviet Foreign Minister Gromyko complained to American ambassador, J. L. Beam: "You're so unpredictable. We can't count on American policy."[5] Until late July it remained unclear whether the Czechoslovak army, perhaps the best in eastern Europe, would resist a Soviet invasion, which might spread hostilities into Austria and West Germany. As evidence mounted that the Czechs would not fight, any sharp American response was discouraged. At that time President Lyndon Johnson wished to begin strategic arms talks and hold a summit with Premier Kosygin before the U.S. presidential elections in November. Reinforcing Washington's caution was its deep and unpopular military involvement in the Vietnam quagmire. "Even without Vietnam and the appalling domestic situation," concludes the American scholar Adam Ulam, "the United States government could and would have done nothing to stop the Soviet move."[6] Thus Moscow believed that it could act with impunity in Czechoslovakia.

---

[5] Foy Koehler and Mose Harvey, eds., *The Soviet Union Yesterday, Today, Tomorrow* (Miami, 1975), p. 146.

[6] Adam Ulam, *The Rivals: America and Russia Since World War II* (New York, 1971), p. 380.

In July 1968 a crucial confrontation occurred at Čierna-nad-Tisou, just inside Czechoslovakia, between Czech leaders and virtually the entire Soviet Politburo. Brezhnev and other Soviet leaders, not yet having resolved on intervention, acted very nervous. On the first day President Dubček received solid support from the entire Czech Presidium. Because the Soviets had expected opposition to Dubček to emerge, this unity compelled a Soviet backdown. Dubček later confirmed that he had tried to outplay the Soviet leaders at Čierna with vague promises to stabilize Czechoslovakia. The communiqué at the end of the meeting suggested that an uneasy compromise had been reached.

However, by August all major Soviet leaders had concluded that intervention in Czechoslovakia was unavoidable. At a conference of Warsaw Pact leaders in May the Soviets had not advocated force, but after they conferred with Czech leaders that same month, Soviet President Nikolai Podgorny adopted a tough public stand and Shelest of Ukraine accused the Czechs of "directly hostile, nationalistic and chauvinistic attacks."[7] However, as late as June Brezhnev still compared the Czech situation with that of Poland in 1956, where intervention had been avoided.

Soviet leaders had interpreted the verbal agreement reached at Čierna as a final effort to avert invasion. Meanwhile the Soviet ambassador in Czechoslovakia was sending alarming reports that greatly exaggerated the danger to Soviet security in Czechoslovakia. Pressure applied by Gomulka and Ulbricht likewise influenced the Soviet decision. On August 16–17 the Soviet Politburo resolved reluctantly on military intervention after concluding that Dubček was breaking his promises and that a "counterrevolutionary coup," allegedly instigated by West German militarists, was imminent. Final details of the invasion, notes Kiril T. Mazurov, a hard-line Politburo member, were decided only the night of August 20.[8]

The invasion of Czechoslovakia by Soviet and Warsaw Pact forces was sudden, massive, and unopposed. However, Czechoslovak passive resistance was widespread and proved morally effective, and the Soviet invaders found very few Czechs willing to cooperate in any way. Declared the Czech newspaper, *Reportér*, of August 26 just after the invasion:

> A country that does not need to be saved from anything or freed from anything, that is not asking for it and is actually rejecting it for weeks in advance as an absurdity—such a country cannot be "liberated." Such a country can only be occupied—unlawfully, brutally, recklessly. . . .[9]

Afterwards Brezhnev and Kosygin insisted on a compromise that allowed Dubček and President Ludvik Svoboda, after they had been brutally

---

[7]Quoted in Jiri Valenta, *Soviet Intervention in Czechoslovakia in 1968: Anatomy of a Decision* Rev. ed. (Baltimore, 1991), p. 169.

[8]Interview with Kiril Mazurov, *Izvestiia*, August 20, 1989.

[9]Quoted in Robin Remington, ed., *Winter in Prague* (Cambridge, MA, 1969), p. 407.

interrogated in Moscow, to retain their posts for several months. The Kremlin used them to "normalize" the situation, then removed them and installed an obedient hard-line regime, under Gustav Husak, as first secretary of the Czechoslovak Communist Party, that retained power until the anti-Communist revolution of 1989. Seeking to justify the invasion, Moscow's *Pravda* trumpeted:

> In discharging their internationalist duty to the fraternal peoples of Czechoslovakia and defending their own socialist gains, the USSR and the other socialist states had to act decisively, and they did act, against the anti-socialist forces in Czechoslovakia.[10]

In Moscow, however, some brave Soviet intellectuals protested the invasion and demonstrated. Evgenii Yevtushenko, a leading Soviet poet, telegraphed Leonid Brezhnev:

> I understand only one thing, that it is my moral duty to express my opinion to you. I am profoundly convinced that our action in Czechoslovakia is a tragic mistake. It is a cruel blow to Czechoslovak-Soviet friendship and to the world Communist movement.[11]

Roy Medvedev, a dissident Marxist historian, asserted in Moscow: "Our action in Czechoslovakia was not the 'defense of socialism' but a blow against socialism in Czechoslovakia and throughout the world."[12]

The invasion had mixed results for the USSR. Undoubtedly, the successful military operation that was unopposed restored the confidence of Soviet leaders. The restoration of direct Soviet control over Czechoslovakia halted liberalization in most eastern European countries and recemented temporarily Moscow's sway. Yugoslavia and Romania, which had expressed support for the Czechs, were ignored and feared that Moscow might invade them too. However, President Johnson warned Moscow diplomatically against such moves. In Prague liberal reform yielded to reaction and repression under Husak. The Soviet invasion provoked almost unanimous denunciations by Western Communist parties and in Asia and eroded their electoral support. The intervention smashed a carefully cultivated Soviet image as a responsible global power and exposed Moscow as a blatant violator of international law and threatened to derail Soviet-American détente. Once again it was revealed that the USSR could act at will within its own sphere and that even a collective leadership would do so to prevent the collapse of a Communist regime. The invasion changed the strategic balance of forces in eastern Europe since six Soviet divisions

---

[10]*Pravda*, September 26, 1968.

[11]Quoted in Stephen Cohen, ed., *An End to Silence: Uncensored Opinion in the Soviet Union* (New York, 1982), p. 279.

[12]Cohen, p. 284.

remained in Czechoslovakia where previously there had been no occupation forces. The Soviet press even quoted the nineteenth century German "Iron Chancellor," Otto von Bismarck, who allegedly declared: "Whoever rules Bohemia holds the key to Europe."

DÉTENTE WITH THE WEST BEGINS, 1969–1974

Moscow's invasion of Czechoslovakia caused tension temporarily with the West and the United States, but soon progress towards détente resumed and the relaxation of superpower relations became a major achievement claimed by Brezhnev. Early in his rule it became evident that both sides had rejected the use of nuclear weapons, except as a deterrent. As Washington realized the virtual impossibility of remaining dominant once the USSR achieved nuclear parity, both powers became content with a balance of power. Soviet-American relations became increasingly pragmatic as crusading fervor to make the whole world communist or democratic cooled. Their competition in the Third World slackened also as they saw that even massive economic and military aid could not insure a country's loyalty. Above all continuing Chinese hostility pressured the USSR to improve its relations with the West and to secure its own western frontiers.

Another factor, curiously, that promoted détente was Brezhnev's major military buildup that allowed the USSR to speak more softly while carrying a big stick. Recalling the humiliation of having to back down in Cuba because of nuclear inferiority, the Brezhnev leadership rapidly increased the Soviet military budget from 1965 to 1970. By early 1967, as the United States concentrated increasingly on Vietnam, the Soviet Union had largely closed the missile gap. The following year Moscow achieved rough numerical parity with the United States in land-based ICBMs, thus creating a basis for negotiations on an equal footing. Remaining markedly stronger than the West in conventional arms, the USSR also developed a substantial airlift capacity revealed in Czechoslovakia. The USSR also built a navy second only to America's and capable by the late 1960s of upholding Soviet influence throughout the world. By 1969 the power situation differed radically from that of 1962. In any future confrontation the superpowers would be roughly equal in overall military strength. The American industrial lead had also narrowed significantly: Soviet steel production almost equalled American output. However, Soviet Gross National Product (GNP) remained far smaller. Decisions in Moscow and Beijing to reduce tension with the United States suggested that they no longer viewed America as an immediate threat. Instead each viewed the other Communist power as the primary danger.

The Brezhnev regime sought to exploit cooling Franco-American relations stemming from President de Gaulle's nationalist and independent policies and his concept of Europe for the Europeans. Moscow welcomed enthusiastically France's withdrawal in 1966 from the military aspects of NATO. Although talk of a new Franco-Soviet alliance came to naught, by fostering warmer relations with Paris, Moscow sought to undermine NATO and Franco-German cooperation. Franco-Soviet relations cooled somewhat thereafter, but de Gaulle's resignation as French president in May 1969 was viewed in Moscow as a reverse; ties with his successor, Georges Pompidou, were less intimate.

After the Social Democrats won the West German elections of 1969, Premier Willy Brandt moved to implement his *Ostpolitik* by restoring closer ties between the two Germanies and normalizing relations with Moscow. Earlier, the Soviet press had depicted West Germany as a major potential threat to the USSR by greatly exaggerating militarism and neo-Naziism there. This pursued the goal of solidifying the Soviet bloc and keeping Czechs and Poles, fearful of a German revival, dependent on Moscow. The Soviets also feared the impact of the dynamic West German economy on East Germany and Bonn's aim to extend its influence in eastern Europe through trade and by obtaining diplomatic recognition.

However, the crisis in Sino-Soviet relations that peaked in 1969–1970 induced Moscow to welcome Brandt's *Ostpolitik*. On August 12, 1970, the USSR and West Germany concluded the Treaty of Moscow whose preamble and five articles constituted the basis for what amounted to a European peace settlement. Renouncing the use of force in their relations, they recognized existing eastern European frontiers, including the Oder-Neisse line between East Germany and Poland and the boundary between the two Germanies. These were to remain "inviolable now and. in the future."[13] However, Bonn was careful to preserve Germany's right to ultimate reunification. Defending this treaty in West Germany's parliament (the Bundestag), Brandt argued that nothing had been lost that had not been gambled away by Hitler long before. In December the Treaty of Warsaw between West Germany and Poland marked the logical continuation of the Moscow-Bonn accord. Because of conservative opposition in West Germany to renouncing the eastern territories, the Bundestag took two years to ratify these agreements. Creating greater security for the Soviet Union and Poland, they represented a radical turning point in the relations of both with West Germany. The Warsaw Pact's Political Consultative Committee then confirmed the approval of these accords by eastern European governments.

An indispensable part of improved Soviet-American relations were the negotiations leading to the first Strategic Arms Limitation Treaty (SALT I) of 1972. In mid-1968 Soviet leaders decided to enter such talks instead of continuing unrestricted arms competition with the United States, which Moscow could ill afford. However, because of the invasion of Czechoslovakia, the talks were postponed for a year. When SALT negotiations did begin in November 1969, the American lead for all three categories of nuclear missiles had shrunk to 2,275 (U.S.) to 1,650 (USSR) giving Moscow a virtual parity. The Soviets had started building an anti-ballistic missile (ABM) system around their capital city and the United States had launched

---

[13]Quoted in Edmonds, p. 94.

the "Safeguard" ABM program. Moscow's main objective was to achieve and maintain a stable Soviet-American mutual strategic deterrence by agreed limitations on deploying offensive and defensive missiles. The Soviets sought to preserve maximum freedom for military research and development, prevent extensive ABM deployment by the United States, and retain the right to deploy nuclear forces against third countries, notably China. Prominent in the Soviet delegation was General N. V. Ogarkov, then first deputy chief of staff, showing how seriously the military regarded the limitation talks.

When Richard Nixon was inaugurated as American president in January 1969, Moscow immediately announced its readiness to start limitation talks. The Nixon administration, which had adopted the concept of strategic sufficiency towards the USSR rather than nuclear superiority, responded that the new president favored concluding a limitation treaty. Soviet Foreign Minister Gromyko told the Supreme Soviet in July: "In questions of the maintenance of peace, the USSR and the USA can find a common language."[14] When the American and Soviet teams finally began the SALT I talks in Helsinki, Finland, in November 1969, each side could destroy the other many times over. Suggesting the danger that a first nuclear strike might succeed in destroying the opponent and implying the likelihood of vast new expenditures for useless nuclear weapons were: 1) new more precise guidance systems, 2) multiple reentry warheads, 3) multiple independently targeted reentry vehicles (MIRV), and 4) ABM systems. These factors helped make the limitation talks highly complex, protracted, and very significant.

Other factors influenced Moscow to enter and persist with the SALT negotiations. In July 1969 the first American troops were withdrawn from Vietnam, and in November President Nixon indicated that the United States aimed to pull completely out of Vietnam before the 1972 elections. As the end of this American involvement in Indochina approached without any end in sight to the Sino-Soviet quarrel, Moscow became more anxious for direct understandings with Washington. Then followed the crucial agreements over German and eastern European frontiers. This period of 1969–1971 marked the beginning of genuine Soviet détente with the West and the United States. In March 1970 the Non-Proliferation Treaty for nuclear weapons came into effect after being ratified by the United States, the USSR, and Britain. In September 1971 the Quadripartite Agreement on Berlin was signed, ensuring improved communications between East and West Berlin and bringing the Berlin issue close to solution.

By 1969 Soviet military leaders had concluded that neither superpower could achieve strategic nuclear superiority and realized that the existing nuclear balance could be upset if either side developed an effective ABM defense system. Thus Soviet military leaders advised the Kremlin to avoid

---

[14]Quoted in Edmonds, p. 80.

the heavy expenditures required by further strategic arms competition with the United States provided an equitable limitation agreement could be reached. The SALT talks continued in Helsinki and Vienna during late 1969 and 1970, then were adjourned until March 1971.

The Soviet commitment to SALT I remained rather tentative until the Twenty-fourth Soviet Party Congress of March 1971. In his report there, Brezhnev, outlining the basic tasks of Soviet foreign policy, alluded to "the great alliance of the three basic revolutionary forces of our day—socialism, the international workers' movement, and the peoples' national-liberation struggle."[15] While condemning China's ideology as incompatible with Marxism-Leninism, Brezhnev left the door open to further improvement in Soviet-American relations. After the congress, Brezhnev openly championed détente with the United States and urged a successful conclusion to SALT I.

Meanwhile Beijing, with the Cultural Revolution a clear and admitted failure, was also seeking to normalize relations with Washington and thus strengthen its position vis-à-vis Moscow. The Chinese viewed the SALT negotiations as a sinister Soviet-American conspiracy: "They mainly hope to maintain a nuclear monopoly and carry out nuclear blackmail by nuclear threats against the Chinese people and the people of the world."[16] However, on July 15, 1971, Nixon's executive secretary of the National Security Council, Henry Kissinger, after a brief visit to Beijing, exploded a bombshell: President Nixon had accepted an invitation from Chairman Mao Tse-tung to visit Beijing in 1972 in order to restore normal Sino-American relations. That paved the way to end the American efforts to isolate China and permitted China to enter the United Nations. All this posed a major danger for the Soviet Union which faced a nuclear China and a unified Western Europe backed by the United States and Japan. Responding quickly, Brezhnev in October invited Nixon to Moscow and the Soviets quietly dropped any claims to having an ABM defense around their capital.

By the end of 1971 a SALT I accord was virtually complete facilitated by an agreement that each side would rely on its own technical means of verification and not interfere with the other party's methods. SALT I granted the USSR quantitative superiority by freezing the number of fixed ICBM launchers in 1972 at 1,618 for the Soviet Union and 1,054 for the United States; the latter would retain an advantage only in heavy bombers. American military experts argued, however, that the United States was considerably ahead in nuclear technology, MIRV development, and that its nuclear submarines were better constructed and harder to locate. However, SALT I reaffirmed Soviet military superiority in Europe over NATO forces. The formal acknowledgment of a balance of nuclear strength between the two

---

[15]Quoted in Edmonds, p. 89.

[16]Gerald Smith, *Doubletalk: The Story of the First Strategic Arms Limitation Talks* (New York, 1980), p. 35.

Map 11–1   Sino-Soviet frontiers

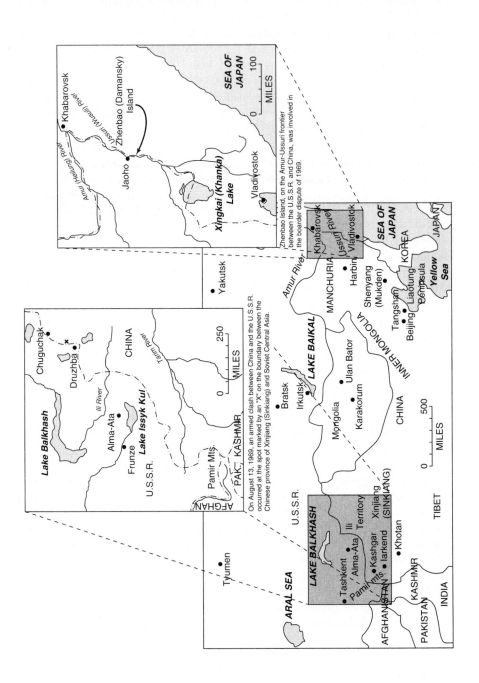

superpowers caused worry in western Europe. In case Moscow struck against the West with its superior conventional forces, would the United States launch a nuclear strike on the USSR?

President Nixon sought to employ the SALT talks to obtain a favorable settlement of America's disastrous involvement in Vietnam. Before his early 1972 visit to Moscow, Henry Kissinger, at Nixon's instructions, warned Soviet leaders that the SALT I agreement could not be concluded while the Vietnam war continued. Thus Moscow sought to help arrange a Vietnam truce without sacrificing Hanoi's basic interests. Soviet leaders concluded that the benefits of détente with the United States would outweigh its costs and risks and hoped that it would also loosen United States ties with its NATO allies. Thus in Moscow Kissinger found Foreign Minister Gromyko anxious to end the Vietnam war so that SALT I and trade agreements could be signed. Indeed, at the Nixon-Brezhnev summit of May 1972 in Moscow this was achieved. As détente entered outer space, President Nixon from the Kremlin addressed the Soviet people on television with a moving appeal for peace and friendship between the Soviet and American nations.

Georgii Arbatov, director of Moscow's Canadian-American Institute, commented in February 1973: "Important and manysided as the achievements of 1972 were, they may be viewed as but the first steps on the path" of rapprochement. The Soviet-American struggle, he predicted, would continue since it was "historically inevitable." However, détente would replace danger of military conflict with "ideological rivalry and competition in many spheres," combined with limited cooperation.[17] A *Pravda* editorial, "Peaceful Coexistence and the Class War," which praised highly the Nixon-Brezhnev summit as a breakthrough in Soviet-American relations, likewise revealed Soviet ambivalence over détente, warning: "The struggle between the proletariat and the bourgeoisie, between international socialism and imperialism, will continue until the complete and final victory of communism throughout the world."[18]

Actually, it was the wicked imperialists who kept the "land of socialism" from going hungry. A serious agrarian crisis in 1972 induced Moscow to seek large amounts of American grain despite simultaneous intensive American bombing of North Vietnam. Affirmed NSA advisor Kissinger with considerable exaggeration: "The Soviet Union quite literally had no other choice than to buy our grain or face mass starvation."[19] Moscow avoided food shortages and possible food riots by swiftly closing deals at bargain prices with several American companies in the so-called "great grain robbery." The Nixon administration, anxious to extricate the United States

---

[17]Georgii Arbatov, "Sovetskie-amerikanskie otnosheniia," *Kommunist*, no. 3 (February 1973), quoted in Adam Ulam, *Dangerous Relations: The Soviet Union in World Politics, 1970–1982* (Oxford, England, 1984), pp. 83–84.

[18]*Pravda*, August 30, 1972, quoted in Ulam, *Dangerous Relations*, p. 87.

[19]Henry Kissinger, *The White House Years* (New York, 1979), p. 1270.

from the Vietnam imbroglio, concluded that expanding trade, credits, and technology for the USSR would break down barriers between the superpowers and promote a peaceful settlement in Vietnam. Soviet-American trade expanded considerably between 1972 and 1975, although the American Congress failed to ratify an October 1972 trade agreement. Capitalist credits and technology from the United States and western Europe propped up faltering Soviet and east European economies.

Moscow reciprocated by inducing North Vietnam to conclude a truce in the war with the south, enabling Nixon to claim that under the Paris accords of January 1973 the United States had concluded an honorable settlement. Nonetheless, the Soviet press rejoiced at America's failure in Vietnam: "The results of the war have demonstrated the futility of the imperialist practices of repression and interference in the internal affairs of nations." The "historic victory of the Vietnamese people" had been facilitated by "the manysided assistance and support rendered by the Soviet Union."[20] However, Soviet leaders praised the Nixon administration for its realism in halting the war and for creating better relations with the Soviet Union. In April 1973 a plenum of the Soviet Central Committee urged that the recent positive changes in the international situation be made irreversible. Nuclear war, it admitted, would be a catastrophe for everyone: "History has fully demonstrated that the policy of peaceful coexistence is not a tactical measure, but a basic necessity, for in our days it has become the only alternative to a thermonuclear catastrophe."[21]

Erupting in the spring of 1973, the investigation into the Watergate break-in gradually eroded the Nixon administration's prestige and freedom of maneuver. At first Moscow downplayed Watergate's significance and did not allow the gathering American domestic crisis to interfere with Brezhnev's June 1973 visit to the United States. In his televised address to the American people Brezhnev emphasized the solid personal links between the two countries and credited President Nixon with leading Soviet-American relations onto a new friendly path. The two leaders, noted Brezhnev, had agreed to continue meeting regularly; he was looking forward to Nixon's visit to Moscow in 1974. Soon, however, even Moscow realized that Nixon's power was waning. Nixon's June 1974 state visit to the USSR was his swan song. Although he was well received and stressed his personal ties with Brezhnev as the foundation for Soviet-American cooperation, no important results were produced. Accords limiting underground nuclear tests and reducing ABM sites were signed in Moscow, but they had been agreed to months before the summit. Nixon's resignation in August 1974 in the face of pending impeachment charges stemming from the Watergate affair ended the honeymoon period of Soviet-American détente. When Congressional critics of the 1972 Soviet-American trade bill made granting most favored nation status to the

---

[20]*Pravda*, February 15, 1973.
[21]Quoted in Ulam, *Dangerous Relations*, pp. 98–99.

USSR conditional on its permitting unrestricted Jewish emigration, Moscow in January 1975 refused to accept this and the trade agreement lapsed.

THE USSR AND THE THIRD WORLD, 1964–1974

The Brezhnev regime swiftly renounced what it considered Khrushchev's overly generous aid and spectacular visits to Third World countries and sought to place Soviet relations there on a pragmatic, businesslike basis. Soon realizing that the USSR could not control countries outside the bloc when it was struggling to keep bloc members loyal, Moscow no longer anticipated dramatic results or great victories in the uncommitted world. Scaling down Soviet foreign aid, the collective leadership sought limited diplomatic and commercial gains without great expense to the Soviet Union. Moscow concentrated its attention on consolidating Soviet influence in nearby countries, such as India and Afghanistan, that subsequently might be brought into the Soviet sphere of influence even if Communism did not triumph there. The failure of Khrushchev's largesse was demonstrated in 1965 by the collapse of several pro-Soviet regimes in the Third World. The most grievous and expensive blow to Moscow was the fall of President Ahmed Sukarno in Indonesia. Following an abortive coup in September 1965, more than 100,000 Indonesian Communists were killed in fighting there, and Sukarno early in 1967 was deposed as president. The new Indonesian regime continued to obtain much Soviet military equipment, but Moscow, saddled with Indonesian debts of more than $1 billion, saw Indonesia turn toward the United States. Also in 1965 President Kwame Nkrumah of Ghana, after absorbing large amounts of Soviet foreign aid, was removed from power and succeeded by an anti-Communist military regime. Confirming the Kremlin's policy shift in the Third World, a *Pravda* editorial in October affirmed that forcibly imposing one country's will on another was alien to Marxism-Leninism; instead socialist countries should concentrate on building socialism at home.[22]

Soviet foreign aid under Brezhnev became less generous than that of China or the United States with repayment of loans required over ten to fifteen years at 2.5–3 percent interest. Reduced Soviet grants and rising repayments from Third World countries cut the Soviet net outflow from a high point of some $300 million annually in 1964 to less than $100 million in 1972.[23] Cuba remained the conspicuous exception as Moscow purchased rising amounts of Cuban sugar at prices above the world level. By 1973 Cuba was costing the Soviet Union an estimated $1.5 million daily.[24]

India became especially important to the Brezhnev regime, which viewed it as a bulwark against excessive Chinese influence in Asia. After a Pakistan-Indian war over disputed Kashmir (September 1965), both sides

---

[22]*Pravda*, October 27, 1965.

[23]Edmonds, pp. 54–55.

[24]Edmonds, p. 56.

accepted Premier Kosygin's mediation offer, and their heads of state met with him in January 1966 in Soviet Tashkent. Kosygin's successful mediation, enhancing Soviet prestige as an Asian peacemaker, discomfited Beijing. Subsequently, India grew increasingly dependent on Soviet military equipment and diplomatic support against China. Moscow invested heavily in building Indian industrial plants, their trade expanded greatly, and a major Soviet propaganda effort portrayed the USSR as a progressive and reliable friend. There was an increasing Soviet naval presence in the Indian Ocean. On the eve of another Indian-Pakistan war in August 1971 the Soviets concluded a friendship treaty with India. The United States and China both backed Pakistan, but Soviet-supported India gained a swift and decisive victory. The Soviets also supported India diplomatically in the United Nations, engaging in verbal battles with the Chinese. The Indian-Soviet Treaty of 1971 was an initial step in Soviet efforts to contain Chinese power in Asia.

In the Middle East, under Brezhnev Moscow continued efforts to penetrate the Arab world and to undermine shrinking Western influence there. This pro-Arab policy involved major risks and costs while direct returns were miniscule; but, already involved in the region, the USSR could not withdraw nor cut its commitments without severe loss of prestige. The apparent aim was not outright Arab victory over Israel since that would end Arab dependence on Moscow and fuel traditional Arab xenophobia and suspicion of atheistic Communism. Instead Moscow sought to keep the Middle East in turmoil and to discredit the West. Also Soviet leaders recognized the great strategic importance of the Suez Canal. Soviet access to bases in Libya and the United Arab Republic (Egypt and Syria) and a sizable naval presence altered the balance of power in the Mediterranean and worried American military leaders.

After fostering a major buildup of Egyptian forces under the aggressive President Gamel Nasser, Moscow failed to dissuade him from abruptly closing the Tiran Straits in May 1967. Apparently the Soviets misassessed the military balance in the region. After a quick and shattering Israeli victory in the Six Day War of June 1967, Moscow had to press for a quick cease-fire. The Arab defeat represented an embarrassing setback for the USSR, but the Arabs, still more embittered towards Israel and the West, became more dependent than ever on Soviet military aid. Afterwards Soviet leaders visited their Arab clients while replacing huge Egyptian losses in military equipment. In November 1967 Moscow intervened in the civil war in Yemen and in 1968 agreed to provide military and technical aid to the new pro-Soviet government of South Yemen formed after the British withdrawal from Aden.

President Nasser's sudden death in August 1970 weakened the Soviet position in Egypt. His successor, Anwar Sadat, viewed Soviet policy as seeking to keep the region unsettled without real commitment to the Arab cause. In 1971 Sadat purged pro-Soviet personnel from his regime, but Moscow felt compelled to retain ties with Sadat since he remained militantly anti-Israel. However, then the huge Soviet investment in Egypt was lost. After visiting Moscow twice early in 1972 without obtaining the military aid he had requested to counter Israel's power, on July 18, 1972, Sadat expelled all 20,000 Soviet military "advisers" from Egypt. Moscow then hastened to reinforce its ties with Syria and Iraq.

In October 1973 the Arab-Israeli "Yom Kippur" war revealed continuing major Soviet involvement in the Middle East balanced by a determination to prevent a breach with the United States over it. The Western alliance reacted to the crisis with confusion and indecision. In January 1973 Moscow had resumed heavy arms shipments to Egypt. A few days in advance of its October 6 surprise attack on Israel Cairo informed Moscow. The Soviets failed to warn the West of this and claimed falsely: "Israel has attacked Egypt and Syria."[25] While the Arabs were still winning, the Soviets proposed a cease-fire while airlifting arms to them in large quantity. Then after Israel counterattacked, Brezhnev exchanged messages with Nixon as they strove to preserve détente. Major airlifts of American supplies to Israel aided the Israeli army win victories that threatened Cairo itself. On October 20 Secretary Kissinger agreed with Soviet leaders in the Kremlin to press for a cease-fire in the United Nations. With fighting continuing and Egypt facing total defeat, Soviet-American pressure induced Israel to halt its advances and end the war.[26] Moscow and Washington credited détente for resolving the worst crisis in their relations since 1962. Thereafter, realizing the West's vulnerability to threats to cut off Middle East oil, the Soviets acted with less constraint in the region. Although the October war represented another Arab defeat, it pleased Moscow by weakening the Western alliance. Afterwards President Sadat, pursuing a more balanced foreign policy, restored Egyptian ties with the United States while Moscow reinforced its relations with militant Syria and Iraq.

Suggested Readings

Amalrik, Andrei. *Will the Soviet Union Survive Until 1984?* New York, 1970.
Brezhnev, Leonid I. *Peace, Detente and Soviet-American Relations.* New York, 1979.
Davisha, Karen. *Soviet Foreign Policy Towards Egypt.* London, 1979.
Deutscher, Isaac. *Russia, China, and the West.* London, 1970.
Dornberg, John. *Brezhnev: The Masks of Power.* New York, 1974.
Edmonds, Robin. *Soviet Foreign Policy 1962–73: The Paradox of Super Power.* London, 1975.
―――. *Soviet Foreign Policy: The Brezhnev Years.* London, 1983.
Ellison, Herbert. *The Sino-Soviet Conflict: A Global Perspective.* Seattle, 1982.
Eran, Oded. *The Mezhdunarodniki: the Assessment of Professional Expertise in the Making of Soviet Foreign Policy.* Ramat Gan, Israel, 1979.
Garthoff, Raymond. "SALT and the Soviet Military," *Problems of Communism* (January–February 1975), pp. 21–37.

---

[25]*Pravda*, October 7, 1973.

[26]See Walter Laqueur, *Confrontation* (London, 1974); Ulam, *Dangerous Relations*, pp. 103–110.

Gelman, Harry. *The Brezhnev Politburo and the Decline of Détente.* Ithaca, NY, 1984.

Golan, Galia. *The Czechoslovak Reform Movement: Communism in Crisis, 1962–1968.* Cambridge, England, 1971.

Goldman, Marshall. *Détente and Dollars.* New York, 1975.

Hutchings, R. L. *Soviet-East European Relations: Consolidation and Conflict, 1968–1980.* Madison, WI, 1983.

Kanet, Roger. *The Soviet Union and the Developing Nations.* Baltimore, 1974.

Kissinger, Henry. *White House Years.* New York, 1979.

Laqueur, Walter. *Confrontation.* London, 1974.

London, Kurt, ed., *The Soviet Union in World Politics.* Boulder, CO, 1980.

Luttwak, Edward. *The US-USSR Nuclear Weapons Balance.* Beverly Hills, CA, 1974.

Nogee, Joseph L. and Robert Donaldson. *Soviet Foreign Policy Since World War II.* 4th ed. New York, 1992.

Pipes, Richard. *US-Soviet Relations in the Era of Détente.* Boulder, CO, 1981.

Remington, Robin, ed., *Winter in Prague.* Cambridge, MA, 1969.

Smith, Gerald. *Doubletalk: The Story of the First Strategic Arms Limitations Talks.* New York, 1980.

Ulam, Adam. *Dangerous Relations: The Soviet Union in World Politics, 1970–1982.* Oxford, England, 1984.

Valenta, Jiri. *Soviet Intervention in Czechoslovakia in 1968: Anatomy of a Decision.* Rev. ed. Baltimore, 1991.

Zartman, William, ed., *Czechoslovakia: Intervention and Impact.* New York, 1970.

SOVIET STAGNATION AND DECLINE, 1975–1985

Early in 1975 Leonid Brezhnev suffered a severe stroke, forcing him to remain politically inactive for several months. A concealed power struggle over the succession began at the top of the Soviet power pyramid, though Brezhnev subsequently reappeared to accumulate more high posts, honors, and military medals. However, after 1975, Brezhnev was elderly and sickly, able to work only a few hours per day, and signs of his advancing senility multiplied. This inaugurated a decade of rule over the Soviet empire by aged and infirm leaders incapable of dealing innovatively with increasingly grave economic and social problems at home. Whereas the Bolshevik Revolution of November 1917 had created a Soviet regime led by energetic, idealistic revolutionaries with a messianic vision of a socialist future for their country and the world, less than sixty years later it had degenerated into a stagnant bureaucratic regime based on privilege, gross inequality, and pervasive corruption. At Brezhnev's death in November 1982 the average age of Politburo members was almost seventy. By 1975, despite its continuing awesome military power, the USSR entered a period of political and economic stagnation soon reflected in declining prestige abroad. The Marxist-Leninist ideology had become ossified and lifeless as it grew evident that Lenin's messianic goals were simply unrealizable. Polycentrism developed within a Soviet bloc whose disintegration was merely concealed by censorship and repression. Nonetheless, the Brezhnev regime, utilizing détente as a facade to conceal its imperial goals, adhered stubbornly to expansionist aims, pursuing them aggressively in portions of the Third World.

THE DECLINE OF DÉTENTE, 1975–1979

For Brezhnev's USSR the signing of the Helsinki accords on August 1, 1975, by the leaders of 33 European states, U.S. President Gerald Ford, and the Canadian prime minister marked a high point in the process of détente. After ten years of effort the Soviets and Warsaw Pact countries had obtained legal recognition of postwar boundaries in Europe, establishing a basis for obtaining the advanced Western technology their lagging economies needed desperately. Although the United States refused to recognize the annexation

?: if US. didn't recognize the Baltic.— USSR then chechnya is not a civil war.

of the Baltic countries to the USSR, the accords appeared to consolidate détente. The agreement stated:

> The participating states regard as inviolable all one another's frontiers as well as the frontiers of all States in Europe. . . . They consider that their frontiers can be changed . . . by peaceful means and by agreement.[1]

Optimistic expectations that the Helsinki accords would ensure arms control, increased East-West cooperation, and improvements in civil rights in the Soviet bloc were not realized. From the start the agreements were violated in eastern Europe and, most blatantly, in Afghanistan, because the Brezhnev Doctrine conflicted directly with Helsinki's provisions on non-intervention in the internal affairs of other countries. Early on, President Jimmy Carter of the United States condemned Moscow's repeated violations of its citizens' civil rights, notably the arrest in May 1977 of Iurii Orlov, heading a Soviet dissident group to monitor the Helsinki accords, and the trial that July of dissident Anatolii Shcharanskii for defending the right of Soviet Jews to emigrate. Soviet ambassador Anatolii Dobrynin protested sharply the reception of dissident Vladimir Bukovskii at the White House. Dobrynin accused President Carter of interfering in Soviet domestic affairs "based on the fictitious pretext of protecting human rights."[2]

Carter's foreign policy focused on Human Rights.

In February 1976 at the Twenty-Fifth Soviet Party Congress Brezhnev boasted that the USSR's international position had never been more stable or favorable. World capitalism, he claimed, was in irrevocable decline:

> It is precisely during the past five years that the capitalist world has experienced an economic crisis the seriousness and depth of which . . . can only be compared with the crisis at the beginning of the 1930s.[3]

Contending that capitalist society had no future, Brezhnev nonetheless praised détente as being advantageous to both superpowers "in lessening the danger of a new world war and in strengthening peace." Displaying nervousness and irritation towards China, he claimed that Beijing

> has been trying feverishly to destroy détente, to sabotage any disarmament efforts, and to sow distrust and hostility between various states. Its basic aim is to provoke a world war, and to exploit it for its own purposes. . . .[4]

Brezhnev urged the Chinese to normalize relations with Moscow by returning to true Marxism-Leninism.

---

[1] Quoted in Robin Edmonds, *Soviet Foreign Policy—the Brezhnev Years* (Oxford, England, 1983), p. 148.

[2] *Pravda*, February 19, 1977.

[3] L. I. Brezhnev, *Following Lenin's Path*, vol. 5 (Moscow, 1976), p. 497.

[4] Brezhnev, pp. 471, 459.

At the time of the death of Mao Tse-tung in September 1976, the persisting bitterness of the Brezhnev regime towards Maoist China was revealed clearly. On September 10, the day following Mao's death, only a six-line report graced the back page of *Pravda*, and no Soviet leader bothered to visit the Chinese embassy in Moscow to mourn the deceased "great helmsman." On October 1 *Pravda*, listing alleged previous Soviet services to China and recent Soviet efforts at rapprochement, urged Beijing either to confirm the continuing validity of the Sino-Soviet Treaty of 1950 or to sign a nonaggression pact with Moscow. However, anti-Russian feeling was so deeply imbedded in Beijing that the emerging leader, Deng Xiao-ping, declined to support any rapprochement. The continuing stubborn opposition of the number two Communist power undercut the Soviet theory of Maxism-Leninism that predicated the inevitable cooperation of socialist states. However, weakened seriously by Mao's extreme policies during the Cultural Revolution, China then did not yet represent a major military threat to Soviet Russia.

The Brezhnev regime was equally unsuccessful in normalizing relations with Japan. Moscow sought a formal peace treaty with Japan but refused to retrocede the southern Kurile Islands (seized by the USSR at the end of World War II) to Japanese control. A major setback for Moscow was the Sino-Japanese Peace and Friendship Treaty of 1978 concluded despite repeated Soviet warnings. Moscow interpreted correctly the two signatories' denunciation of "hegemonism" as referring to Soviet policies abroad and worried about possible major Japanese economic aid to China. In February 1978 this Soviet concern deepened when President Carter opened diplomatic relations with the new Chinese leadership thus raising the threat of a Sino-Japanese-U.S. partnership.

Despite slowing economic growth, the Brezhnev regime, in order to expand its influence in the vulnerable Third World, continued its vast and diversified military buildup. "Discounting inflation, since 1960 Soviet military spending has actually doubled . . . while our own military budget is actually lower now than it was in 1960," noted President Carter in 1978.[5] At the Twenty-Fifth Congress Brezhnev had claimed that the USSR had increased amounts spent for social and welfare purposes but not its military budget. However, in order to conceal a massive arms buildup, much Soviet military spending was carried out by agencies other than the Defense Ministry.

After Portugal's forty-year-long dictatorship collapsed in 1974, Portuguese Angola in southern Africa became independent as revolutionary factions competed for power. The United States and China supplied arms to one faction, but Moscow backed the group that triumphed—the Marxist Popular Movement for the Liberation of Angola (MPLA). Moscow flew in almost 12,000 Cuban troops, inducing then Secretary of State Henry

---

[5]*New York Times*, March 18, 1978.

Kissinger to urge that large-scale American aid be channeled to their opponents. The U.S. Congress refused to appropriate such assistance and the MPLA won out. However, soon the Angolans turned to Washington for technological aid, thus frustrating Moscow's design to create a significant sphere of Soviet influence in western Africa.

Between 1977 and 1979 the Brezhnev regime, tempted by vulnerable regimes in northern Africa, undertook several ventures that departed markedly from its initial cautious policies on that continent. In the Horn of Africa Moscow for some time had cultivated close ties with the government of Somalia, providing it with economic and military assistance in return for naval and air facilities in a region close to important oilfields vital to the West. However, then even brighter prospects suddenly appeared in neighboring Ethiopia when Colonel Mengistu Haile Meriam achieved power at the head of a military regime that soon adopted Marxism-Leninism. However, Mengistu failed to halt Ethiopia's territorial disintegration, especially in the northeast province of Eritrea, and economic decline. Efforts to apply state socialism in Ethiopia provoked serious famine. After Mengistu visited Moscow early in 1977, the Soviets supplied him the following year with more than $1 billion in military aid. By February 1978 almost 11,000 Cuban troops were in Ethiopia, commanded by senior Soviet officers fighting against insurgents and Somalia.[6] However, most Arab states, alarmed at these Soviet military moves, backed the Somalis and Eritrean rebels against Ethiopia. In November 1977, because of Soviet backing for Ethiopia, President Ziyad Barre of Somalia expelled the remaining Soviet advisers and refused the Soviets the use of the port of Berbera. Nonetheless, by February 1978 the triumphant Cuban and Ethiopian forces were threatening to invade Somalia. Moscow restrained them since such an invasion would have strained Soviet relations with its clients, Syria and Iraq, fellow members of the Arab League, but the Soviets continued to employ large Cuban forces to implement its designs in Africa.

On March 15, 1976, President Anwar Sadat cancelled Egypt's treaty of friendship and collaboration of 1971 with Moscow, inflicting a major setback on Soviet policy in the Middle East. Since 1972 Soviet-Egyptian relations had been deteriorating, and the final element was Moscow's refusal to reschedule the large Egyptian debt owed to the USSR. Sadat's move, after accepting billions in aid from the USSR, revealed the perils of Soviet efforts to expand their influence in the Third World. The Brezhnev regime nonetheless continued to believe that the Soviet Union had to expand its influence there in order to demonstrate the superiority of socialism and the decline of the West.

After breaking with Moscow, Sadat drew closer to the United States and intimated that he would seek to settle Egypt's long-standing quarrel

---

[6]Colin Legum and Bill Lee, *The Horn of Africa in Continuing Crisis* (New York, 1979), pp. 13ff.

with Israel. This defection of the Middle East's most populous and militarily strongest country threatened to deprive the USSR of much of its leverage in the region. Thus Moscow, intriguing to undermine Sadat as an Arab spokesman, insisted on Soviet participation in any Middle Eastern settlement. Responding to Soviet overtures, the United States agreed to Moscow's suggestion to reconvene the Geneva conference on Middle Eastern issues that had not met since the October 1973 war. Falling into a cleverly laid Soviet trap, Washington agreed that all outstanding issues would be discussed there including "evacuation by the Israeli troops of the territories occupied in the 1967 conflict [and] the Palestinian problem including the securing of the rights of the Palestinian nation."[7] That Soviet-drafted formulation provoked anger in Israel, which denied the existence of a Palestinian nation. While Washington pressured Israel to join the Geneva talks, Sadat on November 19, 1977, announced he was prepared to go to Jerusalem for direct Egyptian-Israeli peace negotiations. Soviet newspapers promptly denounced Sadat as an accomplice of the Zionists and a tool of the United States.[8] That torpedoed the Geneva conference. Sadat's courageous trip to Israel isolated him in the Arab world but spared President Carter major embarrassment. Carter followed up on Sadat's initiative in September 1978 by bringing Egypt and Israel together at Camp David near Washington. Reacting angrily to the agreements reached there by Sadat and Israel's Premier Menachem Begin, *Pravda* characterized them as "a deal reached behind the back of the Arab nations" that betrayed the Arab and Palestinian cause. "This sellout serves the interest of Israel, American imperialism, and the Arab reactionaries."[9]

Moscow gloated over the forced departure from Iran in January 1979 of the pro-American but dictatorial Shah Mohammad Reza Pahlavi and the triumphant return of the Muslim fundamentalist, Ayatollah Ruhollah Khomeini, to lead an anti-Western revolution. However, the Soviets had carefully hedged their bets by remaining on friendly terms with the shah until his sudden flight. Khomeini's fanatical regime was as anti-Communist as it was anti-Western, but he deliberately made the United States his chief target.

As to nuclear arms limitation negotiations—the centerpiece of détente during the 1970s—after taking office in January 1977, the Carter administration sought somewhat overhastily to conclude a new strategic arms limitation treaty agreement before SALT I expired in October. In March Secretary of State Cyrus Vance rushed to Moscow with proposals designed to set a basis for SALT II talks. However, Moscow quibbled and raised objections. The United States was chiefly concerned by the recent Soviet development of the multiple-warhead weapons, SS-18 and SS-19, and by

---

[7]*Pravda*, October 2, 1977.

[8]*Pravda*, December 7, 1977.

[9]*Pravda*, September 21, 1978.

the advanced Backfire bomber placed in service in 1974. For their part the Soviets worried about the new American cruise missile, a guided weapon that flew close to the ground to avoid radar detection, and demanded that limits be placed on its range. Vance first suggested that SALT II talks should follow guidelines established in Vladivostok in 1974 at the summit between President Ford and Brezhnev that had deferred discussion of cruise missiles and the Backfire. The Soviets abruptly rejected that proposal. Vance's alternative plan provoked this outburst from Foreign Minister Andrei Gromyko:

> They [United States] now propose to reduce the strategic weapon carriers to 2,000 or 1,800, and those MIRVed to 1,100–1,200. Furthermore, they want us to dismantle half of those missiles of ours that some people in the US happen to dislike. Can such a one-sided approach to the issue lead to an agreement?[10]

Moscow eventually agreed to discuss these problems, with technical experts participating, but the initial Carter effort on SALT II was a failure. Gromyko stressed that Carter's determination to press the issue of Soviet human rights violations had complicated the negotiations: "We do not need any teachers [from abroad] when it comes to the internal affairs of our country."[11]

Nevertheless, Soviet-American SALT II talks opened in Geneva on May 18, 1977. Foreign Minister Gromyko warned that the USSR would not permit the United States under a SALT II agreement to provide "any other country" (notably China) with nuclear technology or weapons. Should the United States object unduly to the Soviets' SS-18 and SS-19 and Backfire bomber, Moscow would demand that American tactical nuclear weapons be removed from Europe and from naval vessels in the Mediterranean and North Sea. The Carter administration decided not to press for major cuts in Soviet nuclear forces for fear that Moscow would insist on virtually disarming NATO in a nuclear sense. During Gromyko's talks with leading American officials that fall, some progress was scored on SALT II. Both sides agreed to observe the limitations on nuclear arms imposed by SALT I that had just expired until a new treaty could be concluded. In a conciliatory move Gromyko suggested a possible Carter-Brezhnev summit. (Brezhnev had just assumed the Soviet presidency.)

During 1978 a controversy developed over the American neutron bomb, a powerful weapon that had the advantage of avoiding radioactive fallout. Gromyko denounced it as an inhuman weapon while Brezhnev warned the heads of NATO governments not to install it. President Carter responded in April 1978 that its production would be deferred. Meanwhile the Soviets were busily modernizing their tactical nuclear weapons and installing SS-20 mobile multiwarhead missiles that could reach any part of Europe. During

---

[10]*Pravda*, April 1, 1977.
[11]*Pravda*, April 1, 1977.

the year Moscow strove to loosen the Western alliance by emphasizing pacific Soviet intentions while impressing Europeans with the USSR's strength. Elaborate ceremony surrounded a much heralded state visit to West Germany in May 1978 by Brezhnev and numerous officials and experts.

By the end of 1978 SALT II was virtually ready for signature; on many disputed issues the Soviet draft had prevailed. Earlier, Brezhnev, deploring the slow pace of negotiations, asserted that some American circles did not appear to want "a stable peace and mutual cooperation."[12] Late in 1978 reports circulated that Brezhnev would be invited to Washington for the signing of SALT II in January 1979, a treaty that Carter and his advisers believed was in the America's best interest.[13] However, then Carter announced that full American diplomatic relations would be opened with China and that its new leader, Deng Xiao-ping, would visit Washington late in January. National security assistant, Zbigniew Brzezinski, believed that this overture to Beijing would force Soviet concessions on SALT II. Deng warned the West not to trust the USSR on international issues and called for Sino-American cooperation to "check the ambitions of the 'polar bear'" and castigated Soviet actions in Afghanistan and Ethiopia. "Deng didn't find a single word to say about socialism, or the peoples' struggle for national liberation," complained *Pravda*.[14] Brezhnev deplored a Sino-American statement opposing any power seeking "hegemony" in Asia and elsewhere (clearly the USSR), and Moscow broke off the Geneva negotiations.

After numerous delays SALT II was finally signed in May 1979 at the Vienna summit of Carter and Brezhnev. SALT II would allow each side 2,400 strategic launchers until 1981; from then until January 1985 the number would fall to 2,250. Of these, 1,320 could be fitted with multiple warheads (MIRV) including heavy bombers with cruise missiles. As under SALT I, verification was to be conducted "by national technical means" with neither side interfering with the other's verification measures. At the signing a ponderous, ancient Brezhnev epitomized the stagnation of the Soviet political leadership and system. That December, after the Soviet intervention in Afghanistan, Carter withdrew the SALT II treaty from consideration by the American Senate. Before that debate had raged in the American public and Congress around the claim that the accords would leave the United States exposed to a possible Soviet preemptive nuclear strike.

INSOLUBLE CRISES IN EAST AND WEST, 1979–1982

Undermined by Soviet intervention in Angola and Ethiopia and by Sino-American rapprochement, superpower détente finally collapsed in December 1979 after the Soviet invasion of Afghanistan. Over that neighboring

---

[12]*Pravda*, September 23, 1978.

[13]Strobe Talbott, *Endgame: The Inside Story of SALT II* (New York, 1979), p. 229.

[14]*Pravda*, January 31, 1979, quoted in Adam Ulam, *Dangerous Relations: The Soviet Union in World Politics, 1970–1982* (Oxford, England, 1984), p. 213.

country of primitive Muslim tribesmen, Russian and British imperial interests had clashed in the late nineteenth century. Thereafter Afghanistan remained, at least nominally, independent under a monarchy until 1973, then a so-called republic. During 1977, apparently under Soviet pressure, competing factions of the Afghan Communists—the Khalq under Nur Mohammed Taraki and the Parcham under Babrak Karmal—reunited. In April 1978 army officers and Communists overthrew the unpopular republic headed by an elderly dictator, President Mohammed Daoud. Taraki quickly set up a Communist dictatorship, "the People's Democratic Republic of Afghanistan," and aligned it closely with the Soviet Union. His regime removed army leaders, political opponents, and finally leaders of the rival Parcham group, whose leader, Babrak Karmal, sought refuge in Moscow. Khalq leaders—notably Hafizullah Amin, Taraki's assistant—moved hastily to convert a backward tribal society to socialism violating every Afghan cultural and religious norm. The Taraki-Amin regime's atheism, subservience to Moscow, and open brutality alienated most of the population.

In August 1978 Afghans under Muslim leaders revolted in every province, proclaiming a holy war against the godless Communists. Soviet leaders, initially delighted by the Communist takeover and providing extensive aid, were dismayed at the alienation of the population blaming chiefly Amin who made Taraki a figurehead.

By September 1979 the Brezhnev regime apparently had decided to remove Amin in favor of Taraki. However, that same month, after a shootout at the presidential palace, Amin removed Taraki and ruled as dictator with even more ruthless policies. As the popular revolt against Amin intensified, Moscow escalated its military role until by November there were more than 4,500 Soviet "advisers" in Afghanistan. Soviet pilots flew bombing missions against rebel positions. Step by step the USSR was sucked into a bitter Afghan civil war much as the United States earlier had been drawn into the Vietnam quagmire.

The Soviets prepared that fall for possible full-scale military intervention to prevent the fall of the Communist regime. As he had done in Czechoslovakia before the Soviet invasion of 1968, General Ivan G. Pavlovskii, Soviet deputy defense minister, examined the situation on the spot. The Soviets then tried unsuccessfully to remove Amin in favor of Babrak Karmal. The decision to intervene was blamed subsequently on a small group of Kremlin hawks headed by Defense Minister Dmitrii Ustinov who allegedly induced a seriously ill Brezhnev to sign the order.[15] The day before the invasion *Pravda* wrote falsely:

> Recently the Western . . . media have been intentionally spreading deceptive rumors about the "interference" of the Soviet Union in the internal affairs of Afghanistan. They have even asserted that Soviet "combat troops" have been

---

[15]Joseph Collins, *The Soviet Invasion of Afghanistan* (Lexington, MA, 1986).

MAP 12-1   Afghanistan in the 1980s

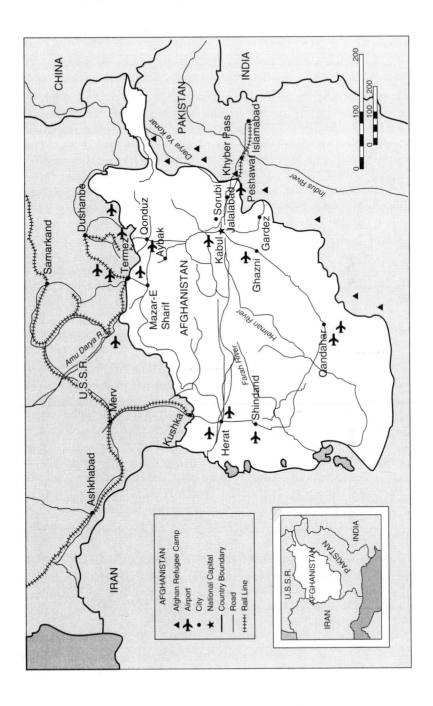

moved into Afghan territory. All this, of course, is pure fabrication. . . . It is well known that relations between the Soviet Union and Afghanistan are based on a solid foundation of good-neighborly relations and non-interference in the internal affairs of one another. . . .[16]

Events would soon contradict these assertions completely. Returning to the USSR General Pavlovskii claims that he reported to Defense Minister Ustinov: "There is no necessity to introduce our troops into Afghanistan"; Ustinov refused to follow his advice.[17] Amin's brutal execution of Taraki may have shocked the Kremlin into concluding that only massive Soviet military intervention would prevent total chaos in Afghanistan. The final decision to intervene was reached evidently in late November, followed by a major increase in Soviet military activity near Afghanistan.

On December 24, 1979, large Soviet forces, mostly Central Asians, began moving into Afghanistan. Three days later a special assault force attacked the presidential palace, and, after a sharp fight with loyal Afghan army elements, killed Amin and members of his family. It took several weeks for the Soviets to control fully the capital of Kabul and provincial centers, and by the end of January 1980 there were more than 50,000 Soviet troops in the country. As in the Czech case, the Soviet invasion was militarily efficient and achieved the objective of eliminating Amin, but once again the political and psychological aspects were handled clumsily. Thus the Afghan "request" for military "assistance" reached Moscow three days *after* the invasion began. Only hours after a Soviet minister had made a courtesy call on President Amin, Moscow announced that Amin had been executed for crimes "against the noble people of Afghanistan." Yet only three months earlier, upon becoming president, Amin had been congratulated by President Brezhnev. Babrak Karmal, installed as the new Afghan leader, arrived from Moscow four days after the invasion began in the baggage-train of the Soviet army, pegging him immediately as a Soviet stooge. Moscow asserted that the Soviets had intervened and had had the president killed in order to prevent "foreign intervention" in Afghanistan adding the fantastic charge that President Amin, at the orders of the American CIA, had planned to nullify the socialist achievements of the 1978 coup.[18]

The Carter administration reacted swiftly and punitively to the Afghan invasion. Earlier, Washington had rationalized Afghanistan's abrupt move to socialism on the basis that the country was unimportant, had already been under considerable Soviet influence, and that the 1978 coup had been exclusively internal. President Carter now declared that the Soviet invasion caused a more dramatic change in his assessment of ultimate Soviet goals

---

[16]*Pravda*, December 23, 1979, quoted in Thomas Hammond, *Red Flag Over Afghanistan* (Boulder, CO, 1984), p. 97.

[17]Scott McMichael, *Stumbling Bear: Soviet Military Performance in Afghanistan* (London, 1991), p. 3.

[18]Hammond, pp. 99–100.

why? CIA —No info

than anything Moscow had done during his previous years in office. Despite much credible evidence, Carter and Secretary Vance did not realize until the last moment that Moscow was preparing a major invasion. They issued no credible warning to Moscow against intervention unlike the strong warnings issued later over Poland.[19]

Washington responded promptly and effectively. Carter urged Brezhnev to withdraw Soviet forces or face unspecified "serious consequences," adding, "Such gross interference in the internal affairs of Afghanistan is in blatant violation of accepted international rules of behavior."[20] When Brezhnev sought to justify the invasion, Carter in effect called him a liar. In his State of the Union address on January 23, 1980, Carter warned that "the implications of the Soviet invasion of Afghanistan could pose the most serious threat to the peace since the Second World War," inasmuch as the Persian Gulf region was of vital strategic importance to the West. The key passage in this "Carter Doctrine" read:

> An attempt by any outside force to gain control of the Persian Gulf region will be regarded as an assault on the vital interests of the United States of America, and such an assault will be repelled by any means necessary, including military force.[21]

Carter then imposed a series of sanctions on the Soviets. American grain shipments to the USSR for 1980 were reduced by more than two-thirds and exports of high technology items to it were prohibited. The SALT II treaty was withdrawn from the Senate, although it probably could not have been ratified in any case. Carter cancelled an agreement to open consulates in New York and Kiev and banned flights into the United States by Aeroflot, the Soviet state airline. Washington soon increased the U.S. defense budget and decided to install new missiles in Europe. Most damaging to Soviet pride was the American boycott of the 1980 summer Olympic Games to be held in Moscow for the first time. West Germany, Japan, and China followed the American lead, seeking to punish Moscow for the Afghan invasion. The United Nations Security Council and General Assembly urged the "immediate and unconditional withdrawal of foreign troops" from Afghanistan, but Moscow paid this no heed. American economic sanctions were weakened since some other countries continued to sell grain and technology to the Soviets.

Was the Soviet invasion of Afghanistan part of an aggressive design to dominate the Persian Gulf region, as some observers concluded at the time, a defensive move to prevent the fall of a client Communist regime to Muslim fundamentalism, or simply a blunder? Was Moscow's move unprecedented,

---

[19]Hammond, pp. 105–06.
[20]*The Washington Post*, December 29, 1979.
[21]Quoted in Hammond, p. 122.

as some claimed, and thus a major turning point in Soviet foreign policy, or was it merely the Asian counterpart of the Brezhnev Doctrine invoked a decade earlier in Czechoslovakia? Because Afghanistan had been within the Soviet sphere even before the invasion, argued the American scholar, Thomas Hammond, this military intervention was really nothing new. It continued traditional Russian imperialism in the region and was consistent with previous Soviet actions in the Third World. It was designed primarily to protect Soviet frontiers by surrounding them with friendly and sub-servient states and thus prevent the fall of any Communist regime. Contributory factors included Soviet fears of Muslim fanaticism spreading into vulnerable Soviet Central Asia, and the desire to end potential chaos fostered by Amin's policies by replacing him with the obedient Karmal.[22] President Brezhnev asserted that the decision to move in had been carefully considered: "The Party's Central Committee and the Soviet Government-... took into account the entire sum total of circumstances."[23]

Babrak Karmal assumed the top posts in the Soviet-installed Afghan regime, named a few token non-Communists to his cabinet, and protested that he was a good patriot and Muslim. He failed to win much support because he was known to be an atheist, a Communist, and a Moscow puppet surrounded with Soviet advisers carrying through progressive Sovietization of the country. Feuding Afghan factions and tribes meanwhile achieved unprecedented unity in their holy war and national liberation struggle against the Russians whom they hated and despised. The rebels *(mujaheddin)* soon controlled about 80 percent of Afghanistan despite a continued influx of Soviet troops reaching a total of some 115,000 men "advising" a weakening Afghan army which by 1984 had dwindled to about 30,000 men.

Soviet forces in Afghanistan utilized massive firepower, saturation bombing, and scorched earth tactics against the rebels. By 1985 some 3 million Afghans—roughly one-fifth of the population—had fled their increasingly devastated homeland, mostly into neighboring Pakistan. Mean-while two years of military buildup and repeated major Soviet offensives against the guerrillas produced few results. Rebel resistance increased as they secured more and better weapons, partly supplied secretly by the United States, and became tactically more skilled. At Brezhnev's death in 1982, the Soviets were no closer to consolidating control over Afghanistan than when they had intervened, nor were they willing to commit sufficient troops to do so. Conventional heavy Soviet weapons proved ineffective against guerrillas who melted into the mountains. Nor could Karmal unify the Communists or organize a regime acceptable to the Afghan people.

Ronald Reagan's accession as American president in January 1981 confirmed the demise of détente. During 1980 he had referred to the USSR as "a hostile imperial power whose ambitions extend to the ends of the

---

[22]For a discussion of the factors in the Soviet decision to invade see Hammond, pp. 130ff.
[23]*Pravda*, January 13, 1980.

SOVIET PRESIDENT LEONID BREZHNEV (LEFT) JOINS EAST GERMAN PRESIDENT ERICH HONECKER IN OCTOBER 1979 FOR THE THIRTIETH ANNIVERSARY OF THE CREATION OF THE GERMAN DEMOCRATIC REPUBLIC.

earth."[24] He accused Carter during the 1980 campaign of a foreign policy "bordering on appeasement," referring notably to his failure to resolve the Iranian hostage crisis. At his initial news conference as president, Reagan accused the Soviet leaders of "reserv[ing] to themselves the right to commit any crime, to lie, to cheat." Later, Reagan described Soviet Communism as "the focus of evil in the modern world."[25] Furthermore, the Reagan administration accelerated the American military buildup begun under Carter.

As the Soviets invaded Afghanistan, major trouble was brewing once again in Poland symptomatic of Communism's inexorable decline in eastern Europe. The election on October 16, 1978, of Karol Woytyla, former archbishop of Krakow, as Pope John Paul II—the first Pole to be elected to that office—may well have triggered this new ferment. His visit to Poland in 1979, strengthening nationalism among all Polish classes, contributed significantly to a major outbreak of worker strikes and the rise during 1980 of the independent labor movement known as Solidarity. After the Polish government suddenly raised meat prices on July 1, 1980, strikes erupted

[24]*New York Times*, February 29, 1980.
[25]*New York Times*, January 30, 1981; March 9, 1983.

immediately; by late August some 640,000 workers were involved.[26] The price increases were designed to help pay off Poland's burgeoning foreign debt to Western banks. In late September 1980, when the Silesian coal miners who had been his strongest supporters joined the strikes, Party chief Edward Gierek resigned, ostensibly for reasons of health. His successor, Stanislaw Kania, was a moderate, colorless Party bureaucrat who adopted a middle course to try to calm the rising storm.

Meanwhile Polish workers took bold and unprecedented action for a Communist country by creating Solidarity as an independent trade union that was formally registered by Polish courts in October. It expanded quickly to several million members and reached almost 10 million at its peak in 1981. As government-sponsored unions disintegrated, the Polish economy sagged into crisis. In the face of this genuine proletarian revolution, Polish Communism appeared on the verge of collapse. Early in December 1980 an emergency meeting of the Warsaw Pact convened in Moscow which insisted that Poland must remain a socialist country. As the Kremlin mobilized additional troops, the danger of a Soviet intervention mounted. However, Polish generals apparently warned Moscow that the Polish army would resist any Soviet invasion. President Carter also sent private and public warnings to Moscow. Recalled Carter in his memoirs:

> We were monitoring Soviet military preparations very closely. Fifteen or twenty divisions were ready to move. . . . The Soviets were surveying invasion routes, had set up an elaborate communications system throughout Poland, . . . and were holding their military forces in a high state of readiness. . . . I sent Brezhnev a direct message warning of the serious consequences of a Soviet move into Poland, and let him know more indirectly that we would move to transfer advanced weaponry to China.[27]

Carter's admonitions may well have helped deter any Soviet action.

All during 1981 Poland remained in turmoil and Soviet leaders in perplexity as to how to handle the crisis. In March major Warsaw Pact military maneuvers were announced to be conducted in the USSR, Poland, Czechoslovakia, and East Germany. As Party chief Kania sought to keep the Polish Workers Party together, a series of premiers sought unsuccessfully to cope with the crisis. Dissent swelled as intellectuals, journalists, students, and finally peasants joined protests by industrial workers. Their chief leader was Lech Walesa, an electrician from the Gdansk shipyard, who displayed much political ability in leading Solidarity. In desperation the Polish authorities in February 1981 had General Wojciech Jaruzelski named as prime minister. He had been defense minister since 1968. In September Solidarity held its first national congress, and when the government refused to yield to its demands for free parliamentary elections and workers'

---

[26]George Sanford, *Polish Communism in Crisis* (London, 1981), p. 48.
[27]Jimmy Carter, *Keeping Faith* (New York, 1982), pp. 584–85.

self-management, it threatened a general strike and the overthrow of Communism. The congress issued an open letter urging eastern European workers to form their own independent labor unions. *Pravda* denounced this letter as "provocative and impertinent" and characterized the Solidarity congress as "an anti-socialist and anti-Soviet orgy."[28]

After the Solidarity congress, Kania resigned as Party first secretary, and General Jaruzelski replaced him in that post in October 1981. He now held all top posts in Poland: Party first secretary, premier, armed forces commander, and defense minister. On December 13 Jaruzelski proclaimed martial law in order, he claimed, to avert a Solidarity coup. Brezhnev in a "Dear Comrade" letter, welcomed his actions warmly. Thousands of Solidarity activists and dissidents were arrested; Solidarity was forced underground by a military dictatorship that lasted nineteen months, until July 1983. Jaruzelski claimed, probably correctly, that this solution had prevented a Soviet or Warsaw Pact invasion of Poland.[29]

The moribund Brezhnev's final year in office was a period of continuing tension between the Soviet Union and the United States. President Reagan was busily expanding United States military strength and pursuing a hard line towards Moscow. In the summer of 1982 Reagan extended the ban imposed originally after martial law was proclaimed in Poland to include American manufactured oil and natural gas equipment, only to drop it when the European Economic Community protested. That summer *Pravda* issued a lengthy assessment of United States foreign policy under Reagan by Georgii Arbatov, an expert on the United States and a close Brezhnev adviser. Emphasizing the persisting danger of nuclear war, Arbatov accused the Reagan administration of "periods of uncontrollable political lunacy. . . . The current United States administration is a highly ideological group of people holding what are perhaps the most right-wing views of any current in the West today."[30] The Brezhnev regime became pessimistic about reaching any real accommodation with Washington.

As Brezhnev's health deteriorated and he became senile, many expected that he would step aside in favor of a younger leader at the Twenty-Sixth Party Congress in February 1981. Instead, he clung stubbornly to power and all members of his Politburo and Secretariat—all elderly—were re-elected. During 1982 evidence mounted that Brezhnev was no longer in real command of the USSR. The death of Mikhail Suslov, the Kremlin's chief ideologist, that January paved the way for change by undermining stability and balance in the ruling elite. Returning from Tashkent in March Brezhnev suffered a severe stroke and lay speechless in the Kremlin hospital for several weeks. That permitted Iurii Andropov, former KGB chief, to build support in the Central Committee; in May he was named chief Kremlin

---

[28]*Pravda*, September 11, 1981.
[29]Olga Narkiewicz, *Eastern Europe, 1968–1984* (Totowa, NJ, 1986), pp. 101–05.
[30]*Pravda*, July 16, 1982.

ideologist. That summer, with Brezhnev ill and on vacation in the Crimea, Andropov took charge of the Party Secretariat. Meanwhile Brezhnev's position was undermined by numerous charges of corruption in his entourage and family circle. After appearing in cold weather at the November 7 parade, Brezhnev died of natural causes on November 10, 1982.

Brezhnev's legacy was a mixed one. At home economic and political stagnation prevailed under the rule of elderly, unimaginative bureaucrats holding office under a consensus politician. Initially, Brezhnev had scored important successes abroad through détente with the West and the confirmation of Europe's postwar frontiers. However, then the breach with Egypt and Soviet-Cuban military intervention in Africa undermined Soviet influence. The intervention in Afghanistan destroyed Soviet prestige in the Muslim world and triggered a major United States rearmament. Overall the Soviet position in the world appeared no better at Brezhnev's death than at his accession.

THE SHORT-LIVED SUCCESSORS: ANDROPOV AND CHERNENKO, 1982–1985

Iurii V. Andropov asserted his new leadership swiftly and smoothly, carefully concealing the lengthy power competition preceding Brezhnev's death. As ambassador to Hungary in 1956, Andropov had acquired considerable knowledge of foreign affairs and wisely retained the experienced Gromyko as Soviet foreign minister and Georgii Arbatov as a top adviser. Despite his best efforts, he failed to impart much dynamism or flexibility to Soviet politics or the economy, although he did make many needed personnel changes. Alterations in Soviet foreign policy under Andropov were limited mainly to matters of style. At Brezhnev's funeral Andropov spoke at length with leaders of the unprecedented number of high-level foreign dignitaries who attended, including friendly chats with China's foreign minister and President Mohammed Zia ul-Haq of Pakistan. In his meeting with Vice President George Bush of the United States, Andropov revealed both intelligence and flexibility. He emphasized that he would direct Soviet policy firmly and reasonably and that a period of diplomatic stagnation was over.

Sino-Soviet relations improved somewhat under both Andropov and his successor Konstantin Chernenko although basic problems remained unresolved. Andropov hastened to initiate a conciliatory policy towards China, and articles critical of Beijing ceased to appear in the Soviet press. The Chinese found Andropov much easier to deal with than Brezhnev, but their relations with Moscow remained cool because of continuing friction over Indochina, Afghanistan, and because of Sino-Soviet troop concentrations along their frontiers.

In his dealings with the West, Andropov had the advantage of knowing far more about the United States than President Reagan did about the Soviet Union. By late November 1982 the Western press was already referring to Andropov's "peace offensive" that would continue during much of 1983. Faced with manifold economic and social problems at home, Andropov

Iurii V. Andropov (1914–1984), general secretary of the Party, 1982–1984, (right) confers with Andrei A. Gromyko, Soviet foreign minister, 1957–1985.

pursued conciliatory policies abroad. The bitterest issue then in Soviet-American relations centered around NATO's decision in 1979 to install 572 Pershing II and cruise missiles in Europe to counter Soviet deployment of the powerful new intermediate-range missile, the SS-20. The Reagan administration had begun negotiations with Moscow in November 1981 on this issue, but they soon had bogged down. In December 1982 at ceremonies marking the sixtieth anniversary of the formation of the USSR, Andropov declared: "We are prepared . . . to agree that the Soviet Union would retain in Europe only as many missiles as Britain and France have—and not one more."[31] That would require the USSR to reduce its forces by hundreds of missiles including many SS-20s. Put under pressure by Andropov's proposal, which won much support in the West, in March 1983 Reagan proposed as an interim agreement that the United States would deploy fewer Pershings in return for Soviet reductions. Early in 1983 there was much debate in the West whether NATO would begin installing the new missiles that year, but electoral victories by Helmut Kohl in West Germany and Margaret Thatcher in Britain ensured that such deployment

[31]Quoted in Joseph L. Nogee and Robert Donaldson, *Soviet Foreign Policy Since World War II*, 4th ed. (New York, 1992), p. 349.

would proceed unless full agreement were reached with Moscow. Andropov, until sidelined by ill health in September 1983, displayed a reasonable approach to nuclear issues that won him considerable applause in the West.

Improving Soviet-Western relations were suddenly aborted on September 1, 1983, by the tragic fate of the Korean airliner, KAL-007. A commercial aircraft on a regular flight from the United States to Japan strayed far off course over Soviet airspace and was shot down by a Soviet missile near Sakhalin Island, killing all 269 passengers and crew. At first Moscow denied all responsibility for the plane's destruction, but five days later, facing an aroused world opinion, the Soviets admitted that one of their pilots had destroyed the aircraft but asserted that it had been performing a secret surveillance mission for United States intelligence. In a dramatic nationwide address President Reagan affirmed that KAL-007's destruction constituted a deliberate and brutal act of murder:

> This crime against humanity must never be forgotten, here or throughout the world. . . . There was absolutely no justification, either moral or legal, for what the Soviets did. . . . It was an act of barbarism born of a society which wantonly disregards individual rights and the value of human life and seeks constantly to expand and dominate other nations. . . .[32]

Moscow's response was:

> The Soviet government expresses regret over the death of innocent people and shares the sorrow of their bereaved relatives and friends. The entire responsibility for this tragedy rests wholly and fully with the leaders of the USA.[33]

What shocked American opinion and the international community was a Soviet policy permitting the shooting down of an unarmed civilian aircraft. Moscow then explained that the Korean plane had been mistaken for a United States RC-135 spy plane that was flying a parallel course. Soviet defense forces, asserted Marshal Nikolai Ogarkov, chief of the Soviet General Staff, had merely been protecting legitimate Soviet airspace from intrusion into a sensitive military area. The decision to destroy the plane, stated Ogarkov, had been made by a district commander of the Air Defense Forces, not by the Soviet government. Andropov's first public comment on the incident came almost a month afterwards and merely supported the assertions of the Soviet military,[34] suggesting widespread autonomy by the Soviet military and indicating that Andropov was not as strong politically as had been assumed. Soviet lying about the facts, accusing the United States of using the plane for espionage, and refusing compensation to the victims' families reflected fully normal Soviet practice since Lenin: the Communist

---

[32]*New York Times,* September 6, 1983.

[33]*New York Times,* September 7, 1983.

[34]*New York Times,* September 29, 1983.

Map 12–2 Shooting down of KAL Flight 007

1. At a Soviet air defense base located on Kamchatka Peninsula radar detects a United States RC-135 reconnaissance plane. Its routine flight brings no Soviet response.

2. When another blip shows up on the Soviet radar, the Kamchatka authorities, believing the blip is another American spy plane, instruct their fighter planes to intercept.

3. KAL Flight 007 reenters international airspace over the Sea of Okhotsk. Soviet pilots from Kamchatka watch Flight 007 enter Soviet airspace over Sakhalin Island. Low on fuel, the pilots end their pursuit and inform air defense on Sakhalin of the approaching plane.

4. The United States RC-135 reconnaissance plane lands at its Shemya Island base.

5. The unknown aircraft is overtaken by three interceptors, two Su-15s and one MiG-23, from Sakhalin Island. One of the Su-15 pilots sees Flight 007 1.2 miles distant.

6. With KAL Flight 007 having only a few seconds left in Soviet airspace, the Su-15 pilot approaches it and fires air-to-air missiles, shooting the passenger plane down.

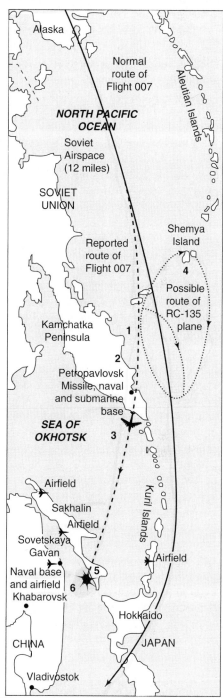

An unarmed Korean passenger plane–KAL 007–was apparently mistaken by the Soviet military for a nearby American RC-135 spy plane. Controversy continues whether the Soviets tried to warn the KAL pilot that he was seriously off course in Soviet airspace before firing. The downing in 1983 created a crises in US-Soviet relations.

was the polito buro Running the country

Party is infallible and therefore the USSR cannot admit an error in judgment to an adversary.[35]

The KAL-007 affair, temporarily reviving bitter Cold War rhetoric and feelings, brought a measured response from the Reagan administration. The 1981 order denying Aeroflot the right to land in the United States was reaffirmed. At Reagan's request, the Congress passed a joint resolution denouncing the Soviet action. The United States suspended negotiations on several bilateral matters and demanded compensation be paid to the victims, which Moscow refused.

On February 9, 1984, after spending most of his final year on a dialysis machine, Andropov died of kidney disease. In the ensuing succession struggle the "old guard" prevailed one last time over the Andropov group whose candidate, the youthful Mikhail S. Gorbachev, became second Party secretary. At age 72 the new leader, Konstantin U. Chernenko, was the oldest man ever chosen to head the Soviet state. A pure product of the Party apparatus, Chernenko believed that all problems could be solved with Leninist ideology and Party discipline. Visibly feeble even when he assumed power, Chernenko was often out of public view with emphysema. During his brief and ineffective rule economic and political stagnation prevailed at home and no important policies were initiated abroad.

Sino-Soviet relations marked time during Chernenko's tenure. The two Communist powers still proved unable to compromise their basic differences. Desirous of some degree of rapprochement with Moscow since it disliked President Reagan's support for Taiwan, Beijing moved during the post-Brezhnev era to a middle position between the two superpowers. Chinese Premier Zhao Ziyang's visit to Washington early in 1984 caused alarm in Moscow. Partly with China in mind, Chernenko agreed to resume arms control negotiations with the United States, but Moscow decided to boycott the 1984 summer Olympic games in Los Angeles, partly to gain revenge for the Carter boycott of 1980. Moscow provided the rather lame excuse: "Chauvinistic sentiments and anti-Soviet hysteria are being whipped up in the [United States]."[36]

In Afghanistan, after five years of intervention, Soviet troops were deeply involved in a ferocious but indecisive war. In 1982 the Soviet command, realizing that stalemate had set in, shifted emphasis from large-scale conventional offensives to long-term economic and political warfare against the rebels and the Afghan population. This involved destroying the rural economy and forcing millions to flee the country. Entire valleys were devastated by saturation bombing and their people were slaughtered or expelled. The loosely organized rebels, aided increasingly with American weapons, nonetheless continued fierce resistance. As one of them noted:

---

[35]Nogee and Donaldson, pp. 343–44.

[36]*Current Digest of the Soviet Press*, vol. 36, no. 19 (June 6, 1984), p. 2, cited in Nogee and Donaldson, pp. 345–46.

"No one has ever conquered the Afghan people."[37] Continued major Soviet involvement in the seemingly endless war in Afghanistan prevented any real improvement in Soviet relations with either the United States or China, and alienated the Muslim world. With the USSR in a condition of stagnation, cynicism, and decline, the Soviet populace awaited impatiently a true leader and reformer.

Suggested Readings

Arnold, Anthony. *Afghanistan: The Soviet Invasion in Perspective.* Stanford, CA, 1985.

Ash, Timothy G. *The Polish Revolution: Solidarity.* New York, 1984.

Bradsher, H. S. *Afghanistan and the Soviet Union.* Durham, NC, 1983.

Byrnes, Robert F., ed., *After Brezhnev: Sources of Soviet Conduct in the 1980s.* Bloomington, IN, 1983.

Collins, Joseph. *The Soviet Invasion of Afghanistan.* Lexington, MA, 1986.

Edmonds, Robin. *Soviet Foreign Policy: The Brezhnev Years.* Oxford, England, 1983.

Ellison, Herbert, ed., *The Sino-Soviet Conflict: A Global Perspective.* Seattle, 1982.

Gelman, Harry. *The Brezhnev Politburo.* Ithaca, NY, 1984.

Gromyko, Andrei A. *Peace Now, Peace in the Future.* New York, 1984.

Hammond, Thomas. *Red Flag over Afghanistan.* Boulder, CO, 1984.

Hauner, Milan. *The Soviet War in Afghanistan: Patterns of Russian Imperialism.* London, 1991.

Holloway, David. *The Soviet Union and the Arms Race.* New Haven, CO, 1983.

Holloway, David and Jane Sharp, eds., *The Warsaw Pact.* Ithaca, NY, 1984.

Hutchings, R. L. *Soviet East European Relations: Consolidation and Conflict.* Madison, WI, 1987.

Johnson, R. W. *Shootdown: Flight 007 and the American Connection.* New York, 1987.

Kanet, Roger. *The Soviet Union and the Developing Nations.* Baltimore, 1974.

Karpinski, Jakub. *Countdown.* New York, 1982.

Legters, Lyman H. *Eastern Europe: Transformation and Revolution, 1945–1991.* Lexington, MA, 1992.

Legum, Colin and Bill Lee. *The Horn of Africa in Continuing Crisis.* New York, 1979.

McMichael, Scott R. *Stumbling Bear: Soviet Military Performance in Afghanistan.* London, 1991.

Medvedev, Zhores A. *Andropov.* New York, 1983.

Narkiewicz, Olga A. *Eastern Europe 1968–1984.* Totowa, NJ, 1986.

Nogee, Joseph L., and Robert Donaldson. *Soviet Foreign Policy Since World War II.* 4th ed. New York, 1992.

Pipes, Richard. *US-Soviet Relations in the Era of Detente.* Boulder, CO, 1981.

Rothschild, Joseph. *Return to Diversity.* New York, 1988.

Rubinstein, Alvin Z. *Soviet Policy Toward Turkey, Iran, and Afghanistan.* New York, 1982.

Rywkin, Michael. *Moscow's Muslim Challenge.* New York, 1982.

---

[37]William Borders, "Afghanistan's Five Year Ordeal," *New York Times*, December 17, 1984, pp. 1, 14.

Sanford, George. *Polish Communism in Crisis.* London, 1981.

Singer, Daniel. *The Road to Gdansk.* New York, 1982.

Stokes, Gale, ed., *From Stalinism to Pluralism: A Documentary History of Eastern Europe Since 1945.* New York, 1991.

Talbott, Strobe. *Endgame: The Inside Story of SALT II.* New York, 1979.

Ulam, Adam. *Dangerous Relations: The Soviet Union in World Politics, 1970–1982.* Oxford, England, 1984.

Yanov, A. *Détente After Brezhnev: The Domestic Roots of Soviet Foreign Policy.* Berkeley, CA, 1987.

13

THE GORBACHEV ERA: TRANSFORMATION AND DISINTEGRATION, 1985–1991

In March 1985, by a narrow margin in the Politburo, Mikhail S. Gorbachev won power as first secretary of the Soviet Communist Party. After a decade of gerontocracy and stagnation, Gorbachev—at fifty-four the youngest man in the Politburo—represented a new generation uninvolved with Stalinist repression. He faced formidable problems of relative economic decline (compared with the West and Japan), a demoralized and corrupt Soviet society, and a growing technological lag. The challenges facing Gorbachev resembled those confronting Tsar Alexander II 130 years earlier when he assumed power from Nicholas I, the "Iron Tsar." Under Nicholas' unreformed autocracy the Russian Empire had fallen far behind western Europe politically, economically and socially, and had suffered humiliating defeat in the Crimean War.

Gorbachev, the most highly educated leader to rule the USSR since Lenin, instituted at first mild, then increasingly drastic reforms at home and abroad in vain efforts to refurbish and revitalize Soviet socialism. Like Alexander II, Gorbachev ended most of his predecessors' manifold restrictions on contacts with the outside world. Both rulers sought to preserve basic Russian or Soviet institutions and the ruling ideology, but Gorbachev lost control of a reform process that after six and one-half years of his leadership led seemingly inexorably to the disintegration of the USSR. In foreign policy Gorbachev placed a liberal team in charge, transformed policy-making and the Soviet image in the world, but full implementation of his "new thinking" destroyed the Soviet Union as a superpower.

NEW MEN, NEW INSTITUTIONS, "NEW THINKING"

Born of peasant stock in a village of Stavropol province in the north Caucasus, young Gorbachev derived self-confidence and satisfaction from hard physical labor helping his father on a collective farm. He completed his secondary education as a silver medalist and received an Order of the Red Banner for dedicated work in the Komsomol (Communist youth organization). Gorbachev attended the Law Faculty of Moscow University,

Gorbachev

1951–1955, joined the Communist Party at age 21, then returned to Stavropol as a full-time Komsomol official. Shifting to the Party organization in 1962, he was promoted rapidly for his intelligence, dedication, and hard work. In 1971 he became the youngest member of the Central Committee of the Party. In 1978 Gorbachev established ties with his three predecessors as Party first secretary, and two years later became by far the youngest member of the Politburo. Following Brezhnev's death, he rose swiftly to the top of the Soviet power pyramid serving as chief spokesman for Andropov, then as second Party secretary under Chernenko.

After Chernenko's death in March 1985, Gorbachev was approved as Party leader over strong conservative opposition after Foreign Minister Andrei Gromyko in a dramatic speech praised him: "Comrades, this man has a nice smile, but he has teeth of iron."[1] The historical dramatist, Mikhail Shatrov, summed up the significance of Gorbachev's confirmation in power:

> March 1985—this was a struggle not for power, but for an idea, for the necessity and possibility for a democratic renewal of the country, a struggle to return to the ideas of October [1917].[2]

In a total contrast with his ill and aged predecessor, Gorbachev at Chernenko's funeral talked energetically and confidently with many of the world leaders who attended; the latter came away much impressed. American Vice President George Bush, following a lengthy conversation there with Gorbachev, returned home "high on hope, high that we can make progress in Geneva, high for an overall reduction of tensions."[3] The first hints of Gorbachev's "new thinking" on foreign affairs appeared just before he took power in a speech of December 1984 on a visit to London. He asserted that the concept of national security had shifted to one of mutual security that could be achieved not by force but by diplomatic and political negotiation. Arms control at all levels between the superpowers was essential in order to prevent a disastrous nuclear war. This "new thinking" would subsequently be elaborated in speeches by Gorbachev, Foreign Minister Eduard Shevarnadze, and in scholarly articles in leading Soviet journals.

In his acceptance speech of March 1985 Gorbachev revealed great impatience to inaugurate a new course: "We are to achieve a decisive turn in transferring the national economy to the tracks of intensive development."[4] During his initial months of rule Gorbachev forced thousands of aged bureaucrats into retirement or to prison for corruption. Despite strong potential opposition from conservatives he transformed the

---

[1] *Mikhail S. Gorbachev: An Intimate Biography* (New York, 1988), p. 134.
[2] *Gorbachev*, p. 135.
[3] *Gorbachev*, p. 136.
[4] *Pravda*, March 13, 1985.

membership of the Politburo and Secretariat with unprecedented speed. In a key move he induced his elderly sponsor, Foreign Minister Gromyko, to become titular president of the USSR, then named as foreign minister the brilliant Shevarnadze, his friend of long standing. A chief rival, Viktor Grishin, was removed as Moscow Party chief and replaced by Boris Yeltsin, a radical reformer. By August 1987 three-fourths of the republic and regional first secretaries had been installed since Leonid Brezhnev's death in 1982.

Preceding the major economic and political reforms, or restructuring *(perestroika)* planned by Gorbachev to rescue the USSR from decline, he launched a campaign of openness *(glasnost)* in order to build support and expose major problems. The Gorbachev regime established new traditions of freedom and tolerance encouraging the press "to fill in the blank spots" in Soviet history and expose fully the monstrous crimes of the Stalin era. Generally, Gorbachev defended Lenin's policies and views as essential for Soviet socialism. However, as Iurii Afanasiev, the liberal head of the Moscow State Historical-Archival Institute, explained in Washington:

> . . . To give a legal foundation to the Soviet regime is . . . it seems to me a hopeless task. To give a legal foundation to a regime which was brought into being through bloodshed with the aid of mass murders and crimes against humanity, is only possible by resorting to falsification and lies—as has been done up till now.[5]

Glasnost contained within itself the potential danger of undermining the legitimacy and viability of the entire Soviet regime. Historical glasnost included denunciations of Stalinist foreign policy—that is, that Stalin's policy of "social Fascism" (see Chapter 4) had contributed to Hitler's seizure of power and eventually to World War II. A leading Soviet military scholar denounced the Nazi-Soviet Pact as a cynical act.[6]

Under glasnost Stalin's leading political opponents, killed off in the purges of the 1930s, were rehabilitated. In January 1988 the Central Lenin Museum in Moscow displayed photographs of Nicholas Bukharin, Grigorii Zinoviev, Lev Kamenev, and Lev Trotskii. Bukharin, a chief architect of the New Economic Policy of the 1920s, was praised for his moderate, gradual rural program that became a model for Gorbachev's own. Nikita Khrushchev now was assessed more positively, whereas the Brezhnev era was depicted as a period of stagnation, and Brezhnev became a convenient scapegoat for Soviet society's manifold ills.

Under Gorbachev political liberalization advanced far more rapidly than economic reforms. In February 1987 competitive elections for some local soviets were instituted. Later, an émigré critic of Soviet policies wrote about the semifree March 1989 elections to the soviets: "For all their unfairness,

---

[5]Iurii Afanasiev, lecture at the Kennan Institute, Washington, DC, October 6, 1988.
[6]General Dmitrii Volkogonov in *Pravda*, June 20, 1988.

fraud, undemocratic framework and stage managing, the present elections will go down in history as the most democratic elections the people have seen under Communist rule."[7] Party conservatives were mostly repudiated, and Muscovites voted overwhelmingly for Boris Yeltsin, who favored radical political change. These elections opened the way for a rapid peaceful evolution toward democracy in the USSR, spurred on by the eastern European anti-Communist revolutions of 1989.* Early in 1990 the Congress of People's Deputies, a new legislative body, revoked Article 6 of the Soviet Constitution, which had guaranteed the leading political role to the Communist Party. As thousands of Party members resigned, a multiparty system began to emerge and the opposition won control of the USSR's three largest cities—Moscow, Leningrad, and Kiev. As Gorbachev's power over the Soviet political system was being undermined, the prestige and influence of Yeltsin and the radical reformers grew.

Meanwhile the major nationalities of the USSR emerged from decades of somnolent obedience to assert long-concealed aspirations to autonomy, then independence. Leading the way were the Baltic republics that were seeking to reassert an independence crushed in 1940. Lithuania's defiance of Moscow in March 1990 provoked a major crisis until Vilnius agreed to defer outright independence. Starting in 1988 Gorbachev faced explosive, bloody ethnic and religious disputes in the Caucasus, notably between Armenians (Christians) and Azeris (Muslims) over Nagorno-Karabakh, an Armenian enclave in Azerbaijan. Moscow sought vainly to calm these conflicts as Gorbachev declared piously in November 1988: "We live in a multi-ethnic state, the Soviet Union is our common home. . . . Our future is not in weakening ties among the republics but in strengthening them."[8] However, during 1990 the USSR disintegrated increasingly as the Baltic and Caucasian republics asserted their sovereignty and the Russian Republic's legislature, under newly elected president Boris Yeltsin, resolved that Russian laws would take precedence over Soviet ones. An irresistible nationalist tide was sweeping over the Soviet empire threatening its very existence.

Proceeding slowest were economic reforms designed to shift the huge but inefficient Soviet economy from full state ownership and management to a market economy featuring individual initiative and local decision making. Initially, Gorbachev tried traditional approaches such as an anti-alcohol campaign, tightening work discipline, and shifting investment. Beginning in 1987 Gorbachev aimed to overhaul the state economy and create a socialist market economy with a significant private sector, but the entrenched Party bureaucracy blocked most real reform. The centralized Stalinist industrial and agricultural system revealed an amazing capacity to

---

[7]Alexander Amerisov, *Soviet-American Review*, vol. 4, no. 2, February 1989.
*See below, pp. 242–44.
[8]*New York Times*, November 28, 1988.

resist and survive. Meanwhile Soviet financial problems worsened steadily as the budget deficit soared.

Hampered and frustrated by conservative opposition to his efforts at economic reform, Gorbachev succeeded in transforming Soviet foreign policy almost beyond recognition. He inherited many difficult international problems including a military stalemate in Afghanistan, tension over the Horn of Africa, a recent Soviet walkout from arms control talks with the West, and a world opinion that condemned Moscow for persecuting dissidents and Jews. Within four years Gorbachev had achieved significant progress on these and other issues with new men, new policy-making processes, and "new thinking." Setting bases for his new course, Gorbachev wrote in his key book, *Perestroika:* "The fundamental principle of the new political outlook is very simple: *nuclear war cannot be a means of achieving political, economic, ideological or any other goals.*" He added: "Nuclear war is senseless; it is irrational. There would be neither winners nor losers in a global nuclear conflict: World civilization would inevitably perish. It is a suicide." From a security viewpoint, "the arms race has become an absurdity because its very logic leads to the destabilization of international relations and eventually to a nuclear conflict."[9] Continued the innovative Soviet leader, breaking from the old confrontational rhetoric: "Security is indivisible. It is either equal security for all or none at all. The only solid foundation for security is the recognition of the interests of all peoples and countries and of their equality in international affairs."[10]

Gorbachev's "new thinking" remained deeply rooted in Soviet domestic problems and requirements. Like Alexander II, he realized the urgent need to reduce external tensions and threats in order to push ahead with major internal reforms. Restructuring in foreign affairs emanated not only from top Soviet leaders but from academic foreign policy specialists, such as those from the Institute of Canada and the USA. "New thinking" meant extending ideas of peaceful coexistence, deemphasizing military force, and fostering superpower cooperation in trade relations even if that implied socialism's failure as a system and undermined pro-Soviet political movements and countries. It signified repudiating class struggle as a primary factor to explain capitalist foreign policies and a stress on achieving security through deescalation and disengagement. Gorbachev also emphasized peaceful resolution of conflicts through the United Nations and a much greater reliance on that organization.[11]

Why did Gorbachev consider the transformation of Soviet foreign policy such an urgent matter? Gorbachev concluded that the foreign policies of

---

[9]Mikhail Gorbachev, *Perestroika: New Thinking for Our Country and the World* (New York, 1988), p. 127. (Italics in the original.)

[10]Gorbachev, p. 128.

[11]Robert Huber, "Perestroika and U.S.-Soviet Relations," in Harley Balzer, ed., *Five Years That Shook the World: Gorbachev's Unfinished Revolution* (Boulder, CO, 1991), pp. 160–61.

his predecessors had failed completely and that major reform at home would require unprecedented changes in Soviet foreign policy. Moscow's draining and expensive involvement in Afghanistan and costly aid to Third World countries threatened to weaken the USSR economically. However, the actual financial burdens of external empire remained stable or even declined during the 1980s partly because of successful Soviet efforts to economize. Total costs for 1984—economic and military—were estimated by the United States Central Intelligence Agency at just over 1 percent of Soviet gross national product, or not sufficient to compel the USSR to relinquish valuable positions on its frontiers or overseas.[12]

In any case, Gorbachev and his advisers moved swiftly to reform the USSR's diplomatic infrastructure. A well-trained post-World War II generation of Soviet diplomats assumed responsible positions as part of a conscious regeneration of the diplomatic corps. Increased emphasis on efficient diplomatic procedures, issues of cost effectiveness in foreign policy, and flexibility and openness in negotiations all reflected the "new thinking." After 1985 there was unprecedented personnel turnover at the Foreign Ministry. Besides the foreign minister were replaced ten of twelve deputy foreign ministers, and nearly all key ambassadors.[13]

A key and brilliant performer in implementing the "new thinking" was Gorbachev's new foreign minister, Eduard Shevarnadze. In his memoirs Shevarnadze noted:

> From the outset it was clear to all that the old methods of confrontation and the elevation of ideology above politics and law were no longer suitable. By remaining stuck in the old positions, we would not stop the arms race which was bleeding our already anemic country or reestablish cooperation with the West. . . . We had to build new relations with the Third World, to search for a new economic order, and to prevent the dangers of global crises.[14]

Quickly Shevarnadze established an unprecedented degree of rapport with U.S. Secretary of State George Shultz and the French and West German foreign ministers based on a mutual trust previously lacking in Soviet-Western relationships. At his second meeting with Shultz in New York in September 1985, Shevarnadze said:

> Much in the world depends on the state of Soviet-American relations. And they in turn depend on the relations that you and I have. I intend to do business as your honest and reliable partner, and if you wish, to be your friend.

---

[12]Dina Spechler and Martin Spechler, "The Economic Burden of the Soviet Empire," in Uri Ra'anan, ed., *The Soviet Empire* (Lexington, MA, 1990), pp. 27–44.

[13]Joseph Whelan, *Soviet Diplomacy and Negotiating Behavior—1979–1988: New Tests for US Diplomacy* (Washington, DC, 1988).

[14]Eduard Shevarnadze, *The Future Belongs to Freedom* (New York, 1991), p. xi.

Shultz then suddenly stood up and extended his palm: "Here is my hand. Give me yours." Thus was established a solid and fruitful friendship: "The obstacles were never stronger than our mutual desire to listen to and understand each other and to achieve a mutually acceptable outcome."[15] Just prior to Gorbachev's report to the Twenty-Seventh Party Congress in February 1986, Shevarnadze received the final draft and saw that it omitted mention of the clear need to withdraw Soviet troops from Afghanistan that had been in earlier drafts. Suggestive of Shevarnadze's influence is his reaction:. "I phoned Gorbachev and told him not a soul in the USSR or outside world would understand us if this sentence were omitted."[16] The foreign minister's public remarks to diplomatic audiences placed foreign affairs on a wholly different professional footing. Restructuring his ministry to make it accountable to the people, Shevarnadze revealed unprecedented openness in dealings with the public. The Gorbachev team strove also to build good media relations with the foreign press and held regular conferences at the Foreign Ministry. Within the USSR, radio and television coverage of foreign affairs was upgraded and expanded.[17]

At Gorbachev's accession, the intelligence analyst, Paul Dibb aptly characterized the Soviet Union as an "incomplete superpower," potent militarily but weak otherwise.[18] Soviet scholars were warning that the country's global influence depended on its ability to make economic and technological advances. Writing in *Izvestiia*, the commentator Alexander Bovin warned that failure to revive the Soviet economy was causing economic stagnation "bringing our society to the brink of a crisis, and weakening the Soviet Union's prestige and influence in the international arena." Warned Bovin: "Socialism has not yet been able to acquire the force of example of which Lenin spoke." Without sweeping economic reforms, "the worldwide balance of power could change in favor of capitalism."[19]

SOVIET RELATIONS WITH THE UNITED STATES AND THE WEST, 1985–1990

During the Gorbachev regime from 1985 to 1991 basic Soviet and American assumptions about each other's foreign policies changed almost beyond recognition. At Gorbachev's accession in March 1985 Washington viewed the USSR as the greatest threat to American interests in the world and argued that United States military power had to be modernized and updated to confront a growing Soviet military arsenal. Pro-Soviet regimes, especially in the Third World, were allegedly threatening America's global interests and regional stability and needed to be contained or if possible overthrown.

---

[15]Shevarnadze, pp. 70–71.

[16]Shevarnadze, p. 47.

[17]Huber, pp. 163–65.

[18]Paul Dibb, *The Soviet Union: The Incomplete Superpower* (Chicago, 1986), pp. 35, 264.

[19]*Izvestiia*, July 11, 1987.

Washington believed that the use of force against the USSR and its allies was justifiable if employed in self-defense. For its part, Moscow assumed in 1985 that the two superpowers would remain permanent adversaries until the final inevitable triumph of socialism over capitalism. Soviet leaders believed that President Ronald Reagan's apparently aggressive policies were blocking arms negotiations. American military modernization aimed at achieving military superiority over the USSR, especially the strategic defense initiative (SDI) and popularly known as "Star Wars," necessitated further Soviet buildups. As the socialist superpower the USSR claimed the right to protect socialist eastern European countries against efforts by the United States to undermine their stability. Six years later most of these assumptions by both sides had become irrelevant. The USSR had thoroughly revised its military doctrine, cut its defense budget, and reduced sharply its support for national liberation movements and pro-Soviet regimes. Soviet withdrawal from Afghanistan, removal of Cuban forces from Angola, and U.S.-Soviet cooperation to prevent another Middle East war had virtually ended American concern about the USSR as a source of regional instability.[20]

In April 1985 Gorbachev declared in a *Pravda* interview that confrontation was an "anomaly" in Soviet-American relations.[21] He criticized Washington's seeming pursuit of military superiority through Reagan's "Star Wars" scheme for a defensive missile screen as the chief obstacle to better relations. In July the superpowers announced that Reagan and Gorbachev would meet in Geneva, Switzerland, that November. At the Geneva Summit of November 19–21, 1985, the two leaders held extensive private talks and issued a positive joint statement. Soviet newspapers described Gorbachev chatting amiably with Reagan, previously depicted as a trigger-happy cowboy. At his press conference Gorbachev concluded: "This is unquestionably a significant event in international life." After Geneva both sides moderated their rhetoric, but Gorbachev displayed impatience over President Reagan's stubborn adherence to "Star Wars" and his refusal to join Moscow in a nuclear test ban moratorium.

Seizing the initiative, Moscow in the fall of 1985 proposed a 50 percent reduction of strategic nuclear delivery systems to limit warheads to 6,000 for both sides for all delivery systems, provided an agreement could be reached on banning research and deployment of "offensive space weapons." In January 1986 Gorbachev outlined a grandiose scheme to gradually eliminate all the world's nuclear weapons by the year 2000. The first stage would involve a 50 percent reduction within five to eight years of all superpower strategic systems. At the Twenty-Seventh Congress in February Gorbachev cited "all embracing, strictest verification" as a precondition for true disarmament, signifying the application of glasnost (openness) in the

---

[20]Huber, pp. 157–59.
[21]*Pravda*, April 8, 1985, pp. 1–4.

military field. Reflecting Gorbachev's emphasis on the growing interdependency of the major world powers Evgenii Primakov of the Institute of World Economy and International Relations declared:

> Instead of viewing ongoing events in different regions through a prism of American-Soviet confrontation, the United States and the USSR should work together to solve regional conflicts.[22]

New Soviet arms control proposals that June revealed greater flexibility on "Star Wars" to permit research, testing and development of its components in the laboratory provided the United States pledged to observe the Anti-Ballistic Missile (ABM) treaty for fifteen to twenty years.[23]

Those were preliminary moves. In September 1986 Gorbachev suddenly proposed holding a summit meeting with Reagan in a third country. Meeting in Reykjavik, Iceland, October 11–12, the two leaders came very close to agreeing to ban all their nuclear weapons within a definite time span. For Gorbachev the entire deal depended on agreement on strategic missile defenses. The fatal stumbling block again proved to be "Star Wars." After this apparent failure, President Reagan became preoccupied with the Iran-Contra affair, causing Moscow to doubt the chances of reaching meaningful agreements with his administration.

However, after an interlude, Soviet-American relations again began to warm up. President Reagan now displayed a remarkable ability to abandon his formerly hostile views towards the USSR and to reach meaningful understandings with Gorbachev. During Foreign Minister Shevarnadze's talks in Washington in September 1987 the hitherto tough Soviet line on "Star Wars" moderated as Moscow agreed that some SDI components might even be placed in space if the ABM treaty were confirmed and reinforced. At their summit in Washington in December 1987 Reagan and Gorbachev achieved a highly significant breakthrough by signing an Intermediate Nuclear Forces (INF) Treaty to eliminate altogether medium- and short-range nuclear missiles with a range from 300 to 3,400 miles. Scoring an amazing triumph with the American public and media, Gorbachev declared that the two sides were now finally emerging from their protracted Cold War confrontation. At his press conference of December 12 Gorbachev confirmed that there had been a deepening of political dialogue with Reagan. The Soviets viewed the INF treaty as a first major step toward complete nuclear disarmament. In the spirit of glasnost the USSR, to ensure compliance with the treaty, accepted on-site verification. Simultaneously, the Soviet press and television for the first time provided positive coverage of

---

[22]*MEMO*, no. 5 (1986), p. 13, quoted in Jan S. Adams, *A Foreign Policy in Transition: Moscow's Retreat from Central America and the Caribbean, 1985–1992* (Durham, NC, 1992), pp. 10–11.

[23]Roy Allison, "Gorbachev's Arms-Control Offensive," in Carl G. Jacobsen, ed., *Soviet Foreign Policy: New Dynamics, New Themes* (New York, 1989), pp. 70–71.

the United States as a positive example for the USSR in restaurant service and individual initiative.

The growing flexibility and innovativeness of Soviet arms-control policy under Gorbachev owed much to changes in policy-making institutions that brought diverse views from the outside into the process of designing policies. In September 1988 Gorbachev assumed the Soviet presidency, and policy-making shifted quickly from the Politburo to Gorbachev and the Foreign Ministry. Foreign Minister Shevarnadze emphasized that the policy-making process would now become more democratic. The bold and flexible style of Soviet arms-control diplomacy often placed Western officials on the defensive. The new Soviet readiness to abandon or modify former fixed positions and to respond swiftly to American initiatives contrasted sharply with the rigidly conservative Brezhnev approach. Soviet willingness to accept disproportionate missile cuts in intermediate missiles illustrated Moscow's new stance.[24]

The final Gorbachev-Reagan summits during 1988 produced no major new agreements but deepened their close personal relationship and mutual trust. Thus the primarily ceremonial Moscow meeting of May 1988 featured Reagan lecturing Soviet citizens on American democracy in Red Square, quite a turnaround for a president who only a few years earlier had denounced the USSR as an "evil empire." Gorbachev also met briefly with Reagan and President-elect George Bush in New York in December to arrange continuation of this new high level of Soviet-American contacts. When Reagan left office in January 1989, the Soviet press praised his evident ability to shift his approach in response to major Soviet reforms. The massive outpouring of American aid to refugees of the Armenian earthquake in December 1988 amazed Soviet citizens by its generosity. The Soviet authorities welcomed this aid with almost unprecedented openness.

This transformation of Soviet external policies under Gorbachev prompted George F. Kennan, an architect of America's post-World War II containment policy (See Chapter 8), to urge Washington to negotiate major agreements with Moscow to reduce nuclear and conventional forces as steps toward creating a normal great power relationship. In April 1989, appearing before the U.S. Senate Foreign Relations Committee, Kennan declared:

> What we are witnessing today in Russia is the break-up of much, if not all, of the system of power by which that country has been held together and governed since 1917.[25]

Kennan stressed Moscow's abandonment of revolutionary ideology and rhetoric and of its political and military efforts to achieve world domination.

---

[24]Allison, pp. 61–64.

[25]George F. Kennan to U.S. Senate Foreign Relations Committee, April 4, 1989, cited in *New York Times*, April 5, 1989.

U.S. PRESIDENT GEORGE BUSH (LEFT) AND SOVIET PRESIDENT MIKHAIL GORBACHEV EX-
CHANGE SMILES AS BUSH TRIES ON A HEADPHONE DURING A PRESS CONFERENCE AT THEIR MALTA
SUMMIT MEETING OF DECEMBER 1989.

He warned that three factors remained to still trouble Soviet-American relations: excessively large Soviet armed forces, especially conventional forces; continued Soviet hegemony over eastern Europe (soon to end); and the arms race (soon to be controlled). Praising Gorbachev's dramatic initiatives on arms control and criticizing American responses as too slow, Kennan concluded that the United States should no longer regard the USSR as an enemy but as just another great power with its own interests conditioned by geography, history, and tradition. Kennan called on both powers to reduce abnormal military tensions and to establish a constructive and cooperative relationship. The Bush-Gorbachev summit at Malta in December 1989 reflected the new era of mutual trust and cooperation between the two superpowers.

Even before his accession to power Gorbachev realized that western Europe was not the way it was depicted in official Soviet writings of the Brezhnev era. Through personal travel and conversations with scholars at the Academy of Sciences, Gorbachev knew the significance of European integration and about the success of the Common Market, which he viewed as a possible model for the USSR and eastern Europe. Already in December 1984 in London Gorbachev emphasized that the USSR was a European power and first used the phrase, "our common European home," derived from Brezhnev. Gorbachev interpreted that concept initially as stimulating western Europe to contribute more to eastern European economic development. He implied that this gradual rapprochement between the two halves of Europe might culminate in the unification of Germany. Initially vague as to the United States role in such a common home, by July 1989 in a speech to the Council of Europe, Gorbachev stated: "The USSR and the United States are a natural part of the European international political structure. And their participation in its evolution is not only justified, but historically conditioned."[26]

During his first four years in power Gorbachev pursued an active policy toward western Europe, with the aim of undoing much of the harm inflicted during 1975–1984 by excessive Soviet rearmament. His major successes there included bilateral agreements with France and Britain and the COMECON-EC Treaty of June 1988. Gorbachev followed this up with a Soviet treaty with the European Community (EC) in December 1989 that reversed thirty years of Soviet disregard for European economic integration. His speech at the Council of Europe in July 1989 showed how seriously he now took that European trend. At first he followed a cautious course toward West Germany, formerly the USSR's *bête noire*, but rapprochement gained momentum in 1987, and finally in June 1989 he capped this with a state visit to Bonn. As Communism deteriorated in eastern Europe, Gorbachev sought actively closer economic ties with western Europe and between western and eastern Europe. By summer 1989 he had fostered a Soviet image in western Europe as a country that wished sincerely to relax tensions in Europe and pursue arms control agreements.[27]

GORBACHEV AND THE EAST EUROPEAN REVOLUTIONS, 1988–1990

A great movement of reform and democratization swept over eastern Europe during 1988–1990 that Moscow, after initial hesitations, allowed to proceed unchecked. Soon that meant abandoning Soviet control over the region and scrapping long-standing definitions of Soviet security. The eastern European revolutions could not have occurred without profound changes within the USSR and a transformation of Soviet attitudes and policies toward that area.

At Gorbachev's accession Soviet-eastern European relations badly needed repair. Economic conditions in most east European countries appeared even worse than in a stagnating USSR. COMECON, the Soviet dominated agency for coordinating the eastern European economies, was shaken by growing recriminations. Moscow was much dissatisfied with a trade structure under which the USSR exported valuable raw materials, notably oil and natural gas, at low prices in return for inferior eastern European products. The Warsaw Pact represented an alliance in decay. Eastern European leaders, except for Poland's General Wojciech Jaruzelski, feared that their close identification with Brezhnev's repudiated policies and

---

[26]Gorbachev's speech of July 6, 1989, quoted in Angela Stent, "Gorbachev and Europe," in Balzer, pp. 143–44.

[27]Stent, p. 145.

advancing age would doom them. However, initially Gorbachev opposed leadership changes and seemed unwilling to rock the boat.

Since the mid-1950s Moscow had employed the Warsaw Treaty Organization to preserve pro-Soviet eastern European regimes forcibly if necessary, to prevent German reunification, to deter western Europe from supporting those challenging existing socialist regimes, and to undermine NATO's willingness to support West Germany in case of a Soviet-West German conflict. All this required maintaining large Soviet and east European conventional forces, making preparations in case of nuclear war, and maintaining large internal security forces. Gorbachev started out as if to make a new reality out of the Warsaw Pact and COMECON. In December 1985 he persuaded COMECON members to approve a comprehensive program for scientific and technical progress for the year 2000 to ensure "technological independence from and vulnerability to pressure and blackmail by the imperialists."[28] However, such rhetoric soon disappeared as Gorbachev realized that no technological revolution was possible without the West, and that it was only possible to slow a widening economic gap between West and East.

During his first two years in office Gorbachev pursued policies designed to reorganize, modernize, and coordinate eastern Europe as the extension of Soviet perestroika. By doing so he became the chief inspiration for reform movements there and for growing social dissent. As the USSR then left eastern Europe increasingly to its own devices, Moscow became regarded as promoting, not blocking change. At the Twenty-Seventh Soviet Party Congress in February 1986 Gorbachev's criticism of the Soviet system implied an indictment of the fragile existing eastern European regimes as well. Failing to mention "socialist internationalism," which implied armed intervention, Gorbachev instead stressed "unconditional respect in international practice for the right of every people to choose the paths and forms of its development."[29] He failed to anticipate that from this would stem a movement for change that within a few years would destroy socialism in all of eastern Europe. For most eastern Europeans Gorbachev's aim of a regenerated socialism was most inadequate. Instead they sought democracy and independence from Soviet control. Until 1989 Gorbachev, arguing that there was nothing wrong with socialism as a system, insisted that it be preserved. Thus in April 1987 he declared in Prague, Czechoslovakia:

> Of course it is not the socialist system that is to blame, as our ideological opponents claim, but miscalculations among the leadership in the running of the country about which we have openly told the party and the people.[30]

---

[28] J. F. Brown, *Surge to Freedom: The End of Communist Rule in Eastern Europe* (Durham, NC, 1991), p. 65.

[29] Political Report to the Central Committee of the CPSU, February 25, 1986, cited in Stent, p. 146.

[30] *Pravda*, April 11, 1987.

As late as July 1989 with Poland and Hungary moving rapidly away from Communist rule, Gorbachev on a trip to France repudiated any idea of rejecting a socialist order. He warned that any Western attempt to destroy it in eastern Europe would produce a "confrontation."[31]

Between 1987 and 1989 the general political and economic situation in eastern Europe deteriorated swiftly as elderly Communist leaders refused to change and their countries fell into crisis. Increasingly absorbed in turmoil at home, Gorbachev found himself compelled to abandon the effort to control eastern Europe. Moscow signified that it would no longer employ force to maintain unpopular regimes in power. During his June 1989 visit to France, Gorbachev repudiated the Brezhnev Doctrine as outmoded. In November he stated that the "Prague Spring" of 1968 had been justified as was the Czechoslovak revolution of 1989. Semi-free elections in Poland in June 1989 represented a key turning point for the political transformation of eastern Europe, followed in October by the dissolution of the Hungarian Workers' Party and the formation of new political parties. In East Germany, the fall of Erich Honecker on October 18 began rapid political change. In Czechoslovakia, change began on November 17 with the suppression by the police of a public demonstration in Prague. In Romania the brutal dictatorship of Nicolae Ceausescu was overturned in December with the approval of the Gorbachev regime.

It is essential to look in somewhat greater detail at the instructive cases of Poland and East Germany, the twin keys to the Soviet position in eastern Europe and to Soviet reactions. By summer 1988 President Jaruzelski's program in Poland of continued economic centralization had clearly failed as the initiative passed to the Solidarity movement. Attending the Tenth Congress of the Polish Workers' Party in June 1986, Gorbachev had backed Jaruzelski but had strongly advised a change in course. However, the martial law regime spurned a reform package prepared by Solidarity featuring independent enterprises, flexible prices, and economic openness. Pope John Paul's third visit to Poland in June 1987 had helped revive Polish national determination. Thus in January 1988 when Jaruzelski imposed steep price increases on basic commodities, a chain of events began, leading to the regime's collapse in mid-1989. Late in 1988 Lech Walesa reemerged as popular national strike leader and hero. At roundtable talks between Solidarity and the regime early in 1989, it was agreed to hold parliamentary elections in June with 65 percent of the seats allotted to the "ruling coalition" led by the Communists. In a peaceful parliamentary revolution only one of fifty regime candidates received the mandatory 50 percent of the votes. Meantime Poland was staggering under a massive hard currency debt to foreign banks of more than $38 billion (compared with $1 billion in 1970). This was accompanied by rampant inflation and advancing economic destitution. After August 1989 Communism became increasingly

---

[31]Moscow TV, July 6, 1989, cited in Brown, p. 56.

irrelevant in Poland, although President Jaruzelski, still a Communist, remained to reassure Moscow and as a guarantor of stability.

Few observers either in the USSR or elsewhere believed that German unification would be completed only a year after the destruction of the Berlin Wall in the fall of 1989. The revolution that deposed First Party Secretary Erich Honecker of East Germany in October was an indigenous movement produced by long resentment at a repressive system that had made the populace involuntary prisoners. At the decisive moment in mid-October when Honecker ordered force used against growing East German demonstrations, the Soviet Red Army was instructed not to aid in the repression. When Egon Krenz replaced Honecker on October 18, Gorbachev's congratulatory telegram urged the new leadership to prove "sensitive to the demands of the time."[32] Clearly admired by many East Berlin demonstrators, Gorbachev approved the ouster of Honecker anticipating that reform Communists would replace Stalinists and maintain East Germany as a separate socialist state. Surprised by the subsequent opening of the Wall, Moscow refused to become involved. When Hans Modrow replaced Krenz in December 1989, Moscow believed that he would survive in power for some time. Thus when Chancellor Helmut Kohl of West Germany issued a plan for German unification and federation, Moscow initially rejected it. Foreign Minister Shevarnadze stressed that two German states were required to insure the security of Europe.[33] However, by late January 1990 the official Soviet view softened, and on February 10 Gorbachev assured Kohl he would not seek to block the achievement of German unity.[34] Moscow adopted that view reluctantly only when it realized that momentum toward unification was unstoppable.

Putting the best face on a disastrous situation for the USSR, Gennadii Gerasimov, a spokesman for the Foreign Ministry, termed the new Soviet policy the "Sinatra Doctrine," implying that Moscow would allow eastern European governments to develop in their own way. Actually, in the fall of 1989 Gorbachev had intervened at key junctures to support the reformers and to undermine conservative Communist regimes, apparently believing that this might rescue his stalled policies of perestroika at home. The sudden collapse of Communist rule in eastern Europe had resulted from internal decay, external influences, and the "domino effect." By the end of the year multiparty systems were developing throughout the region. Accused by conservatives during 1990 of having "lost eastern Europe," Soviet leaders protested that it had not been their fault. Prompt reforms would have saved those regimes, they asserted. In an interview on February 20, 1990, Shevarnadze declared:

---

[32]*Radio Free Europe*, report 14, no. 42 (October 20, 1989).

[33]*Radio Liberty*, report on the USSR, no. 49 (December 8, 1989), p. 20.

[34]*The Washington Post*, January 31, 1990; February 11, 1990.

There was a lag, but not on our part. I am convinced that if the leaders of the GDR had embarked on reforms say two years ago, the situation today would be different. But they doggedly stuck to their viewpoint: "We have built socialism, we do not need any amendments. . . ." Honecker was not aware of the sentiments of his people. As a result, the time for reforms was lost, never to return.[35]

Gorbachev at first resisted the creation of a multiparty system, both in eastern Europe and in the USSR, then he finally accepted it early in 1990. By then all eastern European countries were virtually independent of the USSR. Gorbachev finally realized that Soviet-style Communism had failed so completely in the entire region that it could not be salvaged. Foreign Minister Shevarnadze was brutally frank in informing the Twenty-Eighth Congress of the Soviet Communist Party in July 1990:

> Is the collapse of socialism in eastern Europe a failure of Soviet diplomacy? It would have been if our diplomacy had tried to prevent changes in the neighboring countries. Soviet diplomacy did not and could not have set out to resist the liquidation of those imposed, alien and totalitarian regimes.[36]

The eastern European revolutions of 1989 undermined the Warsaw Pact by depriving it of all purpose and power. The Brezhnev Doctrine that had authorized Warsaw Pact intervention to preserve a Communist regime had been repudiated. By the end of 1989 Moscow merely insisted on formal Pact membership for eastern European countries and that they honor bilateral treaties with the USSR. Soviet passivity in the face of Communism's collapse in East Germany removed the last doubts about Soviet policy, since Moscow had neglected to act in order to preserve its greatest historical gain from World War II and the focal point of its European security. Gorbachev relied instead on improved East-West relations.

How would the new eastern European multiparty regimes view the Warsaw Pact? In Hungary, possible neutrality was suggested as a long-term goal, but Budapest quickly renounced any hasty, unilateral moves. In Poland, Solidarity, recognizing Polish membership in the Warsaw Pact, merely insisted upon equal relations between Poland and the USSR. Initially, Premier Tadeusz Mazowiecki and his foreign minister announced that Warsaw did not intend leaving the Pact, while opposing any external intervention in Polish affairs. The East German collapse faced Moscow with the most serious challenge. The impending unified Germany and the loss of this key Soviet power position threatened an emotional catastrophe endangering the Gorbachev regime's survival. Also involved was the future of 380,000 Soviet troops in the former German Democratic Republic. Most leaders, East and West, wanted at least some of these soldiers to remain

---

[35]*Izvestiia*, February 20, 1990.
[36]*New York Times*, July 4, 1990.

temporarily to ensure stability, whereas most East Germans wanted them out. How could the Warsaw Pact evolve into a political alliance without an official ideology to hold it together?

The new east-European leaders after 1989 devoted their efforts to maximizing Western contacts. Thus COMECON virtually died at its Sofia meeting in January 1990. However, eastern European countries still required cheap Soviet energy and COMECON markets for their low-quality products. In a special COMECON commission a Soviet proposal to shift to hard currency prices in their economic relations beginning in January 1991 triggered objections. The Czechs argued that this would benefit Soviet energy exports while penalizing east European products, and thus Moscow should subsidize the difficult east European transition to global competition. Moscow ignored this objection and insisted on payments in hard currency.

Innovative Soviet policies toward a rapidly changing eastern Europe provoked differences and splits in Moscow. Egor Ligachev, the leader of the more conservative wing of Soviet Communists, while approving grudgingly changes in the Hungarian leadership when the regimes in East Germany and Czechoslovakia faced collapse, strongly supported the old system. As Soviet power crumbled in eastern Europe, Gorbachev's supporters split much as they did over internal Soviet changes between "Leninist reformers" and "social democrats." The latter at least tacitly supported multiparty systems, and introducing capitalist practices and privatization of industry. "Social democrats" such as Shevarnadze and Alexander Iakovlev advocated revisionist or even revolutionary approaches. Events soon forced Gorbachev himself into that group as he zigzagged domestically seeking to retain the center position.[37]

Disagreements persisted in Moscow over Germany's place in the European alliances. The Soviet position early in 1990 was that a unified Germany must remain neutral and demilitarized, as Shevarnadze told Chancellor Kohl during his February trip to Moscow.[38] Later, he modified this stand by dropping references to neutrality. On May 18, 1990, the two German governments signed a state treaty outlining terms for a new economic and monetary union. Whereas unofficial spokesmen such as Viacheslav Dashchichev declared in March that Moscow would accept a united Germany in NATO,[39] in May Defense Minister Dmitrii Iazov reiterated Soviet opposition to this. Negotiations among the four occupying powers and the two German states ("Four plus two") intensified. Bonn finally offered Moscow major economic incentives to make concessions on NATO agreeing to meet all of East Germany's economic obligations toward the USSR. During Chancellor Kohl's visit to Stavropol in July 1990, Gorbachev officially accepted the West's demands: a united Germany would remain

---

[37]Brown, pp. 62–65.
[38]*The Washington Post*, February 11, 1990.
[39]Interview in *Bild Zeitung* (Hamburg, Germany), March 18, 1990.

within NATO and Soviet troops would evacuate East Germany by 1994. Subsequently, the West Germans pledged large sums to help repatriate Soviet troops and agreed to reduce united Germany's armed forces to 370,000 men within four years. Thus the Soviet Union helped create what formerly Moscow had depicted as a nightmare scenario: a united capitalist Germany allied with the United States and anchored in the European Community.

The most important lesson of the Revolutions of 1989 was that the Communist experiment had clearly and utterly failed. "We have made one important contribution," stated Soviet reformer, Iurii Afanasiev. "We have taught the world what not to do."[40] Gorbachev's momentous decision to let eastern Europe go its own way was original, unexpected, and traumatic.

GORBACHEV'S POLICIES IN THE THIRD WORLD

The most difficult problem Gorbachev inherited in the Third World was the stalemated war in Afghanistan. At first he tried to resolve it by applying greater military power, increasing Soviet troop strength to about 115,000 men. Although this forced almost one-third of the Afghan population to flee, the Muslim rebels, aided effectively by American Stinger anti-aircraft missiles, continued staunch resistance; the Soviets could only control the major towns. At the Twenty-Seventh Party Congress in February 1986 Gorbachev proclaimed the Afghan conflict "a bleeding wound," but took no definite action to end it despite considerable support within the Politburo. In February 1988 Gorbachev announced that the USSR was prepared to remove its forces under United Nations auspices over a ten-month period, beginning on May 15 without demanding guarantees for the pro-Communist regime of Najibullah who replaced Karmal in 1986. This withdrawal was completed early in 1989, although Soviet military advisers remained and Moscow continued to supply the Najibullah forces with large quantities of arms and equipment. Expectations abroad that Najibullah would soon fall initially were deceived since the Afghan rebels remained fragmented, but in 1992 his regime collapsed.

The Soviets had suffered considerable casualties in the Afghan war: a total of 13,310 killed; 35,478 wounded; and 311 missing in action.[41] The Soviet failure to score a military victory damaged the Red Army's reputation, but the war had caused even greater harm to Moscow's standing in the Third World, notably among Muslims. Furthermore, the war had constituted a major obstacle to improvement of relations with the United States and China. The Soviet withdrawal therefore, involving a short-term blow to Moscow's prestige, created many compensatory advantages for Soviet

---

[40]Quoted in Robert Kaiser, *Why Gorbachev Happened: His Triumphs and His Failure* (New York, 1991), p. 228.

[41]Joseph L. Nogee and Robert Donaldson, *Soviet Foreign Policy Since World War II*, 4th ed. (New York, 1992), p. 372.

foreign policy. Producing improvements in Soviet-American and East-West relations so important to Gorbachev, it enabled Moscow to relax tensions with Beijing and to begin reducing the Sino-Soviet military confrontation along their frontiers. The Soviet image among Muslims, especially with Iran, was enhanced. The Afghan war had become highly unpopular within the USSR. Now the Gorbachev regime could blame the 1979 invasion on a small hawkish Politburo group around a senile Brezhnev. Reputedly very ill at the time of the invasion, Brezhnev had unwittingly signed an authorization document slipped to him hastily by then Defense Minister Dimitrii Ustinov. Finally, the Soviet withdrawal from Afghanistan ended Western fears of Soviet aspirations to expand southward to the Persian Gulf.

Elsewhere in the Middle East the lengthy Iran-Iraq War of the 1980s induced Moscow to balance carefully between them. The divisive effects of that conflict on Middle Eastern countries inhibited Soviet efforts to mobilize Arab countries against the West and Israel. Soon that was no longer Gorbachev's aim. His major initiatives in the region included opening diplomatic relations with Israel and exerting pressure on Syria and the Palestine Liberation Organization to recognize Israel. Such departures from traditional Soviet Middle Eastern policy reflected Gorbachev's more sophisticated assessment of the Third World. In July 1987 an official Soviet delegation visited Israel for three months. A year later an Israeli deputation visited Moscow. Emigration restrictions were eased on Soviet Jews, and in the fall of 1990 the USSR and Israel formally restored consular relations.

Until almost the end of the Iran-Iraq War, Moscow avoided choosing sides while supporting United Nations efforts to arrange a cease-fire. Moscow also undertook its own mediation efforts: In June 1987 Deputy Foreign Minister Iuli Vorontsov went to the region as Gorbachev's personal envoy. When those talks produced beneficial economic accords, Moscow became increasingly pro-Iranian leading some Arabs to question Soviet support for their cause. The end of the Iran-Iraq War in July 1988 gave Moscow greater flexibility to pursue mutually beneficial economic relations with Teheran. Seeking to restore the USSR's Middle East standing, in February 1989 Foreign Minister Shevarnadze met with top Middle Eastern leaders and urged them to agree to an international conference on peace in the Middle East. Moscow also moved to restore its shattered ties with Egypt, rescheduled the Egyptian debt to the USSR, and in spring 1990 Gorbachev hosted Egyptian President Hosni Mubarak in the Kremlin. In the Persian Gulf region Gorbachev by 1990 had established relations with Saudi Arabia and the small sheikdoms and sought to mediate their disputes. As Soviet trade with the Middle East increased, Gorbachev kept the USSR involved there.

In Africa the Gorbachev team quickly reversed the aggressive policies associated with the late Brezhnev years. In Angola the Soviets helped resolve the crisis and arranged to have Cuban troops removed. Soviet military aid to Ethiopia (still struggling with break-away insurgents) continued until 1991, but Moscow stressed its desire to reduce its involvement. Soviet leaders viewed participation in such regional disputes as inhibiting normalization of relations with the West and the USSR's full entry into the international community. Here too "new thinking" produced new behavior.

Early in Gorbachev's rule Moscow instituted moves to improve Soviet relations with China and Japan. On July 28, 1986, in a major speech in Vladivostok, Gorbachev declared that the USSR "is prepared at any time and at any level to discuss with China in the most serious way questions of additional measures to create an atmosphere of good neighborliness."[42] Later, he revealed his sincerity by agreeing to redraw a disputed boundary with China in the middle of the Amur and Ussuri rivers. For years China had posed three conditions for normalizing relations with Moscow: a Soviet withdrawal from Afghanistan, a Vietnamese withdrawal from Cambodia, and reducing Soviet forces on the Chinese border. Late in 1989 Moscow pressured Hanoi to withdraw its combat troops from Cambodia. With Soviet troops out of Afghanistan and reduced along their frontiers, Beijing agreed to receive Gorbachev in May 1989 in the first Sino-Soviet summit in thirty years. Announcing a reduction of some 200,000 troops in the Soviet Far East and demilitarization of the Sino-Soviet frontier, Gorbachev soon had normalized relations with China. Chinese Premier Li Peng returned this visit in spring 1990 in Moscow. Sino-Soviet trade increased ten-fold during the 1980s.[43] However, the persisting dispute over the Kurile Islands, taken by the USSR from Japan at the end of World War II, hampered normal relations with Tokyo. Strong Soviet patriotic feelings prevented Gorbachev, and later Yeltsin, from yielding the islands and thus he failed to obtain Japanese loans. Gorbachev visited Tokyo in April 1991 but was unable to settle the islands dispute, as did Yeltsin, as Russian president, more than two years later in October 1993.

Still causes tension

In Latin America Gorbachev's "new thinking" was slow to be implemented. Numerous articles in the Soviet press from 1985 through 1987 continued to condemn American policies there, arguing that Washington remained the source of all the region's problems.[44] Meanwhile the Soviet Party maintained close links with Communist parties and leftist groups in Latin America. Cuba still received about $4.5 billion in annual Soviet aid, about half of all Moscow's foreign aid. Major Soviet arms shipments to Cuba and Nicaragua persisted. However, by 1987 Gorbachev's new course began to take effect as Soviet economic aid to Nicaragua was reduced. In April 1989 when Gorbachev visited Havana to sign a Soviet-Cuban Friendship Treaty, Article 7 pledged that both parties would "spare no efforts in . . . rejecting the use or threat of force . . . and fostering the settlement of conflicts between states solely by peaceful and political means."[45]

---

[42] *Current Digest of the Soviet Press*, vol. 38, no. 30 (August 27, 1986), pp. 1–8.

[43] Nogee and Donaldson, pp. 373–74.

[44] *Pravda*, March 19, 1987.

[45] TASS (Moscow), April 5, 1989.

Dramatic and unprecedented events in Central America such as the democratic transfer of political power in 1990 from the Sandinistas to President Violeto Chamorro in Nicaragua resulted partly from Gorbachev's innovative, pacific policies.

Finally, under Gorbachev, Soviet policies toward the United Nations were transformed. For years the USSR had remained behind in its payments to the UN and had been prominent chiefly by its frequent vetoes and obstruction. A Gorbachev article in *Pravda* in September 1988, however, contained an amazing list of proposals, including: enhancing the secretary-general's role in preventive diplomacy; greater use of peacekeeping forces in regional conflicts; mandatory acceptance of the International Court's decisions; developing a global strategy for environmental protection, a movement scorned earlier by the USSR; and negotiations to bring national laws into conformity with international human rights standards.[46] Previous Soviet leaders had held almost diametrically opposite views on all of these issues and had opposed efforts to make the UN an effective force to preserve world peace. Requiring many years to implement his reform program, Gorbachev sought to utilize the United Nations partly in order to extricate the Soviet Union from overextension abroad.

Gorbachev followed up this program with a major address on December 7, 1988, to the UN General Assembly, emphasizing full Soviet cooperation with the world organization in order to achieve a peaceful world:

> We have come here to show our respect for the United Nations which increasingly has been manifesting its ability to act as a unique international center in the service of peace and security. . . . It is obvious . . . that the use or threat of force no longer can or must be an instrument of foreign policy.[47]

Gorbachev announced a unilateral reduction of 500,000 men from the Soviet armed forces over the next two years.

MIXED SIGNALS, 1990–1991

Controversial Soviet policies in eastern Europe, accelerating demands by national groups, and Gorbachev's failure to implement promised economic reforms by mid-1990 had seriously eroded his position. Only after taming a conservative revolt at the Twenty-Eighth Party Congress in July could Gorbachev accept Western terms for German reunification in NATO. That summer Gorbachev initially approved the radical "500 Days Plan," drawn up by economist Stanislav Shatalin, calling for extensive privatization of enterprises. Then Gorbachev backed away from it. As the reformers' position weakened, an increasingly vocal debate raged within the USSR over foreign policy. Foreign Minister Shevarnadze was accused by military leaders and

---

[46]*Pravda,* September 17, 1988.
[47]*New York Times,* December 8, 1988.

conservatives of abandoning Soviet security interests in eastern Europe by permitting the demise of socialist regimes, unilaterally withdrawing Soviet troops, and abandoning pro-Soviet allies' interests in the Third World. Shevarnadze claimed that his critics were seeking to undermine and discredit Gorbachev's leadership and the foundations of reform.[48]

During the fall of 1990 Gorbachev retreated towards more conservative policies as disturbing rightist and militarist trends developed. In June a "Centrist Bloc" formed of hard-liners from the Party, security service, and military seeking a return to centralized authoritarian rule. In December, the so-called Committee of National Salvation from that bloc pressured Gorbachev to impose a state of presidential emergency, suspend political parties, and remove elected officials in more democratic republics. Soon thereafter Foreign Minister Shevarnadze, a chief architect of an open and pacific Soviet foreign policy, resigned his post warning of impending dictatorship. By the end of the year, five Soviet republics—the three Baltic states, Armenia, and Georgia—had declared their independence. This prompted a military crackdown against Lithuania early in 1991 that imperilled Gorbachev's support in the West. However, in the spring of 1991 Gorbachev shifted course once again, and under strong foreign pressure the independence of the three Baltic republics was approved. Actual political power was passing increasingly to Boris Yeltsin, who in June 1991 was elected overwhelmingly as president of the Russian Republic.

As these internal developments constricted Soviet foreign policy, President Bush strongly supported Gorbachev. The Gorbachev-Bush summit of May 31–June 3, 1990, in Washington confirmed the continued warmth of Soviet-U.S. relations. President Bush had moved during his first two years in office from caution to commitment; he and Gorbachev were on close terms. In an effort to shore up Gorbachev's weakening position, the Moscow summit of July 30–31, 1991, featured the signature of the START II Treaty, providing for a further major reduction in nuclear arms. During the crisis in the Persian Gulf over Iraq's invasion of Kuwait, the USSR loyally supported the United States against its former ally, Saddam Hussein of Iraq, despite conservative criticism. In the summer of 1991 the fate of Gorbachev and the future of the USSR remained highly uncertain.

Suggested Readings

Adams, Jan S. *A Foreign Policy in Transition: Moscow's Retreat from Central America and the Caribbean, 1985–1992.* Durham, NC, 1992.

Babbage, Ross, ed., *The Soviets in the Pacific in the 1990s.* Elmsford, NY, 1989.

Balzer, Harley, ed., *Five Years That Shook the World: Gorbachev's Unfinished Revolution.* Boulder, CO, 1991.

Bialer, Seweryn and Michael Mandelbaum, eds., *Gorbachev's Russia and American Foreign Policy.* Boulder, CO, 1988.

---

[48]*Izvestiia,* February 19, 1990.

————, eds., *The Global Rivals.* New York, 1989.

Brown, J. F. *Eastern Europe and Communist Rule.* Durham, NC, 1988.

————. *Surge to Freedom: The End of Communist Rule in Eastern Europe.* Durham, NC, 1991.

Brzezinski, Zbigniew. *The Grand Failure: The Birth and Death of Communism in the Twentieth Century.* New York, 1989.

Clemens, Walter C. *Can Russia Change? The USSR Confronts Global Interdependence.* Boston, 1990.

Collins, Joseph. *The Soviet Invasion of Afghanistan.* Cambridge, England, 1986.

Crozier, Brian. *The Gorbachev Phenomenon: Peace and the Secret War.* London, 1990.

Davies, R. W. *Soviet History in the Gorbachev Revolution.* Bloomington, IN, 1989.

Desai, Padma. *Perestroika in Perspective: The Design and Dilemmas of Soviet Reform.* Princeton, NJ, 1989.

Eklof, Ben. *Soviet Briefing: Gorbachev and the Reform Period.* Boulder, CO, 1989.

Gati, Charles. *The Bloc That Failed: Soviet-East European Relations in Transition.* Bloomington, IN, 1990.

Gorbachev, Mikhail S. *Perestroika: New Thinking for Our Country and the World.* New York, 1987, 1988.

————. *At the Summit.* New York, 1988.

Gwertzman, Bernard and Michael T. Kaufman, eds., *The Collapse of Communism.* New York, 1990.

Harlo, Vilho, ed., *Gorbachev and Europe.* New York, 1990.

Hiden, John and P. Salmon. *The Baltic Nations and Europe in the Twentieth Century.* White Plains, NY, 1991.

Hough, Jerry. *Russia and the West: Gorbachev and the Politics of Reform.* New York, 1988.

Jacobsen, Carl G., ed., *Soviet Foreign Policy: New Dynamics, New Themes.* New York, 1989.

Korbonski, Andrzej and Francis Fukuyama. *The Soviet Union and the Third World: The Last Three Decades.* Ithaca, NY, 1987.

Levin, Moshe. *The Gorbachev Phenomenon.* Berkeley, CA, 1988.

McGwire, Michael. *Perestroika and Soviet National Security.* Washington, DC, 1991.

Nogee, Joseph and Robert Donaldson. *Soviet Foreign Policy Since World War II.* 4th ed. New York, 1992.

Olivier, Roy. *Islam and Resistance in Afghanistan.* Cambridge, England, 1986.

Saivetz, Carol R. *The Soviet Union and the Gulf in the 1980s.* Boulder, CO, 1989.

Shamsab, Nasir. *Soviet Expansion in the Third World.* Silver Springs, MD, 1986.

Shevarnadze, Eduard. *The Future Belongs to Freedom.* New York, 1991.

Urban, Mark. *War in Afghanistan.* New York, 1988.

Wettig, Gerhard. *Changes in Soviet Foreign Policy Toward the West.* Boulder, CO, 1991.

Zacek, Jane S. *The Gorbachev Generation: Issues in Soviet Foreign Policy.* New York, 1988.

EPILOGUE: DEMISE OF THE USSR AND THE COMMONWEALTH, 1991–1993

At the end of 1991 the USSR was dissolved after a life of almost seventy years when its component parts, the fifteen former Soviet republics, achieved independence. The USSR was replaced by a very loose, inchoate political entity known as the Commonwealth of Independent States (CIS), which lacked real power or cohesion. Triggering this sudden disintegration of the Soviet empire was an abortive state coup of August 1991 by conservative leaders mostly installed in office by President Mikhail Gorbachev a few months earlier. The swift defeat of this clumsy coup attempt undermined both the Communist hard-liners who led it and its target, President Gorbachev. It reinforced the power and prestige of Russian President Boris Yeltsin. Four months later the USSR dissolved formally and Gorbachev's power and position disappeared. In the immediate post-Soviet era Yeltsin became the dominant political figure advocating a democratic Russia. During 1992 he sought to carry through drastic economic reforms. Despite significant Western support for Yeltsin's reform policies and to other CIS members, his regime came under increasing pressure from strong conservative forces within the Congress of People's Deputies elected in 1990. In September 1993 Yeltsin suddenly dissolved the parliament, then defeated the hard-line revolt that it led in early October. Yeltsin then announced elections for a new constitution and parliament for December.

THE AUGUST COUP AND THE END OF THE SOVIET UNION, AUGUST–DECEMBER 1991

During the first half of 1991, President Gorbachev labored mightily to save the Soviet Union by negotiating a new union treaty among its restive and independent-minded republics. In March Lithuania had proclaimed its complete independence. At a government residence *(dacha)* at Novo-Ogarevo near Moscow in late April representatives of the five largest republics reached an accord outlining a new loose federal union. The new union treaty was scheduled to be signed in Moscow on August 20, 1991, but early the previous day the eight members of a so-called Committee for the State of Emergency (G.K.Ch.P. in Russian) headed by Vice President

MEMBERS OF THE COMMITTEE OF THE STATE OF EMERGENCY HOLD A PRESS CONFERENCE IN MOSCOW ON AUGUST 19, 1991, TO OUTLINE THEIR STEPS IN TAKING POWER. LEFT TO RIGHT ARE ALEXANDER TIRIAKOV, VASILY STARODUBTSEV, BORIS PUGO, GENNADII IANAEV, AND OLEG BAKLANOV.

Gennadii Ianaev, attempted to seize power and establish a conservative and centralist regime. Detaining President Gorbachev at his summer home in the Crimea, the Committee announced that because of illness he had been temporarily removed from power and had been replaced by Vice President Ianaev, appointed by Gorbachev to that post the previous December. The Emergency Committee, composed of conservative leaders of the Communist Party, KGB, and Defense Minister Dmitrii Iazov, asserted that Gorbachev's reforms had "entered a blind alley." It pledged to restore law and order, end bloodshed, and "eradicate shameful phenomena discrediting our society." At a hastily called news conference, Acting President Ianaev announced that Gorbachev was being treated for an undisclosed illness. "It is our hope that as soon as he feels better, he will take up his office again."[1]

The conspirators sought to control the Russian public media, but liberal and independent publications continued to appear and Western journalists broadcast accounts of the coup as it unfolded. Inexplicably, the coup leaders failed to arrest Russian President Yeltsin, who promptly denounced the putsch as illegal and unconstitutional and coordinated public resistance from the Russian parliament. Other republic leaders, including the Mayor of Leningrad, Anatolii Sobchak, openly supported Yeltsin's defiance of the

---

[1]*New York Times*, August 20, 1991.

Emergency Committee. Gorbachev resolved to resist any pressure or blackmail from the plotters and rejected point-blank a demand by the Emergency Committee's delegation to transfer power to it. Warned Gorbachev: "You and the people who sent you are irresponsible. You will destroy yourselves . . . , but you will also destroy the country and everything we have already done."[2] Meanwhile Gorbachev was receiving foreign radio reports describing growing Russian public resistance to the coup and rising support for him and Yeltsin from top world leaders, including American President George Bush. Gorbachev's courage and Yeltsin's leadership helped frustrate the hard-liners' plot.

The trigger that set off this conservative backlash was the scheduled signing of the new union treaty that would have dismantled the old Soviet order and transferred most of its powers to the individual republics. This directly imperilled the institutions represented in the Emergency Committee—the Party, police agencies, technocrats, and some senior military leaders. The "gang of eight" moved to cancel Gorbachev's political reforms that allegedly threatened the existence of the USSR and its own high positions.

On August 20th—its second day in power—the Emergency Committee imposed a curfew on Moscow and sent new armored forces into the city center. Large crowds gathered before the Russian "White House" to protect President Yeltsin. President Bush, calling Yeltsin on an open telephone line, pledged his support and expressed confidence that the coup would be reversed. A crucial turning point occurred when the Committee's tanks failed to assault the Russian parliament. The next day, August 21, the coup collapsed and President Gorbachev returned to Moscow. The coup leaders, fleeing the Kremlin, were soon arrested; some committed suicide. As long columns of tanks, some decorated with Russian flags, moved out of Moscow to cheers by jubilant Muscovites, Communism was the major political casualty. Not even the Emergency Committee had waved the drooping flag of Marxism-Leninism.

Why had the August Coup, engineered by the USSR's most formidable agencies, failed so ignominiously? Directed by lackluster leaders who failed to plan ahead or present any positive program to the Soviet people, the plot amazed observers by its incompetence.[3] The movement's failure testified to the powerful democratic forces unleashed during the Gorbachev era: No longer was Russia a nation of slaves. The methods and even the language of the junta resembled those of the Brezhnev group in ousting Khrushchev in 1964, but unlike Brezhnev, the Committee failed to win support from key military commanders or from the rank and file. Yeltsin's

---

[2]Mikhail Gorbachev, *The August Coup: The Truth and the Lessons* (New York, 1991), pp. 15–22.

[3]Jerry Hough, "Assessing the Coup," *Current History*, vol. 90, no. 558 (October 1991), pp. 305–10.

Russian government, with greater legitimacy, resisted the junta successfully. The military of the future, led by General Evgenii Shaposhnikov, defeated the army of the past headed by older officers such as Marshal Iazov. The latter, believing Gorbachev was a traitor for yielding Soviet gains from World War II, had aimed to suppress democracy and restore a centralized Soviet Union.

The failed August Coup sounded the death knell both of Soviet Communism and of Gorbachev's authority. He returned to Moscow deeply shaken whereas President Yeltsin's power and popularity emerged much enhanced. Yeltsin promptly asserted control of the central government and issued decrees banning the Communist Party in Russia and closing down its news organ, *Pravda*. However, eschewing dictatorial methods, he soon allowed opposition newspapers to reopen and decided wisely not to challenge the boundaries of other republics. At first Gorbachev still strove to salvage his union plan, but in early September the Congress of People's Deputies in special session confirmed that the entire political organization of the USSR had been fatally weakened. The individual republics hastened to proclaim their independence, and their presidents were now equal to Soviet President Gorbachev on a newly created State Council. An agreement for an economic community that Gorbachev hoped would be the prelude to a union treaty was signed in Alma Ata, capital of Kazakhstan. Ratified in Moscow on October 18, this provided for an economic community of "independent states, members or former members of the USSR." However, Ukraine, the second most important republic, refused to join it.[4]

Gorbachev, continuing to press desperately for a federal union, warned that full independence for the Soviet republics would lead to anarchy and even civil war. However, the republics simply ignored the new State Council chaired by Gorbachev. By discrediting central Soviet agencies—the Party, state bureaucracy, and KGB and splitting the army—the August Coup shifted most actual power to the republics. It remained uncertain whether the vast Russian Republic with over one hundred distinct nationalities could remain united. The final blow to the Soviet Union and to Gorbachev's hopes of preserving the center was Ukraine's overwhelming vote in a referendum on December 1, 1991, for full independence. Without Ukraine the USSR could not continue. Elected Ukraine's president was Leonid M. Kravchuk, longtime Soviet bureaucrat, who after the August Coup converted suddenly to Ukrainian nationalism. Responding to reality, Gorbachev dissolved the Soviet Communist Party, and sought to create a loose economic and military structure to replace the USSR and to coordinate the various regions.

What implications did the August Coup have for Soviet foreign policy? The question was posed whether there could be a single Soviet foreign policy at all. At first President Gorbachev, and foreign supporters such as President

---

[4]Helène d'Encausse, *The End of the Soviet Empire*, Trans. Franklin Philip (New York, 1993), pp. 248–49.

Bush, insisted that the center would continue to direct Soviet international relations. Gorbachev summarily removed Foreign Minister Alexander Bess-mertnykh, implicated in the coup, and replaced him with Boris Pankin, an obscure Soviet diplomat in the Prague embassy who had vigorously opposed the coup. Lacking any international clout, Pankin could only conduct a weak holding action. In November Gorbachev reappointed Eduard Shevarnadze as foreign minister, but he remained in office only a month because of the USSR's final dissolution.

The August Coup accelerated the sharp reduction of Soviet power and international influence evident since the eastern European revolutions of 1989. Now the Warsaw Treaty Organization was dissolved, and Soviet troops began withdrawing from eastern Europe aided by generous financial inducements from a newly reunified Germany. The formidable-appearing Soviet bloc constructed by Stalin after World War II was dismantled and all its members achieved full independence. Warmer relations with western Europe were established by parts of the fragmenting USSR, especially by the westward-looking Baltic republics. By the end of 1991 Soviet influence in eastern Europe had virtually vanished in one of history's most startling power reshuffles.

To the bitter end President Gorbachev sought to assert for the USSR a significant role in world affairs. During the Persian Gulf War of 1991 he aligned Moscow closely with the United States and the West, cut ties with Iraq's Saddam Hussein and with Syria, and played as large a role in the United Nations as dwindling Soviet resources permitted. Finally, the August Coup gravely undermined most remaining Communist regimes. Cuba's Fidel Castro, still defiantly Communist, saw Soviet aid to his shattered economy virtually disappear. North Korea's aged hard-line leader, Kim Il-sung, was shocked out of compacency by growing Soviet overtures to prosperous South Korea. Communist Vietnam, deprived of Soviet economic aid, turned increasingly towards the West.

RECAPITULATION AND LEGACY OF SOVIET FOREIGN POLICY, 1917–1991

What did the Soviet Union contribute over its 74-year span to a turbulent twentieth century? In 1917 imperial Russia had collapsed unable to fight a total modern war with a semi-developed economy and incompetent military and political leadership. In November 1917 Vladimir I. Lenin and Lev Trotskii inaugurated Soviet foreign policy with appeals for a democratic, non-imperialist peace and announced a new type of open diplomacy. During "War Communism," accusing the Allied powers of seeking to overthrow the new Soviet regime, they fostered messianic dreams of world revolution coordinated by the Comintern, an increasingly disciplined Soviet instrument. From 1917 to 1921 Lenin and Trotskii believed fervently that socialist revolutions must either spread to Europe and eventually the world, or Soviet Russia would soon succumb to predatory world capitalism. They outlined a protracted, ruthless conflict with the capitalist world that deepened war-torn Russia's misery. After 1921 a chastened Lenin and Foreign Commissar Georgii Chicherin sought accommodation with the West and aid to rebuild devastated Russia. Before his death, Lenin—through pressure and force—had reconstituted most of the former Russian Empire in a pseudo-federation, dubbed the Union of Soviet Socialist Republics, that subjugated non-Russians to concealed but pervasive domination from Moscow.

Directing Soviet foreign policy as autocratically as had Peter the Great more than 200 years earlier, Joseph Stalin transformed the Soviet empire into a "prison of peoples," exterminating millions and deporting entire nationalities. He helped Adolf Hitler into power by undermining German Weimar democracy. Later, Stalin concluded the Nazi-Soviet Pact of 1939, which ignited World War II and cost the USSR over 20 million lives. The great coalition of the United States, USSR, Britain, and France defeated Germany and created for Stalin a favorable power situation comparable to Imperial Russia's in 1815 after the Napoleonic Wars. Instead of pursuing postwar cooperation with the West, Stalin—partly for ideological reasons—provoked a lengthy, needless, and incredibly costly "Cold War" with the West. That conflict saddled the Soviet and Western peoples with huge financial burdens to pay for bloated military forces and nuclear arsenals of mass destruction. Meanwhile, utilizing the Red Army and local Communist parties, Stalin subjugated eastern Europe, imposing puppet Communist regimes subservient to the USSR. Under Stalin Soviet foreign policy featured monstrous lies mouthed by thousands of obedient Soviet diplomats, many of whom were masquerading secret police operatives.

Stalin's successors, while avoiding his worst blunders, continued the protracted conflict with the West. Three times the Red Army intervened with massive force—in East Germany (1953), Hungary (1956), and Czechoslovakia (1968)—to suppress popular east European revolts and perpetuate Soviet-controlled regimes without local roots. The short-lived Georgii Malenkov regime brought the Soviet Union out of Stalinist isolation, repudiated terror, and recognized the terrible dangers of nuclear war to both sides. Under Nikita Khrushchev the USSR gyrated between "peaceful coexistence" with capitalism and continued rivalry with the West, notably in the Third World. In 1956, proclaiming "peaceful coexistence" the basis for Soviet foreign policy, Khrushchev sought to recement Soviet preeminence in eastern Europe by a socialist commonwealth but had to use force to prevent Hungary from breaking away. Khrushchev could not prevent a fundamental schism from growing within world Communism in a first concealed then an open ideological and power competition with Red China. Erupting openly in 1960, that conflict refuted the Marxist-Leninist thesis on the inevitable harmony of socialist states. Instead, rampant polycentrism, fostered by Mao Tse-tung's China and Josip Broz Tito's Yugoslavia, splintered the Communist bloc. Khrushchev's reckless attempt in the Cuban Missile Crisis to solve manifold problems with a foreign policy coup nearly provoked a nuclear Armageddon with the United States. However, the peaceful resolution of that crisis produced policies designed to prevent a recurrence. Khrushchev and U.S. President John Kennedy established a measure of rapport and trust that anticipated subsequent positive relationships between Soviet and American leaders.

Under Leonid Brezhnev, although the Czech intervention preserved remnants of Soviet power in eastern Europe, the Sino-Soviet quarrel deepened ominously to the brink of war in 1969–1970. Influenced by that conflict, Brezhnev adopted a more pragmatic, power-oriented foreign policy and reached agreement with the West on postwar boundaries in Europe. In the 1970s Moscow achieved a measure of détente with the West based on a rough parity in nuclear weapons that encouraged arms limitation. However, a simultaneous massive Soviet military buildup under Brezhnev greatly overstrained the inefficient Soviet economy. Risky adventures in the Third World and corruption at home produced irreversible Soviet decline concealed temporarily by enhanced military strength. Despite increasing pragmatism, Brezhnev's foreign policy still fostered the myth of inevitable conflict with, and victory over, world capitalism.

During a decade of gerontocracy (1975–1985) the USSR's world role gradually declined as Lenin's original messianic goal of a Soviet-led world socialist system proved unachievable. An ill-conceived intervention in Afghanistan (1979) and Soviet-Cuban military involvement in Africa torpedoed détente. Warmer Sino-American relations after Mao's death (1976) and an American military buildup left the USSR hemmed in between economically more dynamic powers to the east and west. Events in Poland after 1979 heralded the impending collapse of Communism in eastern Europe.

Under Mikhail Gorbachev Moscow's policies abroad were transformed. As Foreign Minister Eduard Shevarnadze reached out to the West, Gorbachev stressed "our common European home." However, despite Gorbachev's success in liquidating the Afghan war and in keeping hands off eastern Europe, the failure of his economic reforms doomed the USSR to eventual disintegration. Gorbachev's major achievements abroad included important nuclear arms agreements with the United States and full cooperation with other countries in the United Nations. Nonetheless, his "new thinking" dissolved the Soviet empire and cost it its territorial gains from World War II.

Where did the demise of the Soviet Union in December 1991 leave Russia? With the independence of Ukraine and Belarus, Russia's frontiers in the west resembled those of 1613, leaving her partially isolated from Europe. While retaining the St. Petersburg region and access to the Baltic Sea, Russia, after the Baltic republics' independence, lost much of Peter the Great's "window to the West." In the south, Ukraine's fragile independence cost Russia clear access to the Black Sea, the Crimea, and other territories won by Catherine the Great. Only in the Far East did Russia retain the imperial boundaries of 1914, including Siberia, plus the Kurile Islands. Most of Transcaucasia and Central Asia, acquired by tsarism in the

MAP 14–1   Russia's western borderlands, 1992

nineteenth century, became independent depriving Russia of direct access to the Near and Middle East. In the west Russia's geopolitical situation resembled that of 1918 after conclusion of the Brest-Litovsk Treaty. Its geographical power position approached that of the early Romanov predecessors of Peter the Great.

RUSSIA AND THE COMMONWEALTH OF INDEPENDENT STATES, 1991–1993

On December 8, 1991, the presidents of Russia, Ukraine, and Belarus, meeting in the latter's capital of Minsk, declared that the USSR no longer existed (slightly premature) and announced the formation of a Commonwealth of Independent States (CIS). The leaders of those three Slavic regions, linked historically for centuries, favored creating "coordinating bodies" for finance, defense, and foreign affairs in Minsk and a common "economic space" featuring a ruble currency. President Gorbachev denounced these actions as illegal, but only two weeks later in Alma Ata, Kazakhstan, this Slavic Commonwealth was enlarged to include the Central Asian republics; by the end of December all former Soviet republics except Georgia had joined it. On December 25 Gorbachev resigned as Soviet president and transferred control of Russia's nuclear arsenal to Yeltsin, and the Soviet flag was replaced over the Kremlin by that of Russia.

However, that promising beginning to the Commonwealth was not adequately followed up as discord flared among the former republics of the Soviet Union. CIS was created largely to keep Ukraine in a type of federation with Russia, yet their "civilized divorce," as Ukrainian President Kravchuk put it, provoked disputes over boundaries and control of the armed forces. Ethnic disputes elsewhere escalated in several areas into armed conflict, notably in Nagorno-Karabakh, Moldova, and Tajikistan.

The banning of the Soviet Communist Party, leaving Russia without a major nationwide political organization, threatened to lead to the breakup of the Russian Federation. Thus Chechnia in the north Caucasus declared its independence, expelled Russian officials and forces, and in fall 1992 ceased paying taxes to Moscow. Tatarstan on the Volga, refusing to sign the Federation Treaty, insisted on its own "sovereignty" and "equality" with Russia. Some other areas, including huge Iakutia in Siberia, sought changes in the Federation Treaty that would transform Russia into a loose confederation. Even primarily Russian regions sought greater autonomy from an inept and divided government in Moscow.[5]

Lacking his own political party, Russia's President Yeltsin soon encountered major and frustrating opposition from the Congress of People's Deputies, a legislature elected under Soviet rule in 1990 and composed largely of former Communist apparatchiks jealous of their power. During 1992 Democratic Russia, Yeltsin's main support in the Congress declined

---

[5]Dimitri Simes, "Reform Reaffirmed," *Foreign Policy*, no. 90 (Spring 1993), pp. 41–42.

MAP 14–2   Armenian-Azerbaijani conflict

In 1990, after a Soviet attack in Baku, Nakhichevan proclaimed independence. Nagorno-Karabakh, an Armenian enclave within Azerbaijan, became the chief area of conflict between Armenia and Azerbaijan which became independent in 1991.

from more than 300 backers to less than 200 in a body of 1,040 deputies. Yeltsin's chief backing came from the Russian people that had supported him during the August Coup of 1991. However, public suffering from the drastic economic reforms of 1992 gradually eroded his once enormous popularity. Would Russia have a presidential or a parliamentary system? Would the chief power reside with the president or parliament, with the central government or in Russia's eighty-eight regions? President Yeltsin handled the congressional session of December 1992 ineptly, but a referendum in April 1993 strengthened his position. Led by the speaker of the parliament, Ruslan Khasbulatov, and Russia's Vice President Alexander Rutskoi, Congress sought to undermine Yeltsin's authority. This conflict virtually paralyzed the central government and slowed the process of economic reform.

On September 21, 1993, President Yeltsin ordered the Congress dissolved and announced new parliamentary elections for mid-December. Denouncing this as a coup d'état, Vice President Rutskoi declared he was assuming power and the parliament, consisting chiefly of hard-liners, voted to strip Yeltsin of his powers as president. A week later the Yeltsin government sealed off the parliament building and surrounded it with troops and barbed wire. The thirteen-day standoff ended after anti-Yeltsin protesters and gunmen broke the siege of parliament and an exultant Rutskoi from its balcony called on his forces to storm major government centers. With the firm support of Defense Minister Pavel S. Grachev and the military,

Boris Nikolaevich Yeltsin (1931–   ), president of Russia.

Yeltsin ordered an assault on the parliament building on October 4 resulting in its capitulation and the arrest of the hard-line leaders. This abortive coup enabled the triumphant Yeltsin to destroy many of the remnants of the Soviet system that had survived the end of the USSR. Declared the mayor of St. Petersburg, Anatoly Sobchak: "This is now the end, the dying agony of the Soviet system."[6] Ruling by decree, Yeltsin announced simultaneous elections for a new constitution and a two-house legislature for December 1993 and presidential elections for June 1994. He also decreed the dissolution of regional soviets. Work on the new constitution was speeded up. With the full support of the United States and European Community, Yeltsin had triumphed over his opponents.

Economic reform likewise encountered rising opposition from former Communist bureaucrats in the Congress. In January 1992 Yeltsin and his youthful Premier Egor Gaidar, an economist, launched Russia toward a market economy. Sweeping economic liberalization removed remnants of central state planning and granted wide freedom to individual enterprises to plan production and sell their products, fostering a rapid increase in private firms. However, in December 1992 strong pressure from

---

[6]*New York Times,* October 10, 1993, p. 9A.

congressional conservatives brought about Gaidar's removal. Higher inflation threatened promised financial assistance from the West. Nearly all land remained publicly owned. A powerful obstacle to real economic reform remained former Communist industrial bureaucrats heading huge inefficient state enterprises consuming huge state subsidies. The return to power of the ardent reformer, Gaidar, in October 1993 accelerated once again moves toward a genuine market economy in Russia.

After December 1991 a crucial question for Russians was whether they could accept as legitimate genuine independence by the other fourteen former Soviet republics. Almost 20 percent of the Russian Federation's population was non-Russian, whereas some 25 million Russians lived outside the Federation's new boundaries. Under the Soviet state, Russians had been favored people wherever they lived. Before the Gorbachev era, Moscow and the Russians had issued orders to the other nationalities. Previous economic integration of the fifteen republics rendered their continued cooperation essential, yet their new frontiers were viewed widely as artificial and unfair provoking resentment and threatening conflict. Some nationalistic Russians dreamed of reconstructing the Soviet empire and urged Moscow to exert financial and military pressure on the newly independent states. They regarded the CIS as a potentially integral confederation in which most former Soviet republics could be unified in a Russian-dominated entity. CIS military commander Marshal Evgenii Shaposhnikov argued that Commonwealth control over nuclear weapons could serve as a first step along that road. Sergei Stankevich, a political adviser to Yeltsin, urged that Moscow deal with other republics not via its Foreign Ministry but through a future Ministry of Commonwealth Affairs that would emphasize the republics' continued integration. However President Yeltsin and his close advisers recognized the independence of the other republics as wholly legitimate. Any attempt to apply a single approach towards them all would require a major application of force. Such a reliance on compulsion could result in authoritarian rule in Russia, spark opposition within other republics, and endanger their Russian minorities. During 1992 and 1993 Yeltsin was careful to avoid any aggressive policies by Russia.[7]

Relations with its immediate neighbors have always been a high priority for Russia, but the declaration of full independence by the other republics complicated that traditional interest. Russia under Yeltsin strove to create the bases for a democracy whereas some of its new neighbors, including Ukraine, remained dominated by former Communist elites. Given the heterogeneous nature of the Russian Federation, its political and economic transformation had to be achieved gradually and without any detailed or specific blueprint. Russia's relations with the former Soviet republics remained fraught with numerous dangers and complexities. A major potential source of conflict with Ukraine remained the Crimea, joined

---

[7]Paul A. Goble, "Russia and Its Neighbors," *Foreign Policy,* no. 90 (Spring 1993), pp. 79–85.

arbitrarily with Ukraine in 1953 but roughly two-thirds Russian in population. A related problem was control of the Black Sea fleet and access to its bases, notably Sevastopol. Beginning in May 1992 negotiations on the fleet between presidents Yeltsin and Kravchuk culminated in their agreement in 1993 to divide it between Russia and Ukraine. Escalating ethnic conflicts in Georgia, Azerbaijan, and Moldova—to mention a few—confronted Russia with a difficult dilemma: Passivity by Moscow would threaten Russian minorities there, but military intervention would risk full-scale conflict. Disputes with the former Baltic republics centered around the promised withdrawal of Russian troops, nearly completed by late 1993, and the rights there of longtime Russian residents. Russia's new foreign policy had to find ways to eliminate or alleviate these perils.

The problem of collective security within the CIS also had to be faced. The Tashkent Treaty of May 1992 provided for nonaggression and mutual assistance in the event of an external attack. In July 1992 Russia and some other republics agreed tentatively to create a Commonwealth peacekeeping force. That would work only if Russia confirmed its non-imperial character and induced its neighbors to lose their fear of the Russian military. Russia retained much the largest military machine, although some of its best-equipped forces were stationed outside its borders. Ukraine moved swiftly to create its own independent army and was the first of the other republics to seek to put Russian forces there under its control. Russian troops became involved in local armed conflicts in Armenia, Georgia, Moldova, and Tajikistan.[8] As to nuclear weapons Kazakhstan, Ukraine and Belarus agreed to send all tactical nuclear weapons to Russia by July 1992 to be dismantled. They also pledged eventually to remove all strategic nuclear weapons from their territory, but Ukraine especially sought to exploit its possession of a sizable nuclear arsenal politically and financially.

Since the demise of the USSR, Russia's foreign policy has not been clearly defined. Nonetheless, its diplomacy directed by liberal and pro-Western Foreign Minister Andrei Kozyrev has sought to restore Russia's benign and democratic reputation, partly to ensure receiving major Western economic assistance. Declared Foreign Minister Kozyrev:

> Russia will not cease to be a great power. But it will be a normal great power. Its national interests will be a priority. But these will be interests understandable to democratic countries and Russia will be defending them through interaction with partners, not through confrontation.[9]

Whereas Kozyrev constantly lived up to this prescription, prominent conservative Russians, such as former Vice President Alexander Rutskoi,

---

[8]Vladimir P. Lukin, "Our Security Predicament," *Foreign Policy*, no. 88 (Fall 1992), pp. 59–67.

[9]Quoted in Daniel C. Diller, ed., *Russia and the Independent States* (Washington, DC, 1993), pp. 194–95.

Map 14-3   Nations of the former Soviet Union

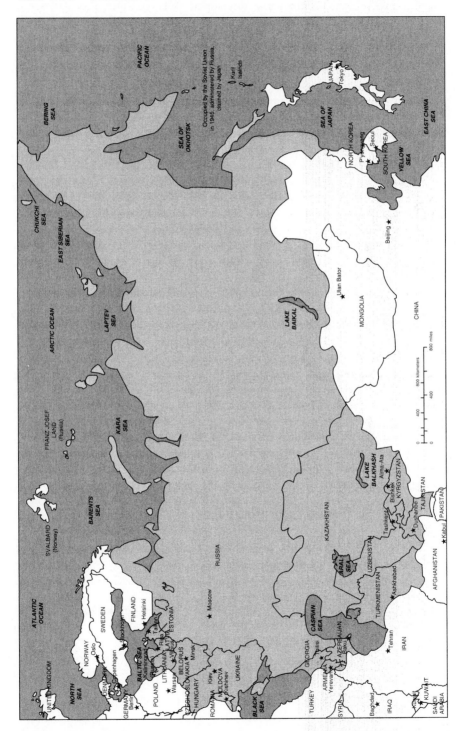

engaged in polemics with Ukraine in contradiction with official policy. During 1992 bitter controversy developed over Kozyrev's pro-Western course which Russia's ambassador to the United States, Vladimir P. Lukin, described disparagingly as "infantile pro-Americanism." Gathering under the banner of "enlightened patriotism," Kozyrev's nationalistic critics in the Congress accused him of following blindly the United States' lead on sanctions against Serbia with which tsarist and Soviet Russia had long-standing sentimental ties, on nuclear arms control, and by accepting accelerated Russian troop withdrawal from the Baltic republics. Ex-Communists and extreme nationalists complained that Russia, having lost its direction in world affairs, was being treated by the West as a second rate power.[10] Reflective of Russia's new course in foreign policy in cooperation with the West was President Yeltsin's statement in his historic speech to the United States Congress on June 17, 1992: "I am inviting you and through you the people of the United States, to join us in partnership in the name of the worldwide triumph of democracy."[11] The issue was joined between Yeltsin's striving for a democratic Russia and his pro-authoritarian opponents. The defeat and dissolution of a hostile Congress in September 1993 dramatically reinforced Yeltsin's position.

The stake of the West in promoting a democratic solution to the Russian question and the viability of the CIS remains great, but its ability to influence the outcome appears limited. With the end of the Cold War and the elimination of ideological or political causes of confrontation, strategic Soviet-American rivalry has become outdated and the centrality of Russian-American relations has diminished. As Secretary of State James Baker expressed it at Princeton University in December 1991: "If during the Cold War we faced each other as two scorpions in a bottle, now the Western nations and the former Soviet republics stand as awkward climbers on a steep mountain."[12] Nonetheless, Russia and the United States possess enough common and parallel interests for a meaningful partnership, something championed enthusiastically by President Bill Clinton of the United States. Russia depends on the United States and the West as its major source of economic and technical aid in its painful transition to a market economy. Washington needs Russia as a partner to resolve dangerous regional crises inside and outside the CIS and as an enormous potential market.

Suggested Readings

Allison, Graham and G. Yavlinsky. *Window of Opportunity: The Grand Bargain for Democracy in the Soviet Union.* New York, 1991.

Aslund, A., ed., *The Post-Soviet Economy: Soviet and Western Perspectives.* New York, 1992.

---

[10]Simes, pp. 14–15.

[11]Quoted in Diller, p. 215.

[12]Quoted in Diller, p. 216.

"The August Coup," *New Left Review.* no. 189 (September–October 1991).

Colton, Timothy J. and Robert Legvold, eds., *After the Soviet Union: From Empire to Nations.* New York, 1992.

Diller, Daniel C., ed., *Russia and the Independent States.* Washington, DC, 1993.

D'Encausse, Helène Carrère. *The End of the Soviet Empire: The Triumph of the Nations.* Trans. Franklin Philip. New York, 1993.

Goble, Paul A. "Russia and Its Neighbors," *Foreign Policy.* no. 90 (Spring 1993), pp. 79–85.

Gorbachev, Mikhail S. *The August Coup: The Truth and the Lessons.* New York, 1991.

Krasnov, Vladislav. *Russia Beyond Communism: A Chronicle of National Rebirth.* Boulder, CO, 1991.

Loory, S. H. and A. Imse. *Seven Days That Shook the World: The Collapse of Soviet Communism.* Atlanta, GA, 1991.

Lukin, Vladimir P. "Our Security Predicament," *Foreign Policy.* no. 88 (Fall 1992), pp. 59–67.

Lynch, Allen. *The Cold War is Over—Again.* Boulder, CO, 1992.

"Moscow, August 1991: The Coup de Grace," *Problems of Communism.* vol. 39 (November–December 1991), pp. 1–62.

Peck, M. J. and T. J. Richardson, eds., *What Is To Be Done?: Proposals for the Soviet Transition to the Market.* New Haven, CO, 1991.

Simes, Dimitri. "Reform Reaffirmed," *Foreign Policy.* no. 90 (Spring 1993), pp. 41–42.

Smith, Alan. *Russia and the World Economy: Problems of Integration.* London and New York, 1993.

Solchanyk, Roman. *Ukraine: From Chernobyl to Sovereignty.* New York, 1992.

"The Soviet Union, 1991," *Current History.* vol. 90 (October 1991).

Yeltsin, Boris N. *Against the Grain: An Autobiography.* Trans. Michael Glenny. New York, 1990.

Young, Stephen, Ronald Bee and Bruce Seymore II, eds., *One Nation Becomes Many: The ACCESS Guide to the Former Soviet Union.* Washington, DC, 1992.

APPENDIX

Soviet Leaders

(All except Lenin were general or first secretaries of the Soviet Communist Party.)

V. I. Lenin	1917–1924
J. V. Stalin	1924–1953
G. M. Malenkov	1953
N. S. Khrushchev	1953–1964
L. I. Brezhnev	1964–1982
Iu. V. Andropov	1982–1984
K. V. Chernenko	1984–1985
M. S. Gorbachev	1985–1991

Chairmen of the Council of People's Commissars

(After 1946, prime ministers)

V. I. Lenin	1917–1924
A. I. Rykov	1924–1930
V. M. Molotov	1930–1941
J. V. Stalin	1941–1953
G. M. Malenkov	1953–1955
N. A. Bulganin	1955–1958
N. S. Khrushchev	1958–1964
A. N. Kosygin	1964–1980
N. A. Tikhonov	1980–1985
N. I. Ryzhkov	1985–1990

Soviet Foreign Commissars

(After 1945, foreign ministers)

L. D. Trotskii	November 1917–March 1918
G. V. Chicherin	March 1918–July 1930
M. M. Litvinov	July 1930–May 1939
V. M. Molotov	May 1939–March 1949, March 1953–June 1956
A. Ia. Vyshinskii	March 1949–March 1953
Dmitri Shepilov	June 1956–June 1957
A. A. Gromyko	June 1957–July 1985
E. A. Shevarnadze	July 1985–December 1990, November–December 1991
Alexander Besmertnykh	January–August 1991
Boris Pankin	August–November 1991

INDEX